NORWOOD IN THE TIME OF HOCKEY

NORWOOD
in the Time of Hockey

Don Reddick

Nauset Sound
Publishing Company

Copyright Don Reddick, 2022

All rights reserved. No part of this work may be reproduced or used in any form or by any means, electronic or mechanical, including photocopying, recording, or any information storage and retrieval system, without the prior written permission of the publisher.

Published by Nauset Sound Publishing Company

Reddick, Don, 1954-
Norwood in the Time of Hockey

ISBN 978-0-9842380-3-3 (0-9842380-3-4)

Visit the author's website at www.donreddick.com

Printed in the United States
10 9 8 7 6 5 4 3 2 1

Cover Painting by Tom Dunlay, used by permission from Katherine and Charles Donahue.
Back Cover Photograph by Terry Reddick
Edited by Pat Burns, with assistance from Bob Mulcahy, Peter Brown, Ed King, Bob Thornton, and Charles Orcutt
Book design and layout by Cynthia Ryan, Edgeworks Creative LLC

to the boys of winter

INDEX

Prologue	1
The Land	9
The Town, and Imagination	13
Elders	27
Kids	51
1965	71
The Street	91
The Legend	107
The Programs	127
Frank Wall	143
1967	153
The Game	173
Baseball	189
The Coach	205
The Higgins Mask	223
1968	233
Tragedy	251
The Other Town	271
The Ice Adonis	283
Our Town	303
1971	321

History, Hockey, and Imagination	**351**
The Great "What If?"	**357**
Norwood at the Movies	**373**
1972	**389**
Arlington, and Imagination	**415**
Game Day	**419**
Norwood Hockey and the Arts	**439**
Requiem for Memory, and Imagination	**449**

PROLOGUE

You can't go back home to your family, back home to your childhood ... back home to a young man's dreams of glory and of fame ... back home to places in the country, back home to the old forms and systems of things which once seemed everlasting but which are changing all the time—back home to the escapes of Time and Memory.

— Thomas Wolfe,
You Can't Go Home Again, 1940

In the beginning were the words. And phrases and sentences and thoughts and dreams, and they came when young, and I sensed I should scribble them. There was no inclination that they were exceptional or unique, momentous or memorable, but more the fashioning, the structuring of an order in my mind, an unrefined but undeniable urge to write down words and phrases and sentences and thoughts and dreams. What they would become took years, metaphorical rambles through brambles. I was never taught to write. Never a creative writing class during my stint at the University of Massachusetts, never mind the Iowa's Writers' Workshop. Never a helping hand from family or friends, merely the son of a Bird & Son foreman.

What evolved was an incessant interest in words and phrases pursued through purchase of books on plotting, on characterization, books on every aspect of writing. I bought a Thesaurus and dictionary. I bought Strunk and White's tiny masterpiece on form; I bought the *Chicago Manual of Style*. I read Mencken's incomparable, *The American Language*. I began watching movies with an eye toward character and story; began re-reading comedic novels and studying what made them funny. I listened carefully and watched closely those who attracted eyes in the crowd, early sensing a correlation between characters who told stories around town and characters who held a reader's interest, buried between borders of a book's binding. During this journey I discovered verification of one of writing's most weathered, withered, and over-wrought cliches: write what you know.

How does a writer determine what to write next? Many assess in terms of career success, wedded to a notion that a perceived path to fame and fortune comes before personal interest, or experimentation. I have no writing "career" as such, nor am I famous or inordinately fortunate, and so options are as varied as imagination. I am sixty-seven years old, past the age at which unfulfilled dreams of fame and fortune slip away as swiftly and easily as years themselves. I am untethered to previous success, nor am I guided by agents or editors. What am I interested in? What are my capabilities? What is my definition of success?

I am not the first to consider these issues. "Writing a best-seller with conscious intent to do so is, after all, a state of mind that is not without comparison to the act of marrying for money only to discover that the absence of love is more onerous than anticipated," Norman Mailer once wrote. "The ideal, and as you get older you do try to get closer to the ideal, is to write only what interests you. It will prove of interest to others or it won't, but if you try to steer your way into success, you shouldn't be a serious writer. Rather, you will do well to study the tricks of consistent best-seller authors while being certain to stay away from anything that's well written."

Write what you know...
...and what do I know?

There is a history of the history of Norwood. Like most colonial towns bereft of flame or flood, the town retains an archival paper trail of meetings and minutes, court proceedings and land conveyance registries, as well as a significant amount of recorded hearsay and social cant which those interested can peruse and organize. We are indebted to these organizers, without whom an appreciation of a time-line record would remain beyond grasp of pedestrian readers.

Erastus Worthington's 1827 effort, *The History of Dedham*, as well as 1887's *The Clap Board Trees Parish*, regarding formative events of Westwood by George Willis Cooke, are invaluable resources. The early history of Dedham village, from which Norwood was calved one hundred and fifty years ago, is the focus of Kenneth A. Lockridge's brilliant 1970 treatise, *A New England Town, The First Hundred Years*. Reading these histories, one appreciates both their research and writing. Yet I sense a flaw in the flow, a gentle murmur of rocks in the stream, calling for care in our footing.

The problem with town histories is that once the last recorded deed is considered, once the last word written, once the last edit completed, once the tale printed and paper dried, folded, bound and delivered, the town, the tale, has frozen in time. It instantly becomes a John Singleton Copley 1767 painting, a blurred 1846 daguerreotype, a black and white 1944 snapshot, or a faded Jack Reddick moving picture of a 1964 Norwood Little League parade, never to improve. The moment these are finished is the last second before the next second...and the next, and next, so that truthfully no town history can be complete. In Matthew Brady's admonition to parents of Union soldiers to get an ambrotype photograph of their sons, because "You cannot tell how soon it may be too late," lies the essence of the flaw in flow, our gentle murmur of rocks in the historical stream. Many of Brady's prospective clients were going to die, and the photographer understood the value in preserving these boys and young men before any coming changes. Brady recognized the value of the present because he understood an inevitable future. There is no final, completed history possible of anything ongoing. Argued with merit is that this doesn't matter, that the purpose of a history is just that of providing what is known at a given time. Yet there is an alternative. I would contend that town histories, that *all* histories of active organisms whether physical or societal, could be construed as a *continuing education*, with periodic visits to time and place.

...*and what do I know?*

Great stories abound. Which one to choose? I realized early an ability to recognize good ones after sensing the worth of a remarkable early hockey story and the resulting publication of my first novel, *Dawson City Seven*. I then stumbled upon the story of a slave ship overtaken by its cargo, who were then represented in court by a former President of the United States. I began researching the incident in earnest until abruptly halted by news that a movie, by no less than Steven Spielberg, entitled *Armistad* was being released. There is no market for struggling writers illuminating the recently illuminated efforts of famous directors. After overcoming disappointment and shock of losing a year's research and work, came consolation that my literary instincts were good. *If Steven Spielberg liked the story…*

I am acquainted with the foremost hockey historians in Canada. I have experience in successfully writing on the subject. I grew up in the same neighborhood with several of Norwood's most gifted athletes. I participated in the formative programs of Mr. Higgins, Mr. Clifford, and Mr. Brown, I skated for three years on Norwood's varsity team. I have written historical novels, the value of which includes an appreciation of time and place, as well as a weathered education in the earnestness and seriousness of those discussing family members. But this dog's breakfast of artificially cooled memory still did not convince to write of my hometown. One out-of-the-blue email, and two incidents remained to convince that, despite lack of market appeal or financial gain, this was a story worth investing years in, a story with value, and most importantly a story that I could tell. The email I received in March of 2018 from Paul Flaherty, Norwood High School class of 1971. With limited editing, it read:

Hi Donnie,

Don, we ran into each other at my sister Gail's luncheon after Billy Barrett's funeral. You were nice enough to run out to your car and grab copies of your book, *Travelogues of America*. Thanks for sharing. I just finished reading this book, and I must admit I read it over just a few days, as I found it continuing to keep my interest. It was pretty neat to come across references to several Norwood folks. Your work as a printing engineer/troubleshooter was unique and led you to have many varied and unusual meetings with so many people.

You did quite a bit of research, as in the Yukon, Vermont military, and on the Canadian hero. You made it so believable in how you incorporated your own real lifetimes visiting these locations throughout the world. I found how you ended many of the chapters to encapsulate the essence of that particular story in such a compact and simple way.

I especially enjoyed your story of Richie Hebner and your brief meeting with Mickey Rooney. Yes, I suppose it must be tough to be famous, quite a journey for an old grave digger! I remember at the time Hebner elected to follow a career in baseball, and I was like what the heck, he was such a dominant hockey player, but he chose the right path for sure.

Speaking of hockey, have you ever given any thought to writing a book about the glory days of Norwood High School hockey? You mentioned Rusty Tobin, and I can see him in my mind playing a solid "D" with his pants somewhat drooping, if I recall correctly.

I think it would be special for you to speak with and research the fun times and no doubt recapture and articulate the hilarious stories from the period of Richie Hebner to the '72 team winning the State title. Here are just a few memories that come from a huge fan, and one who was fortunate enough to play some hockey for the school, but not gifted enough to have made the varsity, every kid's dream who laced on the skates in Norwood. Here are a few story lines for you to consider...

— the corner work done by the small in stature Paul Angelo, who played with a huge heart.

— the Maus brothers...Dana, Gary, and Blaine...the precursors to the Reddick boys.

— the Richie Hebner teams featured guys like Richie Lovell, Hasenfus, Donahue, Billy Crowley (soon to be more known for running Gillooly's Funeral Home), Tommy Smelstor, etc.

— Ernie Higgins making one of the first tight white face-fitting goalie masks...perhaps one to be worn by both his son, Neil, and maybe Gerry Cheevers with the Bruins (not sure about that)...but it was revolutionary at the time.

— it was such a treat playing at the Boston Arena...freshman and JV teams practiced there on very early Saturday mornings, not so much perhaps with the varsity...upon returning to Norwood and getting dropped off at the old Jr. High, we meandered over to the Norwood Hospital lobby to call for rides home...we had a special piece of the telephone book cover that we slid into the phone and we would not have to pay, what all of 10 cents...we felt like we were ripping off the phone company, and would leave it in the book for the following weeks...not sure the hospital would allow a bunch of high school hockey players to hang out in their lobby these days.

— speaking of the Jr. High, I recall as a third or fourth grader of riding on the student fan buses into the Boston Arena to watch games...the high school students would be singing in the back of the bus...I thought it was awesome to be riding with high school girls with my friend Billy O'Brien...we only got to go because Billy had like five older sisters that were supposedly watching us...again, letting a kid this young go into Boston unsupervised would not happen these days.

— other names that flood the memory bank...Jack Cronin who never seemed to come off the ice.

— what was in the water on Crestwood Circle to have so many hockey stars...the afore-mentioned Reddick boys, Neil Higgins, Dickie Donovan, Richie and Dennis Hebner just a stone throw down the street...

— can you see Tommy Taylor flying down the wing?

— my class, 1971, featured Phil Nolfi and Bobby Thornton who both made the varsity as freshmen which was highly unusual...others to follow like John Lawrie, Jack Clifford, Bobby Rosata, Billy Sullivan.

— your 1972 State Champion class had guys like Bill Pieri in net, Peter Brown, Alex Skene, Mike Martin, Billy Clifford, Eddie

King and yourself with some younger ones in Danny Bayer, Paul O'Day, Greg Walker, followed by Mike (Quickie) Costello.

— you mentioned the joy of skating on clear pond ice, so that brings back memories of games played at places like New Pond, Pettee's, Froggies...it was amazing to skate at length on those crystal-clear ice surfaces vs. the days at Four Seasons with the fence as side boards or freezing skating against the wind at the outdoor rink at Noble & Greenough for practices.

Anyway, my mind was wandering, Donnie, sorry about that. What do you think, do you think you could enjoy researching stories about the old Norwood Mustang hockey days? There must be plenty of locker room and other funny stories of the days spent doing Canadians for coaches Wheeler, Gormley, Arvidson etc. I think there could be an audience out there of folks from Norwood and elsewhere who would enjoy reading about the different escapades and short story lines you could recreate!

Anyway, Donnie, thanks for giving me a copy of your book. I enjoyed turning the pages to follow yet another part of your life's journey on the roads of America and beyond. Take care,

Paul Flaherty

An email and two incidents: the first incident occurred one winter afternoon as I perused my old neighborhood. Having returned to my hometown after a decade-long sojourn to the state of Vermont, it was not unusual to revisit, every few months, the street from which I had emerged. As I slowly passed homes frozen in 1960s memory, past the Praino's, the Brownes, past my own house at number 57, I turned the corner, passing the Sortevik's, and there, in front of the old Flavin house, was a teenager bedecked in goalie gear—years later I would learn it was a fifteen or sixteen-year-old Joe Sullivan—pulling a shiny new net from the street to allow my passage.

A smile emerged; I looked past the Flavins to the Moloney's, whose two sons had donned goalie gear for both Norwood and Xaverian High

Schools, then glanced to the right, across the street from the Moloney's, to the former home of one of the greatest goalies in Massachusetts' history. I slowed to a halt and lowered my window. I wanted to encourage the kid, wanted to tell him, if he did not already know, that he lived across the street from where Neil Higgins grew up, the kid who to this day, a half century later, still holds the Massachusetts high school record for most career shutouts, and whose father Ernie's famous goalie masks adorn the Hockey Hall of Fame. I wanted to give cheer and encouraging words to this latest generation inhabiting Crestwood Circle. When I said 'Hello', he backed away. Taken aback, I curled my finger and said, a bit louder, "Hey, c'mere!"

The kid receded further.

"C'mere!" I repeated, then suddenly realized—*stranger danger!*—that indeed I could not go back home to places in the country, back home to the old forms and systems of things which once seemed ever-lasting but which are indeed changing all the time...I suddenly realized this street I'd grown up on with the Donovans, the Higginses, the Sorteviks, the Hebners was no longer the place carried in memory.

The second incident occurred in our new home on Summit Ave., as my wife and I settled in for "movie night."

"Let's watch *Hoosiers* tonight," Terry suggested. I shrugged.

"Have you seen it? You'll love it, it's about a high school basketball team in basketball-crazy Indiana that goes to the state finals."

"Naw..."

"Why not? You'll love it! Basketball in basketball-crazy Indiana, a high school team that goes all the way, a bunch of kids who live their dream!"

"I don't need to watch that movie."

"Why?"

"Because I lived it."

THE LAND

Massachusetts ...was born of a great ice whale. The vast Moby Dick of glaciers, pushing dark silt before it plowed homeward to the sea to die. With transparent lips it sucked the ocean, while its gaunt sides withered inward, leaving around them a narrow shroud rimmed by tallow-white beaches, plumed with blue fire of waves and flanged by the smoky sea.
— Elizabeth Reynard, *The Narrow Land*, 1934

James Mitchener began his epic historical novel *Centennial* with a full eighty pages of geography relating to the Colorado area in which his tale occurs. As a writer I respect what Mitchener attempted. I suspect he reached for the *Moby Dick* of historical novels; he reached, as writers should, for the stars. And one never knows, when reaching skyward, how far one's hand will extend, what realms of diamonds or darkness fingers may grasp or breach, whether nails will hammer home essential truth, or scratch the chalk board of failure.

I sensed the correlation the novelist drew, that of a land and its people. Our land is rich with geographic history, a history of ancient movement and change, a history whose stony character includes moraines and eskers, forged during seasons of varying heat and cold. That we border a great salt sea is relevant; that we bordered vast, unknown wilderness for the first centuries after European arrival also material. As a historical novelist, or in this case as a historical non-fiction writer, I look to masters and try to learn. I do not begin, as Michener did, 70,000,000 years in the past, but a mere 18,000, when geological events defined our land, and whose lingering effects bequeathed the ground we stride upon and the ponds we skate upon.

Ice that crept from arctic lairs in relentless, crushing, gouging manner was the extension of the Laurentide ice cap. Over time immeasurable by human instrument, it simply inched southward, pushing all that was push-able ahead of itself until its journey was abrogated when, presumably, longitude overcame amplitude. At its fullest, the ice mass extended from today's Massachusetts to the eastern edge of the Dakotas, its crescent's apex nudging southern Illinois. How long it remained miles thick over New England is uncertain, but certain is its ablation, or what it left strewn in its inevitable retreat, creating many landmarks of today.

Several of New England's prominent landmarks survived the ice invasion, rather than were sculpted by it. New Hampshire's Mount Monadnock and Mounts Greylock and Wachusetts in Massachusetts, as well as more familiar Blue Hills, are considered inselbergs, or island peaks of ancient rock so hard they resisted glacial eradication. Cape Cod and its outlying islands of Nantucket, Martha's Vineyard, and the Elizabeth Islands are parts and parcels of great ice sheets' terminal moraines, that pile of pushed debris gouged, scraped and driven from all northern New England. Drumlins, low, oval mounds formed in retreating glaciers, have attained significance, Charlestown's Bunker Hill and South Boston's Dorchester Heights historical examples. Islands dotting Boston harbor and Massachusetts Bay are a cluster of drumlins. Concord's Walden Pond is a perfect example of a kettle pond, a pond formed by the process of disarticulation, or abandonment of a large chunk of ice which, during the course of melting, creates a hole in the ground devoid of supporting springs or streams, and sustained primarily by ground water. But most obvious over the extended area is what is called drift, or till, that mess of accumulated debris scattered haphazardly upon the barren zone, revealed by retreated ice.

In Gloucester on Cape Ann peninsula, itself a terminal moraine, lies Dogtown Common. The site is littered with unusual erratics, or large rocks dissimilar to underlying bedrock, indicative of foreign origin and glacial transfer. In Madison, New Hampshire lies the largest erratic in New England, measuring eighty-three feet long and weighing an estimated ten *million* pounds. The White Mountains' famous notches, Pinkham, Franconia, and Crawford are u-shaped valleys created by retreating glaciers. The fine fingers of land forming peninsulas in lower Maine, the Harpswells and Boothbays, are eskers, long lines of gravel deposited by tremendous under-ice rivers spawned of melting ice packs.

These rivers were the result of water probing the least resistance through a glacial barren zone, seeking return to its ocean home. As thousands of years saw southern seed blown north and as vegetation emerged, fell, and accumulated into soil over the land, these waterways wore themselves into the landscape, becoming today's Merrimack, Charles, and Neponset Rivers. An ancient tributary of the Neponset was Hawes Brook, an early site of burgeoning colonial economic development. In 1913 the Winslow Brothers and Smith Company dammed the stream creating Willet Pond, to support their downstream tannery. Locals immediately referred to the newly created reservoir as "the New Pond," and refer to it as New Pond to this day.

Of local interest was Frog Rock, an oft-painted erratic on the pathway, wagon road, and ultimately asphalted Brook Street, whose bridged causeway today separates New Pond from original Pettee's Pond. Ubiquitous stone walls crisscrossing remaining Norwood woodland, as well as lining many of its ancient roads, are reminder of our rural forebears' struggle against ancient ablative drift.

18,000 years after defining geological events and at a latitude conducive to winter cold, it was upon frozen sheets of New Pond ice and a kettle pond named Spy, that Norwood and Arlington kids learned to skate.

THE TOWN, AND IMAGINATION

*We all got holes to fill
And them holes are all that's real
Some fall on you like a storm
Sometimes you dig your own*

— Townes Van Zandt, *To Live is to Fly*, 1977

Pebbles Folan walked into the Shamrock Pub on Railroad Ave., sat down and pulled the stone artifact from his jacket pocket. It fit easily into the palm of my hand, and even to amateur eyes appeared man altered. Pebbles was a Silver Street kid, a near-mythical figure to me as were all members of Norwood's first state finalist hockey team, whose photograph on the steps of Washington's Capital Building had hung in my Crestwood Circle home since 1965. In the photo Pebbles' head is cocked to one side in classic cockiness, but the man today is grayer, any chip on his shoulder long ago smoothed by time.

"Some call it the swamp, but it was Father Mac's when I was growing up," Pebbles recounted. "It was a pond before they put the drain in. It was fed from Germany Brook, it was a low-lying area, swampy. There was an elevated path from Irving Street to Father Mac's, came out by the pool, but we had our own little path from Silver Street that led to the pond. We used to skate there, Fred Kinsman, the Hebners, Billy Hasenfus. Dave Dooley from Hawthorne Street. In the summer we used to skip rocks across the water, that was what I was doing. I think it was 1960.

"They had dredged it, they got the weeds and everything out, and they put a dam in, had turned over the dirt where they were putting in two-by-fours. Two of us were skipping stones across the water and I was by the dam, and I picked up this rock and I was gonna throw it, and I looked at it and thought, *this is an Indian artifact*, and I put it in my pocket.

"Ask the Historical Society, they say the area from Father Mac's back over Spruce Road up to Winter Street toward the dump is the area that most Indian artifacts are found. I took it home, I just kept it. Couple of years after I found it and I could drive, I took it in to the Museum of Science and I had somebody look at it and they said yes, it's a net sinker. He said it was maybe 1840-1860, it was well-worn. Apparently, there had been small fish, or they used it as a practice area."

In the Shamrock that afternoon Pebbles Folan told a story a few months shy of sixty years old. It triggered memory of another story slightly younger, of nine-year-old Teddy Mulvehill telling this wide-eyed friend about an ancient Indian burial ground discovered in woods near his Spruce Road home. Appreciated today as much as Teddy's youthful imagination, was realization that it had an underlying reality and *again*, over a half-century later, sparked *my* imagination of a walk through our town, before its first structure raised:

I turn full circle, aware that I must appear nonchalant, attuned to my surroundings. Yesterday I had driven Dedham center to South Norwood along what was first known as Sawmill Road, then the Norfolk and Bristol Turnpike and familiar today as Washington Street and its short stretch of Upland Road. The original road followed ancient Indian paths, but what confronts now intimidates. I am reminded of Douglas Leach's *Flintlock and Tomahawk*, in which he surmised what one would observe from the air of a 1675 New England,

> He would have been most vividly impressed by the almost unbroken expanse of forest which lay over all the land like a shaggy carpet. Here and there the monotonous wilderness was broken by a few acres of cleared land and a small cluster of houses—a village set down in the middle of the forest. New England was a land of isolated villages and occasional towns, interconnected by a network of woodland paths which served as virtually the only means of access to most of the inland settlements.

Dedham is forty years old, and outside of swelling populations in Plymouth Colony and Massachusetts Bay, one of only a handful of outlying villages. Plymouth's frontier now includes Rehoboth, Dartmouth, and Swansea. Northampton, on the Connecticut River, is twenty years old, boasting a population of five hundred. This year adventurers, husbandmen pressured by a new generation's desire for their own land, are planning a settlement called Framingham. Within Dedham's town boundaries, outlying clusters of homes now rise in the Clapboardtrees, as well as at Hawes Brook. Medfield and Wrentham have small but clinging communities.

There is much to distract, and truly I know not what time I have. It is early spring. Medfield will soon be devastated, burned to the ground. Wrentham will be abandoned in fear, unable to defend itself in the coming fury. What I'd give to see young Medfield and its struggling farming community, knowing what we know now! King Phillip's head now sits securely on his shoulders. How I'd love to see the man, of whom no likeness has come to us through the ages. But it is Tiot, the future South, or Second Parish, one day to become South Dedham and eventually Norwood, that I have come to see.

Peering about Dedham village, I am struck by its simple poverty. Remnants of rotted, forty-year-old stumps stubble house lots and line lanes. Curiosity makes me pause; in historical research, I have always been enamored of the unthought-of fact in description which authenticates. *Tell me something I don't know...* and here, to great satisfaction, I see it. There are no clotheslines, but nearby trees are studded with wooden pegs to the height of five or six feet, on which hang laundry.

I am anxious to leave Dedham village, the thought of encountering anyone daunting. I know not the vernacular, nor possess their syntax or accent, and do not wish to appear foreign to stalwart Puritan's intent on village purity, and wary of the foreign. I am aware of cruelty fostered of a religious and cultural mindset, difficult to comprehend today, that would allow inhabitants to cut off the ears of transgressors. Robert Hanson relates a remarkable example in *Dedham, 1635-1890*, "...at Dedham, on a cold frosty morning, they laid on Elizabeth Hooters aged limbs ten lashes more with exceeding cruelty, at a cat's tail; and being thus torn and beaten...they put her on horseback and carried her on a weary journey...many miles into the wilderness, and towards night left her there, where many wolves, and bears and wild beasts which sometimes set upon living persons, and many deep waters to pass through..." It occurs that many miles into the wilderness very well may be the place

I seek, as the northern access to Dedham was the Charles River, and the primary avenue into the wilderness this southern cart path, many miles into at which, adjacent the deep waters of the Neponset River, lies Tiot.

Intimidated by the woods' depth, worried that I might take a wrong trail or become disoriented in the shaggy carpet, I have little to aid other than my recent drive during which I measured distances from Dedham center to various significant points. Gay Street, named for the family of farmers who would struggle with soil and stone here for three centuries, breaks to the right toward the Third Parish, future Westwood, at 1.5 miles. Clapboardtree Street, also leading uphill toward the Third Parish meeting house, whose brick-and-mortar progeny still sits atop Nahatan Street's highest rise, lies 2.6 miles out. Norwood center at Nahatan Street, the future "Hook", lies exactly 4 miles down-path, and finally Hawes Brook and the seeds of Tiot, 5.5 miles away.

I think of the man I wish to see, and his time. Had Ezra Morse the inclination, he could have travelled to Plymouth Colony in 1676 to watch a Pilgrim procession march through streets carrying King Phillip's head on a pike, where it remained in public view a quarter century. Henry White could have left his tavern on the banks of the Neponset River, or Morse his sawmill on Hawes Brook, in 1692 to visit Salem—present day Danvers—to witness innocents hanged as witches. As late as 1755 twenty-seven-year-old Aaron Guild, had he been so disposed, could have abandoned plow and oxen and traveled dirt paths to Charlestown Common—present day Somerville—to see, as colonial justice meted for murdering their owner, a colored slave named Phillis burned at the stake, or her hanged accomplice Mark's remains now wrapped in chains at a street corner, where they would molder twenty years.

I set off into forest, alive with wonder. The most striking characteristic of these woods is the disheveled mayhem of fallen forefathers, rotting large and grounded, leaning caught and angled, a confusion of forested ruin. So different from this very ground I grew up on, overgrown pastures of Gay Farm and the Forbes estate lightly spaced with second generation growth. I marvel that these woodlands I enter stand in stark contrast, this a true wilderness gleaned not from two generations, but from *one hundred* generations of reign and ruin.

I had imagined walking virgin Washington Street as a luxury of summer days wandering familiar woodland, determining future locations of, say, Norwood's town hall and the intersection of churches, or where my boyhood home would lie. I had imagined seeing our town primitive and post-glacial unaltered, where for thousands of years only aboriginals had ventured.

Orientation would be difficult, water courses and ponds key, as well as distinctive rocks. I wanted time to meander forests and follow streams, searching for those erratic unmoved through the course of South Dedham's, and then Norwood's, history. Frog Rock, located on the Indian path leading to Pettee's Pond might be identified, as well as other distinctive rocks in the Crestwood Circle area. On the Forbes estate, just over the line created by Dedham's Third Parish and future Westwood, toward today's Clapboardtree Street and adjacent one leg of Plantingfield Brook, sits the split-rock hill—a drumlin? —where as children we dropped pennies into the crack, to be lost to eternity. Certainly, in its virgin state it would be identifiable, and with a triangulation of existing 1675 roads entirely possible to locate.

As I walk this uneven cart path, it becomes apparent that any measurement of time and distance, or recognition of landmarks, will be difficult. Nothing appears familiar. With heart-pounding apprehension, I realize I have no watch to time progress, a normal fifteen-minute-mile surely underestimated, not to mention the diversion of fleeting thoughts that lose time and distance to imagination. My mind drifts to Worthington's 1827 assessment of 1736, where he states the number of persons taxed in Dedham to total 259, with 129 in Dedham village, 52 in the Clapboardtrees, and 78 in the Second Parish, the future Norwood. Worthington states,

> During the last fifty years (1686-1736), the inhabitants must have endured great hardships, and enjoyed few of the comforts of life, now within the reach of their posterity. They were continually employed in clearing and subduing their lands, planting orchards, making roads, building fences and houses. In their situation, they derived only a bare subsistence from the fruits of their labor... they were nearly all husbandmen; they had in the last fifty years

extended their settlement six or seven miles from the village, which was not abandoned except by a few farmers...amounting to about fifteen hundred souls...

George Willis Cooke's 1887 book, *The Clap Board Tree Parish*, observed life in rural Dedham after a two hundred-year-long agrarian period of little change. Writing from the perspective of the Third Parish, known also as Clapboard Tree Parish and West Dedham, ultimately to become Westwood in 1897, he hints at emerging internecine prejudices between rural Dedham parishes, prejudices whose remnants whisper to this day. Cooke writes,

> In 1765 there were forty-two houses in the parish and three hundred and thirteen inhabitants. The people were nearly all farmers, lived very simply, and enjoyed life under humble circumstances... Much that seems necessary to our life was then wanting. The books were few and poor. There were no daily newspapers, and the few issued weekly were not much worth the reading.
>
> In his history of Dedham, Worthington speaks of this period as one of great disorder and ignorance. He says the schools were at their lowest stage, and that "few could have had any instruction." He mentions the fact, as an indication of the people at about this time, that the town records were poorly kept. The penmanship was poor, the spelling antiquated, and the grammar not correct. In the second parish (South Dedham, now Norwood) in all these respects the records show an absence of education. As a specimen of the spelling, the word *oathordocts* will suffice. In the Clapboard Trees parish, however, the records were well kept, and in a manner superior to those of the town or the first and second parishes. The penmanship was excellent, the language good, and the spelling fairly modern. The old spelling and the use of contractions were not so common as in the town and first and second parishes.

As I continue my journey through the forest primeval, the murmuring pines and the oaks, avoiding mossed rocks littering the forest path—agrarian impediments which for the next three hundred years will be pulled, dragged and piled into stone walls—I think of Norwood's most vexing historical mystery.

There is no definitive account of how Norwood acquired its name. Difficulty in determining the source of ancient, aboriginal place names such as Tiot is understandable; less forgivable is the ensuing confusion over the naming of Norwood itself. At a time of newspapers, at a time of a rural parish "putting its best foot forward" to demonstrate it could keep records and minutes and provide necessary governmental infrastructure, it is disconcerting that no reliable record exists of the origination of the name, "Norwood."

The name itself is said to date from 7th century Old English, "nord" for north, and "wuda" meaning woodland, or forest. Medieval villages of Nordwuda, through time's oral metamorphosis, became villages of Northwood and Norwood, having existed a millennium in Middlesex and Surrey, as well as other English counties. But the name's application to a calving township in the New World bears no convincing relationship either historical, or geographic.

North Wood, or Norwood lies *south* of both Dedham and Westwood, which would have logically engendered, "Southwood." Nor exists a determinable link between a corresponding Norwood in England. Dozens of Commonwealth towns derive their names from English place names, most, however, obtaining these names in the first generations of Pilgrim and Puritan immigration, when personal attachments to the homeland were fresh. Plymouth, our first settlement, was named for the port from which the adventurers set out. Boston was named by the leadership of Massachusetts Bay Company, several of whom came from Boston, in Lincolnshire. But two hundred and fifty years and ten generations—as well as a revolution—had eroded emotional ties to Mother England.

Handbills printed by T. O. Metcalf & Co. in March of 1872 listed nominees for the new town's name, careful to disclose, "The names proposed were suggested by different citizens of the town, and not by the printer." They served notice of a meeting to determine the name of the new town by vote, to be held in late March. Of twenty-four suggestions, many were names of prominent individuals, including the familiar Ames, Balch, Day, Lyman, Prescott, Vernon and Winslow, as well as Nahattan, an ancient local Indian chief. Sites were acknowledged; Hook, Tiot, and Judea making the list, but also one whose rationale eludes contemporary analysis, Queertown. Tucked in the middle of the alphabetically listed nominees was a seeming outlier, Norwood.

No contemporary rationale of the final decision has been uncovered. What little information historians consider appeared primarily in two newspaper articles, the first appearing thirty years later. In 1903 Mrs. Marcia Winslow, in a talk to the Norwood Woman's Club, claimed local builder Tyler Thayer was responsible, having determined that there was only one town in the entire United States named Norwood. She offered that Thayer had argued that Norwood "looked well in print (no I's to dot or T's to cross), had a pleasing sound, and was easy to write." Almost a quarter century later, however, Francis Winslow was quoted as declaring the name "Norwood" was put into nomination by Universalist Minister George Hall, after Henry Ward Beecher's 1868 novel *Norwood; or Village Life in New England*.

Beecher was a Congregationalist Minister whose theatrical sermons supporting abolition and the Union Cause had earned him the moniker, "the most famous man in America." His literary effort, a paean to Union sentiment and idyllic return to lost innocence, was released directly after the Civil War. It garnered great local interest, as Dedham had sent dozens of men to the Grand Army of the Republic. It is reasonable to believe that Mr. Thayer was investigating the name proposed by Minister Hall, rather than coming up with it on his own. As many as seventeen towns across an expanding nation appropriated the name "Norwood" in the decade after the book's release. This explanation of its final decision comes from the website of Norwood, New York: "Reverend Chase liked the name and proposed that it be adopted. He pointed out *that it was an easy name to write* because *there were no T's to cross or I's to dot and no letter went above or below the line*. Mr. Chase's proposal was promptly adopted and that is how Norwood got its name." (emphasis mine)

This is remarkably similar to Mr. Thayer's *"looked well in print (no I's to dot or T's to cross), had a pleasing sound, and was easy to write,"* as reported in 1903. It is likely not coincidence that two ministers both supported a third, invoking the same reasoning with almost identical language. It suggests the possibility of a coordinated and novel effort by Beecher and his publisher to promote the book. Of equal interest, however, is how did Henry Ward Beecher come up with the name, "Norwood?"

Henry Ward Beecher, brother of author Harriet Beecher Stowe, was educated in Amherst, Massachusetts. At age fourteen Henry was sent to boarding school there, and subsequently was graduated from Amherst College in 1834. His seven-year sojourn in rural Amherst proved influential when, thirty years later, he needed to site the mythical town of Norwood. "I used to look across the beautiful Connecticut River valley," he wrote in 1849 to his wife Eunice, almost two decades before writing his novel, "and at the blue mountains that hedged it in, until my heart swelled and my eyes filled with tears; why, I could not tell." And while at Amherst, his eyes focused across the Connecticut River upon the idyllic country village of Northampton, Massachusetts.

There is little wonder as to why Beecher's eyes were initially drawn to the quiet community. One of thirteen children of a minister, he had attended a college created to assist "indigent young men of promising talents and hopeful piety, who shall manifest a desire to obtain a liberal education with a sole view to the Christian ministry." And it was in Northampton a century before that Jonathan Edwards began preaching sermons that evolved into, "The Great Awakening."

It is difficult today to appreciate the scope of the religious "awakening" that swept colonial America in 1734. To a divinity student a century later it was of substantial ecumenical import. Recognized as a founder of evangelical Christianity as well as transcendental movements, Jonathan Edwards' influence was well-known. In homage to the preachers' influence, the Northampton Association of Education and Industry was created, a transcendental utopian community of abolitionists existing from 1842-46. In 1851, in recognition of Northampton's growing reputation as a cultural center, Jenny Lind, the "Swedish Nightingale", performed there. Observing the beautiful New England hamlet, she declared it to be "the Paradise of America," a phrase retained to this day as Northampton's motto.

In the introduction to *Norwood; or, Life in a New England Village*, appears this description of the location of Henry Ward Beecher's mythical Norwood,

> A traveler going north from Springfield, in Massachusetts, soon perceives before him an abrupt barrier, running east and west,

which, if compared with the country on either side, might be called mountainous. The two westernmost summits are Mount Tom and Mount Holyoke. By a narrow passage between them comes through the Connecticut River. Passing between these hill-mountains, we enter a great valley or basin, some twelve miles long and thirty wide, which one might easily imagine to have once been a lake; the Pelham hills on the east, Sugar-loaf on the north and the Holyoke range on the south, forming barriers on three sides, while its waters on the west were stayed by the slopes of those hills which, in the middle of western Massachusetts, are all that remain of the famous Green Mountains.

Look with my eyes, good reader, upon the town of Norwood…

It may appear curious that the naming of Norwood should focus on Henry Ward Beecher and the town of Northampton, but there is circumstantial evidence that indeed this is the genesis of our town's name. In his introduction, Beecher mentions that Norwood "was early settled, not far from thirty years after the Pilgrims' landing." Northampton, Massachusetts was settled in 1654, thirty-four years after the Pilgrims' arrival. His introduction mentions, "Norwood, a town of 5,000 inhabitants…" The 1850 population of Northampton was 5,278; in 1860, at the beginning of the decade during which Beecher wrote his novel, 6,788.

An online description today describes the town's location as, "Northampton was settled in 1654 on a low rise above the rich meadowlands by the Connecticut River." Beecher's description of mythical Norwood matches and may contain a winking reference to the town's transcendental colony of the 1850s. "Norwood…refusing to go down upon the fat bottom-lands of the Connecticut, daintily perches itself upon the irregular slopes west, and looks over upon that *transcendent* valley from under its beautiful shade trees and you will say no fairer village glistens in the sunlight, or nestles under arching elms!"

In a chapter entitled, *Leaving College*, Beecher has his characters travel to Amherst College from mythical Norwood. "They soon came to the bridge across the Connecticut," Beecher wrote. "Hiram must have a word with the woman who took toll." In 1867 the only Massachusetts bridge spanning the Connecticut River north of Springfield was the

Northampton Toll Bridge—today's Calvin Coolidge Memorial Bridge—built in 1808.

Other lines in the novel suggest Northampton as the model for mythical Norwood. The author mentions that from the vantage point of Amherst's chapel tower, Norwood's "distant buildings, which he had often looked at through his spy-glass," can be seen. The only two villages within spy-glass distance of the chapel tower in 1868 were the sparsely populated farming community of Hatfield, and the village of Northampton.

Henry Ward Beecher's novel *Norwood; or Life in a New England Village* appears the most logical genesis of our town's name. It is evident that he focused on the lovely village of Northampton as model for mythical Norwood. Theological interests, coupled with a local education, made him knowledgeable, if not expert, on Northampton history. Which defines the final correlation.

When colonials first pushed into western Massachusetts, the Connecticut River proved the most accessible avenue. The rich bottomlands of today's Pioneer Valley were a desirable destination and the tribe inhabiting the area, sharing its aboriginal name with the location itself, was known as the *Norwootuc*. The name appears in archival papers as Norwootuc, Norwottuck, Nonotuck, and several minor variations of the general spelling. James Russel Trumbull, writing Northampton's town history thirty years after the release of Beecher's novel, characterized the area,

> The Nonotucks owned the lands on both sides of the river, from the falls at South Hadley to Sugar Loaf Mountain. The name Nonotuck signifies "the midst of the river." The name was applied to that part of the valley extending north from Mts. Holyoke and Tom to the confines of Deerfield. Its spelling differed at different times, though Nonotuck was always used to designate Northampton.

Seizing the most anglicized variation of the name, Beecher's *Norwood* was almost certainly derived from the Native American town and tribe, *Norwoo*tuc.

I enter the clearing just past the stream, to the right. I recognize the rising slope of Morse Hill. It is difficult to imagine what lies here today... the stubble of stumps, the mounds of piled branches and brush disorient; certainly, the stream is Hawes Brook, the Coakley school must be right *there*...and before the brook the forest lies thick where Hawes Pool and Alandale Parkway lie. In that direction there is a suggestion in the treetops of an opening, perhaps a small pond. I turn around and look in the direction traveled, *and King's Market would have been right about there...* But here is a busy clearing, the forest perimeter leaning into it, grasping for exposed sunlight.

The man sees me and stops, his posture one of alert caution. As I approach, I see his body lithe and sinewy, a body which has never carried an extra pound. His eyes are direct and dull as though unencumbered by waste, or excess. He is business and busy, though pauses at my draw nearer. He appraises me, my extended hand, without hint of the appraisal.

"Don Reddick, of Norwootuc," I say to the man, my hand reaching in eternal, ubiquitous manner. Then, perhaps full of cheeky enthusiasm with an improper anachronism, I add, "Ezra Morse, I presume?"

"Morse," he responds, without raising a hand. Myriad thoughts as the man stares, dispelling any fragile confidence. *Flight...flight...* Then, with a narrowing of eyebrows, "*Where* didst thou say you were from?"

Retracing steps toward Dedham village, I passed the divergent cart path called Wrentham Road, today's Walpole Street. A bit further was noticed a fainter opening to the left. With hours of daylight remaining, I decided to follow it. In retrospect it was probably the course of Vernon Street, as it led directly west up a long, gradual incline. Foliage closed in upon the trail, so I could only imagine streets of the future, crossing— maybe here—Nichols Street, and then about here, Prospect. The path veered toward the right, now sloping downhill, until suddenly opening upon a small pond. In utter fascination I spied a young Indian on the far side wading slowly, peering into the water. He held something which flashed with a splash as he twisted it from his hands, the net dropping with the weight of stone sinkers.

I watched the boy, obscured by centuries of foliage, transfixed. Water shimmered with early spring sunlight, reflecting greenery crowding the shore. Turtles and snakes sunned themselves on shore rocks. It was a slow process of quiet movement, his silent wade through water, hands expert at the task, what bounty easily grasped and placed into a small wicker basket slung over his shoulder. It was the moment I conjure most of my imaginary journey, the quiet, the calm, the woods.

In one of the first books written of the New World, Pilgrim Edward Winslow's 1624 *Good News From New England* contains a fascinating account of aboriginal pre-literary memory,

> Instead of records and chronicles, they take this course. Where any remarkable act is done, in memory of it, either in the place, or by some pathway near adjoining, they make a round hole in the ground about a foot deep, and as much over; which when others passing by behold, they inquire the cause and occasion of the same. Being once known, they are careful to acquaint all men, by which means many things of great antiquity are fresh in memory. So that as a man travelleth, his journey will be less tedious, by reason of the many historical discourses which will be related unto him.

Thus is provided another wonderful metaphor; traveling through time with imagination correlates a static past with a fluid present. Not often does an old hockey player from Silver Street sit next to you at the bar and produce a direct link to the past that you can actually turn in your hand and inspect. But neither the anonymous Indian fishing Father Mac's pond, nor Ezra Morse and his sawmill on Ed Hawes Brook, are truly my destination. As I retrace steps from the pond toward Norwood center and today, I pause.

I've got a hole to dig.

ELDERS

We old men are old chronicles, and when our tongues go they are not clocks to tell only the time present, but large books unclasped; and our speeches, like leaves turned over and over, discover wonders that are long since past.
— Elizabeth Reynard, *The Narrow Land*, 1934

Much has been written of the 1950s and '60s father, his quiet, steadfast aloofness and emotional distance, as well as mothers of the era and their submission to what today are considered quaint cultural norms. Our parents' coronation as The Greatest Generation for efforts during World War II remains their brilliant outward architecture; their foundation was of much grittier matter, and weight.

Parents and grandparents that raised us experienced not just World Wars, but the 1919 Spanish flu epidemic, the economic collapse of 1929 and ensuing Great Depression, as well as the cultural tectonics of mass immigration. These disparate experiences coalesced into the familiar, into us.

My father John Reddick's eighty-fifth birthday was celebrated at the Horse and Carriage Restaurant in Norfolk. Before dinner, to which a large group of family and friends had been invited, I was approached by a friend of my father's named John Martin. A builder long retired, Martin was an avid reader, had read one of my books and knew of my interest in local hockey history. Martin exemplified the best traits of his generation; sober and serious, formal and courteous, the man a consummate gentleman. And he had something for me.

"I have a friend named Vinnie Fitzpatrick," the octogenarian explained, handing me a manila folder. "He's one hundred and one years old, and lives in assisted living in Norton. You should interview him, he is a remarkable man and has great stories of growing up in Walpole, and the first hockey played in the area. I can arrange to go over with you."

Living at the time in Vermont, I never arranged our visit, and Vinnie Fitzpatrick passed away in 2013 at the age of one hundred and two. I had missed a great opportunity. But I retained the document inside the manilla folder, which provided a wonderful individual example of the mass Irish immigration into the Norwood-Walpole industrial area, as well as a glimpse of early hockey.

RECOLLECTIONS AND COMMENTS FROM MY CONVERSATIONS WITH VINNIE

By JOHN MARTIN

Recently, my friend Vinnie Fitzpatrick celebrated his 99th birthday July 11, 2010 with family and friends at his assisted living residence in Norton. He continues to be a remarkable and grand person. His attitude is uplifting, his kindness a joy, and his story unique and wonderful.

On occasion Vinnie and I get together to reminisce and remind each other of old friends and events. Sometimes we talk about books we have read and things we have done during our lives. Occasionally he recommends books he thinks that I will enjoy, and he always makes excellent choices. There is no way that I could read all the books suggested, but I do make every effort to get through the ones he thinks will really interest me, so we can compare each other's reaction to the author's thoughts.

However, more interesting to me than the books are Vinnie's own personal stories. When our talks include personal recollections, I make note of the details, and hope that they will at some time help me give others an appreciation of what a family and individuals can accomplish no matter the adversity. Vinnie, like most of his generation, is a product of a former small-town America. But also like each of us, he is a product of individual life altering circumstances.

Born in a house on Main Street in Walpole, now Watson's Candy Shop, he grew up in Walpole, and married a Walpole girl, Barbara Cole. They reared their children in Walpole, where Vinnie was employed for his entire after-college working career at the Kendall Company within walking distance of his home. Unsurprisingly, he and Barbara chose to retire in Walpole.

In 1906, before Vinnie was born, his mother and father together with their five children, William (1897), Patrick ('98), Mary ('01), Margaret ('02), and Francis ('05) emigrated from Ireland. During the voyage, Vinnie's brother Joseph was born. So, the Fitzpatrick family, father, mother and six children settled in Walpole in 1906. The 1910 town census indicated that they lived on Main Street. Brother Ambrose was born in 1907, sister Eleanor in '10 and Vincent was born in '11—all born in Walpole.

Vinnie's father was a carpenter who worked at the railroad yards in Readville and managed to purchase a small farm on East Street. The farm had a small barn with four connecting sheds. One of the sheds had a well, one an outhouse and the farmhouse had running water. The property bordered railroad property, had a large vegetable garden and stone walls helped set the property off.

In 1914, when Vinnie was three or four years old, his mother died. In 1915, his father had to be taken to the hospital. When his father left for the hospital, he told the children he would either walk through the front door or should things not go well he would be carried through the door in a box. Well his father died because of his illness, and the young family was left on its own.[1]

Perhaps a natural resourcefulness, courage, and hopefulness nourished by their parents helped the young family work together to help one another, or perhaps these characteristics combined with necessity and the help of relatives, friends, and neighbors played a part. But for whatever reasons, the children managed to overcome their adversity, and they did so magnificently.

An important person in this story is Mr. McCarthy, a successful local businessman who lived on Lewis Avenue. When Vinnie's father died, Mr. McCarthy bought the mortgage on the

---

1   The father's death, ironically, may have saved his nine orphaned children. Four years later, in September of 1919, the great influenza epidemic emerged in this area from the Readville railroad yards, workers spreading the disease to family and friends at home. Norwood's first three fatalities included two men employed in the Readville yards, and the spouse of a co-worker.

family property and proceeded to explain to the family that they all must find work of some sort to pay family expenses. He told them that he would come weekly to pick up the mortgage payments and to see how well they were doing. At times when they were short on a payment, Mr. McCarthy would help them work out the shortfall.

Vinnie remembers that the family looked to his sister Margaret as the little mother and called her "Saint" Margaret. The two older boys were his father figures. William, the oldest brother, was a boxer and fought in club matches. He had a punching bag hanging in the cellar, and had the boys learn to box. Vinnie said that he and his brothers never had to fight, because everyone knew they could box. The older brothers watched over Vinnie pretty closely. One time when he was with Patrick, he called someone a "bugger" and received a quick slap. He had no idea what the word meant, but that was the end of using bad words.

Among the many friends and local people who came to the family's aid was Mrs. Allen who put Vinnie to work caring for two Roundy children. As part of the job, he would have lunch at the Allen's when he was caring for the children. And when jobs were scarce there was always the vegetable garden, or in blueberry season they would gather blueberries to sell to neighbors and near Christmas they gathered greens to make wreaths to sell.

Vinnie didn't play sports much in the spring, summer, and fall because there were always chores or jobs that might help out the family, but in the winter when chores and work let up, he could play hockey. He was a member of Walpole High School's first hockey team and played on the team for its first three years. There is a great story about Vinnie's hockey and football experiences at Walpole High in the *Walpole Times* of March 31, 1988. The story also provided remarks from Vinnie about his family, work, and retirement. I'm attaching a copy of that article to this paper.

After high school graduation, Vinnie found a job at the Holliston Mills in Norwood. About the time of his graduation, one of his Walpole coaches, Evan Johnson, asked him where he was going to college. Vinnie told him he couldn't go to college because there was no way to pay for it, and even if he could pay for it, he had not taken the necessary courses to qualify. Well, Vinnie worked for a year while his former coach arranged a hockey scholarship at Hebron Academy in Maine, where he could earn the necessary college credits.

After completing his two years at Hebron, coach Johnson helped Vinnie with his application to Dartmouth College. Vinnie was a credit or two short, but he received a letter from the president of Dartmouth telling him that they were impressed with his work at Hebron and were making an exception in Vinnie's case, and they were accepting him and providing a hockey scholarship on a probationary basis.

Hockey, class work, and on-campus jobs kept Vinnie out straight, so he missed some of the social business of college. But he stayed focused and along with a summer job at the Holliston Mills (forty cents an hour for 10 weeks, $160.00), work on the school campus and help from sister Margaret, he was able to earn his degree.

After graduation at Dartmouth, Vinnie returned to Walpole in 1936 to job hunt. The country was mired in the unemployment and economic concerns of the Great Depression, and for most these were dark times. However, Vinnie was young with a great naturally positive attitude, had successfully worked his way through extraordinary obstacles, and was ready to show what he could do.

Walpole was typical of then small-town New England. Local businesses employing college graduates were, for the most part, family owned manufacturing firms whose owners were residents of the communities where the businesses were located. These firms had grown over time through the efforts of local owners and local employees. Most of these firms were struggling to survive the poor economy. Some would fail and some few would work through hard times and prosper. The Kendall Company was the successor to a failing manufacturing firm employing about 75 people in a rundown facility off West Street in Walpole. Harry P.

Kendall, who was brought up in Walpole and had strong local family connections, had taken over the failing business in 1903.

When Vinnie went to The Kendall Company in 1936, he wasn't focusing on future possibilities. He went to find work, just hoping to qualify for any opening that might be available. He was interviewed by Harold Young, plant manager at the time. Mr. Young asked him what type of work he felt best qualified for, Vinnie said that he just needed a job, and would try anything. Mr. Young said that they had a crew that was going to work that weekend clearing debris from the river and that if Vinnie was interested he could work with that crew and come back on Monday and they would talk.

After clearing debris from the river for the weekend, Vinnie and Mr. Young had another talk. They agreed that Vinnie would work in different departments at the plant and decide later what work would best suit Vinnie and the Kendall Company. Vinnie first worked in manufacturing tending carding machines on the night shift. The machinery was located in a small, old wood building which at one time was known as Chandler Mill.

It was at some point during these job moves that Vinnie met Barbara. And in 1939 Vinnie and Barbara had the good sense to become man and wife. They lived on East Street in Walpole in a house that Vinnie and his brother, a carpenter, had built, and their three children, Betsy, Gayle and Jack, grew up in the very same area that their father had always called home.

Vinnie's retirement continues to be blest with family and friends, with rich memories of relationships and accomplishments and with undiminished personal goodness. When I asked how his 99th birthday party went, he said, 'It was very nice, but I'm really going to celebrate next year!' And he did!

This brief account of some of my friend's life experiences is offered as an attempt to acknowledge some of the extraordinary accomplishments of my friend and those with whom he has shared and those with whom he continues to share his goodness.

HELEN JOHNSON

"Helen was born Helen Marie Johnson on March 17, 1922 in Norwood, Massachusetts. She was the 6th child of 7 born to John Oscar and Hannah Maria Anderson Johnson. All of the children were born in Norwood and attended Norwood schools.

"Helen's father, Johan Askar Jansson (Swedish spelling) was born 21 Apr 1889 in Ljusnarsbert, Orebro, Sweden. He immigrated to Massachusetts from Sweden in 1907. Sometime after he arrived the name was changed to John Oscar Johnson. Four of his sisters also immigrated to the Boston area. Marie married Peter Wallin, a machinist, who immigrated in 1900; Hulda married Otto Benson, a house painting contractor who immigrated in 1905; Signe married Paul Siegismund who immigrated in 1923. Paul was from Freiberg, Germany and worked for the Salvation Army in Boston. John was a brick mason by trade, and he built many brick and rock walls around Norwood until he died at fifty-six years of age in 1944.

"On April 4, 1914, in Norwood, John married Hannah Maria Anderson who was born October 18, 1891 in Frykerud, Varmland, Sweden. The children born to the Nilsson's used the surname of Anderson, so I'm assuming they used the traditional naming method in Scandinavian countries of adding 'son' to their father's first name. Hannah Maria immigrated at the age of twenty on the boat *Campania*, arriving in New York City on September 23, 1911. Her final destination was Norwood, Massachusetts where she lived with the Anders Kallgren family.

"The Kallgrens were also from Frykerud and immigrated to America in 1895 on the ship *Rhynland* and landed in Philadelphia with their destination being Michigan. Their first child was born there, but one year later their 2nd child was born in Norwood, Massachusetts. Helen's mother immigrated and she may have come to help Mrs. Kallgren with the duties of taking care of a large family and a new baby, as well as being a twenty-year-old wanting to come to America. Even though both of Helen's parent were from Sweden and spoke Swedish, she and her siblings never learned to speak the language. Helen said the only Swedish words she knew were swear words.

"Like so many people during the depression, John Oscar developed a drinking problem and often people would hire him and, instead of a paycheck, he would accept a 'bottle of booze', as Helen put it. This put the family at risk and Hannah had to work hard to keep a roof over their heads and food on the table for their growing family. Hannah worked for a Newman family as a domestic worker. She did laundry by scrubbing on a wash board, and ironing in their home for working or wealthy women that she knew. She worked hard to help keep her family afloat during the depression and after her husband died. In about 1931, her son, Billy, developed polio and she nursed him back to health with the help of a friend and/or the Kallgren's daughter, Vivian, who was a nurse. All this she did while raising her own large family. In her later years, after her husband passed away, she would live, for a spell, at each of her children's and her brother's home. She died in June 1961. She is buried with her husband John Oscar, in the Highland Cemetery in Norwood.

"Growing up in the 1920s and '30s was a struggle for this Johnson family. They started out living on East Cross Street in Norwood. Then John Oscar either built or bought a home at 33 Cross Street. Originally, the house had a wrap-around porch that is missing today. It was a cozy little place to play. The house has been added on to, so it doesn't look like it did when Helen lived there. There were apple trees in the yard that one could sit under on the warm, humid days of summer. The neighborhood was made up of many immigrants. Right next door was the Martin and Julia Folan family from Ireland. They had a son John that was Helen's age and a younger son, Martin Jr. James Cuff who also lived nearby, with his two sisters, worked for the Post Office. His sister Gertrude was a schoolteacher and Catharine was a store clerk.

"The Johnson family home set further back from the street than the other homes and there was an open field in the back of the house where a creek ran through and blueberry bushes grew. Helen remembers picking blueberries when they were in season and they ate them on their cereal in the morning. This area is near Hennessey Field today. Summertime they played baseball in the front yard. They liked going to watch the baseball games at the Civic Center.

"In the winter, when it was freezing, the boys in the neighborhood would dam up the creek in the field behind their house where the blueberries grew. The dam made a pond that froze over and was used to skate on. As far as Helen knew, none of them played hockey, but some may have been on a team at school. At first she didn't have ice skates, but had the type that would strap or clamp onto her shoes. Later Helen inherited a pair of the much more stylish shoe ice skates which made it much easier to skate.

"They also had sleds and would go sledding on a downhill part of Cross Street. Someone at each end would stop traffic when a sledder was soaring down the hill to keep everyone safe. It took the whole neighborhood to make it fun. The kids built igloos and snow forts and had many snowball fights. Snow boots were not in style then, so they had rubber boots that fit over their shoes with metal clamps that would hold them snuggly on her foot. If they didn't have the boots, they would put bread wrappers over their shoes to keep their shoes dry, but that was a hazard since they were very slick.

"In the fall, football was the game of choice in the neighborhood. There were many different games, over the years, the kids liked to play. In the outdoors, one of the games Helen called 'Peggy' was a game where they would break a clothes pin in half and would put it on a stick and try to hit it to land in a circle drawn on the ground. Ollie Ollie Ox in Free, Stick Ball, Red Rover, Blind Man's Bluff, Tether Ball, and Kick Ball were also very popular. Boys played cowboys and Indians and girls played house, carving out the rooms on the ground and using plants to represent foods to serve. They loved it when blueberries were in season! Jumping rope was also popular with the girls. It was such good exercise. As Helen got a little older, she would venture out and ride bikes with her friend Blanche Dallalis, who lived by a store and was in her class in school. She was the daughter of Jerome and Adela Dallalis who lived on Lenox Street. She would borrow a bike from her brother, so she had to ride a boy's bike. She never had a bike of her own.

"Times were tough, and her family didn't have a car. The First Baptist Church had a Christian Endeavor group, for the teenagers who were good friends. A couple of guys in the group had cars and they would all pile into a couple of cars and go on excursions, to ball games, and community events. Along with Helen, she remembers the group consisted of Rose James, Harold Fillmore, Doug Ross, Mary Town, Joe Belotti, Jenny Tobin, Eleanor Tomasillo, Nita Steward, and Blanche Dallalis. They had a lot of fun together.

"Some favorite memories she has are when the neighbor kids would hear the ice cream truck coming down the street and waiting for a treat when it got to their house. The kids liked splashing in the warm water when summer rainstorms would fill the street gutters and flood the sides of the street. She also remembers visiting older neighbors on their front porch in the evening, who would pass out candy to them when they went to visit. Christmas was always special when family would come. Helen's Aunt Signe would bring the family clothing and other things that were probably purchased at the Salvation Army in Boston, where her husband worked. Signe was able to pick out nice things that were like new for them to wear. Signe, who had no children, would knit mittens and things for Christmas gifts. Helen said that she wished she had appreciated them more then, since she now knows the love and time put into making them, but as a child she longed for brand-new things.

"As a poor family during the depression, they always had clothes to wear and food on the table. There were people at the church that would help with food and there was a neighbor who worked at a bakery who would bring cookies and baked goods that were a day old, because she knew Helen's mother was having a hard time. She is sure that her mother helped other people with things that she knew she could do for them in their times of need. It was a time of sharing what you could share.

"Everyone in the family did work at some time, while living at home, to help their mom keep food on the table. Helen's sister, Ruth, lived with Doctor Harwell's family, taking care of their children and housekeeping. Ruth gave Helen a little red trinket box full of pennies for Christmas. Helen kept pennies in the box for a very long time. She said as long as she had money in that little box, she felt rich! The pennies are gone today, but she still has the little red box.

"Her brothers Oscar and Bert both worked at Holliston Mills. In 1940 Bobby worked as an office boy at the Norwood Press at the age of nineteen. For a time, Helen lived in Needham with a Newman family and took care of their children and did housekeeping, paying her $7 a week. She also worked as a domestic helper in the Allan and Natalie Haskell household in Norwood, caring for their son William and helping with preparing food for Mrs. Haskell to cook. Allan Haskell was the proprietor of Codex Book Company in Norwood. As soon as Helen finished high school in 1940, her Sunday School teacher helped her to get a job at

Bird & Son in Walpole, where she did office work. It was too far from home, and she didn't have a car, so Arnold Schaier helped her get a job at Bendix Aviation in Norwood, where she was able to walk to work. After three years working there, in 1944, a gal that had worked with her at Bendix Aviation joined the Navy and talked Helen into joining up. So she did.

"Helen spent about a year and half as a W.A.V.E. working in the Washington, DC area, in the Medical Records Department, during WW II. She wasn't in the service for very long before her father died. So she got to go home for the funeral. Helen was in Washington, DC during the time that Franklin D. Roosevelt was president and when he passed away she marched in the military parade during his funeral procession. She met her husband to be, Jack Jansen, in Washington, DC and they were married in 1945, in Norwood after the war ended. Jack was a divorced father of two children and he worked at Plimpton Press until he made enough money to make the train trip home to Idaho, where they started their life together with the two children.

"Helen has outlived two husbands and now lives in Grants Pass, Oregon in an Assisted Living facility near her daughter and will soon be 98 years old, as of this writing in February of 2020. She and her sister Sylvia are the only survivors of her immediate family. Sylvia now lives in Maine. Helen's memories were told to her daughter, Sondra Appel, who wrote this piece."

LINDA VENSKUS

"The Swedes and the Finns mainly settled in the Savin Ave., Chapel Street, Winslow Ave. area. The American Legion, which has been turned into condos, at one time was the Finn Hall. This was back in the early 1900s. Runeberg Hall was on Wilson Street. The order of Runeberg included both the Finnish and Swedish! As kids, we had a lot of fun up there. Many Scandinavian dances and dinners took place on Saturday nights and Scandinavian dance classes were offered for the children on Saturday mornings. A favorite memory of mine of Swedeville was going to Grandma's house on Friday nights for supper where we were served *plattar*—Swedish pancakes—with Lidonberries, rye bread, and Lutefisk, a form of fish well-known to Scandinavians.

"My mother Ruth W. Mattson was born on May 26, 1914, in the family homestead, 11 Johnson Court, located off of Savin Ave. in Swedeville. She was the 7th born child of eight children. Her parents emigrated from Sweden, father 1892 and mother 1897 and were married shortly after they settled in Norwood. Their first apartment was on Sturtevant Ave. in South Norwood where the first three children were born. They bought a brand-new two-family house in Swedeville in 1905 and the other five children were born there.

"Grandpa worked at the tannery and Grandma stayed at home to care for the eight children. They rented the first-floor apartment and also took in boarders in order to make ends meet. They had outdoor toilets due to the fact that there were so many people living in this house. There was also a closet in the back hall of the side entrance of the home where it was converted into a portable bathroom toilet without running water. There a large piece of oak with a round opening served as the toilet seat. Below contained a large bucket for human waste. There was not any running water and they used kerosene lamps for lighting. They had a chimney pipe that both of the wood burning stoves were attached to for their heating. The water was boiled from the heat produced from the wood burning stoves. They had four Macintosh apple trees on their property, raised turkeys and chickens and grew several types of vegetables. Also had some grape vines.

"Also the steam baths were very famous and the male Swedes and the Finns often frequented the steam bathes which were located right behind the now Colonial House Restaurant. Since people did not have running water, the steam baths were a great place to frequent plus they are widely used in Sweden and Finland to this day! The now Colonial House Restaurant was called Costello's back in the 1930s and probably remained under that name until Paul Angelo bought the place back in the late 1960s, early '70s. I have pictures of my mother and her sister taken around 1938 at Costello's where the exact same wooden booths remain as of today! Oak lasts forever! Costello's was the first restaurant-bar in the area and opened around 1934.

"My father, Andrew T. Venskus, was the first child born to Lithuanian immigrants in South Norwood on January 16th, 1913. Both of my paternal grandparents emigrated to the U.S. from Lithuania, Andrew Sr. arrived to the USA approximately 1907 along with two of his brothers and a male cousin. I believe that Grandpa Venskus' first job was at the Morrill Ink

Works. He sent for Grandma Domicella Razulevich who was still in Lithuania around 1910 as he wanted to marry her. She had relatives living in Lawrence, Mass. who I believed sponsored her. She lived with them for a while and then she and Grandpa Venskus married in 1912. They rented an apartment on the corner of St. George Ave. and Washington St.—right over the bakery—and my dad was born there. My grandfather lost his job as I believe the Morrill Ink Works folded around 1914 or 1915. The family was forced to move to Hyde Park from 1915 through 1921 as jobs were not plentiful.

"My father's family were Catholic. They returned back to Norwood around 1921 where I believe that my dad attended the Winslow School. He had to stay back in the first grade when they lived in Hyde Park as he only spoke Lithuanian and the parochial school expected him to be able to speak English. The nuns thought that my father was just faking it and would punish my dad by lifting him up in the air and smashing his butt over the steam radiators. They also beat him with the rattan and tied him up to a chair making him sit in the corner of the classroom. Once these nuns finally realized that my father did not speak a word of English, they kicked him out of 1st grade and told my grandparents that he had to learn the English language. He was tutored but lost an entire year of school. My dad went through so much pain and agony in his life.

"Since we are presently experiencing a flu epidemic, I want to share what my father's family went through while living in Hyde Park during the Flu Epidemic of 1918. My grandparents lost a baby boy in August of 1918 who only lived for one month. Grandma became pregnant right away in August of 1918 and was carrying twins. She became pregnant while the epidemic was still active. She lost one of the twins, a boy that lived only one day and baby Annie survived for a few months but died right before Christmas of 1919. My Dad often spoke of his memories of baby Annie's funeral procession led by horses and buggy as they transported her to Fairview Cemetery in Hyde Park. I also have a professional photo that was taken of baby Annie reposed in her baby casket with my dad, Uncle Ben and Aunt Gene standing behind her. The photo is such a treasure! I have a copy of it that was taken of the original that is inside of a glass frame. My cousin wouldn't take the original copy out of its original encased glass frame so there is quite a bit of glare in the photo. Maybe that is good because most of the glare is of baby Annie and her casket. Not many people display pictures of deceased relatives in their homes!

"A lot of what I am writing about is just information to differentiate my mother as a Swede and my father as a Lithuanian. They lived so close to each other growing up yet the families did not associate with each other. My dad went to high school with my mother and both graduated from Norwood High School class of 1932. They both went their separate ways but met up at the Norwood Sports Center when my father was home visiting as he was stationed in Biloxi, Mississippi during World War II. She was Protestant and he was Catholic. Boy, that was not a good combo back in those times. They did get married and my father left the Catholic Church where he was very disliked by many of the Norwood businessmen, as well as a few in his extended family. One was considered a real sinner if one married outside of the Catholic faith. My father attributes his success in his jewelry business from his patrons who were mainly the Congregationalists and the Lutherans. Catholics would not frequent my dad's store and took their business to other jewelers that were located in Norwood center. That was how different things were back in 1940s up through the late 1960s, early '70s.

"So upon moving back to Norwood in 1921 my father's family bought a home across the tracks, on the other side of Cedar Street near Savin Ave.—not in South Norwood—because there was a housing shortage in South Norwood. Consequently many Lithuanian and Polish families moved to the upper side of Cedar Street and also onto Saunders Road and Winslow Ave.

"When I read about what some of our ancestors went through, having to say good-bye to loved ones, enduring that trip over the Atlantic Ocean by ship, and not necessarily a non-stop trip, and many had to change from vessel to vessel in other countries, truly amazes me! Yes, most had sponsors, but the process to enter America at Ellis Island did not necessarily go smoothly and did not work out for some.

"My uncle lost his eye as someone threw a baseball at him. He was discharged from the Army Air Corps as a result. This truly upset not only my uncle but my grandma who was left to support eight children as my grandpa died from an abscess tooth. Several of my aunts and uncles were older as my mom was the second youngest of eight. Very sad when one has been permanently injured at such a young age. At least families were so tight-knit back in those days and neighbors all watched out for each other. If someone was ill, often a neighbor would stop by to drop off a fresh batch of soup. Women were often seen sitting out on their front porches working on their crocheting or needlework projects. Quilting Bees were often held at a neighbor's home one night a week where a group of women met to stuff down feathers into a quilt in order to make the process move faster. Then the following week another neighbor would hold the Quilting Bees with the goal that every family involved would receive a completed down feathered quilt after the course of many weeks of hard work. I am sure you have heard stories similar.

"When we were very young these stories shared by our folks and relatives may have not been 'that interesting to listen to.' As one grows older, one begins to appreciate what our families and relatives had to endure in order to survive and continue with their mission to move forward."

DON HAMLIN

Heroes walked among us, some in unlikely form. On Winter Street lived my mother's best friend Barbara Hamlin, whose husband Don was a fellow United Church member and frequent guest in our home. The diminutive man's quiet and reserved demeanor belied his World War II deeds. His daughter Nancy Hamlin Jones, Norwood High School class of '77, spoke reverently of her dad.

"He grew up on Washington Street, his family had a, remember Dr. Howard, the dentist? Where his house was on Washington Street? My father lived in a house diagonally across from that. His parents owned a gas station, they owned the gas station at the corner of Railroad Ave., across from where the Mobil station is now. There was a gas station on the other side. And then it got sold when my grandparents died, and from then on, he worked at the Plimpton Press until it closed. He was a book binder. Dad would have been happy to talk to you. When these people are gone, the stories are gone."

Don Hamlin graduated from Norwood High School in the spring of 1942. At 5' 4" tall, his subsequent enlistment in the U.S. Army found him designated a ball turret gunner on a B-17 bomber nicknamed, *Heavens Above*. In one of those wonderful discoveries for gatherers of Norwood lore, Don Hamlin's stories are not gone, because he had dictated them to son

Don Jr., who wrote them down. The following describes the action for which Don Hamlin received the Distinguished Flying Cross, awarded to those who "distinguish themselves by single acts of heroism or extraordinary achievement while participating in aerial flight."

Stories from a very big "Little Man"

Imagine, if you can, what it was like to fly over enemy territory, during what some call the greatest war of the modern era, at forty thousand feet with nothing between you and certain death but some thin sheet metal, plexiglass, and a few thousand rivets that they called a B-17 Flying Fortress.

This was a time when flying was very young and had no modern conveniences which we have all grown to know such as heat, comfy seats, restrooms, and such. This was a time when planes were being built in a few days to support the war effort and creature comforts were not part of the thinking process. By today's standards, these planes would never be allowed to leave the ground never mind fight our war. And just to make you understand what it was like, think of flying from Boston to L.A. and back, non-stop, with no heat in the plane, no comfy seats to sit on, no in-flight meals served by a pretty stewardess with a friendly smile on her face, and best of all no bathroom on board to use when the action got intense... This was the place I knew as my workplace for some time.

One of these workdays I remember quite well was a time coming back from a daylight raid over Augsburg, Germany when we ran into a flight of six Messerschmitts—German fighters—and they were very angry that we had just bombed their homeland and looking to take some revenge on us. They broke into our formation and began to shoot us up. I guess it was our lucky/unlucky day as one of the German fighters has shot our pilot, wounded our co-pilot, navigator, bombardier and top turret gunner. Being as I was also taught as flight engineer; it was my duty to take control of the aircraft and bring our crew home. I got out of my position as ball turret gunner and climbed up to the cockpit to see the lifeless form of my pilot at the controls and the severely wounded form of my co-pilot. I reached up to release the seatbelt of my pilot and dragged his body out of his seat, letting it slowly drop on the metal decking, then climbing into his seat and trying to get this hulk of a plane back on track. Our windshield has been smashed and the control panel has been blown to bits by the enemy bullets, our plane has been shot up pretty badly and full of holes making the plane hard to control. I strap myself into the seat and get this bird under some kinda control and level flight.

Right about then I see three of our P-51 Mustangs take up the fight with the Messerschmitts, and of course saving our sweet little butts. Surely put a smile on my face as the P-51s were now taking the heat off of us and I now being able to concentrate on flying this bird. I headed the plane in the general direction of my base in England and shortly after leaving the fight area, was joined by our P-51s, which took up escort positions on our wingtips. We all headed toward our base and I thought the worst was over and I just have to land this crate. As we cross the channel I'm thinking we're home free and we'll be in the bar soon enough, well I was in for a very large surprise. I see the base in the distance and I know it's time to drop the landing gear so I begin to proceed with this task as I fly over the field.

Through my headset I hear the control tower telling me we only have one wheel down and to fly by the field until they get ready on the ground. Well this is not what I wanted to hear but still flew by the field. Knowing that we cannot land on one wheel, I retract the one wheel and tell the tower we're coming in, I need to get this crate down.

As I approach the field on my fly-by, I see every piece of emergency equipment lining the field and begin to think, *Is this the way I'm going, never to see home again?* I hear through my headset a full bird Colonel trying to calm me down and land this monster, but I know it's all up to me to bring this plane and her crew home safely. I line up the runway and pull my harness tighter as I know it's going to be a bumpy ride in. I start looking around the shattered cockpit making sure everything is as it should be and let the plane sink into the runway, belly dragging on the ground, sparks showering the ground like fourth of July fireworks. We slide for some distance and come to a stop way down the field. The plane is surrounded by rescue and fire trucks and medics scramble into the plane to get the wounded out. I try to move but I'm frozen to the seat, just can't believe what had just happened and I'm still alive. Next thing I know, up pops a medic up through the passageway and hands me a bottle of whiskey and says, 'Here, get drunk...' This little adventure earned me the Distinguished Flying Cross as well as giving me new respect for my plane.

HENRY VALENTINAS

Locked in a corner cabinet in the Sarah Bond Morrill Reading Room in Norwood's Morrill Memorial Library is a wonderful book by William Wolkovich-Valkavicius, entitled, *Lithuanians of Norwood, Massachusetts, A Social Portrait in a Multi-Ethnic Town*, in which Wolkovich-Valkavicius writes,

> The surname "Tumas" that has appeared in this text can serve as an introduction to a post-World War II phenomenon, the influx of the Displaced Persons. Commonly called the DPs, the Tumases were among thousands of Lithuanians who fled their homeland in the face of returning Soviet invaders in 1944. First these displaced people lived mostly in refugee camps of Germany for several years. There, as best as circumstances allowed, they reconstructed their religious, social, and cultural lives, as extant in Lithuania. As it gradually became evident that Lithuanians could not return to their native land, an estimated 30,000 such refugees emigrated to the USA, while another 20,000 found haven in Canada.
>
> Agencies handling this type of relocation included "War Relief Services"—an arm of the National Catholic Welfare Conference collaboration with diocesan bureaus of Catholic Charities. The key to the success of the programs was the local, giant-hearted person or family responsible for finding living quarters, or a job, and

at least temporary support so that the recipient would not become a financial burden on the community. The standard form for the benefactor asked if the "home opportunity" compared favorably with other homes in the vicinity, and if school and church were accessible. Furthermore, the applicant had to specify a potential employer by name, address, and job description.

Altogether, among the many such uprooted, some thirty-five families made their way to Norwood and surrounding towns. This influx took place between 1948 and the early 1950s. An undated list in St. George Parish files lists sixty-eight displaced persons who gained their start in the New World here in this town.

The standard form asked if the "home opportunity" compared "favorably" with other homes in the vicinity. This was the reality of Lithuanian relocation,

> Typical of fresh arrivals, Lithuanians found the cheapest apartments in the south end of Norwood, pejoratively long known as "The Flats," at one time designated "the dumping ground of the peasantry of Europe." These Lithuanians occupied quarters next to Italian and Syrian neighbors, somewhat earlier arrivals. Sites such as Lenox and Dean Streets, and Oolah Avenue, as well as the principal route of Washington Street became home for the Lithuanians. They found themselves in a district described as "a shabby, unsanitary, and poorly provided place to live" in the words of town historian Bryant Franklin Tolles.

Though the largest percentage increases in Norwood and Walpole populations came during the industrialization era toward the end of the nineteenth century, the largest per capita increases occurred post-World War II. Not only was the "baby boom" booming, but the mass assimilation of European refugees combined to create the 1950s surge that brought Norwood's population to the level it has maintained these past seventy years. And here-in lies a remarkable tale of a future Norwood hockey captain, that of Henry "Hank" Valentinas, whose son Matthew provided the following narrative from his Newton home:

"My father was born in Radviliskis, Lithuania, just outside of Siauliai. One of the reasons my family could escape the Russians was it was a train town, the biggest rail area. Actually, when the Russians came in, they tried to throw my grandfather on a train to Siberia because he was educated. The Mayor of the town pulled him off and saved his life. But they went to Germany, they got out in '41. If you got out before June '41, you could get citizenship.

"A horrible experience he never got over. One story from the labor camps was my grandfather spoke seven languages and he was spokesman of his group. They weren't given utensils to eat the food with, so my grandfather wrote Himmler and asked for utensils, said if they were going to work them to death, at least they should be able to eat. Himmler wrote back, and they got the utensils. But they sent him to the sulfur mines to kill him, basically to work him to death, but he came back.

"My grandfather was smart enough, he had traveled to St. Petersburg and Berlin, he was a worldly guy. He always knew what was going on, they stayed along the Baltic seacoast. The whole family was in labor camps. Looking back, he would have stayed and fought, but a daughter was born in a labor camp in Poland, and he stayed for the family.

"So, like I said at the end of the war they ended up in Flensburg, where the official Nazi government was operating out of after Hitler killed himself. They just got out of Hamburg two days before they bombed it. He was strafed three times. As he got older he talked more of the war, like he told me toward the end of war the Russian prisoners were walking through and they were all starving, and the story changed, his wife went to give a bowl of rice to one of the Russians and he pulled her back and he originally told me the guard hit the Russian in the head, but later he told me he hit him so hard he bashed his head in and his brains came out.

"Then they were in the DP camps, the Displaced Persons camps. From '45 to '51 they were there. There was no food and they almost starved, he told me they were eating grass.

"Then they came over to America, and they were sponsored by a Lithuanian family in Norwood, I think it was St. Georges. And they lived with them for a while, my grandfather was a successful businessman, but he went to work in the shingle factory. They called him a Nazi because they didn't know.[2] And my father would work there summers, too, they bought a house across from the shingle factory, the one by Morse Street, and he was smart enough to buy a triple decker. They lived in the top floor and rented out the two others.

"I think when my father first came here there was no English as a second language, and he taught himself English from TV. He got beat up a lot by the Walpole kids, the Irish and Italians, so sports sort of changed that for him. Said he went out for football once but got hit so hard he said enough of that! Then he went out for hockey and the first time he didn't make the team. But he really loved it, and he kept at it and by sophomore year he made the team and was captain his junior and senior years. I think he was a leading scorer of the Bay State League. My grandfather never supported him in that, he couldn't understand why anyone would play games, you should be studying engineering or something. But I think he worked out a lot of anger he had. But he just loved it, he just loved it.

"He was offered a scholarship for hockey from Princeton, but it didn't pay room and board and he went to Northeastern. There were not many rinks around then and it was really hard, and he was working too, so I think he lost interest. He still played hockey until the late '70s in the rec leagues.

"He said he got his revenge on the guys who beat him up earlier in life, but hockey made him—he was a pretty tough guy. He was about 5' 8" and one-eighty, he really had a passion for it and it gave him an identity here in America. He was Lithuanian, immigrant groups always were together, and he wanted to get away from that. Lithuanian men married Lithuanian women, he wanted to get away from that. Hockey gave him his own identity, and he embraced that.

"He ended up getting drafted in '62, and he had just graduated from college. He was made a citizen before he got shipped out. He was in the

---

2 The taunt was ironic. Aleksandras Lileikis, a Lithuanian refugee brought to the U.S. under auspices of the Refugee Relief Act in 1955, lived for 40 years in Norwood before authorities identified him as a Nazi war criminal. He was de-naturalized and returned to Lithuania in 1996. He was quoted, "All of us were collaborators, the whole nation, since it was acting according to Nazi laws. I needed to clothe myself and eat. I was offered a job, and I accepted it. I got into a mess, and I got stuck...So probably I made mistakes. Mistakes, or let's say the 'crimes' which I am accused of."

8th infantry in Germany, and they wanted him to become a helicopter pilot. My grandfather said you've already seen enough war, don't do it."[3]

Our elders entered, established, and conveyed an ethnic Norwood that fast faded with my generation's assimilation. Anecdotes abound of our parent's elbowing; a mother on Crestwood Circle sending her (unknowing) Protestant son to school on St. Patrick's Day in an orange shirt; a Catholic neighbor organizing his (unknowing) children into a wagon-pulling, sign-wielding parade in support of the first Catholic presidential candidate. But to us, the delineation of neighborhoods, of Dublins and Germantowns and Swedevilles, seemed a quaint aspect of fading generations.

William Wolkovich-Valkavicius, in his book *Lithuanians of Norwood, Massachusetts*, discussed inter-Eastern European assimilation which can be extrapolated to all of Norwood's ethnic embraces.

> Lithuanian-Polish ties in Norwood long ago resumed an air of civility, and then cordial cooperation. Inter-ethnic marriages have helped to topple barriers as exemplified by the mild-mannered Polish American Walter Gotovich, Esq., who took a Lithuanian-American bride, Anne Smolski, on the 4th of July 1943. While the immigrant parents remained deeply divided between church people and agnostic or atheist socialists and free thinkers, their children found common ground in sports and fraternal societies, cordial relations among the youths proved to be a welcome result of baseball and similar athletics as well as participation in community organizations. These adolescents did not necessarily worship together, they learned to get along on and off the diamond and in various social settings. These second-generation Lithuanians learned to shrug off the hard feelings that lingered among their parents.

Hockey played its part, the Lithuanian community producing the Tamulionises and Smelstors (originally Smelstovius), Wheelers, Higginses

---

[3] The advice was sound. In short years to follow, of approximately 12,000 helicopters used in Vietnam, nearly half were destroyed in combat, with over 2,000 pilots Killed in Action.

and Reddicks reflective of Protestant Christian Hill; Ranallis, Angelos, and Rosatas distilled of Italian immigration; Hebners, Hasenfuses, and Mauses representing Germantown; the Arvidsons Swedeville; the Thorntons, Tobins, and Lawries of Cork City stride-for-stride with Donovans, Dempseys, and Feeneys of Dublin, all melding into 1960s Norwood hockey.

In 1982 an article appeared in the *Norwood Messenger* detailing an Irish reunion of Dublin neighborhood residents. "Five years ago they were all able to recapture those days," it read. "A reunion at Concannon's Village brought together 'Babe' Feeney, 'Butch' Lydon, 'Zark' Connolly and five hundred other Dubliners." In 1982 I had three girls under four years of age, lived on North Ave. in a second-floor apartment, and cleaned up job sites for a living. Old Patrick Naughton, whose brogue rang with rhythms of County Cork, lived next door, and I was surrounded by a Dublin neighborhood so familiar there seemed nothing remarkable about it...*these stories shared by our folks and relatives may have not been "that interesting to listen to"...*

What I would give to attend that reunion today.

KIDS

What I want to know is how people were living, what they were thinking, how they expressed themselves. One problem with some recent Western movies is that the writer or director has tried to impose a late-twentieth century viewpoint on a nineteenth century situation, and it won't work. A person or a situation can only be understood against the background of its own time.

— LOUIS L'AMOUR, *EDUCATION OF A WANDERING MAN*, 1939

My mother, tasked with creating, corralling, and correcting three boys under six without benefit of the modern-day babysitter nicknamed TV, used to affix rope to my belt and tie me to a tree in the yard. Thought bizarre if not criminal today, I never once heard a disparaging word regarding the practice in my youth, and it remains a small example that child-rearing has changed through the years. Evidence abounds, as in this recounting of 1830s Ohio from Ulysses S. Grant's memoir,

> When I was seven or eight years of age, I began hauling all the wood used in the house and shops. I could not load it on the wagons, of course, at that time, but I could drive, and the choppers would load and someone at the house unload. When about eleven years old, I was strong enough to hold a plough. From that age until seventeen I did all the work done with horses, such as breaking up the land, furrowing, ploughing corn and potatoes, bringing in the crops when harvested, hauling all the wood, besides tending two or three horses, a cow or two, and sawing wood for stoves, etc., while still attending school. For this I was compensated by the fact there was never scolding or punishing by my parents; no objection to rational enjoyments,

such as fishing, or going to the creek a mile away to swim in summer, taking a horse and visiting my grandparents in the adjoining county, fifteen miles off, skating on the ice in winter, or taking a horse and sleigh when there was snow on the ground.

While still quite young I had visited Cincinnati, forty-five miles away, several times alone; also Maysville, Kentucky often, and once Louisville. The journey to Louisville was a big one for a boy of that day. I had also gone once with a two-horse carriage to Chillicothe, about seventy miles, with a neighbor's family, who were removing to Toledo, Ohio, and returned alone, and had gone once, in like manner, to Flat Rock, Kentucky, about seventy miles away.

General Grant was subtle in his pride of childhood work ethic and responsibility; R. E. Gould, author of Maine's *Yankee Shopkeeper*, in a 1930s letter to novelist Kenneth Roberts, was more direct,

My recollections include the story of grandmother's uncle, who was attacked by Indians while mowing near Fort Popham, and killed six Indians with his scythe before they got him. Of my grandfather taking a load of salt back into the interior to swap for corn when he was nine years old, and incidentally swapping a pair of steers for a pair of oxen that the owner couldn't winter out on account of a shortage of hay. Of my great grandfather who, as a boy of eight, followed his father to the siege and capture of Quebec under Wolfe—and then to read that present-day eight year old boys are overtaxed when we ask them to do anything useful, such as bringing in an armful of wood!

Like DNA defining their bodies, the thread of boyhood cultural Darwinism replicates through the years. The book, *The Real Diary of a Real Boy*, an 1866 diary of a twelve-year-old New Hampshire lad, serves as an example.

Dec. 1 Skinny Bruce got licked in school today.

Dec. 2 Pretty near had a fite in school today. Skinny Bruce and Frank Elliot got rite up with there fists up when the bell rung. It was too bad, it wood have been a buly fite. I bet on Skinny.

Dec. 8 Skinny Bruce got licked in school today.

Dec. 17 Tady Finton got licked in school today. Snowed today a little.

Dec. 18 Bright and fair. Nothing particular. O yes, Skinny Bruce got licked in school.

December 20 Bully skating, went after school and skated way up to the eddy, was going to skate with Luey Watson but Pewt and Beany hollered so that I dident dass to. Johnny Toomey got hit with a hocky block rite in the snoot and broke his nose.

December 23 Saturday and no skating.

Jan. 1 I went home mother said something was the matter and I told her and then I cried, I don't know what I cried for, because I dident ake any. Father said he would lick me at home when I got licked at school and perhaps that was why I cried. Ennyway when father come home I asked him if he was a going to lick me and he said not by a dam sight . . . I went to sleep. I drempt I was fiting all the time.

Jan. 19 Nobody got licked in school today, gess why, becaus there wasent enny school.

June 16 Dennis Cokely and Tomtit Tomson had a fite behind Hirvey's resterent today. Hirvey stopped them jest as they were having a good one. That's jest the way. I don't see why they always want to stop a fite. All fellers fite for is to see which can lick, and how can they tell unless they fite it out?

Such was the tenor of typical 19th century New England adolescence. *Nobody got licked in school today, guess why, because there wasn't any school...* While acknowledging poor spelling skills—as well as a questionable penchant for betting on Skinny Bruce[4]—do not doubt the "class" or intellectual veracity of the author, for Henry A. Shute would graduate from Phillips Exeter Academy and Harvard University, before becoming a lawyer, judge, and author of twenty books.

So common was fighting that in *Tom Sawyer*, Mark Twain's quintessential tome to American boyhood, the first altercation appears on page three. Evidence that a pugilistic atmosphere extended beyond adolescents is found in a letter Henry Ward Beecher wrote his wife in 1832. Shortly after accepting a position in the Hopkinton, Massachusetts public school, the young teacher was confronted in class by a student bully. "A battle commenced (you know I box a little) and I beat him still over shoulders, arms, side and finally broke the ruler over his head. I then seized a club of wood which lay upon the floor and smote him again hip and thigh. The school was all in an uproar. The girls screamed, the little boys cried. Some boys went to help me, some to fight me." When Beecher appealed to the Hopkinton school committee for assistance, he was told they did not want to get involved, and that he must deal with the situation himself.

In his biography of infamous Boston politician James Michael Curley, Jack Beatty indicates not just the fighting spirit of adults in turn-of-the-century Boston, but its *leaders*:

> Each campaigning season now brought renewed brawling...In 1910 Curley was approached at the bar of the Parker House, the watering hole for Boston's politicians, by six-foot-plus, three-hundred-pound Big Bill Kelliher, the brother of a Boston congressman whom the Tammany Club had heckled off the stage in a recent campaign appearance. "I suppose I shall have to chastise you publicly," Big Bill said to Curley, then knocked him to the floor. Most men would have stayed there; Curley got up swinging. They traded

---

4   Even 150 years ago men remembered their youthful athletic pursuits later in life. When Henry A. Shute's book was published in 1902, he included a "Dramatis Personae" appendix which includes, "Skinny Bruce," Wm. J. Bruce, A tinsmith of Exeter who still thinks he could have licked Frank Elliot." Next is, "Frank Elliot. A successful mechanic in Boston, who is confident that he could have licked "Skinny" Bruce.

punches at the bar, but Curley landed the heavier blows, and the brute went down...Curley was good with his fists. In his autobiography, he tells a brutal anecdote about inviting a heckler up to the platform ("make a path for the gentleman") and when he reached the top step giving him "a wicked uppercut." Some might call that a sucker punch and feel a twinge of shame about it. Not Curley.,,the sucker punch, the knee in the groin—his fighting was along these Darwinian lines. He was a tough man in a tough country...

Teddy Roosevelt wrote in 1900, "what we have a right to expect of the American boy is that he shall turn out to be a good American man. Now, the chances are strong that he won't be much of a man unless he is a good deal of a boy. He must not be a coward or a weakling, a bully, a shirk, or a prig. He must work hard and play hard. He must be clean-minded and clean-lived, and able to hold his own under all circumstances and against all comers. It is only on these conditions that he will grow into the kind of American man of whom America can be really proud."

Ingrained in American culture was the belief that boys required toughening. Charles Lindbergh recalled his father admonishing that boys "must get knocked and knock back, in order to stand the world's knocking later." Preeminent historian William Manchester wrote of his own upbringing in Springfield, Massachusetts, "'Hit back,' my father sternly told me. 'Never forget that you are a Manchester.' Somebody was always 'after' me; I was in a state of more-or-less continual terror, a fugitive from punishments I did not understand. What I couldn't grasp was that it was my refusal to hit back which enraged them, not my physical frailty."

"No ballplayer ever went through any harder struggle or suffered more heavy burning than myself in earning a place in the big league," legendary baseball star Ty Cobb wrote. "Others have gone through struggles as hard, but none harder... In those days a young fellow had to fight his way through almost insurmountable obstacles—obstruction that the fans never see—to get any kind of a start at all. It was, in other words, a survival of the fittest."

This unrelenting cultural manifestation of toughness was not restricted to politicians and athletes but shared with those achieving acclaim in the arts. "When our school started," Woody Guthrie wrote in *Bound for Glory*, "the kids got more excited about fighting than about books. New kids had to fight to find their place on the grounds, and the old bullies had new fights to settle who was still who. Fights had a funny way of always ringing me in. If it was between two kids that I didn't even know, whoever won, some smart aleck kids would holler, 'Yeah, yeah, I bet ya cain't lick ol' Woody Guthrie.' And before long I'd be somewhere out across the playgrounds whaling away and getting whaled..."

Ernest Hemingway was accused of being a lousy football player in high school. He recounted, "I couldn't figure out the plays. I used to look at my teammates' faces and guess who looked like they expected the ball. I was called Drag-Ass when they put me at guard. I wanted to play backfield but they knew better. There was one guy on the team beat me up in the locker room every day for two years, and then I grew up to him and I beat the be-Jesus out of him and that was the end of that."

Teddy Roosevelt encapsulated the atmosphere in a 1907 speech to the Harvard Union in Cambridge, when he said, "We cannot afford to turn out of college men who shrink from physical effort or from a little physical pain. In any republic courage is a prime necessity for the average citizen if he is to be a good citizen, and he needs physical courage no less than moral courage; the courage that dares as well as the courage that endures, the courage that will fight valiantly alike against the foes of the soul and the foes of the body. Athletics are good, especially in their rougher form, because they tend to develop such courage...I emphatically disbelieve in seeing Harvard or any other college turn out mollycoddles instead of vigorous men, I may add that I do not in the least object to sport because it is rough. Rowing, baseball, lacrosse, track and field games, hockey, football are all of them good."

Many, having endured the process, ultimately agreed. Biographer William Manchester wrote of Winston Churchill, "Wrenched from her (his nurse) while still a child, he was sent to a brutal boarding school in Ascot, where the sadistic headmaster caned him until his back was a mass of welts. His treatment at the hands of the other boys was, if anything, worse. Toward the end of his life, in halting tones, he told his doctor about it. Sickly, an uncoordinated weakling with the pale fragile hands of a girl, speaking with a lisp and a slight stutter, he had been at the mercy of bullies. They beat him, ridiculed him, and pelted him with cricket balls. Trembling and humiliated, he hid in a nearby woods. This was hardly the stuff of which gladiators are made. His only weapons were an unconquerable will and an incipient sense of immortality."

Churchill, in his biography of the first Duke of Marlborough, wrote, "famous men are usually the product of an unhappy childhood. The stern compression of circumstances, the twinges of adversity, the spur of slights and taunts in early years, are needed to evoke that ruthless fixity of purpose and tenacious mother wit without which great actions are seldom accomplished."

Cobb, after completing perhaps the greatest baseball career of all and recognizing the slowly easing of cultural harassment and violence, wrote, "I sincerely believe that I was a much better ballplayer for all those hard knocks. ... The rough days of hazing are gone. As a result, the ballplayer of today...is not heckled and roughly treated by his teammates. By not having to go through the grind, the hard knocks, these new players . . . have not the groundwork and tenacity of such men as Walter Johnson, John McGraw...or any of that school."

It is one thing for the ultimately successful to ruminate on adolescent conflict, but what of the average kid?

Civil War historians were at first baffled by accelerated rates of mortality due to disease suffered by Vermont's Grand Army of the Republic volunteers. It was only with emerging understanding of immunities that the mystery was resolved. Despite being reared in strenuous farm communities, breathing the cleanest and healthiest mountain air, they had succumbed in far greater numbers during the Civil War than those born and bred in confined, unhealthy, coal-dusted eastern cities, because they had not developed those immunities that come with constant germ exposure. In much the same way were adolescent social immunities developed. Corollary bullying, as well as a universal ritual of hazing newcomers, informed a millennia of boyhood experience, preparing them for manhood.

A Cambridge lad named Richard Henry Dana touched upon this in his 1834 masterpiece, *Two Years Before the Mast*: "Wednesday, October 1st. Crossed the equator...I now, for the first time, felt at liberty, according to the old usage, to call myself a son of Neptune, and was very glad to be able to claim the title without the disagreeable initiation which so many have to go through."

The benefits of harsh upbringings, hazing, and bullying were not restricted to those who eventually achieved eminences, but also to every-day souls. *Across the Plains in Forty-Nine*, written by Bostonian Rueben Cole Shaw on his experiences during the California gold rush, contains this: "Applicants for membership in our company were subject to rigid examination by the surgeon and many were rejected on account of physical disability; yet it is a noteworthy fact that those who seemed the most robust and, to all appearances, best able to battle with the hardships of the journey, were the first to succumb to disease and death."

Military analysts were surprised to find, upon investigating First World War shell-shocked nerves, that it was not the most robust and, to all appearances, those best able to battle with the hardships that successfully managed PTSD, but more often the beaten upon, the bullied, those who had been inoculated against the fear of intellectual and physical punishment.

William Manchester touched upon this in his memoir of the Pacific war, *Goodbye Darkness*: "In the jungle I also learned that my timidity was actually an asset. Because of the beatings I had taken as a boy, I had become a master of evasion. And I was seldom startled. If I was about to be cornered, if danger was close, I knew it before anyone else...because I was young and frightened and had youthful reflexes, I responded instantly to those flickers of warning. It was a sense I cannot define, a kind of pusillanimity on a subliminal level."

At the same time cultural re-enforcement of prevailing norms thrived. American icons in the 19th century, and entering the 20th, included brawny Paul Bunyan, as well as one of the most enduring legends in the sledge-hammering railroad worker named John Henry, an individual of such extraordinary brute strength that he was immortalized in the era's most common social media, *song*. From this cultural realm Norwood boys of the 1960s emerged. More than a few threads held them fast to the past; one the traditional violence of the playground, where the mightiest neighborhood legends defended, as well as *offended*, turf.

A subtle thread to these origins can be found in the silent film, *With the Movie Man, Norwood, Mass., 1914.* It is exciting to recognize Norwood buildings still existing over a century later. Crowds leaving the United Church and St. Catherine's are recorded, as well as Norwood Printing and great shots of children exiting the Balch and Shattuck schools. These last images are relevant; in them, live and in action, are Norwood boys behaving in ways if not quite unimaginable, at least unusual in modern time. They look a hard-scrabble, working-class lot, many the grandfathers of the 1960s. The girls filing from school in disciplined and tidy twos are in stark contrast with their incorrigible counterparts. The boys are pushing and shoving, rowdyism rampant.

"At Plimpton Press there were two brothers who happened to be Irish," Dave Early, class of '71, related. "My father told me they used their lunch breaks to practice bare-knuckle boxing on each other. I think it was before World War II, he said they were brutal on each other!"

Ken Reddick recalled witnessing an epic battle. "I'll never forget it, it was Jay Dixon against Donnie Perry at the Shattuck School. I thought they were gonna kill each other! If you remember, there was a stairwell on the side with the baseball field, and they started at the top and rolled down the stairs, it was unbelievable, screaming at each other. I don't even know who won the fight, or what their beef was, they just kicked the crap out of each other! That was sixth grade, so that's what, eleven years old, 1960. They were the two toughest kids in town. Jay of course was a great athlete, but Donnie Perry wasn't, I don't remember him ever playing any sport. It was just a classic, the fight of the century..."

"I think I heard about that," Dennis Hebner mused. "Donnie Perry was a tough bastard. I remember a story about a fight, this was a long time ago. I think we were living on Nahatan Street at the time but we still hung around with the kids around Prospect Ave. where we first lived in Norwood, and we were down playing baseball at Shattuck and my brother Richie got into an argument or a fight with—what the hell was his name, they lived downstairs—Manning, John Manning was the father, his son was older than Richie and taller, and he started picking on Richie, started fighting him, hitting him pretty good, and my brother Robert who's like a pacifist, Robert saw this and jumped in and beat the fuck out of this kid, actually pounded him! And Robert, I don't think I've ever seen him fight, that's probably the only fight he had in his life and I remember that night the father came up to our house on Nahatan Street, *your son beat up my son down at the playground,* my father said *yeah your son was beating up Richie so we're even!* I remember that fight, Jesus Christ, I was probably about seven or eight years old then."

"I'm eight or nine," Peter Brown recalled, "and Timmy Flynn was there, I don't know if you know Timmy, he was a Diner Boy, remember the Diner Boys? And I was like eight. I walk up there and go to the football game at the high school. Timmy Twomey, who I knew was a hockey player, my brother was like Timmy Twomey is the best defenseman ever, you should see this guy play, so I'm up at the game, oh there's Timmy Twomey, right? Evidently Timmy was with the Diner Boys up there, and Timmy gets in a fight, a big crowd circles around, so I'm like eight, I'm in the front row and Timmy's going at it. Fair fight. I think they were playing Milton High School, this is during the game! A circle forms, they let it go, Timmy gets his front teeth knocked out. These two guys are going at it, dust and blood and everything. I think it was Odie Cook and Timmy Flynn grabbed him and at the end of it Timmy Twomey turns, he's all fucked up, and shook his the guy's hand and says, *good punch.* Heroes? Timmy was an early one."

These tendencies, unsurprisingly, crept into high school athletics. A 1946 *Boston Globe* article headlined, "Norwood Attacks Winning Waltham Team at Arena/Police Quickly Quell Riot After Hockey Tilt" described our high school skaters, including sixteen-year-old John Monbouquette, at perhaps less than best behavior,

> Seconds after Waltham High had registered a decisive 4-0 triumph over Norwood High in a Bay State League game at the Arena yesterday afternoon, members of the losing team sought revenge with their fists in a ramp leading from the rink.
>
> As the Waltham players were trooping toward their locker room through the southeast exit, a pair of Norwood puck-sters, whose dressing room was at the opposite end of the building, followed their conquerors from the ice and began swinging at the startled Watch City Skaters.
>
> These soon were joined by other members of the Norwood squad and scores of schoolboy fans who poured from the

grandstand, despite the notes of the National Anthem, which the management played over the public address system in effort to quell the riot.

Police and Ushers Stop Riot. The battle was stopped in minutes by ushers and police. No players were injured in the melee, for the Waltham lads, wisely obeying the advice of their coach, refused to retaliate against their attackers. The postgame activity climaxed a hard-fought contest that became rough in the final period after Charlie Metz had scored Waltham's fourth goal. Several Norwood players began massaging their foes with body checks and, following the final bell, Joe Wall and Captain Frank Seastrand launched the attack on the visitors.

The venerable venue saw tables turned on a Norwood sextet a decade later.

"I remember I was in I think my freshman year of high school," Jim Gormley recalled, "and I was on the hockey bus the night the Norwood hockey team got jumped by kids at the Boston Arena. Norwood had the last game and they came out of the locker room, there were these kids with broken sticks. They were city kids, somebody said they were Southie kids, somebody said they were Dorchester kids,[5] I don't know where they were from. They had hockey sticks and they split Gussy Purpura's head open from here to here, and they had to take him to I think City Hospital. I'm guessing it was '58 or '59. John Monbouquette was the coach, and he grabbed one of those kids, he had him in a headlock and he was punching him, and the Norwood guys had to break-up the coach, say coach! *Coach!*

---

5   Editor Patti Burns send along this comment when working on this section: "It must have been about 1961-2, we used to go to dances at BC High on Friday nights. BC High was at Columbia Point near the *Globe*. A lot of locals also came. Mostly, the priests would chase them out. They wore leather jackets and had taps on their heels—simply not our kind. One night it was pretty boring and a bunch of us took off with a guy and his friends. They came from Dorchester. We headed up toward Savin Hill. There was some kind of Dorchester-wide intramural football game going on. 'We don't always win the game,' bragged this guy, 'but we always win the fight after.' As we approached the game, the guys in the group started pulling the pickets off of people's fences. One guy was all excited because his picket pulled off with a nail in it. Tough crowd. Discretion being the better part of valor, my friends and I turned around and headed back to the dance. Where I grew up, in Milton and Weymouth, Norwood was looked upon as a tough town.

Eddy Feeney was on the team, I think Pete Curtin was on the team, Bucka Fanning I think was a sophomore, Bucka was a sophomore or a junior. I forget if Charley Donahue was on the team, or Donnie Smith...I remember we were on the hockey bus, and we went to the hospital. Gussy had his head wrapped when he came back in, and I think Eddie Feeney might have had some stitches."

"I seem to recall that Artie Walker or someone was jumped by irate fans of a non-Bay State League team we had played at the Arena," Pete Curtin affirmed. "The jumping occurred as players straggled out of the locker room and were heading to the bus. Either coach Monbouquette or the bus driver prevented those already on the bus from getting involved. Try Artie, Gus Purpura, Bunny Griffin, Jackie Taylor. They might remember something."

"I remember playing at Boston Arena too, that was a pretty heady experience," Jack Cronin said. "I remember we beat Boston Tech, a good Boston Tech, Billy Shandly was on that team, Steve Cedorchuk, and we beat them, and the fans were not happy that we won. And I remember there was a riot in the stands, and I remember there on the ice, and a chair coming out of the stands and crashing two feet away from me. That was rough, we had to get a police escort out of there, we had some moments, because other teams didn't like us."

"I was at the game, Tech," Peter Brown recalled. "At the Tech game, they didn't throw the chairs because they were metal and they were bolted to the floor. What they did, they were wooden fold chairs, they smashed all the wooden slats, and threw the fucking slats out on the ice! I was at the game, *go Tech, go!* They were all city rats! I was a little kid. Tech was a good school back then, believe it or not, the whole upper balcony—*go Tech go!*—I swear, this is a memory of mine, it might collapse! I go *wow*, this fucking place might *collapse!*"

"A couple of my brothers took me in," Jerry Drummey recalled. "We got there at 4:30 and this is at the Boston Arena, this is the quarter-finals and they're playing Boston Tech. They supposedly turned away 6 or 8,000 people that year, that was the last year they had the quarterfinals at the Arena before they moved to the Garden. Ah, the boys were a little bit misbehaving up in the horseshoe, yeah. Matter of fact, Cedorchuk was the big star for Boston Tech, I remember the refs called time out and they went to the bench, and they called Cedorchuk out and he went out and he went right down to the end, right at the end of the horseshoe and he said, *hey, assholes, knock it off, will ya? Okay, Steve!* And that was that. That's a true story."

"We had to get a police escort from Framingham my freshman year, '65," Jack Cronin continued. "Richie Hebner was in the penalty box and people were spitting on him, and Richie would not take crap from anybody. I don't know if he climbed the fence, but he was trying to climb the fence and all hell broke loose. I remember our bus was stoned at the Boston Arena, state tournament, I don't know who the hell, maybe it was Tech, but people did not like us."

"We did that in 1968," Bobby Dempsey recalled. "A fall league game in Melrose against Needham. It ended up spilling from our bench onto the locker room area, thank God we had Sails Wall and Joe Curran to make things right. A flat-out brawl... by the way, Artie Harris saved my butt! There's a scuffle on the ice, it was Peter Tamulionis and some guy who was about eight feet tall and Peter goes *oh jeesh*, and they got in another scuffle and the ref said let 'em go, let 'em go. So he tangled for a bit with him and they end up in the box, jawing at each other, one jumps out, the other jumps out, and they start to go at it again, ended up going through our bench into another locker room area, so naturally all of us went right into the locker room area and Needham came right back into it, and it was a full brawl, and the only two guys were Joe Curran and Sails Wall trying to keep peace. Jimmy Gormley mighta been there, too. Everybody's swinging, so some guy starts whacking me in the head so Arthur grabs him by the shoulders and throws him down on the ground with his goalie pads on, and starts to hit him, and the guy looked like he was in turmoil, and Arthur stopped and says, are you okay? He goes, yeah I'm okay, so Arthur says okay, and *boom* he starts hitting him some more! He was a tough son of a gun, boy. Oh, *oh!* You better believe it!"

"Artie Harris, I was talking to Arthur," Phil Nolfi recalled, "I think when he got married, and I said you know, Arthur I said, looking through the scrapbooks you were the all-star goalie your senior year, you never got credit for that, that was a pretty big deal. *Nah* he goes, that was all right he goes, but remember we had a fall league game up in Melrose we had a fight with Needham, we were kicking the shit out of 'em, *that was a good time!*"

"Growing up in Norwood was such a unique experience," Jack Cronin related. "It was a great time to be a kid. As a young kid I moved to Norwood from Jamaica Plain, I think I was eight. Living in the city there was very little opportunities, particularly at that age, to play any sport. Little League, hockey, I had no idea what that was, so when I came to Norwood it was like, oh my God, Little League, skating on the pond, which was totally foreign to me. We used to go to Father Mac's, behind the swimming pool on the little swamp down there, and skate. And guys like Richie Hebner was there, Dennis Hebner was there, Billy Hasenfus, all ages, didn't matter if you were young or old, everybody was just on that pond skating. And I fell in love with skating.

"I fell in love with playing hockey there, having never played it before, and of course being in Norwood...and this would have been in the early '60s, and the high school team was a big deal. I can remember going with the Flaherty's, Mike and Jack Flaherty, going to Boston Arena to watch Norwood play and it was like I was going to the Stanley Cup playoffs, it was incredible. Especially since it was kids that I knew, whether they were the older brothers, it was really a great time. It was a great motivation to become a better hockey player cuz you could only dream of someday playing on the high school team. It's funny, I never started playing hockey thinking wow, I want to be a Bruin, I want to be in the NHL. My horizon was Norwood High School. That was all I knew."

"That's where it started, back in the day was on the ponds," Leo McInerney said. "You had the one at Father Mac's, you had Froggies, you had Dunn's, there was a pond down the Flats. That's where Taylor started, on the pond down there behind Hawes Pool."

"I grew up until second grade on Pleasant Street," Charlie Donahue said, "when there was still a house on Nahatan Street where they were going to put the street through to the circle over Rt. 1. I used to walk up to St. Catherine's and we'd go by Dunn's Pond and I'd ask my father, what is that Daddy? What are they doing, and what are they holding? Those are sticks, they're playing hockey, and I'd go skating and you'd meet other kids. I played with the Kellys, and Jack Taylor, Mike Graney...

"First game I ever went to in Boston Arena I saw all those guys. As a little kid I'd seen them on the pond, and now they were like the Bruins, and I thought someday I could be like them. In those days, every neighborhood had a pond. We moved up to Bond Street and the good thing about St. Catherine's was they had no gym. All the Catholic kids had no gym, so we'd go to the ponds. I'd rush home as soon as I could and go up to Father MacAleer's. You'd have to wear hip boots to go into the pond to retrieve the pucks along the edge. And it was older kids, when it snowed we'd go over and shovel the pond off. We were little kids up there freezing our butts off. My father built a hockey net, and we'd shoot a thousand pucks a day. And I met Kenny Arvidson, and we'd go to Father MacAleer's together, but we never knew we were developing a trade, developing a skill."

"I grew up on Rock Street," Rusty Tobin remembered of his Cork City neighborhood. "The pond we skated on was Dunn's which is now the police station. I grew up in a very sports-oriented neighborhood and everybody played hockey. Basically it was the kids around here, the Sweeney's, of course my brother Dennis and the Lauries, and Abelys, and gee I'll think of them afterward…George Hawley…but most of the older kids were on Norwood's hockey team. The Graneys, the Kellys, Mike Kelley and Mike Graney were both captains at Norwood at one time.

"So I grew up kinda looking up to those guys. And my mother would take us into the Arena, and she didn't know anything about hockey of course but became one of the biggest fans, because the Graneys played and they were a lot older than us and we looked up to them. In fact we used to shoot across the street in the driveway because Tommy Faulkner was one of the Norwood goalies and they'd have a bunch of the team there most of the week shooting, and they'd let me and my brother, and we'd kneel down beside them with our mouths open in awe how they could shoot, and they let us chase the pucks, you know, we thought it was a big deal, that is a good memory. They were real good to us. You know how older kids treat younger kids, treat them good and you never forget, you know?"

"Russ lived on Rock Street right behind Star Market and he brought great 'street cred' to the pick-up games we had at Dunn's," Bobby Thornton remembered. "His legendary temper was on full display on a couple of occasions. Why was our friend George Hawley the all-too-frequent recipient of Rusty's ire at Dunn's Pond? Probably because George had a Donny Marcotte-like peskiness about him whenever the puck was dropped, which just might have rubbed Rusty the wrong way at times. But Mr. Tobin taught the Dunn's Boys how to play with *attitude*."

"We grew up skating on Dunn's," Rusty Tobin continued, "and Mr. Hawley the fireman or Mr. Lawrie the policeman would turn on the streetlights in the winter for us—no one would question *them*—so we skated nights. It was one section that we called the Chinese laundry, the water would never freeze and the only kid in the neighborhood that didn't skate would put on weighters and go in there and get all the pucks. In those days if you had one puck that was a big deal and he used to try to sell them back to the older kids, and they used to stand on the edge and not let him out until he handed over the pucks!"

"There was a water well located at the far end of Dunn's Pond," Bobby Thornton affirmed, "about fifty yards behind the house of one Charlie Allen. The well-known idiosyncrasy of playing at this venue is that you always had to bring a ton of extra pucks to play there, because the slight turbulence over the water well would always prevent the ice from freezing fully in that small area. And of course, no matter how hard everyone tried, missed passes and puck shots would always find their way into this obscure little hole above the well. That was the bad news. The good news—at least for Charlie—was when the ice would thaw in March, he would always walk out to the well in his hip boots and collect hundreds of collector's item pucks for next year.

"We loved playing there *so* much that we would often play there way too late into the afternoon, early evening until dark and much too late into March when the season, and the ice, were diminishing quickly. So, one late March afternoon when I was about twelve, I pushed the limits a little too far and went through the cracking ice into the freezing cold water. My friends were laughing so hard at me that I got a bit miffed and stormed off. The only problem was it was so cold, and my skate laces were so wet and freezing and my skates could not be removed. To this day, I remember crossing Nahatan Street to go to Star Market to call for a ride home, totally embarrassed about the absolute sparks that were generated from my angry skate blades as I went on an enraged search of a pay phone!"

"I grew up on 4th Street down by Froggies," Leo McInerney recalled, "and it all started for me with Donnie Smith. I don't know if you remember, he was the goalie on the 1960-61 team, and he introduced me to, cuz we always played on Froggies, and he introduced me to Tom Clifford's program, Norwood Hockey Club, and he used to get up at four o'clock in the morning and take his brother Steven and I over to Mr. Clifford's at Tabor. It's St. Sebastian's, but it was Tabor rink back then in those days, and of course growing up on Froggies we spent every waking minute down there. We had great games against the Dunn's Boys, the Dunn's Boys were up in the old, where the police and fire station is now. It was Dunn's Pond, and they had some really good pond skaters up there, Rusty Tobin, the Abely brothers, Lanzoni, Ralph Lanzoni was a great skater. So we had great games, and the thing with Froggies was as little guys we used to stand on the side, stick around and wait to see if we could get in the big game, you know, where the big boys were playing, and every once in a while you'd get promoted so to speak, and they'd say all right come in and play. And you'd get into the big game and Christ that was the best thing in the world!

"That was in late '50s, early '60s, the big guys were like Donnie Smith, Mike Falcone was always on the pond, great pond skater, his brother Ricky was down there. Donnie used to bring down some of the boys from the team from the '60s like Monk Jessick and Charley Donahue, when those guys came down they were big, big games, those were your idols, right?"

"We had some great hockey games up there!" Dennis Hebner recalled of Father Mac's pond. "Oh we had some great hockey games up there, the kids from the North Ave., Silver Street, I remember we'd go up there on Saturday and we'd stay all day. In fact, then you didn't bring food or water, I remember a couple of times I got so thirsty I broke a hole in the ice and drank it! And that was run-off water from the streets! Never got sick! It was probably '59, '60, '61. And the big thing was if the weather got real good and if we got someone to drive us we'd go to Pettee's, that was the premium thing, to go to Pettee's on New Pond. As long as you don't fucking fall in! (laughs) I used to love skating on New Pond, especially on a windy day, you could almost skate forty miles an hour with the wind but coming back was like walking up a hill."

"I do remember Ed King," Tommy Taylor said. "We used to skate down at Hawes Pool, Freddie Carbone, Phil Nolfi. Phil Nolfi lived in the Saad house, he'd be out there shooting pucks all day long, I started skating behind Hawes Pool, Phil, myself, Eddie King, the Saads. There was one guy that played, he played there, Jackie Koval. He used to skate, and another guy was Laddy Baxton, but they only played JV.

"There's a little pond, used to be two ponds that the river flooded into, right behind Hawes Pool. There was one other kid from South Norwood that played hockey, his name was Foley. We used to play with the Saad brothers, they had nothing, but they were always there. Pete Larson was the playground instructor at Endean playground. At that time, I don't know, I'll tell you who I used to hang around with, the O'Connells, Tommy O'Connell and Franny O'Connell, Stevie Costello, Billy Costello. I think your brother hung out with Stevie Costello. Billy Costello used to take me to the Norwood hockey games in at the Arena all the time, really early to get front seats. They were the guys who brought me along, know what I'm saying?"

"So it was unique," Jack Cronin continued, "and that was just hockey. Baseball was great. When I was a freshman, my father passed away, so I was young, and I had the support of so many people, Mr. Higgins was one of the biggest, Jimmy Gormley, he was the assistant hockey coach at the high school, people that influenced me. I had role models, people I could look at, I didn't know really what they did but they were good people, you know, like Mr. Curran, Mr. Dempsey, and they all went out of their way to offer support to me along the way in some shape.

"Summers were busy, you had the parks, Father Mac's they had baseball there and there was a swimming pool, it was active, there were so many things to do. You know there was Little League baseball, so many parents were involved, it was a great time to be a kid. I lived on Spruce Road, my back yard backed up to Father Mac's, so I could walk out my back door and be on the ball field, or the swimming pool. We didn't have much, but I didn't realize, I think it took me until I got to BC to realize there were people that had money. Living in Norwood I never felt like I was a poor kid, and apparently, I must have been pretty poor, but I never realized. So it, like I said, it was a very healthy, in my belief, time to grow up in Norwood. Great friends, great kids, not a lot of idiots.

"There were a bunch of girls on Spruce Road and in retrospect they were beautiful, but I didn't have time for them. Honest to God, I was so focused on sports, but I would go cut through Father Mac's and go up to North Ave. where the Flahertys, Mike Flaherty, Jack Flaherty, Mark, I spent many hours in that kitchen, Mrs. Flaherty fed me a lot. We played baseball a lot at Hebners', Richie and Dennis. In back of the Hebner house they had a little ball field, and we spent hours there playing baseball, the Flahertys, Neil Higgins would go there, I don't know if the Donovans would go there, but then we had Harry Pascoe, he lived by Father Mac's. I had a lot of friends, and so it was a real good time. My point of reference was just that, I didn't have, I wasn't comparing to anything, I was just living at the moment, I didn't know if we were making history, I didn't know what we were doing. We were just having fun."

No one knows who created the creek, or why. The ribbon of still-water lay a quarter mile into the woods of the Forbes estate behind Crestwood Circle. Fifty yards in length, ten-foot-high banks on each side, it was almost certainly man-made. The forest there is crisscrossed with stone walls indicating former farmland, with a still-viable cart path from the fields of the former Gay Farm to the apple orchard by Forbes's mansion. Stretches of swamp surrounded the creek; surmised is that it was constructed as a drainage system emptying, as it does, into Plantingfield Brook. And when conditions were right, Crestwood Circle boys, skates slung over shoulders and hockey sticks in hand, trod snowy paths to the creek.

Ken Reddick is not particularly nostalgic, but with the subject broached sixty years later he said, "You know, I've sometimes thought about the creek, how we played out there on ice maybe twenty feet wide and a hundred feet long, with bushes and branches of trees overhanging each side, and then we ended up in Boston Garden..."

1965

*I can't get no, satisfaction,
'Cause I try...*

— THE ROLLING STONES,
(I CAN'T GET NO) SATISFACTION, 1965

It was the day every American living at the time remembers. Joe Morgan was home from minor league baseball with the Atlanta Crackers of the International League. "Well in those days, it was November, so I was working for John D. Murphy," the Walpole native and future Red Sox manager related. "He built houses and other things around Walpole, and it was around two o'clock. I happened to go in this little store where I was, and that's how I heard about JFK. I heard it on the radio there. So that was it. I wasn't too happy, I know that. I went home and told my father, I can't believe, I said...I think I cried a little that day. And I don't cry that easy."

Former Bay State League hockey star Ted Casey was with a U.S. Army traveling team in Europe. "We were playing hockey in Munich, Germany. We had just finished the first period. I think we were up 1-0, and when you came off the ice you went through their bar to the locker room. And as we walked through, all the TVs were all on, and it was focused on Dallas, Texas. The president of the United States has been shot. So, we all go in the backroom, we're going wait a minute, some of it was German and some was English, a lot of it was in English so we could listen, and we all looked at each other and said we can't play, we gotta go. We took off our skates, put our boots on, got back on the bus and went home. That was November 22, 1963. We got back to the barracks, and we took the rest of the year off because of that. We had never heard of anything like that, nobody had. Who would do that?"

Arlington's Joe Bertagna: "What I do remember vividly was the day Kennedy was shot. I remember walking home from middle school and a woman rolling her window down and yelling they just shot the president! Up to that point there hadn't been anything like that. Obviously, what happened in high school in 1968 with Bobby Kennedy and Martin Luther King and George Wallace was shot, and all these things that followed, but '63 was a pretty peaceful, pretty comfortable existence. It's funny, when I heard they shot Oswald I was in the Boston Skating Club taking my skates off from a Sunday morning hockey session and somebody walked in and announced on live TV they'd shot Oswald."

"I remember it like it was yesterday," Dickie Donovan recalled. "I was in the seventh grade and the nuns, the superintendent came over, said President Kennedy's been shot. And I was practically crying, you know, I really liked that guy. He was such a charismatic person, the first lady was so charismatic too, and to see him, I was watching. I was addicted to the TV that day and I watched when Jack Ruby—I *saw it*—and I said *oh my God ma, look! He just killed Lee Harvey Oswald!* It was unbelievable! It was like watching a movie, but it was real!"

"Remember Bobby Little?" Peter Brown remembered. "Played for the Indians with Chris Dixon, how's that one for ya! Town champs. Was a good player. I'm walking, as you look at Cleveland school, there's like the front gym and there's a setback, and I was walking across and I was right before the corner of the gym, I was just getting to the corner. Mrs. Little came up to me and she said, Peter where are you going? You need to go home. President Kennedy's been shot, you need to go home. Mrs. Little told me on the Cleveland school playground. She came to school to pick Bobby up because she was so upset. Bobby Little. I remember that whole weekend, right? It was raining, it was grey, literally everybody huddled around the TV, Lee Harvey Oswald getting shot... *What? He shot him on live TV?* That was a big... *Jesus.*"

"I was in my history class at the high school," Ken Reddick recalled. "It was freshman history class 1963 and Johnny Poce was my teacher and some kid was giving an oral report. He was standing in front of the class giving an oral report and all of a sudden over the intercom—I think it was Jack Monbouquette the principle—comes over the intercom and tells us what happened and everyone's like oh my God, this, that, and the other, and they didn't know Kennedy had died at that point. He was shot and in the hospital, and we're all stopped, and as soon as the message was done and Monbouquette got off the intercom, this kid just continued with his report as though nothing had happened and Poce said *sit down you fool!*

"It was a Friday afternoon, and we had a football game against Dedham," Ken Reddick continued. "And we went to the locker room and as we were leaving the locker room after getting dressed, they announced he had passed away, but they didn't cancel the game. We all hopped on the bus, go to Dedham, working out on the field, sitting on the bench and Dad came over, and he kind of leaned over, whispered in my ear, said, *did you hear what happened today?* I said yeah, yeah. He said *oh man, just awful*, and he went back to the stands. So that's how I heard about it. That's my story."

By 1965 America had acknowledged the hand it had been dealt—and was all-in. Enthusiastically embraced was the unfolding of cultural revolution as both salve and salvation from the soul-wrenching, decade-defining tragedy of November 22, 1963. On Saturday evening, September 12th, 1964, four Liverpool lads strode across a stage set mid-ice in Boston Garden for the city's first intimate embrace of a cultural phenomenon. Tickets ranged from $3.50 to $5.50, the event beginning at 8 o'clock sharp with opening acts The Bill Black Combo, The Exciters, Clarence "Frogman" Henry, and Jackie DeShannon. The Beatles set, consisting of twelve songs and lasting all of thirty minutes, began and ended with cover songs, but also included their early hits, as well as Chuck Berry's ode to musical revolution, *Roll Over Beethoven*.

"I was at the Beatles concert with three of my friends," Patti Burns, class of '66 recalled. "We were seated to the left of the stage in the first row of the first section by a metal railing. I couldn't hear a thing for all the screaming. A few minutes into the Beatle's set, a wave of screaming meemies descended upon us from the rows above, sandwiching us against the railing between them and a row of cops wielding night sticks on the floor below. My friend fainted and fell over the rail!"

It was the height of "Beatlemania." So infused was the Beatle's influence, that three months later at the United Church's Christmas Show, with assistant hockey coach Reverend Dan Young among the organizers, Dave Early, Frankie Pascoe, and Donnies Hamlin and Reddick, all ten or eleven years old, donned kimonos and long-haired wigs, and performed as The Japanese Beatles, to howling approval.[6]

The "British Invasion" began in early '64, barely two months after the tragedy, when the Beatles made their much-anticipated appearance on The *Ed Sullivan Show*. To this ten-year-old I confess understanding little at the time. Music to dirty-faced denizens of Crestwood Circle was considered a bit feminine, the ensuing attention disorienting, despite music being part of my family's tradition. My older brothers were required, as much as participation in Little League, to take piano lessons from Alice Beldon in the Talbot Block above Duke Folan's Guild Variety. How they disliked the experience, especially the pressure of "Recitals," solo performances at the end of each year's session. My maternal grandfather Bradbury Jenness was a violinist in the Wellesley Orchestra. My grandmother harbored great fondness for classical music. Every Wednesday was lunch and dinner at our grandparents 444 Prospect Street home, and I recall the day Gramma requested we bring the sensation's new album, *Meet the Beatles*, about which she had heard so much and was interested in hearing herself. I remember clearly the formidable woman, born 1894 and possessing remnants of prim and proper Victorian sensibility, sitting in her rocking chair, slowly moving back and forth listening to the gentle ballad, *This Boy*, until the next song, *It Won't Be Long*, with its sudden, explosive opening lyrics, literally jolting her upright in surprise. Roll over, Beethoven.

"I remember that day," said Ken Reddick. "Afterward she said (mimicking a dismissive voice), 'Well, all the songs seem to be about the same thing...'" Little did kids in 1964 realize that they had been introduced to initial chords of the soundtrack of their lives. Weeks after the Beatles' Boston appearance, on November 5th the Rolling Stones, another group of British lads, graced Boston Garden. A twelve-song set ended with their current craze and the number one song in America, *Satisfaction*.

"Yeah, we went, '65, that was their first U.S. tour," Ken Reddick recalled, "and they played at Boston Garden. Course they had their famous song *Satisfaction*—great song, by the way—and I went with two of my buddies, Bob Fitzpatrick and Al Venskus, Fitzy and Duck as they were known in those days, and we had great seats, we were up in the balcony. They were

---

6 We lip-synched three songs, thankful the record did not skip, *I Want to Hold Your Hand, All My Loving,* and—yeah, yeah, yeah—the song with their then-most signature lines, *She Loves You*. I was John.

in the end zone right by one of the Bruins nets, and our seats looked down right on the stage from the side. It was great seats, they put on quite a show and we loved it. They were huge, they were second to the Beatles in our book, and it was a great night. Other than just being there, that was the best part, it was awesome. And then, who knew but we'd be playing hockey in the same place the next year, and the year after that."

The 1964-65 Norwood hockey team was a bouquet of blossoming and bloomed superstars. Appearing for the first time were freshmen Neil Higgins and Jack Cronin, bracketing in-his-prime junior Richie Hebner with senior tri-captains Blaine Maus, Timmy Twomey, and Paul Angelo.

"I played a CYO game," Richie Hebner recalled. "St. Catherine's, went over at BC, I don't know, I scored four or five goals. I didn't realize Wheeler was there, and all of a sudden, I'm on the varsity team as a freshman. Wheeler must have called my father or somebody and all of a sudden here I am on the varsity team as a freshman with all these older guys, and I'm like, *ahyee*... But I did all right, I guess! I had a few goals as a freshman, that was the start of it. I played four years and I tell people, I'd rather play hockey than baseball. Well, there was two thousand people, if you didn't get to the Four Seasons an hour and a half before the game you weren't getting in the building.

"I had good size, I could skate, I could skate with most of the normal kids in high school, that was it. We were playing a game up in Framingham and I hit a kid, I didn't get a penalty for it, and that night I didn't realize it, I ruptured a kid's spleen. Oh, they thought I was the dirtiest player in the league, but I never got a penalty for it. I musta hit him pretty good, but I didn't get a penalty. My name up in Natick or Framingham, they thought I was the biggest asshole in the world. It was on the ice, he musta got in my way!"

"Jackie Cronin was going to go to Catholic Memorial," Jim Gormley recalled, "and he decided to come to Norwood. I had him on the playground.[7] Babe Ruth had a banquet, and they invited my mother, because

---

7 Norwood had a well-developed summer program for youngsters centered on playgrounds and schools. "Playground instructors" were usually teachers and college students, many former athletes at Norwood High School. Playgrounds included Wilson Street, Ellis Gardens, Pleasant Park, Eliot Park, Father McAleer's, Bond Street, Recreation Center (Civic Center), Endean, as well as Shattuck, Callahan, Winslow, Oldham, Balch, Cleveland, and Prescott Schools.

it was around the time—Jackie's dad was president of the Babe Ruth League, and he invited my mother to come to the award night. And he took me aside, Jackie's Dad did, and he said, Jackie's going to Norwood High School you know, and I said I do. He said well he's going there because of you, and all I ask is you take care of him. And my mother heard the conversation, and we were in the car coming home, she said, I think Mr. Cronin is sick. I said what? And she said, I think he was giving you a message to take care of his son, and I think he's very sick and it wasn't within the year he was dead. Jackie came to Norwood High. First class guy."

"It's kind of funny," Jack Cronin remembered. "Course Don Wheeler, I don't have to tell you, he was a taskmaster, and he didn't play around. He wasn't going to put someone on the team just to have 'em sit on the bench. And he brought myself and Neil onto the varsity as freshman. Neil didn't play much, because he was behind Tommy Smelstor. We had a really good team, went to the state finals. And I didn't play a lot in the beginning, but I would play JV and I would play freshman, so I got a lot of ice time. And then half-way through the season he started putting me in games.

"In those days you played three defensemen and he didn't have to play me, but he played me. And so that freshman year I learned a lot about the game and also a lot about myself. That was the year my father passed away. And I gotta say, hockey, I was just immersed in the sport, physically and mentally. I knew at the time that there was only one other player that played as a freshman, and that was Hebner. So I guess I did realize that was a pretty big deal.

"Timmy Twomey and Bobby Clifford were the two defensemen, I think, I'm trying to think, there's another kid that played, I think I might have taken his place during the year. But anyway, Timmy Twomey was, in my young eyes, the toughest son-of-a-bitch I ever met in my life. I mean he was just... Wheeler loved him because he was so tough, he worked so hard, and Bobby had talent, Bobby Clifford had talent. I don't know how much talent Timmy Twomey had, but he worked so damn hard, he was like a dog on the ice, and so I was behind those two guys."

"Richie was quiet, but a great leader," then-sophomore Rusty Tobin remembered. "I mean everybody just watched what he did, you almost dressed the way he dressed, or how he put on his skates. He was real good to us younger guys, at least to me. Before Wheeler or Gormley would get on the ice we'd have a little free time, and Richie would take me down in the corner and we would work one-on-one, battle, and I'll tell ya, you go into one-on-one with him and it's a battle. And he would help me on body position, and also Twomey was great with me, and Richie Lovell. Richie Lovell came back, and you'd see him at practice every once in a while, he would help with different things. But I remember Richie helping me a lot with that one-on-one. He was such a great competitor, and you know Wheeler loved those one-on-one drills. Richie if you beat him, one-on-one in the corners, if you ever got it by him, he wasn't a happy camper. That was just his competitive nature.

"He was the best in practice, he wanted to be, and it showed. He was first on the ice, last to leave. I remember your first year you're picking up pucks, and Richie would still be out there working on things, his shot, his backhand. I have no real funny stories about Richie. He kept to himself. I mean he was good friends with his friends. Believe it or not he was a shy guy, people think he was stuck up, but he wasn't at all. His friends were Billy Hasenfus, they were good and close. Bobby Donahue, Bobby Clifford, they were all close together."

Blaine Maus remembered The Legend. "Richie, I'm not sure this is something you want to share, but he used to come on the bus and Lovell used to give everybody a hard time. He used to say, hey *Witchie*, what are you doing? Cuz, Richie, he didn't sound out his 'Rs' too well, so with Richie—I mean it was just a speech impediment or speech problem that he overcame later on. The funny thing is, Lovell would give him a hard time and he would yell at him, they'd yell back and forth.

"He was kind of an introverted guy. He was outspoken about certain things, but he was pretty much introverted. He was a little self-conscious about that and other things in his life, and it's like everybody, we all have things that don't make us too happy. The best story I can tell you about Hebby is this. We'd go over to the practices over to the old Tabor rink, and the coach said listen when you get there you can go right on the ice because I might be a little late. We're all out there zooming around, but Richie wasn't. I'd go over, and I'd watch Richie for a while. He'd be in the corner with six pucks, he'd go 'round the circle, go around the right circle all the time, and he'd get to one point, he'd drag the puck in with his right hand, and his bottom hand would *snap* the puck. He could snap the puck with a snapshot on his backhand, everyone could do it on their forehand if they spent time enough like I did, you know, I weight trained and I steel-puck shot to try to help me, so I could snap it pretty good. But on the backhand! Oh my God! You just can't believe how fast the backhand was! I mean, you've seen it in games, right? He'd come down there and he'd be off-angle and *snap*, and upper corner! Up under the guy's arm! It was unbelievable. He's the only one I've ever seen shoot a backhander that well of all the hockey I've seen. I've played with all these other teams all these years, no one was able to shoot a puck like that on his backhand. Amazing, just an amazing feat as far as I was concerned. And he worked on it every practice. He was practicing on locations too, like basketball players do. You know, the best place to take your shot, that you're gonna be more successful. That's the way he was. He was something.

"The one good thing," Blaine Maus continued, "was every time I sent Hebner the puck I knew one thing, if he scored, I was getting a point too! Because I got an assist, I'm a right shot, I'd snap it over the left naturally, I'd do that and usually he didn't give it up. He would go in there and ace one, and that's when I said to myself, *hey shit, this is easy, I'm getting a point every time he scores!* That's what happened. Because of that scenario, I ended up getting the most points in the Bay State League."

"I'll tell you one about Richie," Paul Angelo said. "We were going down to Cranston, and Wheeler said be there at 11:00, the bus leaves at 11:00. *Sharp.* At 11:00 Mr. Hebner pulls in ahead of the bus, but Wheeler says no, you're not getting on the bus. You're not playing. Mr. Hebner follows us the whole way down to Cranston, and Wheeler says no, you're not playing. And he didn't. We were playing Needham, and Richie gets a penalty. He deserved it. But he says to Eddie Barry, the referee, *Fuck you, you son-of-a-bitch!* And Barry is gonna throw him out of the game, and I grabbed him by the shirt and said, you go apologize, and he did!"

"It was just a great opportunity to play with two fabulous hockey players," Blaine Maus continued. "They both deserve all the praise in the world. Angie used to set me up from the corner, he'd go in there, wiggle his way around, give me the puck right at the top of the circle and I'd rifle one upstairs off the pipe, and all I would do coming out of the zone, he would give me the pass, I'd come up over the blue line, I'd look over to my left and of course Hebner's *flying,* and all I had to do is give him the puck! And he'd go in there and dash a goal off, no problem!"

"It was a great deal being a Norwood player," Rusty Tobin explained. "Do you remember going into the Arena? We would always go in the front door. I think Gormley used to pay off the little peanut guy, he was always there every year. He would go, *peanuts a dime, three for a quarter, here comes Mighty, Mighty Norwood!* I think he probably handed him ten dollars' worth, and the guy would say it loud enough so people would stop and, you know, let us through. And you could hear people, people would mumble, who's who? When Richie was there, they'd say which one is Hebner? That must be that big guy. You could hear them saying, Hebner, Hebner. He was known through-out the state.

"It was really a big deal being from Norwood. Special group. We were special... I remember the rides up to Four Seasons on a game night and there'd be traffic all the way back to Norwood. And people honking as we'd go in, but I think after a while we took it for granted that that was the way it is."

"That was another point of pride as a kid," Jack Cronin agreed. "When we walked into a rink, even if it was for practice, everyone knew who we were. And I don't mean they knew who Jack Cronin was, they knew who Norwood High School was. People knew who the elite high school teams were. So that was a point of pride. If you go practice somewhere, and people say *whew* I wanna watch these guys."

"It was a big thrill," Richie Hebner recalled. "Crowds everywhere we went. Not like now, you gotta drive an hour and a half and there's probably thirty people in the stands, but it was packed every night. It was a big thrill to play for Norwood. And there were some good teams, Walpole, Dedham had a good team, Framingham, I mean it was a tough league, the Bay State League was a tough league. You had to play every night to win. It wasn't where you walked on the ice and got a 'W'. It wasn't that case. Some of the teams weren't good, but a lot of the teams in that league were *good.* Billy Hasenfus, Donahue, Angie, Maus, Higgins lived up by you, we had a good team."

"The thing I remember most about hockey in the '60s was how big it was," Ken Reddick recalled. "After playing in Boston Arena in the early

'60s, Walpole Arena opened in 1966 and the Bay State League would bang out 3,000 people every Saturday night. For the big games, Norwood-Walpole or Norwood-Needham. It was standing room only and people were turned away who didn't get tickets in advance.

"How big was hockey in the '60s? In my sophomore year 1965 we went all the way to the state final game—played our arch-rival Walpole—and lost 1-0 to Kevin Woods, Jackie Norwell, Dick Delaney and that great Walpole team. We *lost* the game and yet the town held a fundraiser and sent the entire team plus coaches and chaperones—ha! Frank Wall was one of the chaperones, so you know how that went—on a five-day trip to Washington D.C. and on the way back the 1965 World's Fair in Flushing Meadows, New York City. You can still see the somewhat famous picture of the trip down at Paul Angelo's OCC. We wondered where we would have gone if we had *won* the game."

There was a season to play before any tournament and tour, however, and like any season, there were memorable games. In 1965 one such contest was against a hapless Milton sextet, which fell by a score of 14-0. It was not the lop-sided score which warranted indelible memory, but the ferocity in which it occurred. Frank Wall wrote the following description of the game:

> Norwood led only 2-0 going into third period. Wheeler had sat the first line of Hebner, Angelo, and Maus through the second period. In the second period, Norwood mentor Don Wheeler only used his first line two turns as the second and third waves saw most of the action...Norwood continued to apply the pressure as third liners Ken Reddick, Dave Dooley, and Bob Folan applied the pressure... Then came the third period bombardment. At seven seconds it was Maus from Angelo for a 3-0 lead. Twenty-two seconds later Maus scored again, and the rout was on. Bobby Clifford scored his second of the afternoon at 2:22 and it was 5-0. Next it was Richie Hebner's turn. Richie scored four of the next five goals in a span of three minutes with Maus assisting on three and Twomey picking up two assists in the quick surge. In between Hebner's four goals, Bill Hasenfus took a pass from Bobby Donahue and scored from in close. With the score 10-0,

Jack Cronin hit the upper left with a blazer and then it was Maus and Hebner finishing off the spree with the final score Norwood 14, Milton 0.

"I remember one time we were playing against Milton," Blaine Maus recalled. "Wheeler benched us after the first period. So, we sat the second period watching. And the third period it looked like we weren't gonna play either, but he said, now are you ready to get serious and play? And we're like, *yeah coach!* And we went out and we scored twelve goals. Twelve goals we scored, just up and down, we couldn't get out there enough! I think each one of us had like five points apiece, you know whether it was an assist or a goal, whatever."

Frank Wall wrote after the game, "Norwood now has scored 60 goals in the first 11 games and has allowed only 6... Norwood goalie Tom Smelstor recorded his eighth shutout in 11 games as he was called on to make only four saves..."

Norwood was on a roll, and Don Wheeler continued to do everything he could to improve his team. "Don would set goals for us which was great," Blaine Maus said. "He used to push us, and tell us what it took, he'd tell you what it takes to become a successful team. His rationale would be educate 'em first, or initiate them, and what he's trying to do and the reason you're playing, you have to have goals. And then you also have to have a team mindset to work together, we're in this together, and he was very good, very talented at doing that. And then he'd get you on the ice and work you over pretty good. There was crazy shit... We beat almost everyone else. We beat that Cranston East team; did you ever hear this one?"

Early in his coaching career Don Wheeler came to appreciate the talent of Rhode Island high school teams. He understood that improvement came more from competing against excellent competition as opposed to beating up on hapless Miltons, knew that powerhouse Arlington, for instance, regularly scrimmaged college freshman teams. And this particular Cranston East team excelled. They were not only Rhode Island state champions but defending New England champions. They featured a line considered the greatest in the state's history, with stars Joe Cavanagh, Dan DeMichele, and Rich McLaughlin a worthy match for Norwood's tenacious trio of Hebner, Maus, and Angelo.

How good were these Rhode Island kids? Cavanagh and DeMichele would attend Harvard University where Cavanagh was thrice selected first team All-American. DeMichele would join Cavanagh in Harvard's athletic Hall of Fame for efforts in both hockey and baseball, as well as be selected in the second round of the 1967 MLB draft. A kid named Curt Bennett played defense, a kid who would earn All-American status at Brown University before playing ten seasons in the NHL and becoming the first American to score 30 goals in that league.

"We did a scrimmage with them down in Rhode Island, went down there, and beat 'em up and blew 'em out the door, 6-2," Blaine Maus remembered. "And they were like the best team in New England, which later came true. They won the New Englands. So, the coach down there was pissed, and Don Wheeler was like, oh this is great! He knew the teams down in Rhode Island were that good, cuz we had played Mount St. Charles, Hope, Lasalle, we played 'em all, and Don was really good at getting everybody games, trying to improve us. So that helped, so the coach said we want a rematch. So, they came up and they beat us 6-2. Beat us 6-2, and it was a tough game, I mean, we were banging bodies everywhere, but it was a scrimmage.

"So, they said okay, so we're tied. Wheeler said why don't we rent out Walpole arena, and we'll play you there with referees, full game, scoreboard, everything, and they said, you're on! They said, *you're on!* Cuz, they knew we were that good.

"Two weeks later they rented out the rink, got all the referees, the whole deal. It was like a regular game. And they dropped the puck, and we went at it like the two best teams in the NHL. And it was just phenomenal play, everything was full speed, it was playoff time. We beat 'em 6-2, the same score, and we beat 'em. The only thing we lost, was DiMichele jabbed Hebner right in the mouth and took out two of his teeth. Did it on purpose. Just drove it into his face."

"Lost my teeth there, got hit," Richie Hebner recalled. "I went to school, God, must have been six weeks with my three front teeth missing. I talked like *Elmah Fudd!* I don't remember much, but it wasn't a good feeling."

"So yeah, kinda crazy," Blaine Maus concluded. "Not many people remember that one. This was like middle of the season, like January. We just wanted tough opponents to play against. They hated us, we hated them, it was great!"

Norwood's Mike Crimmins, three-sport star at BC High, recalled scrimmaging Norwood.

"Father Pollard was the coach," the Nichols Street kid remembered. "Here's a guy who couldn't even skate, okay? He would watch us on the ice. He was a German teacher, a Jesuit at BC High. I was up Pettee's skating pond hockey, it was Saturday afternoon, and my mother came up and got me, and she said you have a practice at Walpole. I said we don't practice at Walpole, Four Seasons, and she said well, Father Pollard says the other goalie can't make it.

"She drove me up and the guy is trying to charge us for parking and I said no, I got a practice here, I'm not paying a dime or a quarter whatever it was. So anyway, I got my stuff out, I'm walking in, and Father Pollard came running up to me and said, ah, Mike, I didn't tell your mother, but we're playing Norwood because they were supposed to be scrimmaging Burrillville, but it fell through.

"I turned around and walked out."

"He came running after me. I said oh no, no, I can't do this. I said, we're gonna get *killed!* This is gonna be tortuous! *No, you gotta play, you gotta play!* Anyway, I played, and I had one of the best games of my life. We only lost, 5-1. I think it was forty-nine saves, you know, I got written up in the *Norwood Messenger*, a great article, *Norwood's Crimmins Spectacular With Forty-Nine Saves*, and ah, everyone's saying, why can't we get a guy like that! (laughs) That was with Hebner and the gang, I remember Richie took a shot, I don't even know where it came from, it was like a twelve-foot wrist shot, and he had a blazer as you well know. I was a baseball player and somehow I caught it, and everybody's like looking in the net *where is it where is it!* It was in my glove, I'm like, *thank you, Lord!* I was so dizzy and tired I let in a couple of squeakers that went under me, but it was okay, it worked out fine. But that was something else, man, *ooof....* There was a lot of respect after that, they were all a bunch of good guys."

Norwood began the tournament by defeating two league champions in Boston Arena, previously undefeated Lynnfield, 2-1, and Christopher

Columbus, 3-0. The last barrier to Norwood's longest post-season stint—and their first visit to Boston Garden—was the infamous, aforementioned Boston Tech contest. Frank Wall's *Norwood Messenger* recap of a 3-1 victory noted the intense climate of the high school tournament:

> The Norwood-Boston Tech game was a big win for Norwood but the in-between actions of the Boston fans was uncalled for. They turned away over 3,000 fans and the place was really jammed. Norwood goalie Tom Smelstor was pelted with objects from the Tech fans who were just above him in the stands. They threw firecrackers on the ice and when the call for police was issued the men in blue stood motionless. After the game the same sort of behavior occurred outside the Arena…maybe the ones who said the environment of the Boston Arena was bad were right, but then again it may be a case of just simply what schools are involved in the game and who wins. The Bay State fans did themselves proud as their cheering was in voice only and they had the winners.

"Boston Garden," Blaine Maus mused. "That was one of your goals, to play under the lights. I wanted to stand, you know how they used to have—you'd stand out on the blue line and they had colored lights on each one of the players? My goal was to be there. To have that happen, and it happened. We played well enough to get to the semi's and played Newton." Blaine Maus reminisced of his road to an historic Newton match.

"I started out near the Pond Plain school, we had lived right next to it over Westwood, and we spent most of our time either in school or on the playground. And then in third grade level I moved over to Norwood, actually Norwood and Westwood, it was on the line. We continued going to Westwood schools, took the bus, and then we got a little older and realized that Westwood was a great town, but we needed to play hockey. We were playing with the Clifford group, so at that point we were at a dead end. Westwood wasn't having a team and Norwood had a team, so Dana and I, my brother convinced me to move into the Norwood schools, and I ended up over the Guild school, junior high school, and he was at the high school two years ahead of me.

Well anyways, he convinced me to do that so now we're going to a new school, but we had an opportunity to play hockey, the thing we wanted to do. The rest is kind of history, we went through the school system and got a chance to play hockey for Don Wheeler and stayed with him for four years.

"It happened more when you went in with friends to watch Norwood play, when I was like in junior high school. We'd go into the Arena to watch the games, we were young, screwing around, running around the rink and kicking paper cups, and we'd see all these guys playing out there, great uniforms zooming around, and you're playing against these exciting teams in Boston, it was outstanding. Guys like Grapefruit Johnson, Donahue, Charley Donahue, amazing, we just looked up to all of them. Jim Neilson, he was a defenseman...

"In 1961 I was on the freshman team and freshmen couldn't play varsity. So we thought. That's the way it continued until Al Crowell and the boys, I think the first line on the varsity, as we were watching 'em, broke out in a brawl playing against Framingham and we were up there yelling and screaming and throwing stuff, and watching this amazing fight. There was at least six pairs fighting all over the place and it went on and on and the referee couldn't break it up and we were cheering it on, it was a great time!

"Al Crowell's line and two defensemen, the goalie was in it too. Fanning came from one end of the rink to the other to pummel the guy! Oh yeah, it was a brawl they couldn't break up, it was like the NHL. But we didn't realize that because of that, all those kids got kicked out for the next game, so Don Wheeler brought up five of us from the freshman team to play for the varsity. We played Needham High School at that time, and it was our first introduction to varsity hockey, and it was a tough one. I think the score was 5-0. We got hammered though, and they beat us up and basically threw us out the door and it was interesting. Course we had Smelstor in the net, along with our line that played which was Hebby, Angie and myself and then two of the defensemen. Yeah, so that was our introduction, and so the next year course we played on the varsity."

Patriot Ledger columnist Kevin Walsh described how Blaine Maus performed in Norwood's first Boston Garden contest:

Blaine Maus scored against Newton in overtime to send Norwood to the state finals against Walpole. The most important goal Norwood High School captain Blaine Maus ever scored in his life made the State Schoolboy Hockey Tournament an all-Bay State League final.

Maus, the leading scorer in the Bay State League and a two-time all-star, gave Norwood its third shot at Walpole this season with a "sudden death" overtime goal for a 2-1 win. "It was just fantastic, fantastic," said Norwood coach Don Wheeler. "The kids played their best game; the defense was immense and this win is the most important thing that has ever happened to Norwood High School. I don't think any Norwood team in any sport ever played for the State Championship. I'm so happy I don't know what to say. It's just a great feeling."

How did Maus score the winning goal? The team captain was all smiles as he related the most important goal. "I couldn't believe it went in at first. I picked a corner and just shot as hard as I could. It was a wrist shot off of my forehand. When I picked the corner, I just shot hard. I didn't know that it was in until the players started to rush over toward me. I was really surprised the Newton goalie didn't move out. I faked to one side with my shoulder and shot to the other corner. It really is the only big goal I have ever scored.

That's how Blaine described the goal immediately after the game to a Boston sportswriter in a euphoric Norwood dressing room; excitement remains as he reminisces fifty-five years later. "We beat 'em in overtime, I beat 'em in overtime, upper corner, *inside the bar!* I couldn't believe it, it went in! I just drove that thing it went up and it hit the netting and I says *yaaahhh!* We're screaming, everyone's jumping around, banging on the glass, it was a trip!"

The *Ledger* article continued,

Maus finished the Bay State season with 35 points, to edge Richie Hebner for the title. "I only scored six goals as a junior," confessed Blaine. "This year, over half my points were assists. My objective on the line is to set up my wings Richie Hebner and

Paul Angelo. They are both good scorers and we really work very well as a line."

Hebner scored his team's first goal on a brilliant effort and played the entire sudden death. "He never left the ice," pointed out Wheeler. "I had him playing wing on both the first and second line." Hebner was hit in the face in the opening period, and it took five stitches to close the cut between the first and second periods.

If Norwood's victory over Newton was memorable, Walpole's 3-2 semi-final victory over Hudson bordered the historic. Six overtime periods over two days were played before Dick Delaney scored the game winner, placing two age-old Bay State League rivals in the state final game of March 13, 1965.

"I remember they lost to Walpole in Boston Garden," twelve-year-old spectator Phil Nolfi recalled. "Woods was the goalie. Richie was all over the place. I used to listen to sports radio, one of the guys who used to be on RKO or EEI when it was sports, he was also the announcer for BC basketball, I can't remember his name, I'll remember it tonight having dinner, you know how that goes. And they were talking about when they were closing the old Boston Garden and they were building the new arena, and... Garabedian? I can't remember his name, I'll remember it. Now this was a guy who was a sportscaster, and he did BC basketball, and he said the greatest game he ever saw in Boston Garden was Norwood-Walpole. He said that was the greatest game I ever saw in all the games. That included Orr and the whole bit, I mean, 1-0, back and forth, nobody would go to take a pee, you didn't want to miss anything!"

Gordie Goodband scored the only goal of the game.

"I really remember how Walpole got the goal," then fourteen-year-old spectator Jerry Drummey recalled. "It hit Smelstor like on the shoulder, and it flipped over his shoulder and rolled into the net. It wasn't a very good goal, a classy goal, it hit him in the shoulder, took a lucky bounce over his shoulder and rolled into the net. Norwood couldn't put any pressure on Kevin Woods, the freshman goalie."

"I know I got on the ice, but I didn't play much," Jack Cronin recalled. "That game, someone hit the crossbar from just inside the blue line, someone on our team, that's how close that game was. And Angelo,

Maus, and Hebner, that line was, they dominated. It was a game for the ages. Someone said they had that film somewhere, that would be fun to watch. They had a great team, there was no taking anything away from them. As we did, too. It was an awesome period, and then we lose that game, and the whole time the town is supporting us like it's the Stanley Cup finals, and I didn't know any different, I figured that's what they just do in Norwood, people go crazy for hockey."

"I didn't play that one," then-freshman Neil Higgins said. "We played a great game, we had a lot of opportunities, but Walpole was playing a freshman goaltender, and his name was Kevin Woods. He became a dear friend, too. We loved to dislike one another, and that's how our wonderful friendship came about. But what I remember is we had some opportunities and Kevin Woods just played fantastic, he was terrific. The thing is, he was the first left-handed goaltender our shooters had ever gone against, so our guys were always shooting right into his catching glove instead of into his blocker. So, it really kinda baffled our shooters. That game, once again, could have gone in any direction, but Kevin Woods and Tommy Smelstor played sensational games."

"It put us into the biggest disappointment of my life!" Blaine Maus lamented. "The thing is we lost to Walpole that whole year, we lost three games to Walpole, one was in the finals. It was disappointing to say the least. Walpole was pretty good, but we just didn't play well. I mean, I saw the tape. (laughs) We looked like slow motion for chrissakes. Yeah, we didn't play well."

"I remember being at that game," Jerry Drummey continued. "They lost 1-0 in the finals, and I saw most of the games that year. They lost both regular season games to Walpole that year. It's funny, years later, cuz I used to hang around with Bobby Donahue and Bobby Clifford, they kept saying, we were better than Walpole and I keep saying, you lost three fucking times! *We were better! We were better!* I'm not so sure about that one! (laughs) Great talent up there, they had great talent. They talked about that for years. It was a great time, it really was a great time, 13,000 people watching those games..."

"It was a heartbreaking loss," Jack Cronin added, "but it was also kind of like the pinnacle for Norwood hockey. Because I remember the semifinals, we beat Newton, a good Newton team in the semifinals, and it was the first time Norwood had gone to the Garden, and we won. And

I remember when we came home that night the fire engine met us right at the town line on Washington Street, and we all rode the fire engine through town. It was like, are you kidding me? It was incredible...and of course a week or so later we lost to Walpole, 1-0. Kevin Woods, God rest his soul, he stoned us, he was a freshman playing for Walpole, and he was the real deal. Dickie Delaney was one of the best hockey players I ever played with..."

Paul Angelo deflects when asked about the game. "I mean, we got up, we went out and we tried to be better than the other guys," he said. "That was my theory. Okay? I didn't care how good they were, I just tried to be better. I'm still the same way. It's just something that's in me. When I was in high school, I don't ever remember losing a wind sprint. I wouldn't lose a wind sprint. It was just my drive."

"I remember after the game Paul Angelo and myself driving around," Blaine Maus recalled. "He had a car I didn't, he had the car, we drove around and talked about the game. Tried to talk ourselves down, instead of going home and talking to our parents who were pissed about it too... It was fun, it was nice to be able to talk to your buddy and shoot the breeze and you know, try to work out why you lost.

"Talking about the game. Talking about how we couldn't beat 'em, what the hell. Talking about Kevin Woods, he was instrumental in bringing that team all the way to the finals, he was the main reason. We blamed ourselves for not making the plays, passes, Hebby took the puck and that would be it, he wouldn't give it up. When they isolate you like that...it's a team game. You have to move the puck around, that's what you do. We were a good team, but the great teams play better. And we weren't. And we lost to them twice before! We did all kinds of things to get fired up and just didn't beat 'em.

"Paul Angelo is very, Paul doesn't say much of anything. Every time I go in there and see him, I'd say you were the best right winger I ever had in my life. I do that, I'm truthful about it. He just, *arrgh*, it was just the old days, why are you living in the past, but what the hell? When you see someone that you grow up with, that's what you do. It's all in the past, for a short period of time. He's so modest, he doesn't want to live in the past, he just wants to deal with what's coming at him, and that's it.

"If you've gone through that process, it's so similar, most of it's good memories, I mean the kids that didn't make the team, it was bad memories for them. But I can't do anything about that. Just worry about what you, how you grew up and how things worked out for you. Because when I got to college, things didn't work out as well as I wanted...

"Don Wheeler was a tough person. He used to tell us never settle for second best. *Never*. So, when we lost in the finals it was like, how do you settle for second best? You can't. You find that out. It's truth. But the important thing is, like Angie says, we've all become successful, we're all working trades or doing something, you know, we didn't give in to the pain, give in to the disappointment. What we did was we now know what it's like to be on the losing side. But it didn't ruin our lives. Made you feel very bad, but it didn't...and it also spurred you on because you weren't so successful to a certain degree, you wanna keep going. It prepared you for real life, whether it's disappointments or success. Enjoy your success while you can, because there's gonna be down moments, there's gonna be losing moments where you're not gonna...

"Later when I was coaching the kids, I'd say lookit, think of all the teams you know and watched all these games, and all the teams you've been on, how many times did you win something? I mean, besides winning the game? What else did you win? Did you win beyond what normal people do? You get a win once in a while, their season goes 5-4, and then they fade away. It was a fun experience, it's like a participation trophy. *Yeah, great*. But when you want to be super successful that's what you do, you push the kids...

"How do you settle for second best?"

THE STREET

Crestwood Circle is in a very remote part of town. Infact, fifty per cent of the 30,000 people in Norwood probably have never heard of such a place... In Crestwood Circle there was three groups of kids. The first one was "The big kids." In this group was my brother Kenny, Neil, Kenny Higgins, Brian and Danny Malony, Jerry Flavin, Dickey and Kevin Donavon, Bob Corners, Gary and Steven Sautovick, and near by came Denny Hebner, and his big brother Richie, who is now a profeshonial baseball player with the Pirates. That's the biggest group—13 in all... The big kids were always playing sports games...

— FOUR POOR BOYS, DON REDDICK (AGE 12), 1966

He arrived in America in 1907 as a seven-year-old, his family settling on a chicken farm on Walpole's Granite Street. There his family operated a slaughterhouse and chicken-canning operation, as well as an egg delivery service to Boston. In his late thirties or early forties, he demolished the outbuildings on his family property, replacing them with three houses. The experience demonstrated a more lucrative employment, and Vito Giusti began building houses for others, laying foundations of loves and lives throughout Norwood, Walpole, and Medfield. In 1950 he purchased 6.788 acres carved from the former Forbes estate at the far reach of Nahatan Street, submitted plans for twenty-one simple, identical, and inexpensive cape-style homes, naming the street, in reflection of its horseshoe layout and rural setting, Crestwood Circle.

Giusti Construction Corporation wasted little time. Purchasing the land in April, by year's end fifteen homesites had been sold. Those bracketing the closest entrance to downtown sold first to John Carlson, Joe Mendeloff, and Bob Donovan, quickly followed by lots lining Nahatan Street which, though not technically on Crestwood Circle, nevertheless were part of the project, and to whose deeds were affixed the names George Dennison, Fred DeRosa, and Arthur Early. Giusti worked in from both entrances, building homes that would house Webber, Connor, Higgins, Praino, Browne, Berglund, Reddick, and Sortevik families, finishing in early 1951 the far curve of the Circle, those lots edging the woods of the former Forbes estate and sold to John Sullivan, James Flavin, Daniel Moloney, and Henry Baker.

Demographics of the new neighborhood reflected quintessential baby-boom America. Homes were purchased by blue-collar couples with young and growing families. John Sullivan and Ernie Higgins were plumbers, Bob Donovan and Joe Moloney salesmen. Willis Webber was a maintenance supervisor, Fred DeRosa a contractor. Arthur Early was an electro type finisher at Plimpton Press and Jack Reddick had just been hired as night foreman at Bird & Sons' roofing plant.

The milieu was framed by World War II experience. George Berglund was an Army Air Corps fighter pilot who had flown 110 sorties over North Africa and Corsica. Willis Webber was a gunner's mate in the Navy, and Jack Reddick had rushed to join the Navy out of high school in the spring of 1945. Ernie Higgins maintained U.S. Army U-boat and anti-aircraft defenses along the New England coastline. Eddie Praino had served in Europe, and the most prized artifact Circle boys would seek out was John Connor's Nazi helmet with a bullet hole in it, kept in the Connor cellar.[8] One consequence of "the War" dominated Crestwood Circle, and was colloquially known as, "the returning soldier effect."

Long documented but still not fully understood is the evolutionary tendency of humans to produce more male than female children immediately after a war. The "why" is easily understood, for it replenishes the male half of the equation normally diminished by warfare. The "how" remains elusive.

It has been attributed to "divine intervention." Some, dismissive of other-worldly influence, believed it simply the result of testosterone-enhanced men doing what testosterone-enhanced men do after being

---

[8] When Jack Connor was asked about the Nazi helmet, verifying half-century-old memories, he frowned and shook his head. "I don't remember that..." Then he slowly nodded and said, "Oh yes, that wasn't from my father, but a family friend from Newton who had a large collection of World War II memorabilia. He gave it to us, and we used to play soldiers out in the woods with it. Anyone who wore the Nazi helmet got killed!"

deprived of intimacy for extended periods of time, as though mere desire increased odds of male children. More recently posited are more sophisticated human genome theories. Whatever the cause for this evolutionary tendency, post-war Crestwood Circle bore the effect: the fourteen original purchasing families who remained throughout the 1960s produced twenty-four boys and nine girls. Six families, including the outlying Hebner clan, produced nine hockey players to suit up for a Massachusetts state final hockey game. These six families, remarkably, bore eighteen boys and one girl.[9] The repercussions were obvious enough for even a twelve-year-old to survey the landscape and observe, "...*the big kids were always playing sports games...*"

"I grew up on Crestwood Circle, in Norwood of course," Neil Higgins remembered. "I don't even know how many houses were in that development, I'm gonna guess maybe fifteen, twenty, and in my back yard there was a low-lying area and if we had snow and rain and then a freeze it froze into ice. So I could go out there, I had a hockey stick and just in my sneakers and slide around and hit a puck or a ball and that was fun to do after school or on a Saturday or Sunday. And then low and behold one day my dad came home with a pair of skates. And actually, they were double-runners. And I was probably about six at the time, and that was fun. I think the following year maybe seven or eight years old, then we had snow and Dad and I pushed the snow to the side and made a little ice-skating patch and we flooded it. And then I went to single-runner skates.

"Skating around, my dad, he was from Canada, so he knew a lot about ice hockey. And my grandmother, his mother, when she was going to school and the rivers would freeze up in Canada, she and her girlfriends would ice skate to school down the river, so she knew about it, too. That was Prince Edward Island, Canada. So that little patch of ice, Dad didn't have any skates, but he would pass the puck with me, and I'd pretend like I was a goalie and he'd take shots on me and once in a while I'd make a

---

[9] Billy, Brian, Robbie, Richie ('65) and Dennis ('67, '68) Hebner, Kevin ('65), Dickie ('68), Robbie, and Timmy Donovan, Kenny and Neil ('65, '67, '68) Higgins, Danny ('65) and Brian Moloney, Steven and Gary ('68) Sortevik, Kenny ('65, '67), Gordon, Donny ('71, '72) Reddick, and, the last of this list to be born in 1959, Mrs. Bernie Cooper, the former Connie Reddick. Two girls in the Crestwood Circle development also became cheerleaders, Lynn Winthrop and Darryl Dennison.

save. We'd put a boot on one side and a boot on the other side and that was the net, that's what he could shoot into.

"I had a baseball glove and I used a leather workman's glove, and I taped a *National Geographic* magazine to it so now I had a blocker glove, and I had a baseball glove and Dad would take shots. That was probably at seven or eight years old. And the following year Mr. Tom Clifford had the Norwood Hockey Club and Dad asked Tom if I could go, and Mr. Clifford said yes. And I went, and they needed a goalie and they had some real old goalie equipment and Mr. Clifford let me use it, and I had fun doing it.

"So at that point in time, I started getting a little bit better at it and really enjoyed it. Dad and I agreed that if I would shovel snow or mow lawns or whatever he'd go in halvsies, and I think the first thing we got was a pair of pads, used goalie pads, still using the baseball glove and the *National Geographic* taped to a glove, but we found an old catcher's chest protector, so now I had that. So I was pretty much set to go. Then Dad came home with a pair of used hockey pants and of course a protector for the lower region, Dad made sure I had one of those, a cup. And so there I went, no mask, played with the Norwood Hockey Club for I guess a year and started getting a little bit better, and then Dad got a pair of real goalie skates and because Norwood didn't have a formal program back in those days, there were six teams in what they called the Greater Boston League. It was for peewees and Bantams, and I had just reached the age of bantams which was eleven years old. Wellesley needed one more goaltender..."

"I first started when my father made a rink out back, on 12 Crestwood Circle, probably 1957," Dickie Donovan recalled. "And I used to run on it, I have a picture, my father took a picture when I was about third grade, and I'm leaning on a chair, just pushing the chair around. I mean, everyone up there used to go to my house or Neil Higgins' father eventually built a rink, too, and we had our own places in the swamps.

"Bobby Connor would come over, and the Moloneys come over, and Neil would come over, before, you know, before we had any organized hockey. I finally got to skate with Mr. Clifford when I was in the fourth grade. I used to dress with my pads on the night before, I would tape up my pads, cuz he would come like five-thirty in the morning and my alarm would go off and I would run out the door. It was freezing, but we loved it, you know? Coldest rink in America, Tabor. Unbelievable. But at least I got to practice, skate on the ice. So that was good. My father loved hockey. He coached the CYO to two state championships. He loved hockey."

Growing up on Crestwood Circle in the '50s and early '60s was very much a rural experience. Isolated from town and inserted into almost a square mile of Forbes estate and Gay Farm woods and fields, bracketed across Nahatan Street by a similar stretch of woodland reaching to Father Mac's playground and Winter Street, it was a mile walk down Nahatan Street to Norwood center. News of a recently uncovered pitchfork with "Gay Farm" stenciled on it from the basement of the Early house elicited this email from Gordie Reddick,

> I remember Gay farm with the main outbuildings where they built Oldham School. Used to be an active dairy farm and the milk truck making home deliveries and we would "sneak" in the back of the truck and help ourselves to some ice (like the driver didn't know). We also used to jump off the roof of one of the barns—not that high up—into piles of hay. Then the big apple orchard where I think there's just one apple tree still standing. Then they built the Oldham School in 1962-63 and I was in the first sixth grade class to "graduate" from there in 1964. Then there's Gay St. in Westwood nearby. Fascinating that the Early's would have a stenciled pitchfork—an old piece of Norwood history for sure. Those were the days when we would walk the 3/4 miles to Shattuck school in kindergarten without parents getting arrested. And walk to Grandma's place by the cemetery on Wednesdays for mac and cheese lunch and then George Washington cake after dinner for dessert.

The woodlands dominated our childhood, different locations in different seasons. "The woods," as it was simply referred to, were accessed by two paths, one through a hole in an old, rusted wire fence behind the Sullivan house leading toward "the creek," and the more traveled path behind the Baker house to the "first field." Spring swamps and vernal pools were scoured for bullfrogs and yellow-spotted turtles; in summer, since the late '50s after the cows had finally been removed, the first field became Crestwood Circle's field of dreams. Autumn brought brown paper grocery bags supplied by mothers to gather the bounty from the Forbes, and later United Fruit's apple orchard, to be baked into pies and crisps. And winter saw a rag-tag crowd converge on the nearest possible venue for playing hockey.

"I remember the creek, I sure do," Neil Higgins recalled. "Yeah, we played on the creek behind Jerry Flavin's house. Gary Sortevik, your brother Kenny, Danny Moloney—Brian didn't wanna go—ah, once in a while Jerry Flavin would go, and let's see, myself and Dickie and Kevin Donovan, Gary Sortevik—Steven didn't want to go—and I would say that was it, that was all of us. Because it wasn't really that wide, and it wasn't really that long, and I'll tell you, we would skate. It was a nice place to skate, it was, but the problem was it was into the woods. When you were hot and you're sweaty and then you started walking home your fingers were freezing, you didn't want to take your skates off and put your feet back into cold boots, that's why the longevity of the creek didn't last that long. It was brutal when it was cold in those Boston winters, coming back home. Your fingers, your lips were blue and they were chattering and your feet were frozen, but yeah, we played the creek."

Saturday morning was a structured time of *The Three Stooges, The Little Rascals,* and *Cinema Seven.* TV sets only received channels 4, 5, and 7 and, beginning in 1964 and if your family purchased a UHF antenna, channel 38. Families gathered each winter to watch the once-a-year showing of *The Wizard of Oz.* Parents weren't afraid of letting children play alone outside, or in the woods. We were let loose each morning, only returning home for a peanut butter or baloney sandwich at lunchtime, or when you heard your mother's call or bell at dinner time.

We used to walk to friends' houses and call out their names. It would be a singsong effect: "Gaaahh-*reeeeeee.* Gaaahh-*reeeeeee.*" I'm not sure why we didn't use doorbells, or knock. Kids had great acorn-throwing wars, organized, serious affairs; one side of Crestwood Circle led by the Donovan, Higgins and Connor boys, the other by Sorteviks, Moloneys, and Reddicks. The armies filled bushel baskets full of acorns, reconnoitered and then engaged the enemy half-way, in the Higgins's backyard.

Relievio was a passion. Kids congregated on the rail fence between the Sortevik and Higgins homes, sides were picked and the evening spent running and hiding throughout the neighborhood. It was serious business leading a captured "enemy"—*"one two three caught by me!"*—back to the fence, held securely by the arm, and great excitement when opponents approached the fence—the jail—dashed up and touched it shouting, *"Relievio! Relievio!"* thus releasing captured teammates.

"Who was the fastest guy in the neighborhood?" Dickie Donovan asked, animated with the subject broached. "Playing relievio? I was close, very close. Gary was quick, Kenny could move. We used to play that until nine o'clock at night. It was fabulous! Everything we did was athletically competitive, even playing a game like that. We played relievio every night, and it was competitive! I mean, you'd sneak around the Higgins house and not make a sound...a lotta times the goal was right in front of the Webbers, we had the hydrant out there, and touch that and everyone's free! Oh God, we played all night!"

Humorous memories survive and continue to emerge. We heard parents recall early days when Gay Farm cows breached first field boundaries and milled about the street. Neighborly disputes arose. One father built a chicken coop and had just begun harvesting breakfasts when another objected to being awoken by his rooster's pre-dawn crowing. The chicken coop became a work shed. Two neighbors disagreed on who should pay to paint a newly installed rail fence separating their properties. The installer thought it fair to split the cost, while his neighbor felt it entirely the other's responsibility. When they could not agree, the wearied neighbor finally asked what color the installer wished to paint the rail fence. Black, he was told. Okay, the neighbor agreed, I'll paint my side white. The installer painted his fence.

Circle kids were on the cutting edge of primitive pyrotechnics. One taught how to use candles to delay a forest fire, so that one could be safely seated and unsuspected on front steps when the fire engines arrived.[10]

---

10 Taped to the back of an original page of *Four Poor Boys*, written when I was twelve, is a *Norwood Messenger* article headlined, 28 Acres Burn In Norwood Fire, Arson Suspected. It reads, "Norwood. A fire burned through a 28-acre section of brush and grass off Crestwood Circle before being contained by local and Westwood firefighters last night. Fire officials said the blaze was probably set by youngsters. The fire was burning in several scattered locations when fire-fighters arrived at 5:10 p.m. They were at the scene until 9 p.m. No one was injured and no buildings were threatened, according to fire officials." Nod sagely when one refers to the great men of Norwood like Ernie Higgins and Tom Clifford, who "sought to keep the kids occupied."

Another was known to assemble balsa wood airplanes, douse them with lighter fluid and *alight* them from his second story bedroom window. I myself became fond of placing unwanted plastic soldiers on the end of a stick, lighting them on fire, and napalming a nearby red ant hill with dripping flames.[11]

Conversing with my oldest brother recently, I mentioned a long-ago fall day playing touch football in the first field with "the big kids." Dennis Hebner was the only player that day to wear an actual football helmet, and naturally I lined up opposite him. He promptly planted the top of his helmet squarely in my solar plexus, knocking the wind out of me. Now, when an eight-year-old gets the wind knocked out of him for the first time by a twelve-year-old, it's scary. Your body desperately gasps for air and panic ensues when momentarily it will not come. I remember running home, crying. Ken recalled more.

"I remember that!" he said. "Do you remember what happened at dinner?" Ken explained that my father had listened to me relate the afternoon's atrocity, his right hand slowly closing into a fist as I spoke. When I had finished, he looked at Ken and pounded the table.

"And what did you do about it!" he demanded of my oldest brother, inquiring what retribution had been wreaked upon dastardly Dennis Hebner in defense of a younger brother. Ken looked at my father, glanced desperately at my mother, and stuttered, "...I...I...*I scored three touchdowns!*"

The youngest Hebner brother made a lasting impression on his neighborhood friends. "Dennis was the paperboy in the neighborhood," Mike Lydon remembered. "He used to have a wagon and drag the papers with the wagon he had so many, and we had the swimmin' pool. Dennis always wanted to come up to the pool and swim, and I go no, my mother doesn't want anyone up here swimmin', and he got pissed at that. And one day I'm walking home and *yeah so I can't go swimmin' up your pool* and beat the fuck out of me out on the sidewalk. And I'm whimpering up the sidewalk going home and Richie comes by, and Richie goes hey Mike, what's the matter, oh nothing, did Dennis do this to you? I say no, no, Richie says I'll take care of this. I was limping home before this, and I saw Richie go to his house and I was like a jackrabbit, I went behind

---

[11] This ceased when red ants counter-attacked up my pant legs, breeching my lower region.

the woods, I'm hiding behind the house and Richie whaled the tar out of Dennis! Made me feel...and I get along, I talk to Dennis about that story. Dennis is a fucking riot. I dug a couple of graves with the old man over West Roxbury, *just don't drive over with him, don't drive over with him, drive over yourself!* Oh God, Dennis is a funny bastard. The Hebner family, *Jesus.*"

Today I occasionally encounter Dickie Donovan, normally in Savin Ave.'s Colonial, or Lewis', where we sometimes talk hockey, and neighborhood. Dick is a serious guy with a sharp memory. Ken once suggested he would have made a great Marine officer. One evening Dick seemed a bit harder than usual, a bit more reserved in our casual banter. Sensing this, I finally asked why.

"You stole my soldiers," he declared.

Playing soldiers was a ubiquitous, time-honored avocation of Crestwood Circle kids, raised as we were by the generation that had fought the Second World War. In my bedroom was a toy box full of Indians and Colonials, Bluecoats and Confederates, Axis and Allied troops. We imagined guns from sticks and recreated valiant victories and maudlin defeats in the vast Forbes estate woods. We purchased packets of Civil War cards from C & W's variety store[12] on Nahatan Street after the Shattuck School bell had rung. And we played soldiers earnestly and endlessly, the Donovan backyard a special place to do so, as Mr. Donovan allowed firecrackers. How realistic that was! Firecrackers buried, fuses only sticking above ground and soldiers placed precariously around, so that when we lit the fuses poor plastic souls flew through the air to the delight of imagining kids. And now, sixty years removed and on Savin Avenue, I hear the complaint.

"You stole my soldiers," Dickie said.

"What are you talking about?" I responded, surprised by the accusation, while desperately trying to recall if true.

"You stole my soldiers!" Dickie repeated.

"I never stole your soldiers," I protested. "Honestly, Dickie, I don't know what you're talking about!" Dickie's stare did not relent. "I didn't steal your soldiers!" I insisted.

With bemused indignation, I repeated Dickie's accusation in Ken's

---

12 C & W's, short for Curran and Wall, occupied the building today housing D & G Deli. As a kid I always thought it was, "Sam W's."

living room a few nights later. I rambled on a bit, all the while slowly sensing my brother's silence. I paused when the implication dawned, and facially expressed clarification.

"I stole the soldiers," Ken admitted. "I mean, I *had* to"—he cocked his right arm in the air—"the Indian was holding a *tomahawk!*"

The cows were gone, a Gay Farm real estate transaction beyond grasp of Crestwood Circle boys, who nevertheless reacted by taking possession of the first field. The path behind the Baker house began to broaden, leading through a short stretch of wood past a cluster of wild black and red raspberry bushes, through a stonewall breach and into the open.

Home plate was placed closest the opening, a stonewall perfectly aligned in left field our own Gray Monster, center and right field borders more distant, and falling to briars. The significant blemish was a rock, the tip of an immovable iceberg boulder—an erratic so deep and large our colonial ancestors found impossible to remove to the stonewalls—that surfaced between the pitcher's mound and the second baseman's playing position.

Springtime's sustained sunlight, eradicating the most stubborn splashes of field water, found boys dragging lawnmowers and shouldering sickles down the path. I recall sweeping sand from the sides of Crestwood Circle left from winter sanders, filling buckets and lugging them out and dumping them along baselines. Fathers led a work party constructing a crude dugout one spring; a chicken-wire backstop another, neither lasting longer than the season, their two-by-fours and chicken wire appropriated for hockey nets come fall.

My own recollections, sixty years aged, are mostly fractured, and sometimes poignant. I remember Neil Higgins' older brother Kenny, transistor radio to ear, ranting at the latest perceived atrocity emanating from Fenway Park. I recall standing aside the "big kids," watching two either "buck-up" or perform the unnamed but common custom of grasping a bat, alternating one hand/finger over the other, until one captain claimed the top of the bat earning first choice of teammates, all the while anxiously waiting to see if a captain would choose me to play. This occasioned one of my first inklings that there was more than just winning when I saw, as a learning kid of seven or eight, my oldest brother attain first choice and selecting, against all perceived common sense and over an uproar of objection, the *worst* player available first.

In that era of unquestioned parental authority, I witnessed almost inconceivable rebellion. As my mother's dinner bell rang and I began running toward the path homeward, Ken stood at the plate and refused to drop his bat. "C'mon, Kenny! *The bell!*"

"I'm not going till I get my at-bat..."

Baseball was played day-long, season-long without supervision. Bobby Orr's autobiography noted similar circumstances during the same era, in a neighboring country,

> Parents today might be surprised to discover what kids can do if they are left to their own devices. We certainly learned to figure things out for ourselves. We had to take the initiative, because the odds were that no parent would be available to shovel off the bay or the rink or a stretch of road. If we wanted to play, we had to do the work to make it happen... No coaches to tell you what to do. No parents to tell you how to behave. No referees to tell you what's fair. And no linesman to break up trouble if someone loses his temper...

Tempers were lost in the field behind Crestwood Circle. Embattled neighborhood kids stridently argued everything from balls and strikes to fair or foul, or whether so-and-so touched third base. It was competitive, serious business, engaged by souls whose sole objective was to win. Bats were wood, balls blackened and softened by continuous use, often lost for weeks at a time over the stonewall in left, or in high, uncut grass in deep center, or right. These balls were sometimes found during subsequent mowings or in late August while picking blueberries along the Blueberry Path in woods just beyond left field's stonewall, frequently and to our great remorse a sticky, glutinous ruin. And I remember the Hebner boys, come to visit from Nahatan Street.

The older Hebner brothers were vague, at least to me, though their baseball ability was renown. Richie and Dennis, though, would sometimes come over. They were not regulars because they had their own diamond in the great field behind their next-door neighbor McDonough's house on Nahatan Street, as well as an abrogated infield, complete with real bases, in their own backyard. And they did things no one else could do.

I recall Richie hitting a baseball directly upward into the air seemingly a mile, something no one else could do after much trying, and Dennis the only one who could circle, and catch it as it fell. Even at a young age they possessed a more thorough understanding of the game's nuances. I myself felt the wrath of teammates when tricked by Richie as I passed second base on an outfield hit. As I lumbered toward third, I saw Richie's eyes following the ball almost into his glove, so turned and scooted back toward second only to hear sideline screams that the ball was still in the outfield, so turned and ran toward third where *again* I saw Richie about to catch the ball and tag me out, so *again* turned toward second, when I discovered to my chagrin that the ball was just being retrieved by the outfielder. Naturally I turned and ran toward third base—and was thrown out.

I also recall Richie, after hitting baseballs directly skyward, whacking me across the back with his bat. I was younger than most and wanted to play, so refused to give in to any intimidation. When I didn't react, he repeated the act, a bit harder. "That doesn't hurt?" he asked, and I shook my head. He then repeatedly struck my back, a bit harder each time, calling out, "Hey lookit, *Weddick likes it!*"

"It was in back of the Moloney's, Brian and Danny Moloney," Neil Higgins recalled. "God bless them both they've both passed on, and they were dear friends. It was in back of their house, I think it was called Gay Farm who owned that land, and they let us mow it down and play baseball out there. And that was just, you know, life couldn't have got any better. The Sorteviks, the Reddicks, the Moloneys, Jerry Flavin, Bobby Connor, the Donovans, Kevin and Dickie, we'd just go out there in the morning and play baseball until we were told to come back home for dinner. It was quite a neighborhood.

"In the summertime, we'd say okay, let's have a baseball game. And Dennis would come, Richie would come, Robbie would come—Robbie Hebner would be the umpire—and then maybe a couple of other kids would come, maybe Freddie Kinsman from Nahatan Street would come. We'd play baseball and Richie would have to bat left-handed. And honest to goodness, he could blow it out of that field into the woods! There wasn't much that kid couldn't do. But he would tone it down because he was having fun. It wasn't Little League, it was fun time, it was lot baseball. We all had fun doing it."

"It was great, it was," Dickie Donovan concurred. "We had tons of boys, very few girls, we didn't pay any attention to girls, right? So all we did was play sports all day long. In the winter we'd go out to the creek and make our own little space to skate, horrible, too, but you know, we did all right. I can remember going out to that first field. We were there every day from like spring to fall, and even then, the Hebners would come over and we'd play football. Richie would be throwing a ball like he a was a pro quarterback, he had an arm like that, he was unbelievable.

"It was a great neighborhood, it really was. I still remember going out, bringing water and pistols and we'd go out in the summer, Kenny'd be there, my brother Kevin, me and Bobby, Gary, Gordy was there, and we'd just soak each other. Squirt guns and water balloons. That was quite a place. On this side of Xaverian, remember the old apple orchard out there? It was a beautiful area, wasn't it? We'd make forts and tree huts, it was unbelievable. Kevin was unbelievable. He began a log cabin out by the creek! It's true!"

Winter's game, though, most enthralled Crestwood Circle boys.

"In the wintertime," Neil Higgins continued, "we'd get a couple games going and it was Father MacAleer's. In back of the pool there was a pond there, a tiny pond, and we'd have a little hockey game there. This time it was on a massive scale. Jack Cronin would come from up by where the cemetery was, Harry Pascoe, he lived near Father Mac's, the Doyle's would come, Jimmy Doyle and Allen Doyle would come over, the Hebners, we'd meet them there, all the kids from Crestwood Circle, and there'd be some other kids, Ray D'Arcy sometimes would be there, Jimmy Doyle and Ray D'Arcy had great careers at BC, they were a little bit behind me, so yeah, we, once again, we—it was a kinship, I would call it. All the neighborhoods got together, we were just a bunch of ragamuffin boys playing sports and having fun."

"We were outside all the time, the only time we were inside was when it was raining," Dennis Hebner recalled. "We had the greatest street hockey games in my yard. I don't know if you ever played there with us. I think Dickie might have played, the kids from North Ave., I remember Norman Johnson played once.

"Me and Richie made a net, we found some old wood, I think they were four-by-fours, really thick wood, and for the backing, instead of netting, my father was gonna throw away an old rug, we nailed the fucking rug to it. The thing musta weighed three hundred fucking pounds, you couldn't move it! It just stayed in front of the old post. We had some boards, some wood they use for concrete forms. We had one on each side, and we nailed up some chicken wire above them so the ball wouldn't go down the backyard, and we put boards along, especially if it snowed, we made a little thing."

"Oh, Dennis. Great guy," Dickie Donovan recalled. "What a talent. He was a great baseball player, too. As well as a goaltender, he was not that far behind Neil Higgins. If they had to get another goalie, Denny could have played. Yeah. Me, Denny, and Richie and your brother Kenny would go to their driveway there, and we'd play street hockey as soon as the hockey season ended, and we'd play street hockey for another two months. In the goal was Richie, or Dennis. They loved playing goal. And they were quick as a cat! My God, yeah! It was great!"

"I played street hockey at the Hebners and on Neil's driveway all the time," Ken Reddick said. "The day I remember the most was, we were playing street hockey and every day Ernie came home around the same time so we would move the net around, get out of the way, and we'd all get out of the way, and one of us would go to the door of the garage and open the garage door. For whatever reason this was my turn and I put the garage door up, all the way in, *bang!* against the ending of the track, and came right back down again and *boom!* he went right through it with his car! Everybody ran like hell except me, my feet were like in cement. And Ernie was great about it, he wasn't mad, he didn't give me any grief at all. He might have been a little upset, but he didn't take it out on me. But I was the one guy who didn't run home, I couldn't move a muscle!"

"What I really remember," Neil Higgins said, "and it's funny, I was talking about this with my wife, because our grandson is playing street hockey and I just remembered that. She said, did you have glass windows on that garage door? And I said yeah, we had two garage doors and we had glass windows, and inevitably once or twice a week we'd put a ball through those glass windows.

"So, Dad would bring me down to the Cooper's hardware store right next to the United Church. And they would cut to size, we knew the size, and Dad would tell me buy as many as you've got money for, and they'd be fifty cents apiece but that was a lot of money back then, a gallon of gas was twenty-five cents. Heck yeah, he made me pay for them! Teaching me responsibility. Now, he'd give me a chore and over-pay me, but I did something and he taught me how to work, and what work ethic was.

"I think I bought eight. Eight panes of glass, so we always had panes of glass, we'd break it and everybody'd say let's run home, you don't have to! Now we can continue playing! We got to keep an eye on the clock, so before my dad gets home, we have to sweep up all the glass, make sure there's no glass, and I have to put in a new piece of glass. Okay, all right Neil, that's a plan.

"So not to be left out, Danny Moloney, he broke his leg. I don't know how he broke it; I can't remember how he broke it. But Danny wanted to play street hockey with us, and he was on crutches and somehow, someway he got an old wheelchair. So, Danny Moloney would get in the goal in his wheelchair. He had a baseball glove, had a goalie stick, and Danny was the goalie in a wheelchair. I mean, almost like a sitcom of the olden days. We were a tight neighborhood. Danny couldn't play? Well, we'll figure out how he *can* play. Nobody was being left behind in that neighborhood. Anyone wanted to play baseball, football, hockey, they got to play. That one always stands out. God bless Danny and Brian."

It was a working-class neighborhood whose coming athletic exploits were summarized by a Norwood hockey captain almost sixty years later, after moving into a house developed on the old Lydon compound.

"Living there has given me a belated reinforcement of the following closely-held hockey secret that few in Norwood are fully aware of," Bobby Thornton related. "As I embark on my daily Covid walk—one of the silver linings of Covid—one of my routes is to not just walk straight down Nahatan, but I always take the scenic loop my wife calls 'Crescent Ridge,' a/k/a Crestwood Circle. Invariably when I do, I automatically am reminded that the short little loop of pavement on Nahatan and

Crestwood contained the highest concentration of hockey talent per square foot that could ever exist. I'm sure I'll miss a few names but there were a few Hebners, Donovans, Reddicks, Higgins, Moloneys, Sorteviks, Connors, etc. who all lived within a slap shot of each other and I cannot recall any other area in this former hotbed that can lay claim to such a fact. Dickie Donovan used to go on and on to me about this for years from the next stool at Lewis'. Now that I walk it daily, I realize he was right and should have been proud of it."

"Your neighborhood," Bobby Dempsey said, "look at the talent, look at your neighborhood, my gosh! Crestwood Circle itself could have had a varsity hockey team and done extremely well, not extremely well, might have won! Right? Two solid lines just from Crestwood Circle, couple of good goalies, the Moloneys, Neil...*what was in the water up there?*"

THE LEGEND

Lord, what a ballplayer! I don't believe there's a man over there that can throw and ketch like you; and as for battin', I never see a ball rise so like a bird and sail off through the air as yourn do. Of course you'll take the honors. You pitch quoits to a p'int, and you can wrestle, side-holt, back-hug, arm's-length, any way, I don't care which, and as for a long pull at a race, I guess your breath wouldn't give out sooner than a blacksmith's belluses. Of course you'll be at the head of 'em all—the hull of 'em. I don't b'lieve there's a chap there that can climb as you can, or straddle a horse as well, or hold out as heavy a sledgehammer at arm's length, or throw it half as far, for that matter, as you can!

— Henry Ward Beecher,
Norwood, or Village Life in New England, 1868

The first time I recall ever seeing The Legend was from my perch on the fence separating the Higgins and Sortevik yards. Rounding the curve of Crestwood Circle, walking in the middle of the street past Bobby Connor's house, came strutting—and that word was simply created for this image—Richie Hebner, smoking a cigar. He was followed by what seemed a constant entourage, younger brother Dennis always among them.

Thirteen or fourteen years old, chin raised in his common pose, he seemed always above the fray, carrying himself even at that age with a superior, confident stride, and why not? He knew he was better than anyone else, even his immediate elders, at the only things that mattered to us. Other things mattered to Mr. Sortevik. Dismayed by the cigar but primarily annoyed at lamentable language, Gary's father banned the Hebners from the Sortevik yard. To which the brothers responded by sitting on the Higgins side of the fence tee-ing the adjacent yards, almost as a taunt to the fuming, pipe-smoking father.

The family possessed a reputation for both athleticism and toughness. Billy, the oldest, would one day be signed by the New York Yankees, and eventually enjoyed a career as a minor league umpire. Robbie had the reputation of being a star pitcher, and Brian, a future Norwood firefighter, was said to be the toughest of them all. Then followed the youngest two brothers.

If Richie was above the fray, Dennis *was* the fray. Though he recently denied any memory of the act, it was rumored they'd hung Arthur Dodd by his feet in the woods behind their house and left him there. Notoriously banned from Father Mac's playground one summer—a serious infraction of note in a 1964 Norwood—he prowled the front yard of their Nahatan Street house armed with small, hard crab apples, accosting passers-bye he deemed unworthy, so that passing the Hebner yard on the only street that led to Crestwood Circle and upper Nahatan Street became running a gauntlet. And like all Hebners, Dennis had an *arm*...

"Early memories of learning to skate and play hockey was behind our house in the swamp," Dennis Hebner reminisced. "You remember, did you ever go down that way? Back of Rio's house, Bobby Rio and Richie Rio, where Norwest Woods is, that was all swampland, and we skated between the stumps and the broken branches. We had a little spot no more than twenty-five feet long, we called that the hockey rink, we played hockey there. That's where I learned to skate, and Richie learned to skate in Connolly's house, remember Cindy and Nancy Connolly? They lived two houses away from us, going towards Crestwood Circle. They built a house, Richie was probably nine or ten, so what the hell was that, late '50s, early '60s. They poured the foundation in the fall, and they weren't gonna build till the spring and we had a lot of rain and stuff and it flooded. We used to go over there and skate, that's where Richie learned to skate, in Connolly's basement.

"We skated there, we skated in the swamp and Father Mac's once it got frozen after cold days. After school we'd have like an hour and a half or something because it got dark so early. I'd put my skates on in the house and walk through the fields and the woods with my skates on because it was too fucking cold to put my skates on up there!

"I remember we grew up poor, poor as hell, until my grandfather died, and my father took over the cemetery in '63. We were a little bit better then. But we never had a new car. I remember some nights my mother would heat up two cans of gravy and put bread down and pour the gravy over it, that's dinner. Hot gravy and white bread, that's it! Or couple pounds of pasta, throw some sauce on it, nothing fancy. Unless it was Sunday. Sunday my mother'd go crazy. Oh, yeah.

"One day she'd make a big roast beef, I mean huge, another a leg a lamb, then corned beef and cabbage, and pot roast. Those were the four main things; she'd make them on Sunday. She'd make it and if you weren't there, she didn't give a fuck, you don't get it. You knew it was gonna be around one, two o'clock, we'll eat in the dining room, and if you weren't home for it, tough shit! When most of us were living at home there weren't any leftovers! We used to go through two gallons of milk a day! I used to have to go down to Dacey's on my bicycle with the glass bottles, couple times I broke them. (laughs) But yeah, seventy-five cents a gallon back then, Dacey Brothers. Unbelievable. I don't know how we survived, really, five of us. Food bills, they were outrageous!"

"My favorite meal? Probably steak," Richie Hebner recalled. "My mother would go down Shurfine and buy some steaks, and let me tell ya, with five boys, you better get to that table quick! (laughs) Five boys, you better sit down quick! No, there weren't many leftovers. We had a little dog, and he didn't eat shit after we were done."

"I remember Saturdays was the day my mother would go down to Shurfine and buy the big half ham, Morrell easy-cut ham," Dennis continued. "I still buy Morrell easy-cut hams to this day on special occasions, like Easter and stuff like that. She used to buy it and she'd say there it is, your lunch, dinner. Saturdays, that was her day off. We'd make ham sandwiches, potato chips, that was it, every Saturday.

"We used to play ball in McDonough's field. We used to cut the field, if it got too high, we used to fucking burn it, we'd used to run around and burn it and run home and wait for the fire trucks to come! We did! Oh yeah, we did! My father brought some lawnmowers home and Richie and I would go over there and cut the whole field, it took all day. That was a big thing, I know you want to talk about hockey, but playing baseball on McDonough's field, first sixteen kids or so showed up you played, if you were too late, we didn't need you, you didn't play. All the kids from Silver Street, North Ave., all around our neighborhood, almost every night from

April to when school got out. We played every night. I used to play once in a while behind Crestwood Circle with Dickie and Kevin and those kids up there, you were probably up there. I'm trying to remember who else we played with, oh Harry Pascoe, remember Harry Pascoe? They moved to Seattle or something? Washington? He was a nice kid, pretty good athlete.

"We played whiffle ball in the back yard, oh man, we had some... I don't think anyone could play with us, just me, Richard and Robert played, I mean it was so tough. We used to use the whiffle ball without the holes, you know, just a plastic ball, and we had the big bottle bat and Richard, Robert and I we took turns pitching, and you couldn't catch it, cuz we'd throw so fucking hard. We'd set up a whole canvas so a ball wouldn't get dented by hitting that old shed my father built, and I used to throw curve balls, knuckle balls, I swear that helped Richie hitting, honest to God.[13] I was only forty feet, forty-five feet, and I could throw pretty good, and some days you got hit with it... We used to do a lot of things like that. We used to go over to McDonough's field just the three of us, Robert would take a bat and ball, I'd play third base and Richie would play left field and we'd make believe we were playing a Red Sox game. He'd only hit the ball to me or Richie, and we'd keep track, we'd play that for hours. Yeah, kids don't do that anymore. You go by a field today and it's fucking empty."

"Everyone's got a story about Mr. Hebner, here's one about Mrs. Hebner," Pebbles Folan related. "I go with Dennis up to the Hebner house and Dennis says hey, look at this, Irish bread! It's still warm! You want some? So, Dennis gives me a piece and I eat it. Mrs. Hebner walks in, sees the Irish bread and says, 'That's for the nuns!' The nuns had a bake sale every year, and Mrs. Hebner had made the Irish bread for the sale. And she *whacks* Dennis, she really gives him a good whack, and she turned to me and says, 'And *you* had a piece?' and she *whacks me* like she whacked Dennis!"

"Oh yeah, the Irish bread," Dennis recalled. "She used to make the best Irish bread. When she used to go to Pittsburgh to see Richie play,

---

13 "Hey, let me tell ya," Richie Hebner recalled of those backyard sessions, "Dennis was just as good a hitter as I was. He played about a year and a half with the Pirates (organization), and then they let him go. He was a good ballplayer."

she'd make an Irish bread and give it to Danny Murtaugh. He was the manager there and he'd put it out in the clubhouse, and he loved the Irish bread! My mother's from Ireland, County Mayo, the town of Ballyhaunis. She came over here with her two sisters, she was in her mid-twenties when she got here. Know something? I never knew she had a brogue until she got interviewed after my brother won the World Series in '71. She was on television, I said oh my God I can't believe how she talks! I never knew that in person, yeah, never knew it! I said holy shit, she got a brogue! Didn't know it! Didn't know it!"

Richie told another story about the belle from Ballyhaunis. "My mother and father went to one of the World Series games, the first night World Series game I played in, 1971," Richie related. "So, after the game I went back to the hotel, and I said mom how was the game? She said I don't know, I couldn't pay attention, this guy beside me was driving me up a wall. All he did was talk and talk. I says who was it? My father says, *Casey Stengel! He never shut up the whole game!*"

"She was feisty," Dennis continued. "I'll tell ya, I was afraid of my father, but I was kinda afraid of my mother, too. God, we had that big lilac bush out back, if I pissed her off, she'd go out there and snap off a long fucking whip and she'd say get in this house right now, if you don't get in now you'll get twice as much when I get ya! She'd fucking whip the back of my legs, *owww*... My father used to beat the shit out of us, too. Oh yeah, yeah. But know something? We deserved it! I don't hold it against him at all. I mean, especially having five boys in the family and... I had to share a bed with my brother Robert until Richie moved out. We had a big double bed and Richie had a single bed, and Brian and Billy had a double bed they shared. That was something."

"That had to be a pretty wild household," Jack Cronin surmised. "I remember we used to play in their ballfield behind the house, and I can remember Mrs. Hebner coming out. She'd yell Richie! Dennis! Come in! And they'd ignore her for an hour. Finally, the door would sling open and she'd be like would you get your goddamn...and she'd have like twenty-five swears linked together, stuff I never heard of, *get your asses in here!* And then they'd drop everything and go in. I think it was like the wild west. I'm not saying there was anything abusive, but it was all boys, and they're all rambunctious.

"I have lots of stories of the Hebners. It was a great time to grow up and they were great kids to play sports with, because they loved to win, they loved to compete. We had great battles, we had great battles, Dennis and I were the Park League horseshoe champions! For Father Mac's, Father Mac's would play Shattuck, we just loved to compete, that's what we did. It was fun."

"Richie didn't start playing hockey till third grade because he had a foot infection," Dennis said. "He stepped on a rusty nail and his foot got infected. He stayed back in second grade. Just talent, just talent. Matter of fact, he had an accident, I don't remember, I was really young, we were living on Prospect Ave. at the time, so it was before I was five. He jumped over a fence and landed on a rusty nail in his heel. You ever hear that story? He stayed back his first year because he was too shy, he was too shy, just afraid, afraid of everything, he didn't talk or anything. But a rusty nail went right up into the bone of his heel, and they went to a doctor, as a matter of fact it was Dr. Orme, and he said he needs an operation and all this stuff and needs to go to Children's Hospital. They said well, I dunno, let's give it a little more time, so my mother went to fucking church and prayed for an hour, and the next morning Richie woke up and was fine.

"We used to play baseball over at Shattuck. We cut a hole in the fence, we used to go out our back and onto the field. He used to play baseball on crutches. He had crutches! He'd get up there on the crutches, hit the ball, take the crutches to first base. I was five, he was like seven and a half when he did that. Even at Little League, he won the batting title when he was ten, he won it at eleven, but he didn't win it when he was twelve, Jay Dixon beat him out. Jay was a good ballplayer!"

Mike Crimmins, himself a baseball star who batted over .600 in Norwood Little League, remembered The Legend. "I knew Richie, he was a character! A real character! Everything came so naturally to Richie. When he was playing baseball, he had the hips and he had the wrists. And as you well know, that's all you need. He put all of that into every swing, and it was a very graceful kind of swing, and he just, he made the ball *cry*."

"Wheeler musta knew Richie was pretty good at hockey," Dennis continued, "cuz Richie made the CYO team his freshman year. Wheeler went to the first game, cuz he said I gotta check this kid out, see what he does against kids a little older. Well, that was the only game Richie played for CYO. Richie had six goals. Six goals he got in one game. It was the only CYO game he ever played. I was at that game. Every time he got the puck he scored. He was just so much better, that was the only game he ever played. That Monday Wheeler called and said you're gonna practice with the varsity."

In a 1968 column Frank Wall recalled the kid's debut.

> In his first game as a freshman he scored the first time he came on the ice against Framingham when he took a Dana Maus pass and fired it home. Perhaps his biggest thrill when only a 14 year old freshman came on Saturday, Jan. 19, 1963 when he scored three goals to defeat Natick 4-2 and assisted on the other.

"We used to look forward to Saturdays, especially the first two years Richie played because it was in the Arena," Dennis Hebner said. "We used to go to the games a lot when I was younger, because my brother Billy was into high school sports, and he used to take me into the Arena. Then all of a sudden, the fucking what do you call 'em, the supervisors, the superintendents, *we can't go into Boston, we have to bring the games out here.* It ruined everything. Loring Arena, Ridge Arena—Ridge had a good ice surface, it was cold as a bastard—and they had glass too, which was...matter of fact, I had the paper route then. I had the afternoon paper route. On Saturdays my father would take me down to Welch's, right over here on Broadway. I'd get my papers and deliver 'em real fast, cuz my father would say we're leaving at five, at quarter of five we're leaving.

"My father and mother in the front seat, me and Robert and Jimmy Lennon, remember Jimmy Lennon? And driving with my father, people can tell you stories about that. You know how you're supposed to drive defensively? He was just the opposite. He wanted everyone to get out of his fucking way, I swear if the horn didn't work in the car, he wouldn't drive it. He used to make it from Norwood—we used to park behind the Arena and go over that walk-out bridge, we used to park there—we used to make it in twenty-five minutes! He was crazy, he was absolutely fucking crazy, my father.[14]

"Richie scored some great fucking goals. I remember the Arena, we used to go early cuz we had to sit up on the balcony that overlooked the goal, we sat there every game. They were playing Needham, either Richie's freshman or sophomore year, he got the puck and went around two guys, through the defensemen, went in on the goalie, the fucking goalie never moved, he never saw the puck. He had some great goals.

"After the games, my father would give Richie a beer. Richie drank when I was in high school a little bit, Richie would drink in the house. My father would say you can drink in the house. Me in high school? I never drank in high school. Fuck no, I was afraid of my father, he would have beaten the fuck out of me. I never drank in high school. I didn't even want to go to places where you could get served under twenty-one, nope. I have that guilty look when I go into a place like that, I said I'm not gonna look like a fool and get thrown out."

"He could skate very well," Neil Higgins recalled. "He was powerful. He could hold off with one hand an opposing player with his left hand while he's got his right hand on the stick controlling the puck, okay? And could just lean into, well there weren't many men bigger than him back in those days, but he could lean in and work his way right to the net. Richie could shoot the puck left-handed or right-handed, same as with a baseball bat, and he had the most fierce back-hand shot that you've ever seen in your life. He could pick out the top corner with that back-hand shot, and a back-hand shot for a goaltender is one of the most difficult to stop. Especially when it's coming at you that fast, and it's rising that fast.

"He could control a game by himself because he was so powerful. He also did what a lot of high school kids just didn't wanna do. He was not afraid to go in the corners, he was not afraid to take a hit. I think it got his adrenaline going if somebody did hit him, *that's the last hit you'll get on me, I'm gonna show you*, and he'd come out and score two goals just to show them. He just, he could shoot the puck with one hand, he could shoot it with two hands, and he could go both ways, and he could hold off one or two guys who were trying to double-team him. That's how strong the kid was."

---

14 Almost everyone telling stories about Bill Hebner mentions his driving. "Drove around like it was the Five Hundred Indy. Nobody got killed! Well, they didn't call him Wild Bill for nothing," Richie said.

"Richie was a man among boys on the ice," Jack Cronin agreed. "And on the baseball field. I don't know mentally how mature he was at that time; I was just a kid. I know he had some conflict with Wheeler, but Wheeler wouldn't take anything from anybody. Richie was a superstar even then, everybody knew it. He was never a prima donna; he would always work as hard or harder than anyone else. It was a pleasure playing with him, except he wasn't what you would call a playmaker. (laughs) I'd give him the puck and he would not try to stickhandle around anybody, he'd go right over them, he was a man among boys. He always had a good shot, he used his body well, and people are right when they say he could have played professional hockey, and they're also right saying he made the right decision in not playing professional hockey. I thought it was an honor to be on the ice with him. And I played baseball with him at the time, I was a third baseman, he was the shortstop.

"This is another funny story, they brought me up to the varsity when the state tournament started, and they played me at third base. I don't know if the third baseman got hurt or what, my freshman year, and I remember I had a baseball glove that was old, and I remember in infield practice before the game started, I think we were playing down in Fall River, and Richie's playing shortstop, and in infield practice he's turning a double play, and I'm taking a ball from second base, and I'm gonna throw it to home, and he throws it so damn hard it broke the webbing in my glove! It's a state tournament game! I mean, I had to borrow someone's glove to play the game! Again, he was a man playing with boys."

"I just heard a story about Richie just this year that I had never heard before," Leo McInerney said. "Did you know Pickles Crowell? Gary Crowell? He was on the '64 team, he told me. I actually asked Richie and he said he does not remember this, and Richie was thirteen years old— *thirteen* now—and playing in the Park League and there's a guy pitching for the Johnson Bombers who was an ex-Red Sox pitcher who had retired, pitching because, you know, he loved the game, and Richie goes five for five with two doubles against him. And he comes up against him for the sixth time—the kid's thirteen years old now—and the pitcher walks off the mound and hands the ball to the manager and says, have someone else pitch to that kid."

Yet there were days before he was The Legend, and subject like every Norwood kid to the hard-scrabble, blue-collar give-and-take of '60s boyhood. "I remember your brother used to drive Richie nuts," Leo McInerney recalled. "You know Richie didn't do his 'Rs' at the time very well, and he used to call your brother 'Weddick.' And Kenny would always say, hey *Wichie*, did your dog kill a *wabbit*?"

"Richie lost his teeth," Dennis Hebner said. "That was a story and a half. It was at Four Seasons, but they were playing one of those Rhode Island teams, I think it was Cranston, one of those big teams cuz Wheeler liked to play a good team to see how his team looked. It was Richie's junior year, he already had a reputation that he was one of the best, and so some punk from the other team right in the first period cross-checked him in the mouth, and he had to go to the hospital. His four front teeth are fake. Blood all over the fucking place, so the next year they played the same fucking team, did he tell you this story? Richie got on the ice, he got the puck behind the net, got just over the red line and took a shot and fucking scored, over the goalie's shoulder from half-ice. That was like his payback."

"Richie was just so driven," Jimmy Gormley recalled. "I would have to say he was probably the greatest competitor I ever saw. I mean he really took it personally that he didn't want anyone to be able to beat him. But another side to that was sometimes he wouldn't adjust when he was playing hockey, and I used the example that he loved his backhand move because he was so strong he could just throw the puck to the outside, fend off the defenseman with his right hand, and he had such strong wrists and arms from digging the graves that he could hold onto the puck while he was basically holding the defenseman with his elbow and his forearm to keep him away and cut in on the goalie. But the defensemen got wise to it and they started forcing him closer and closer to the boards, and I remember one time a guy tried to pin him against the boards and he jumped up, he just jumped, and he just stepped on the small of his back and jumped over him, he stepped on his ass, basically, and he just jumped over him! He was just dynamic. And he had such pride. *Not gonna beat me, not gonna beat me...*

"There was a cockiness to him, but I think it was a cockiness based on what he could do. He could have been—he was very driven, and, in hockey

I think it was Bobby Donahue who got the captaincy, and Bobby was more polished, and I think that was part of it. And Bobby was less emotional. You know, Richie could pop sometimes. I remember he hit Jack Garrity with his hockey stick once, and Jack was gonna throw him outta the game. And Don Wheeler went, after the period—this was in Framingham—he went right down to him, and he said Jack, Jack, don't throw him out of the game. Because I think he had already been thrown out of a game that year, and if he got a second one, he was out for all sports for one year and he wouldn't be able to play baseball his senior year, and Jack Garrity to his credit said to Don, just don't play him the rest of the game. He said that will give him the message, but you tell him, no more.

"I remember one night I drove him home, I forget what game it was but, he said don't, I brought him up to his house and there was a whole bunch of cars out there. He said, I don't wanna go in right now. Those guys will want to replay the game in the living room. Can we go someplace? And I said well I don't know what's open now. Was coming back from I don't know, a tourney game or what it was. We ended up going to Dunken Donuts, the only place I could find open, in Westwood, on Rt. 1. And we just sat in the car and talked for a while, and I said Richie I gotta go to school tomorrow, so I gotta drop you off. I brought him home and I remember what he said to me. (laughs) 'Looks like I sleep in the tree hut tonight.'"

When Paul Flaherty sent the email that urged this writing, the Richie Hebner reference he made was to paragraphs in a travelogue I had written about meeting famous people, which follow,

> I have always believed in keeping a distance from famous people. I grew up in the same neighborhood as Richie Hebner, and although I can't call him a close friend, I certainly have known him all my life. The transition from neighborhood tough to schoolboy hockey star to major league draftee to eighteen seasons in Major League Baseball was an interesting metamorphosis to observe.
>
> Watching from a short distance I saw that celebrity has its costs. Anyone you encounter may recognize you. I saw this. I saw

it in Richie's eyes even when he saw me in the back of Shurfine Market—would I say hello? Would the next guy? Richie's eyes always seem to be wandering the faces in a subtle but certain resignation that he'd probably be called upon to greet—and remember—somebody. From such vague realizations came a belief that you should leave celebrities alone, give them some respect, some space.

Growing up in the same neighborhood as a professional athlete allows a view into areas of their life seldom considered. Attending the University of Massachusetts in Amherst, I befriended Mark Procaccini of Walpole, an outstanding high school football player in his own right, but whose twin brother was a superstar quarterback whose feats were well known. One day together in the elevator, rising to the 20th floor of the John Adams dormitory, we stopped at a floor and moved aside as another student entered. As freshmen and introducing ourselves to new faces, the kid responded to Mark and asked, "Are you the football Procaccini from Walpole?" To which Mark replied, "No, that's my brother Gary."

After the kid had exited the elevator and our rise continued, I turned to Mark. "Hey, why did you say your brother was the football player from Walpole, and not you? You're a football Procaccini from Walpole, too..." suggesting, of course, push-back to a much-ingrained deference to more successful siblings. Mrs. Hebner pushed back.

"My mother would go shopping," Richie Hebner recalled, "and people would go up to my mother and say, how's the boy? And my mother would say, which one? I've got five of them, which one are you talking about? That's the way my mother was."

Skip Lockwood's wife Kathleen touched upon peripheral, lesser-realized trials of the professional athlete in her 2010 book, *Major League Bride*,

> A good friend of mine confided in me once that it was not easy being married to the "golden boy" of the family. Family life always centered around the sports schedule and whims of the larger-than-life special son. I'm willing to wager a guess that this white glove treatment is much more the rule rather than the exception for the exceptionally talented athlete...Skip was always the center

of attention and the focus of all conversation when his family joined us for dinner after a weekend day game. He was expected to be their affable star/hero and did his best to live up to those expectations even if he was not in the mood to be sociable after a less-than-stellar performance.

I sat across from Brian Hebner in George's Place, a South Norwood establishment now lost to the stream of time. "Brian got in a car accident in 1971," Richie had mentioned, "he was lucky he didn't get killed. But Brian was off from the fire department, came to Pittsburgh, got in the plane with us, went to the World Series in Baltimore, was in the clubhouse, flew back to Pittsburgh with us, and Brian was in the parade! Brian was a character!"

Though separated by a number of years in age, we nevertheless shared the same childhood neighborhood, and over a couple of beers covered the usual suspects. And when I asked Brian, "What is it like being Richie Hebner's brother?" the flood gates opened.

"It's a fucking pain in the *ass!*" the Norwood fireman responded in typical Hebner directness, now animated. "Every time you meet someone new, every time you see someone, they want to know about Richie, Richie this, Richie that, it's a total fucking pain in the fucking *ass!*" And then, as though his outburst sated long-withheld grievance, Brian Hebner leaned back in his chair and smiled.

"But you know what? I'm proud as *hell* of Richie!"

The most storied hockey career in Norwood history came to a close under heart-breaking circumstance.

"When they lost to Waltham in the quarter-finals in '66, lot of people don't know this, but Richie's skate broke," Dennis said. "The blade broke and they couldn't do anything about it. He tried to skate the whole game with it disconnected from one of the pegs, or whatever you call it. He tried; he couldn't do much about it. That's what fucked that game up. Jeezus..."

Pending decisions for the child hockey-and-baseball prodigy are themselves part of Norwood lore.

"He was a man-child," Leo McInerney recalled. "He was by far and away, until Ftorek came along, he was…I'll tell you a story about Richie. I don't know if he'll tell ya, the last time I had a beer with Richie was Christmas time at Lewis'. He absolutely said he went to Bruins' camp with Sanderson and Westfall, couple of other guys I can't remember, and he said he actually did not feel out of place. He thought he was a better hockey player than he was a baseball player, but he followed the money. He definitely was unbelievable; he had a backhander you could not believe. He could shoot a backhander the length of the ice, and most of us couldn't lift the puck *off* the ice!"

"Years later I played golf with Milt Schmidt," Charley Donahue said. "There were no Americans in the NHL in those days. Milt Schmidt said they really wanted Richie Hebner, that with a year up at Niagara Falls they could have used him." Graduating in 1966, a year at Niagara Falls would have placed Richie on the Bruins roster for their coming Stanley Cup-winning years. But opportunities available for the youngster from Nahatan Street were not binary. There was also the college option. Jimmy Gormley recalls a telling conversation with an eighteen-year-old Richie Hebner.

"Whether it was gonna be hockey or baseball was his dilemma, and it was a nice choice to have because he could have been in either one and made a name for himself. As you know, Richie used to dig graves for a cemetery where his father worked, and he'd go over there and make some money for himself. The problem was, his style of grave digging put a little bit of stress on his back, on his lower back, and there were times it used to tighten up.

"I used to take Richie over to see a cousin of mine, Billy Linskey. He was a trainer for the city of Cambridge. He would take care of all those injured on the job, and he'd also be trainer for the two high schools, Rindge Tech and Cambridge Latin. This was his senior year I was taking him over there and it just so happened that the Boston College hockey coach at that time had been Snooks Kelley. Snooks taught in one of the high schools there. And Richie of course had quite a reputation as a hockey player, and Snooks Kelley was wanting to see if he could get Richie.

"I remember one of the days that I took him over there. My cousin said to me, Coach Kelley would like to see you upstairs. He's very interested in Richie, but he may have to do a year or two of prep school, because he hadn't always taken college courses in high school. And when I went upstairs, I was brought right up to coach Kelley's classroom. He taught social studies, and he saw me and he said, where's Richie? I understand you have Richie with you. I said he's in the hot tub right now. And he said quietly, that's good, he doesn't have any clothes on, he can't go anywhere! And he turns to the class and says, boys and girls we're honored to have with us today a graduate of my alma mater Boston College. Mr. Gormley is now a graduate student in American Studies at Boston College and he's going to speak with you on the upcoming elections. He walked me to the door, and I said coach, what election is this? He said it's a local one, they don't know shit. (laughs) He just said take care of them for me so I can go down and see Richie while he doesn't have his clothes on and can't go anyplace.

"I ended up leading a discussion with the kids about the upcoming election. And he went down to see Richie and about twenty or so minutes later he came back up and he said, Jimmy I think we can get him, but he's going to have to do at least one year at New Prep. I think we can get him in. I went down and when I walked in Richie was talking to a couple of other people. One of them was a guy name Pete Igo, athletic director and coach at a small Catholic high school in Somerville. He said Richie, I know you just talked with coach Kelley, but what is it you're thinking about? He said well, I don't know, he said I like hockey, I like baseball... the Bruins are interested in me too, and they even asked me to skate for them in I guess a practice or something... If I was gonna go to college, I'd have to do a couple years of prep school. He said I'm not a student, I'm a doer. I think I'd like to do the baseball, but the hockey is tempting, too...

"And he was so good at both," Jimmy Gormley continued. "He was All-Scholastic in both. Anyways, he says, I'm torn, I like the hockey, I like the physical-ness, but I like to hit a baseball too. He was a born hitter; I mean I can remember him since he was nine years old. Playing major league Little League as a nine-year-old was a real feat in Norwood. He was just a very good player on a team that had his brother Billy and other brother Brian, he was clearly a star in the making. And Pete Igo said, Richie, when it comes down to it, what do you really like to do? Do you like to study, or do you like the sports more? And Richie said, *I like to hit a baseball.*"

"Well, I lived on Nahatan Street," Richie Hebner recalled. "There was a little woods in the back of the yard and there was some ice on it, and it's where we learned to skate. I mean, you tell that to people they say what are you, crazy? And there was a house two houses up, they were building a house and they had a foundation and it was full of water, we would skate in that! Yeah! No rinks, we just skated where there was ice, and sometimes the ice wasn't that big. That's where the swamp was, in the back yard. It was very unusual, you tell people now and they laugh at you, but it wasn't a big area, but we'd take our skates there, skated until Mom said let's go!

"There were so many kids around that neighborhood, we'd skate, we'd play baseball, we'd do everything together. Played baseball, threw footballs, did everything. You were on Crestwood Circle, there were so many kids around that neighborhood, you came home from school you always had something to do. It was interesting, always had something to do. I tell Dennis, those were the days, no freakin' computers, you did your own thing, and it was fun. Kids come home from school now and get on the computer, TV. It's funny, when I was in the minor leagues I'd go by these playgrounds in North Carolina or wherever I was all over the country, every playground was empty. When we were growing up, you'd get ten kids, buck-up sides and play baseball. It's a shame. Obviously, you and I know it, it's a different world. The kids never knew what we did. Those were the days, couldn't wait to get home from St. Catherine's or the high school, you know, let's go outside and play!

"To me, Norwood was a great town to grow up in, there was always something happening. There was always something happening. Like I said before, you don't come home and get on the computer or the TV. So many kids stay in the house, I mean Jesus Christ, go out and *do* things, it's good for your mind, it's good for, just doing some exercise, it's probably why so many kids are overweight. Back then everybody was doing something, you know, we had five boys in my family, we had half a baseball team. We'd go to a baseball field and say who wants to play against us? Like I said before you go to the playgrounds and they're all empty. It's a shame, really.

"I loved them all, I tell people, some parents want to talk to me, and they put their kids in AAC or baseball for the summer, or hockey. I always said play every sport. Don't depend on one sport, everybody thinks their kid's gonna be the next Mickey Mantle or Bobby Orr. Play all kinds of sports. You meet different kids, it's a nice way to grow up. So many parents put their kids, and they spend a lot of money, and I just don't think it's right. Play football, throw the ball around, skate, play hockey. Over McDonough's, back field. It was fun, we played catch or hit the ball, catch the ball, we thought it was just a great thing to do. I didn't stay in the house too long, I stayed in the house when it started getting dark out. Too many kids stay in the house when it's light out. Which I don't think is good.

"I tell ya, I loved Mickey Mantle. I always wanted to play on a field with Mickey Mantle. He retired about a year before I got to the big leagues. I was a Yankee fan, I thought the Yankees were gonna sign me. It's funny, the Red Sox had me on the second draft, but I was a number one draft pick, I was the fifteenth pick in the country. You know who was the number one pick that year in 1966? Kenny Brett. Kenny Brett was the first pick. The Red Sox told me I was gonna be on the second round, which I never made. I come home, I think someone told me, you're a number one draft pick. Back then, I didn't know, number one draft pick, Chick Whalen who signed me, come over the house and told me I was a number one draft pick. But I think the thing that stood out, I was a junior in high school, went to Natick, Joe Coleman was a great pitcher. I had two hits off him, I hit a home run off him and I had another hit off him, and there were a lot of scouts there and they said geeze, this kid might be pretty good.[15] That's how I think it all started. In baseball, there were parents, there might have been twelve people at a baseball game. My senior year, there were more scouts at the games than parents. So, hockey was to me—I think when I signed with the Pirates, I think a lot of people were pissed-off at me, they wanted me to go hockey. But I signed with the Pirates.

"Baseball was the American game. I was a number one draft pick. I got $40,000 in 1966, which obviously back then it was big money, but you know Milt Schmidt told me, play a year, a year and a half, you don't like it we'll sign you. And a year and a half, two years later, I was in the

---

15 Richie next faced Joe Coleman on Monday evening, June 28th, 1976, in front of 7,370 fans in Pittsburgh's Three Rivers Stadium. Pitching for the Chicago Cubs, the Natick kid struck out the Norwood kid in the bottom of the 1st. Richie grounded out in the bottom of the 2nd, then doubled off Coleman in the 5th.

city of Pittsburgh, Pennsylvania playing baseball in the big leagues. So, it was kind of a no-brainer. I played eighteen years in the big leagues which I never would have thought, and I had some decent numbers.

"In spring training of '86 we're stretching and Dallas Green comes up, says come on in the clubhouse after you stretch. What's up? He says, does your father still have your shovel? Said, I imagine. He said well, we're gonna release ya. Three days later I'm digging a grave with the old man at the cemetery!

"I managed and coached for thirty years afterward. It was good working with Triple A players, they were older guys. A lot of the guys had already been in the big leagues so you don't have to repeat yourself, you don't have to babysit. When guys got called back to the minor leagues, they'd mope around, and I'd be the first one to take 'em into my office and I'd say let me tell ya, you're back here for some reason. I didn't send you back, they sent you back. Now if you wanna play, you play. If you don't wanna play, leave the clubhouse and pack your bags. Lotta guys didn't want to hear that, but I've been around long enough I go right to the jugular vein. I'm gonna tell it like it is. I'm not sugarcoating anything and if you come back here and think you're gonna get some sympathy from me, you're not gonna get it from me. The only way to get back to the big leagues is get better. Then you get back.

"At first I had no clue. First time I ever been on a plane, I fly from Boston to Washington D.C., then Washington to Roanoke, Virginia where the rookie team was. We're going to the gate in Roanoke, and there's about over two or three thousand people, I'm going *Jesus Christ* what do I say to these people? The general manager meets me, and I said what are these people here for? He said Richard Nixon's coming in in a half hour later for re-election, I was the happiest guy in the world. I was the happiest guy in the world! I didn't know what to say!

"I didn't know what to think, to be honest with you. I played probably six weeks of rookie ball and Joe Brown the general manager comes up to me and says next week you'll be in Parris Island. I said Jesus Christ I just signed; I don't want to go on vacation! He said Parris Island is the Marine Corps! I was in the Marine Corps for six months, back then the Vietnam war, they had two openings, they brought me and Bob Moose. I was in for six months and five and a half years in reserves. Half the guys went to Vietnam, a lot of them came back with a tag on their toe. And unfortunately, there were five or six Norwood kids who died in Vietnam. Pat Burke, Fitzgerald. From our neighborhood. Fitzgerald lived right down the street from Shurfine. Nice parents. Got shot down about two or three times in a helicopter, and the third or fourth time, he died. Awful, awful.

"It's funny, I had two coaches in the minor leagues. Joe Morgan in Raleigh, North Carolina '67, and Johnny Pesky in Columbus, Ohio 1968. Joe loves talking to people! Good guy, he's a good guy. Joe was a good hockey player at BC. He's still around, lives in the same house he's lived in for years. It's funny, I walk a lot, and I'm walking down Fisher Street and a guy drives up and puts his car in park and I look and I say, who are you? It was Joe Morgan!"

"He was a really good competitor, I can tell you that," Joe Morgan recalled of Richie's first full professional season in Raleigh. "And he took it seriously. Good line drive hitter, but he could also hit the ball for distance, too. Quite a few home runs. Good low-ball hitter, *real* good low-ball hitter, but he could fight the high ball off until he got his pitch a lot, too. A thinking hitter, a thinking hitter, that's what we like. I definitely knew he was gonna be in the big leagues. He was such a good hitter there, and he was strong, put together pretty good. There was no way he wouldn't make the big time, I figured.

"Pesky loved him, I know that. He used to talk to me about him all the time because he knew that I had come from the same area. When Richie went on to the big leagues, he started hitting really good. He was always a great spring hitter. He was hitting a ton, so I wrote him a letter. I said lookit Richie, it isn't that easy, so remember what you're doing now so when you go bad, maybe it won't last as long. Naturally he tapered down a little bit, he still was hitting really good, but he definitely was a great spring hitter, always started good. Pretty good fielder, he had a good arm, and he worked on his fielding also when I had him, oh yeah. He was like Boggs, he worked at it. Other than that, what can I tell ya? Fairly good runner, us hockey players are not noted for our speed, I don't know if you know that!"

"Our season ended in Columbus, Ohio, and they called Al Oliver and I up," Richie Hebner recalled. "It's funny, Al Oliver and I went to the big league the same day and left the same day. If you have a baseball card, back then the baseball cards there'd be two guys on the card, Al Oliver and myself. Most of these cards when you look at 'em, one guy makes the big leagues and the other guy's fucking pumping gas somewhere a year later. I graduated from Norwood High School in June of '66 and in September of '68 I walked in the Pirate clubhouse, Clemente, Stargell, Mazeroski, and I said to myself, what the hell am I doing *here?*"

I remember a spring day in 1969, delivering the *Patriot Ledger* to the Hebner household. Richie was beginning his rookie season with the Pittsburgh Pirates and hitting a ton. At a time when Boston's Tommy Williams was the only American playing in the NHL, Richie was in The Show, playing alongside Roberto Clemente, beginning a career that would span eighteen playing seasons as well as more than thirty subsequent years managing and coaching at the high professional level. Walking up the driveway, I encountered Mr. Hebner, a wrench in hand and covered with grease, leaning under the hood of his car.

"Hey Mr. Hebner," I called, "that's somethin' about Richie, isn't it?"

"Ahh, *fuggit*" he spit out, dismissing the thought with a wave of a blackened hand. "He could have played with Bobby Orr!"

THE PROGRAMS

I realize I've been celebrating all the things we kids did on our own back then, but the fact is we were surrounded by people who cared about us and helped us along. I couldn't have realized then just how important they would be in my development, both on and off the ice...Neighbors, volunteers, family members—these people are always contributing in ways kids just take for granted. But there are some that stand out in my mind.
— Bobby Orr, *Orr: My Story*, 2013

"I just want to say one last thing, right?"

Billy Sherman would have been class of '73 had he not been expelled from Blue Hills Regional Technical High School, or subsequently dropped out of Norwood High School to join the Marines in 1972. From his home in North Carolina, he was impassioned with memories of his youth.

"The one thing I always think back on is how lucky I was as a child to grow up in Norwood because of the men in Norwood who took care of me. Know what I mean? It could have gone either way, fortunately for me there was a lot of good men. I could have ended up with some kind of pervert or something, but I ended up with Ray Baldwin, Sgt. Travers, Dickie McEachern who was my coach, Minty Kuporatz. That was an important part for me, all these guys who dedicated themselves. They may not have been scholars or technicians or professionals, but they were good people who took care of their kids and took care of the other kids in the neighborhood.

"I can't say enough about Danny Nuzzo, who today they wouldn't let anywhere near kids! But for me, he was the best thing in the world! Because he would get right in your face and tell you exactly what he thought of your performance or whatever, and he wouldn't sugar-coat it. And he'd create this competitive environment, within the team, or within the group of kids that you're hanging out with, even a football game behind his house it was like life and death! Like I said, the guys, the men of that era, of the '60s, deserve a lot of credit for the guys like me who came out of Norwood and contributed to society and became good United States citizens. It wasn't just the Marine Corps, it wasn't just the parade and all that other stuff, I think the real strength of Norwood was in the men. Look at the Civic, look at the guys from the Civic who helped us out, I mean, we were just so lucky, like I said the Ray Baldwins, the Sgt. Travers. I was just lucky; I was so lucky. Think about this, though. Back then we were always outside, always on the loose, and we had these guys, they were kinda like lighthouses for us, to steer us through danger.

"Today kids don't leave their... everything's organized, everything's prescribed. If I went to a baseball game, either Dickie McEachern would pick me up or Minty would pick me up, or I'd walk. We didn't have twenty, thirty, forty people at the game watching. I was a good ballplayer, I played against Joey Sansone, Billy Travers—I actually touched one of his pitches with my bat once—I played with all those guys who were good ballplayers. We didn't have forty or fifty parents down there cheering and screaming, we might have two or three! Because the fathers were working, the mothers were home, so my answer is, if you have it, it's in a different place. You might have the same type of men doing the same types of things, but it's gotta be in a different environment, a different kind of framework. Kids don't go outside today, they don't just walk the streets, they don't walk up to Father Mac's or Hawes Pool, you don't see kids outside playing street hockey. When was the last time you saw a kid outside throwing a football? Look at how hockey today is organized to the tenth degree, you know what I mean? We didn't have that, which is good."

A curious dichotomy emerges in the parallel development of Norwood youth baseball and hockey. Baseball was historically the realm of vacant lot and pasture, a childhood passion little influenced by adults. The advent of Little League, Babe Ruth League, and American Legion games homogenized the local game, and may have actually impeded player development.

"That's been going on for quite a while, the regimentation," Joe Morgan observed. "When we played, there was no automobiles and we had no money, what that hell else can we do? We played every night down at the park from six o'clock until eight-thirty when it got dark. Every single night, well at least six nights a week, anyway. There's a couple of reasons. They don't play enough baseball. With all the cars and all the people looking at the movies and television, that's what hurt a lot of regular sports. I mean, guys that would have been a little better, the average type guy, just didn't put the time into it. That's my feeling."

"Today kids play Little League, they play twice a week," Ken Reddick agreed. "Every kid plays at least an inning in every game. They play seven inning games. The best players, the kids who play the whole game get what, six or eight at-bats a week? Out in the first field we'd play all day, every day, all spring and summer. You'd get *twenty* at-bats a day! *Twenty* a day, all summer long..."

The opposite was true of hockey.

"If I was born in Canada," Walpole's Joe Morgan continued, "I would have played in the NHL for a long, long time. That's the way I see it. I had the ability, all I needed was more ice time growing up." The former MLB player and Red Sox manager succinctly encapsulated the problem. "I would say this, and I could tell you about Hebner, too. If we were born in Canada, we'd a-both played in the National Hockey League for a long time. Guarantee you. We knew how to play the game and we had the ability, so we would'a been skating up there at four or five years old like them kids. The truth would come out, we'd be there in the end! Guarantee ya! It was so much easier than baseball it wasn't even funny. Baseball you have to do everything by yourself, and nobody can help ya. Run, field, throw."

"Remember," Jim Gormley observed, "in the '50s there were no rinks. Every high school game was in Boston Arena. They'd practice on pond ice, at Pettee's, and if the weather was bad... They might practice three or four times a year on indoor ice. There were ten-minute periods, one-minute penalties..."

Thus, as the '60s progressed under increased adult supervision, baseball skills diminished, while hockey skills flourished. Emerging youth programs provided ice time necessary for the acceleration of hockey abilities.[16]

"Know what the biggest influence in Norwood was?" Dennis Hebner said. "You probably heard this from everyone, Tom Clifford. If it wasn't for Tom Clifford, Norwood wouldn't be shit in hockey. Those '60s and early '70s—I don't know when Tom disbanded that Saturday morning over at Tabor—that was the most fun!"

"Oh, Tom Clifford was the best," Richie Hebner agreed. "Go over Tabor, Saturday morning, I couldn't wait to get up. Yeah, a lot of people in Norwood that played hockey owe a lot to Tom Clifford. Tom was one of a kind, I don't think he had a bad word about anybody. And his wife, let me tell ya, they were the nicest family. I'm glad you brought him up. I don't know if you're gonna put it in the book, but let me tell ya, a lot of people in Norwood owe a lot to Tom Clifford back in the '60s. Saturday mornings, Tabor in Needham, was the fucking greatest thing since sliced bread! It was really good; it was really fun. He was a mild, mild person, I don't think he ever yelled, I don't think he ever swore in his life! He was just a good guy. Just a good guy. I don't know if other guys said it, but make sure if you write the book, put Tom Clifford in it. Great guy. He did a lot for the town of Norwood, and I don't know how many people know that, but I'm telling you he did."

"It was older kids," Charlie Donahue recalled, "when it snowed we'd go over and shovel the pond off, and one day an older guy, he was probably thirty-five, was there shoveling snow, and it was Tom Clifford. What are you doing? And they'd come out and play with us. He's the guy who started Norwood youth hockey. We'd play with them, and we started to go to St. Sebastian's and I saw Richie Hebner skating on his ankles, he was the fastest guy on the ice on his ankles! And I saw Blaine Maus with pillows wrapped around his knees because he wanted to be a goalie. How do you get the money? How do you organize? Tom Clifford did this. In high school we go to Pettee's

---

16 The emergence of three MLB players from Norwood during the '60s, Skip Lockwood, Richie Hebner, and Billy Travers, may seem to refute this assertion. Note, however, that before Hebner's 1985 retirement, the longest stretch without a Norwood kid in MLB was 31 years, between John Kiley's 1891 last appearance and Marty Callaghan's 1922 first. There has not been another Norwood kid in MLB since Hebner's retirement in 1985, 37 years and counting.

Pond, and New Pond would freeze in those days. Tom Clifford had it all organized on New Pond."

A 1964 article written by Bob Creamer of the *Boston Traveler*, a framed copy hanging today upstairs in Paul Angelo's Olde Colonial Cafe, discusses the Clifford group, and its eventual merging with Ernie Higgins' program.

> It was just after the war when Clifford wondered why boys weren't skating on all that nice ice around town. But by the time he got 10 boys and formed a team, the nice ice had left town and the best they could find was on Pettee's Pond along the Walpole line. It was only an informal team but the future looked good because of men like Clifford, Dr. William Lovell the dentist, Steve "Zark" Connolly of Plimpton Press, the ex-major leaguer Marty Callaghan, and Tom Lynch, the hockey referee. They were all fathers and the sons were playing hockey but a lot of other boys weren't.
>
> "We always saw the same old faces and the ice outside just wasn't much good anymore. They would skate until they were ready to fall through and that was that," recalled Clifford. "But more boys were getting interested and during Little League they would pester me in the dugout, always asking if I thought we'd have ice next winter."
>
> The search for ice went on. They even took the train to Walpole to find some. Finally, about 1959, two things gave hockey the shot it needed here. Clifford's boys, 11 to 12-year-olds, played three games with Westwood and then they found ice. Dr. Lovell and Tom Lynch got together with the Boston Skating Club and nailed down some inside stuff at the club's rink in Brighton.
>
> "There's only one catch to the deal," Clifford recalled Lovell as saying. "The ice time is for 5 a.m. so we'll have to get up before 4. I made a few quick calls and John Lennon and some of the others accepted the idea. So, in 1960 we formed the Norwood Hockey Club with just one team and 22 boys." A year later the group came back to Norwood and used the indoor rink at the Taber School Camp. That was a big help and we didn't have to be there until 5:30," Clifford said.

My family's involvement began with a telephone ring during the winter of 1960, or 61. "Kenneth," my father called, "Tom Clifford wants to speak with you." My older brother was invited—to his great excitement—to come down to Pettee's on New Pond and practice ice hockey with a group Mr. Clifford was putting together. Without access to a real rink, they were shoveling the snow off the inlet and organizing some drills and scrimmages. My brother is still enthused when speaking of traveling to West Point and playing on their over-sized rink; he remembers one long bus ride home when all the kids were anxiously looking forward to the Ed Sullivan show that evening, when that new long-haired British singing group was scheduled to perform. Virtually every Norwood hockey player of the era has memories of Tom Clifford's group.

"We would get up before my mom and get dressed," Rusty Tobin remembered, "and we'd be waiting in the kitchen in the dark. You know, with your bag packed and your stick, with your jacket on, everything. Dennis in one chair and me on another. She'd turn on the lights, she was stunned, you know, surprised. But after that not surprised at all. The comments, you can't do this for school? (laughs) Those are great days with Mr. Clifford, that's how you got to know all the people in Norwood. Course you knew most, a lot went to St. Catherine's, and the ones who didn't you knew through Little League and Mr. Clifford. I think that was all we had in those days."

The town was in a period of disorganized hockey interest. Various attempts at hockey programs, including efforts by brothers Frank and Joe Wall, were made. "I loved being a forward," Charlie Donahue remembered. "Jack Monbouquette was the high school coach then. He called me up on the bus and said we're gonna make you a defenseman. So I called up Frank Wall and say I'm gonna be a defenseman. Frank said, come to New Pond.

"I went to New Pond and Frank says, this is my buddy Shotgun Seastrand, he'll teach you to be a defenseman. Seastrand had played for Norwood; Frank had been the goalie on that team. My Little League coach was Sails Wall. I didn't even know he liked hockey. There was an advertisement in the newspaper for anyone who wanted to learn to skate at the Boston Arena to meet at the Civic, on Saturday morning at eight o'clock. And we needed two more busses!"

In the early '60s, another group of skaters was formed. Jim Gormley tells of his experience with the Crestwood Circle Higgins group.

"My mother was teaching at the junior high school. And I had worked in the recreation department in the summertime, and I also used to chaperone Friday night dances down at the Civic. So I knew a lot of her students, seventh and eighth graders from the playground, from Little League and stuff like that. My mother would often talk about what I was doing with coaching, she would often talk about the games that I was seeing, things like that with the kids. She had a good rapport with her students, and some of the kids came to her and said do you think he'd take us to hockey?

"So, I got together with Tabor Rink, and I think your dad may have been involved, and I'm trying to think who else was involved, Bob Donovan, Roger Sortevik and Ernie Higgins. We rented ice over at Tabor Academy, this was in '63. Six ices, the last six weeks they were open. And we took the kids over there and just ran a little clinic with drills, and then we'd have a scrimmage. Don Wheeler was with the Norwood hockey program, and he said to my mother, do you think Jimmy would mind if I came over? She said sure, no problem. So he came over.

"We enjoyed doing that, and then Ernie said to me, would you do this next year if we do something? And I said I'd love to. It was a lot of fun. And kids like Stevey Falcone, Richie Graham, Eddie Graham, Peter Oberlander, Kenny Reddick, Sortevik, the older Sortevik, Steven. And then it expanded a little, some of the others were maybe Paul O'Day and Dennis O'Day, and oh, another Norwood hockey player Dave McNamara, who was on the '62 I think, '63 team. He was a good little hockey player. Charley Parker was important in this, too. He was on the staff at the junior high school, and he had played some hockey in high school. And I think he came to one or two of those sessions and he may have brought Ray Martin with him, who was a defenseman on the first hockey team. We had six weeks of hockey and Tabor shut down, and that was it."

Bob Creamer's *Herald* article documented the new group.

> Into the picture strode the other giant, Ernie Higgins, the plumbing contractor. "His boy was in our group and we knew he was a good organizer," Tom Clifford said. "Starting with some 60 boys

and a committee of Joe Moloney, Tom Brown, Dick Gendron and Bill Clifford, Higgins launched the pee-wees with the Norwood Nuggets and got them affiliated with the American Hockey Assn. They started them young, but it worked so well the players stayed on right through high school. The pee-wees were 10 to 12 and some were started in the second grade."

Clifford breathes a little easier today with everything so well organized. There are now 64 advanced pee-wees and this season 50 beginners under 10 started skating. And there are 64 Bantams aged 13 to 14, and the Pee-Wee All-Stars, 16 to 18 boys who represent Norwood in league play with other towns. There is a similar all-star set-up for the Bantams. And Clifford still has 66 boys in the old Norwood Hockey Club who compete among themselves.

"It was Higgins who really opened it all up," Clifford said, "and he hopes that any boy here who wants to play, can."

Financial support of hockey comes primarily from parents but sometimes someone raises money at a dance or the players go around selling candy. And then there's transportation and without drivers like Joe Connolly, Arthur Conley, Marty Callaghan, John Lennon, Gary Maus, Tom Lynch and Franny Whitley, nobody would be going anywhere to play.

Coaches are just as vital, too, and the whole program owes a lot to Noel Doyle, Ed Sweeney, Ed Powers, Bill Hebner, Charlie Parker, Alex Skene and Ed Martin. A man named Joe Wall has started a third group in town for the purpose of teaching the fundamentals of skating and hockey. There's no doubt the vast farm system has been good for hockey here and probably the main reason why Norwood High has won two Bay State League championships in the past five years."

Word of the hockey programs reached every corner of Norwood. "When I got to the seventh grade," Tommy Taylor remembered, "I was kinda lucky and I remember going up there and there was Johnnie Ranalli, Jimmy Scott, and Gary Sortevik, and I went to Wheeler and said can I skate and he said I think I can do something for you, and we played on the freshman team for Jimmy Gormley. That's where we got started. I remember saying to my father all the guys are skating with Mr. Higgins, and my father said well you better get a paper route. We didn't know about Tom Clifford because we were from South Norwood! That's where all the heavy hitters were, with Tom Clifford, the rich kids!"

"One of the great guys I ever met in my life was Ernie Higgins, Neil's father," Dickie Donovan recalled. "What a man. Class man. I played on the first bantam team, that was when Ernie started the Norwood Nuggets with Tom Brown, they were both great guys. And I was the captain of the first bantam team in 1965. We got killed, we didn't win a game. We had Doyle and D'Arcy on the team!"

My earliest memories of learning to skate are of Mr. Higgins' group on Tabor Rink in Needham. I don't remember how young I was, but a family anecdote indicates *very* young, for when we drove into Logan Airport and I saw a line of oval-roofed hangers I had commented, *look at all the hockey rinks!* I was a bit older when I joined Mr. Clifford's group. Memories of rising at 5 a.m., or more commonly a bit later to the sound of Mr. Clifford's, or Tom Lynch's horn out front. Tossing my hockey bag and stick into the rear of a station wagon and joining a row of bundled and mostly silent kids early on a Saturday morning.

These were the mornings that we learned how to play hockey, Mr. Clifford a remote, austere figure guiding all on the ice. Always in the same Norwood jacket. I know now that he was about forty years old at the time, a quiet man, intensely focused, seemingly incapable of anger. He had an almost timid, reserved manner. He spoke softly, never swore, and always had an encouraging word for each of us kids, regardless of ability. He was modest and, off ice, always wore a suit jacket and tie, as though a relic from a previous era. Even then, as a ten or eleven-year-old kid I sensed his genuine interest not only in developing our hockey skills, but our personal and social skills as well. We were admonished when we swore, or when we did something dirty on the ice. Incapable of yelling, his critiques were issued with a sternness, a kindness, and a simple revelation of nothing less than old-fashioned quiet strength and integrity.

Tom Clifford was a selfless man. He ran his program for twenty-seven years without recompense, developing the relationship with West

Point that for years saw a team of youngsters travel to the military Academy to play on their rink. After retiring from active participation, grateful Norwood people planned a night in his honor. Tom Clifford declined. Later, under increased pressure, he acquiesced. At his dinner I stood behind him in line at the buffet table, and once again was reminded of his quaint, simple bearing and humor when he turned to me and whispered, *"Donny, I just love free food!"*

"Mr. Clifford," Leo McInerney said, "they should name the rink down there on University Ave. after him, because he's probably the guy who did more for Norwood hockey than anybody ever and doesn't get any of the recognition that he should. He wouldn't even collect money from you, he'd reach into his own pocket and pay for the ice, just a great, great man. He was just a prince of a guy."

"I remember a couple of times my parents wouldn't let me go because I fucked up at school," Dennis Hebner recalled. "And I was so pissed, and I said I wanna...and they say no, you're not gonna go, you're gonna learn your lesson. I remember I had to ask 'em for $1.35, that's what we had to pay, every kid had to pay $1.35 to Tom when you got there to pay for the ice. I think it was thirty dollars an hour or something. If it wasn't for him, I mean the Maus kids played there, Paul Angelo, I think Timmy Twomey, too."

The Hebner brothers weren't the only ones punished by the withholding of Tom Clifford hockey. It was probably 1966 when Frankie Pascoe ratted brother Gordie and me out to my mother for smoking cigarettes in the woods. At the dinner table that evening, where all such transgressions were adjudicated, my father listened intently to my mother, and then summarily rendered judgement: "That's it, you're not going to skate with Mr. Clifford for a month!"

I started crying.

"Oh, for chrissakes okay," my father relented. "We'll let it go this time..."[17]

---

17 Fifty-five years later I ran into Pebbles Folan in Shaws supermarket. While discussing the progress of this book, Steve DeCosta walked up. I told Steve that there was a story about him in it. But I wasn't sure, I told him, if it was him or Frankie Pascoe who ratted out my brother Gordon and I for smoking in the woods, and that our punishment was we couldn't skate with Mr. Clifford for a few weeks. "Wasn't me," Steve replied, "I would've been with you." He paused, then added, "Pretty stiff penalty."

The final development was the amalgamation of various programs into the Norwood Nuggets Hockey organization.

"I used to go up to Crestwood Circle to the Higgins' with my father where they came up with the name," Peter Brown remembered. "The high school was the Golden Nuggets at the time, did you know that? The Golden Nuggets. And I think the next year they went to Mustangs. I remember Mr. Higgins—Neil was there—talking about what colors, the high school is blue and white, what colors, and I remember my father going well what about purple and gold, it's kind of close to blue and gold, and I remember Neil going that's Latin's colors, *go Latin, go!* And they came up with the blue and gold and the Nuggets at the Higgins' dinner table.

"I used to go up there and see hockey sticks, because I couldn't believe there were hockey sticks, because I had never really seen hockey equipment. It has to be late '63, '64. That was at the old Boston Skating Club, all the peewees and all the bantams had an hour next to each other, and the Norwood peewees all skated on a sheet, and the bantams skated on a sheet. Neil I believe had played for the Wellesley youth hockey, and Mr. Higgins knew those guys, and they were in the Greater Boston League. So Ernie was like, we got a lotta kids in Norwood, so the year before was doing the groundwork, can I get a group from Norwood in the Greater Boston League? So when we started that year, we weren't in the Greater Boston League. The following year, Norwood had the first peewee and bantam teams in the GBL.

"So at the time Mr. Higgins was very busy as a plumber, but also just starting his mask making, transitioning into not full time, but transitioning into making some money. And then became the top guy in the world for goalie masks. And anyway, to make a long story short, my father who'd never played hockey at all, was like, you wanna? Yeah. I know Mr. Higgins put the fishhook in and got him, and he was into it, so it worked out well, and that's how that happened."

"My father signed me up," Billy Clifford recalled. "I don't know who got him involved, he must have met someone, maybe Tom Clifford at the time, I'm not sure. When Mr. Higgins had it, he was getting out, he asked my father if he wanted to run it. My father turned it down, he said no. Then Tom Brown took it over. And my father with Tom Brown was on the board of directors, they were the original Norwood Nuggets. Tom, my father, Al Brown, and Sheila Brown, that was the board, and maybe

Dan Burns was involved in it somehow, too. But those were the, for the Nugget program, that's how it started."

"It was formed in my living room, and I can tell you who was there," Rita Lyons recalled. "My husband Tom, Tom Brown, Dan Burns, Ernie Higgins, and Bill Clifford. We're talking 1960, must be '60. I think it was '61, because Mike began skating at age six.

"Ernie Higgins came because he was well-thought of. I don't know how the group was formed; it was word-of-mouth. The reason Tom Brown took it was because Tom was a salesman and could take time off. A salesman doesn't have a regular schedule. He really didn't want it, it was really kind of forced on him, because they said you've got the time, as a salesman. He wasn't a hockey guy. I am originally from West Roxbury, I never saw a hockey game until I was married, and then I never saw anything else! They just decided that kids needed something to do, and the ice at Pettee's was taken over by the big kids, and they said we'll form a group to help the young kids learn to skate. And it turned into a hockey program within weeks."

In 1972 *The Hockey Times* contained an article documenting the transition.

> "All Star" is an unknown word in Norwood, where quality hockey is a long-standing tradition. The youth hockey program, which began in the fall of 1963, has grown from an organization of 75 boys to its current strength of more than 450 youngsters, and they even found a place for 88 girls in their setup.
>
> Norwood Youth Hockey Program director is Tom Brown, a 6-foot-4" enthusiast whose huge frame is topped by a shock of white hair. He took over the reins in 1965, when the program's first director, Ernie Higgins, stepped down. Higgins is the man who custom-makes face masks for goalies. Brown, who is a charter member, lays no claim to fame as a former player, but puts his administrative talents to good use, along with his board of directors which includes his brother Al, Dan Burns, Bill Clifford, and Don Smith, all of whom oversee the entire operation. "We start with boys who have never been on skates and assist them to master the art of skating and the skill of playing hockey," Brown said.

Norwood was not the only town in the early '60s with developing youth hockey programs. The cost of an hour of ice doubled in just the scant years between the Clifford and Higgins groups' beginnings. With increasing demand for ice time came a corresponding boom in rink-building. The town of Framingham, flush with pride after their first state championship in 1961, built Loring Arena in 1963. Ridge Arena on West Street in Braintree was built in 1965, and at the same time ground was broken off Rt. 1 in Walpole for Four Seasons Ice Arena.[18]

"Did you go with us to see it being built?" brother Ken asked. "You were younger. Roger Sortevik asked me if I wanted to go up and watch it being built, and I said sure! Gary and Steven, Neil, he drove about five of us over."

Effects were immediate. Frank Wall wrote at the beginning of the 1967-68 season,

> Norwood now is considered a state power, and with the various youth programs now functioning in the town Norwood's fortunes should continue to rise. Just take a look at the past three years at Norwood High. With over 200 hockey teams in the state, Norwood has been in the state finals twice and in the quarterfinals once. In fact, the past two years they have had the top hockey player in the tourney. Last year Neil Higgins won the Most Valuable Player award and the previous year it was a kid by the name of Richie Hebner. And the year before would you believe it was a freshman goalie from Walpole by the name of Kevin Woods? It shows you that within a stones-throw we have quite a few hockey players.

Little noticed, except by the kids themselves, was a prescient article in the *Norwood Messenger* of Wednesday, February 1, 1967, containing the headline: "Martin Paces Pee-Wees Over Wakefield Sextet." Rich Bevilacqua, writing in the *Boston Herald* at the beginning of the 1971-72

---

18 These arenas doubled as concert venues for the burgeoning American music scene. On May 5, 1966, Four Seasons Ice Arena hosted Ray Charles; the next night The Beach Boys, and in years to follow, Chicago and Sly and the Family Stone. On November 11, 1968, Ridge Arena hosted Big Brother and the Holding Company, featuring lead singer Janis Joplin.

season, revealed Don Wheeler's recognition of the value of youth hockey programs as well as his growing frustration with the town of Arlington.

> Wheeler's nemesis in past years has been hockey power-house Arlington, the team which dealt Norwood three of its four final round playoff losses, including last year's 3-0 setback. "We're getting better skaters through our Pee-Wee program," Wheeler said. 'Last year was the first time we had a bunch of kids that came up through a group program. I think it was probably Arlington's 20th or 30th."

The Norwood community had recognized these contributions the previous spring during a celebration of the 1970-71 undefeated Bay State League hockey team.

"We had a senior banquet after we lose," Bobby Thornton recalled. "Four hundred people at the banquet, and you know Sails, pictures everywhere. They really did it up with these banquets, it was so well organized. At the beginning of the night, they had three awards that they gave out. And the first one, they called Neil Higgins up from the crowd, they brought Neil back from BC. He comes up before the microphone, and nobody knew he was gonna do this, and presents the first award to his father Ernie. The second one was presented by Jack Clifford to *his* father, Tom Clifford. And the third one Pete Brown to *his* dad, Tom Brown. So, I said to myself, my God, these guys were the ones that got this going. When you look at these trends, Norwood came on in the '60s, and it was these guys. That night, they called Neil and Jackie and Peter up, they passed the torch from Mr. Clifford to Mr. Higgins, to Mr. Brown in the youth hockey, and they all got awards that night, and their kids presented it to them. It was so cool."

Norwood's youth hockey programs are credited with producing the great skaters of the early '70s, but it was the great men behind them who were individually responsible. We honor here their efforts and acknowledge others, in other disciplines. Frank Wall and Minty in Little League, Henry Diggs with his Sea Scouts, Duke Folan in his Guild Variety store, known for helping kids without dads by providing a job, or taking them fishing, Rhoda Linehan and Jean Brown with girls Little League, and the dozens involved with Cub Scouts, Brownies, Boy Scouts, and Girl Scouts. Billy Sherman never skated in any Norwood hockey program, but understood well their purpose, and saw clearly the replicating process.

"Rusty Tobin, another good man," Billy said. "He lived a few streets down from me on Rock Street. He was a 'Diner Boy' with a tough-guy reputation, but he was a sweetheart to me. He is a few years older than me, so I looked up to him. He didn't disappoint me in that regard. Rusty always looked out for me. He is the prodigy of our '60s mentors. Same mold—solid as a rock."

They were kinda like lighthouses for us, to steer us through danger…

SPORT SLANTS

FRANK WALL

Frank Wall covered the *Time of Hockey* era for the *Norwood Messenger*, his column often including "Sports Slants," the town's equivalent of an athletic gossip column. The potpourri was retrospective and informative, often tongue-in-cheek, and always entertaining. Indeed, much was exaggerated, and some patently untrue. Peter Brown's acting career comes to mind—more humorous because eventually Pete *did* have one. But one should respect those movers and shakers of notebooks and typewriters, those who have earned their literary license, acknowledging with shrugged acceptance Walter O'Malley's famous quote, "Only half the lies the Irish tell are true."

"Well, I was a year behind Frank," Joe Curran remembered,[19] "and the thing I remember about Frank is he was just a likeable person. He played three sports; he was just an average guy as far as that was concerned. But Frank being the goalie, they were overshadowed coming from the same neighborhood as Shotgun Seastrand who was an outstanding hockey player. Frank played baseball in high school also. He played his first year for Benny Murray, then his junior and senior year he was playing for Andy Scafati. Frank was a good ballplayer, he wasn't outstanding, but he certainly carried his own weight."

"The hockey was his special sport," life-long friend Bob Ivatts recalled. "When Frank was growing up and playing, he wasn't a very good skater. In fact, most of the time when he was skating, he skated on the side of the shoes, actually, so he turned into a goalie. It was the only place he could play, and he was a very good goalie. Baseball, same thing. Sails was very fast, he was quick running, he was a left-handed hitter and most of the time he could lay down a bunt and he could beat, and he was half-way down before

---

[19] This quote, as well as several others in this chapter, are from the excellent documentary on Frank Wall filmed by Jack Tolman in 2002. The film included several who are no longer with us such as Pete Wall, Bob Ivatts, and Joe Curran, and represents a shining example of why a community's words should be recorded.

the ball hit the ground. He was very good, very fast, an outstanding hitter, but his biggest aspect was he could run very fast."

"Frank went to work down at Birds," Bob Ivatts continued. "Had a funny story down there when in 1950 during the Korean conflict there was a draft and Sails got drafted. And he entered the service with about nine other guys, and I guess when he left Birds, they had a real time for him. They collected money and gave him going away presents, but when he got to Fort Devens, they found he had perforated eardrums, he got rejected and he came home again. And of course, the first day back to work all the guys were after him, they wanted their money back, and so he says, *over here*, they ain't getting that money back! That was his favorite saying, *over here*. I don't know where it came from, but that was one of his favorite sayings."

Frank was quintessential, mid-century Norwood. Born in 1929, he and four siblings grew up on Mylod Street atop Morse Hill, overlooking Endean fields. My first impression of Frank Wall came at my kitchen table. My father had gone to work at Bird & Sons roofing plant in 1950, becoming night foreman in '54. Frank Wall went to work at the mill after high school, and the two became friends. At the dinner table, the scholars of 57 Crestwood Circle had "picking shingles" drilled into our heads as an example of hard, hot work to be avoided by attending college. Dad thought highly of Sails after he had embarked on his journalist career because, as my father phrased it, "He got out."

When Sails first went to work for the *Messenger*, he had a ready-made mentor to emulate. "He got into sports writing," brother Pete Wall recalled. "Frank Karshis used to do it. Sails was working down at Birds and he started doing little specials on high school sports and then eventually they gave him a full-time job and all the rest is history."

Frank Karshis, of South Norwood's Lithuanian immigrant Kiarsis family, penned a column entitled, "Sports Slants". Running from 1952-1964, he regularly "added to his bulging scrapbooks of sports lore," and continued to "contribute feature stories to area newspapers" as of 1987. When Frank took over sports-writing duties, he adopted the column heading. An example of the retrospective, along with the era's "it takes a village" concern with the formative character of local boys, appeared in the same August 1965 column,

> Here's our Little League All-Time team for 1956-60 based on the boys' performances in Little League games, not including any playing after their Little League days. The team is selected by Nick Ferrara, Gus Petrovek and Yours Truly...For catcher we went for two in Dave Heylin and Pete Maddocks; on the mound it's Skip Lockwood, Dave Hardy and Rick Falcone; at first base Paul O'Donnell, at the second base spot Mike Carney. At short Ricky Hebner, and third a tossup between Paul Angelo and Mike Crimmins. In the outer garden we picked four, Bill Bender, Tom Borroni, John D'Espinosa, and Dick Baxter. The latter was a fine pitcher and infielder but certainly belongs on the team, so we switch him to outfield.

Further down the column appeared,

> All students at the high school, especially those graduating next June, are urged to take an interest in helping to promote football. It's discouraging to see groups of "giants" hanging out at various locations day after day with cigarettes dangling from their mouths and doing nothing in particular, or riding around in the family car looking for something to do. Better they were out on the athletic field developing their bodies, learning sportsmanship and promoting school spirit.

Frank brought continuity to Norwood athletics. In a town whose sports culture was necessarily both transitory—the length of a Little League career, the length of a high school career—as well as familial—parents normally participated mainly while their kids played—Frank provided adhesive to bind eras. He remembered legends of youth, the John Dixons and Benny Murrays and Marty Callaghans, as well as his own era's heroes, Dick Bunker, Charley Bowles, Ray Martin. He knew a kid's Little League prowess because he saw it as coach and scribe; he covered that same kid's high school career. His last-page-of-the-*Messenger* columns were of above-the-fold interest to kids. Half the town loved Frank's Christmas edition, when he simply listed everyone's name, hundreds of kids, parents, coaches and teachers scouring the page to locate their own, gleaming with satisfaction when they found it. Indeed, in the era in which most families had one car, one phone, and one TV set, a kid seeing his name in the newspaper was beyond exciting; *it made you someone.*

"It's just not the same to go to a computer screen and print off a story and say hey mom, look, I made a story on bostonherald.com," Hank Hryniewicz told Jack Tolman. "Not the same when you can actually pick up the newspaper and see your name in print, and it's there forever, it's not going to disappear. And it gets put in a frame or it gets put in a scrapbook and it turns yellow but it's still there and it still has your name on it and it still has Frank's name at the top, *by Frank Wall*. It was just really special. It was a blessing, and he blessed many, many people and many, many athletes in this town for many, many years."

"You'd come home," Billy Clifford remembered, "and you'd run to get to the paper and see your name there, and he built you up like you were the best player in the world, there was no one better and you looked forward to that when you had a good game, he took care of you. He wrote you up big time, and you were the celebrity of the town for that day or the week, I have a lot of fond memories of that."

"I'll never forget the first time that my name was in Sports Slants," Peter Brown recalled, "and I tell ya, I thought I was pretty cool. And Frank did that for a lot of people. I will be forever indebted for what he created for us kids in Norwood."

The sentiment was hardly new. Historian Samuel Eliot Morison wrote of his late nineteenth century childhood in newly filled Boston's Back Bay. "At one time we had a small printing press, upon which we printed our names on cards," he recalled. "Incidentally, do my readers remember what a thrill it was first to read one's name in print?"

I remember the first time I saw my own, on October 13, 1967. Bobby Taylor and I, younger brothers of linemates who had led Norwood to the state finals the previous spring in hockey, were the terrors of our eighth-grade football team. We knew an article covering our games was appearing in the *Messenger* that day, and after school had rushed from the junior high to the *Messenger* office, by Clark's Pharmacy. With vast excitement we stood on the sidewalk, huddled together as we opened the newspaper and read the headline, "Junior High Rolls Over Braintree, Milton Teams." The article read,

The two big names as far as the Norwood offense is concerned are co-captain Bobby Taylor and Don Reddick. Taylor went for four touchdowns in the pair of games, and Reddick scored three times. Both boys are averaging over 22 yards a carry. At Braintree Taylor scored on touchdown jaunts of 50 and 8 yards, while Reddick dashed for 75 yards and 13 in a great show of running.

So enthralled were we, so excited—this is a true story—we began stopping people walking by to point out our names!

This synopsis of Frank Wall covers basics, but in danger of being lost—and a considerable danger it is! —is what all who knew him are thinking and grinning as they read these words: the man was the consummate character. Much of it emanated from a now-archaic, mid-century male sensibility.

"My earliest memory of Frank Wall was practice time with the Braves when I was ten years old," Derek Ghostlaw said. "We used to take batting practice and he would walk around the edge of the infield with his cigar in and out of his mouth, and he'd come around and stop with each kid and say, how's the wife? You'd have to answer, which one? He'd say, you got more than one? You'd say, doesn't everyone? I didn't understand it as a ten-year-old, but it was kind of a right-of-passage to be on the Braves."

"There was another time," Lenny Harris recalled, "having the Little League draft and it came down to one of our last picks and Frank said we're gonna pick this kid here. And I said Frank, he was like the worst kid in the tryouts, he doesn't belong in the majors. Frank said no, trust me, you got him confused, he's a great player. Kept arguing with him. Well, Frank was the guy, he made the pick. Sure enough, we show up down here at this field for our first practice, this kid didn't even have a glove. It was a wasted pick, and I kept saying to Frank, jeeze Frank, we made a mistake, we made a mistake, and just before practice got over, car pulled up and this woman stepped out, absolutely, positively gorgeous mother of one of our players and all of a sudden I put two and two together and about the same time Frank turned to me and said, *I guess he wasn't such a bad pick, after all.*"

As Sails Wall became more comfortable in his new career, he honed his creative writing skills. "My wife and I on one of our trips to Hawaii," Joe Curran remembered. "We went out to dinner one night in Honolulu and who was at the restaurant, it was during the Hawaiian Open, Lord who was Hawaiian Five-O, and I think Jack Nicholas was in the same room. We were at this outstanding restaurant, and I come back and tell Sails the story, and next week's column Joe and Betty Curran have just returned from Hawaii where Joe played golf with Jack Nicholas, Jack Lord, and Dano, and I said *Frank*...and there were people who actually believed it!"

"Frank tended to embellish," Ed King concurred. "I think one time I scored a goal; I took a shot at the goalie and I whiffed. It went off my stick and it dribbled through the goalie's legs, and the next Tuesday or Wednesday it was written up I had shot a rocket wrist shot to the upper right-hand corner. Frank was beautiful. No matter what happened, it was the best shot, it was the best game he ever played. He was a character. To look back at the scrapbooks now, yeah, he embellished, and a lot of it was hyperbole, to look back on Frank Wall's articles, you have to chuckle. It's humorous."

"It was great," Mike Martin added. "I couldn't wait to get the paper to read it. Everything was, he made the greatest pass and the shot went into the upper corner when it was like, you know, the puck just dribbled over the red line. And you're saying, is he talking about *me*? I didn't score a goal like that!"

If all looked forward to seeing their names in print, some were disappointed when they found it. The working-class scribe carried a dismissive air concerning finer points of grammar, punctuation, and particularly spelling. He wasted no time verifying names, perhaps his most atrocious attempt suffered by Gary Sortevik, whose name initially appeared as, Gary Sputevic. Consistent, extended malfeasance was endured by Guy Marzullo, variously identified over several weeks in 1969 as Ron Marzuollo, Ronnie Marzuola, Marzuolo, and, finally closing in, Guy Marzuolo. Fellow *Messenger* employee Vin Lembo remembered the scribe's defense of an active imagination. "Frank had a lot of great sayings at the paper, sometimes if you couldn't get a couple quotes that you needed, Frank would just say, make something up. As long as you say something good about somebody, what are they gonna do, deny it?"

In the back of Norwood High School's 1937 *Tiot* yearbook appeared an ad for Orent Brothers clothing store. In part it read,

> To be successful, one must also look the part; perhaps we should say, dress the part. It is generally conceded by recognized authorities that clothes not only "make the man" but they play an important part in this great "struggle for existence". The knowledge that you are correctly groomed creates a feeling of self-confidence and assurance. It likewise creates a favorable impression.
>
> The art of dressing is one that cannot be minimized; it requires the same amount of study that is necessary in the pursuance of the other arts. The danger of over-dressing...wrong ensembles...wrong color schemes present ever-present pitfalls. In Father's generation it was a ritual to keep the shoes shined and the hair combed; but in this era of a style-conscious world, this is hardly enough.

Where to begin?

"Oscar Madison on steroids," was Peter Brown's assessment.

"He was a classy dresser," Mike Martin laughed. "He'd have a Hawaiian shirt on with a pair of shorts that looked like a pair of underwear, you know, with white socks up to *here*. Aw, he was too much. He actually took myself and Chris Dixon up to Hampton Beach when we were twelve years old to golf and have fun up there, and I'll never forget his golf outfit up there. It was like *jeeze*, I was like shying away from him. I didn't want anybody to know I was with him, for God sakes. He was just, he had the Hawaiian shirt and the big white socks, but Frank, you know, he always had the cigar in his mouth..."

Sails Wall was known to mix plaids with stripes, wear two different colored socks, and often advertised what he'd had for lunch by what remained on his tie. Which only lent contrast and color to complexity often accompanying true characters.

"I went out socially a couple of times with Frank," Joe Curran laughed. "I'll say one thing, I went down to Mosely's one night with him. Men walk into a dance hall—he'd try to find a woman he'd like to dance with, and in the same token, when Sails walked in, I can tell ya, there were women hoping he'd ask them to dance. He turned out to be an excellent,

excellent dancer. He was smooth on his feet. Just a, he really was, he stole the show, he'd dance all night long, and he'd dance continually. Just a great guy."

"When we were in Washington," Jimmy Gormley said, recalling the 1965 team trip to the nation's capital, "Frank Wall was one of the chaperones. Sails...we were in this place and there was dancing. And Sails has this little cane, so he pretends he's blind and slowly taps his way over to this beautiful woman sitting in there, slowly taps his way over and says to her, my friends tell me you're the prettiest lady here, and I'd love to dance..."

"One of my more memorable trips was a drive down to see BC play Navy at the Academy in Annapolis. He picked me up about 6 p.m. on a Friday night, we checked in about three a.m. He picked up the key and asked for directions to the lounge. Desk clerk said sir, it is three a.m. The lounge is closed. Frank looked at me and muttered, *dead town*. We went to the room and I can't wait to get to bed. Frank turns on the TV and proclaims, great flick! Edgar J. Robinson and Humphry Bogart in Brother Orchid."

"Frank Wall was the hugest thing in this whole town," Paul Angelo said. "When they lost him, they lost part of Norwood. Everything he did, he was crazy, he was cuckoo, he was the best, the nicest man in the world, but he was for the kids! The kids today, the kids today miss this man, and there'll never be another one like him. Joe Curran, same way. Did it for the kids. Remember the days they'd have raffles, and Frank would raffle a TV and Joe Curran won it? There was no TV! The money was for the kids!"

"I remember his funeral," *Boston Herald* columnist and Norwood resident Joe Fitzgerald recalled for Jack Tolman's film. "Couple people spoke. One guy got up and he said, I couldn't wait to get the paper the next day to see what I said. That was great! But somebody else stood up, a coach, he said often after the game, Frank would come to me and say, what kid needs a boost? I can't think of a higher form of sports writing than that, Frank asking a coach, who needs a boost? Guys like Frank Wall, guys like J. J. Cooke, they're the fabric, the essence of a community. You don't fully appreciate what they mean until all of a sudden, they're not there. The bylines are gone, and you're left doing this, talking about what used to be, who used to be."

In homage to the man who did so much for Norwood kids, for Norwood sports, and especially for Norwood hockey, we wander a bit in our narrative with a nod toward his Sports Slants column. Our own ancillary lies, only half of which are true, fall more favorably under his laudable legacy. For many growing up in the 1960s, Frank Wall was the first true character encountered.

He would not be the last.

1967

I can't get no, satisfaction,
'Cause I try, and I try...

— THE ROLLING STONES,
(I CAN'T GET NO) SATISFACTION, 1965

"I'm loving this piece of leather, workin' its sharp edges off so it's supple and old looking," Hondo Crouch, legendary Texas Hill Country character, once said to his daughter Becky Crouch Patterson. She continued, "I learned from him that the old, used, worn, the crooked and imperfect, has more mellowed beauty and personality than the new, shiny, straight, and slick. 'If you want that rocking chair to be really beautiful,' he said, 'just let it sit there for a long time.'"

No metaphor better conveys the essence of Boston Garden in 1967. The iconic structure had long marinated in Boston cultural history since boxing promoter Tex Rickard had christened his "Boston Madison Square Garden" in 1928. The building was old, used, worn, crooked and imperfect, its mellowed beauty and personality beloved by those arriving on elevated trains at North Station, drifting over after dinner at Caffe Vittoria on Hanover Street in the North End, or hastily downing one last glass of beer at the Iron Horse on Canal Street before striding long ramps to turnstiles, as game time approached. Once inside, the building's flaws, inconsistencies, and idiosyncrasies melded with exceptional traits into timeless character.

The atmosphere was imprinted with impassioned voice of blue-collar fandom who could approach John Kiley at his organ above the loges to request a tune or say "Hi" to WSBK TV announcers Johnny Pierson and Fred Cusick as they made way up stairwells to their media positions. There were not enough restrooms, there was too much smoke. Without air-conditioning, the building could become uncomfortably hot, even creating a fog that hung over the ice surface during spring heat waves. There were blind spots, infamous obstructed view seats, and pride in those hockey-knowledgeable fans who could only afford the highest and cheapest seats, the Gallery Gods.

There were endless stairways, a scarcity of elevators, an absence of escalators. There was the endearing tradition of "the hat-waving Zamboni driver" who for years, during his last, center-ice swipe before the third period of Bruins' games, would rise and wave his fedora to each side of the Garden as he exited the ice surface. There was timeless pleasure of the "Garden Banquet": a dog and a beer. There were rats in the soiled bowels of the ancient building, rumored monkeys in the rafters. But the most dominant characteristic, recognized by fans and players alike, was noise-inducing intimacy created by low balconies. There was no better ticket in all of sports than a front-row, Boston Garden balcony seat.

"I played in the old Boston Garden but that would have been in the fall of 1972, the first year of the WHA," Quebec Nordique Jean Payette related. "The boards would bend-in a good four, five inches when you took or gave a check into them, so they were a lot safer than the rigid boards they have today. But what I remember most is that the crowd was right on top of you."

Don Wheeler was animated when recounting the Garden experience for Jerry Kelleher's film. "Back in the old Garden, you could sit there and it's almost as though you could reach out and touch Bobby Orr!"

"The Boston Garden," Ken Arvidson recounted, "the sound of the crowd, because the crowd was really almost on top of the ice from the balcony, the noise was unbelievable. If somebody scored a goal the sound would be incredible, it would be a roar!"

"Surreal," Neil Higgins responded, when asked his experience. "It was, looking around, what was it, 13,909? And every seat, it was standing room only. But back in those days the old Garden and the old Boston Arena, and actually all of the venues, none of them had air conditioning. None of them had ventilation. And they allowed smoking in all of those venues. And I was wearing contact lenses. When I first stepped on the ice for warmups just to look around, there was a slight haze of white smoke, and that was all cigarette and cigar smoke, but it was surreal. Skating around it was like time was standing still. We were moving but everyone was just sitting there. It was like they were cardboard posters of people kind of like Covid right now, people were just there. It was just totally surreal to me.

"What I always remember every year in the Garden or the Arena, in between periods I had to clean my contact lenses and I had white tissue, Kleenex tissue. And I'd put the contact lens solution on them, and they'd be brown on that white tissue from the nicotine in my eyes, and I'd get gook in the corner of my eyes. It was terrible back in those days. But skating around at center ice, the big "B", the yellow "B" with the black wagon wheel spokes—*Wow!*—*this is where the Bruins play!* It was every kid's dream."

"I loved playing in the Gardens," Dennis Hebner recalled. "Playing in the Gardens was like a dream. I loved playing there, the lighting was so good, and the ice was...it was just amazing. Younger, my father used to take us in to see the Bruins and just knowing I was playing in the same place as Bobby Orr. This was years ago, early '60s, we used to go in there and just walk up and buy a ticket for four bucks, you could sit in a loge seat or something. My father would take us in there quite a bit and just playing on the same surface as the major leaguers was something. It was like first class, plus the people, I mean the people really, I think it helped me, I just loved...you could recognize people. You're skating and you look up and see someone you know from Norwood! I loved that; it was something. We were big shots, that's what it felt like, we were big shots. Now I look back and I was a seventeen-year-old punk going in there and playing hockey..."

"I got to dress, that was a big thing," ineligible sophomore CM transfer Dickie Donovan said. "Got to skate out on the Garden ice, and it was the most thrilling moment of my life. Magical. Just like being in a kaleidoscope, there were so many sounds and pictures coming at you, you just had to figure out what was going on. You're just running around on the ice, I loved it, man did we love that!"

"It must have been terrific, I just don't remember," Rusty Tobin said. "I probably was numb. And then like, I talk to people over the years and they're surprised. They go, *you* played on the Garden? And then you tell them you played six times, and they're just in awe. I do remember Wheeler made sure we walked in and took a look, it was unbelievable. The Garden, of course—13,909, everyone knows that number—it was amazing, and it was starting to fill when we got there."

"Yeah, going into the Garden," Leo McInerney recalled. "I can remember, I'm not sure if it was '67 or '68, because we were seeded number one, they put us in the Bruin's locker room. That was unbelievable, we were sitting there looking around going, wow...well, I had never been in anything like that. I remember Jimmy Gormley's line was 13,909, that's what the old Garden held, and that place was packed to the rafters. It was crazy, people would actually call the house looking for tickets, like we got tickets. I don't have any tickets! I don't have any tickets! But yeah, you come out in that place and...most of us except for Jackie and Neil who were there in '65, the rest of us were awe-struck. I think that's why we played like we did. It was pretty, for a young kid at sixteen or seventeen, it was pretty unbelievable."

Ken Reddick laughs at mention of Cronin and Boston Garden. "Jack Cronin played four years for Norwood," he said. "His teams went to state championship games three times, in '65, '67, and '68, and, including the quarter-final loss in '66, means Jack played ten games at Boston Garden as a high schooler. That has to be a schoolboy record in Massachusetts!"

Jack Cronin laughs when asked his impression of stepping onto Garden ice. "I'll start by saying after my senior year, I won't say it was no big deal, but I played there so many damn times it became more about the game than about stepping on the ice.

"Although the first time I stepped on the ice I was probably so sky-high, I don't know if I can say nervous, probably nervous, excited to be there. It was just incredible, and the games were always packed, 13,909 capacity, everybody knew at the time. That was the culmination of many high school hockey players' careers, playing at Boston Garden. Doesn't matter if you won, lost, whether you played, you can tell your grandkids that you played at Boston Garden. That was a pretty significant honor. And I remember when I went to BC, it would have been my sophomore year—freshmen didn't play on the varsity—and I had some great teammates at BC, you know, guys that played in the NHL, and when I played my first Beanpot at the Garden there were guys that hadn't played in front of more than 2,000 people, 3,000 people, maybe 4, I'll exaggerate, maybe 5,000, and they were just blown away by stepping onto the Garden ice. And not to sound, not to minimize the experience, but me stepping on the Garden ice was, it wasn't like another day at the office, but it wasn't the same pizzaz that some of these guys experienced."

Despite Bob Bartholomew's tongue-in-cheek boast that, "playing on Boston Garden ice was like playing a home game for us," Arlington players shared the reverence. "It was great," Bartholomew admitted. "I mean, you're skating where the Bruins played, and then we got to play. I mean, the place was *jammed*. In front of huge crowds, and it was just an unbelievable experience, I mean, it felt like you were skating and you'd look around and see all these people…"

"Oh, it was like someone spun you around and told you to walk in a straight line," Arlington backup goalie Joe Bertagna remembered. "I'm sure after skating around the rink once or twice I wasn't sure where our bench was, what door you came out of, it was, it really was something special. It's funny cuz years later when I was with Hockey East some of the athletic directors would talk about moving the Hockey East tournament out of the Garden because they thought we could make more money somewhere else, and I'm thinking, what are you guys, crazy? This is where we wanna be! Players don't want to go some other place, they wanna go where they can skate over the spoked "B" and where the Bruins play, and I just thought it was nuts they were talking about moving, and I'm sure my opinion was formed by my first experience."

The 1967 team's make-up developed. "Ken Reddick was one of the best hockey players, I should say one the most underrated hockey players that Norwood has had, that I know of," Jack Cronin continued. "He could put the puck in the net. He had the gift to put the puck in the net. And I remember I guess it was my junior year, he was a significant reason why we were successful. He was with Mousie Graham, he was the reason, he was a significant reason why we went to the state finals that year. Nobody expected us to do anything that year… I don't remember him as much when he was a junior, or a sophomore, but his senior year he was one of the leading scorers in the league. Neil Higgins had set a record for shutouts that still stands, and we would win games 2-1, 3-2, and we had Kenny, we had Mousie Graham, Pete Oberlander. We struggled to score goals, but Wheeler, again, a testament to Wheeler, every game we played we thought we'd win, and we just kept winning."

"Kenny Reddick was a pretty damn good hockey player who went under the radar a lot," Neil Higgins assessed. "He had a really good shot. And he could skate really good, too. He had good size for a kid back in those days. Kenny was probably one of the underrated ones who really did stuff."

"You know what it was with Kenny," McInerney added, "in my opinion, he was the first one who was smart enough to keep it along the goalie's feet. He did it all the time. And I think he did it on purpose, I swear he did it on purpose. Keep them on their feet. Now they all butterfly. Back in those days they were stand-up goalies, most of them were athletes, they wanted to catch things. And he kept it on the ice, boy. That was a great line, him, Dennis and Taylor were a very formidable second line. Ken by far and away was the leading goal scorer on the '67 team.

"Unfortunately, Don's system, you know, it was throw it in and go get it, but Richie Graham was a puck carrier, he was a skill guy and Don wanted Marines. That was a problem, and then he put him on a line with Tommy, you know, Tommy Shea was deadly in the corners. So that was the first line, Tommy Shea, Pete and Mouse, and Jack and Rusty on defense."

"Richie Graham certainly was a high skilled guy," Rusty Tobin said. "Wheeler kinda put a, well, we all thought Wheeler put the brakes on Richie during the season. He was a team player, so he played the way Wheeler wanted him to play. You know how we played, dump the puck and go in after it. But he let him loose in the tournament. I think someone must have woke him up or something, because Richie was just phenomenal, he and Denny Hebner were just awesome. And Taylor was a great player. And I was lucky I had Kenny and Tommy Shea as my backcheckers on my side. When I was with Jack, Tommy Shea I could hear, he would breathe heavy, and I could hear him say *I got him Russ, I got him!* And I could step up.

"I'll tell ya, Richie Graham and Denny Hebner were underrated. I do remember how good they were in every game. I think they were good in every game all year. Peter Oberlander didn't get a lot of press and he was a hard, good hard worker, always, he was our captain, quiet but really good. I don't know, Tommy Shea, well he also never got much press and he was good too, he was a great teammate. And we had two of the best goalies in the state. Artie Harris was every bit as good as Neil I thought, yeah. They worked their butts off, they really did. People think Neil never did but he did, he worked hard. People think these great players, you know the great players work the hardest. At least in my perspective of knowing great players. And I played with the best. I have arguments with people who was better, but I still think Hebner was the best. Timmy Twomey was the best defenseman I ever saw. That's why I got number 7, because he had it. When he graduated, I asked before the season, and of course Wheeler said something like, *if* you make it...of course in those days you didn't talk to Wheeler about equipment, you talked to Jeff Brown. Who by the way, Kenny would tell you on our freshman team, Jeff Brown had the best shot. He was a great guy, yeah. He was a good player, too. I think he had back trouble, but I remember him being a great skater, great shot, I think he even played with us on the CYO.

"Tommy Taylor is another one who didn't get much press," Rusty Tobin continued. "I think he did in his senior year, but when he played with me and your brother, he didn't get much press. You know Eddie Graham, he was under Richie's saddle, and he was also a very good player. And Leo McInerney was a very good player. I should have mentioned Eddie. Eddie Graham stands out for me. He was a hard worker, he hustled, but there were so many good players behind, and if you didn't do the job, there was someone else who'd fill in right away. That's the group we had."

"I just went out for the team," Dennis Hebner recalled. "I knew I was gonna make it. I didn't know I was gonna start playing center though on the second line, which was great. And I think Tommy Taylor was a sophomore, we had a sophomore, a junior, and a senior on that line, and it worked out well. Oh yeah! I wanted to play, and I thought nothing of... I said, well I'll play, I know I'm gonna make the team, I was that confident. And now that I look back at it jeeze, I was fucking cocky. I really don't think I acted cocky, but I said I can do this, I know I could do this. And I did, I did it my own way.

"I watched every game Richie played. I just loved sports, just loved them. I tried to be a goalie, but once I saw how good Neil was, I said well this is a fucking waste of time. I mean Neil was the best, at the time there was no one any better. So, after my sophomore year, that's when Jimmy Gormley was at Father Mac's, remember they had the playground thing? I think Jimmy Gormley was our instructor and he kept telling me, Dennis you gotta go out for defense, you gotta play defense and I said I'd try it, but I didn't like defense. I only played six or seven games and then they put me on the second line with your brother, and we were...I'd get that puck and just give it to him and let Boots go! I'd get a pass up the middle and Kenny would be going down the wing, I'd just hit him and I'd follow and maybe get some rebound or something. We had a good year!"

Assistant coach Jim Gormley recalled a JV game at Noble & Greenough's outdoor rink on the banks of the Charles River, and the introduction of a South Norwood kid who over three seasons would produce one of the most successful careers of '60s Norwood hockey.

"I was waiting for Don's car," Jim Gormley said. "I just wasn't going to put Tommy out there. I said, are you ready? Are you ready? *I'm ready! I'm ready!* I mean, he was just goofing off before the game... He was looking to bring him up, we were playing down in Braintree that Saturday, we had an afternoon game and Don said he was going to come over and look at some of the JVs.

"I said Taylor's not real polished, but he'll work like a dog out there. So I got him good and ready. I went up to him and told him, Mr. Wheeler's on his way in, so get your skates on, you're going out there. Afterwards Don said to me, wow, you were right about that Taylor. He was like a whirling dervish out there, you know, popping guys, and hustling, and backchecking and forechecking. And I went to him and said, good job, Tommy. So I said, Tommy you're dressing Saturday. I am? And Don put him on the second line, and I think he got a goal. That's all Don wanted. He figured, just you play guys who really wanted it. He could take any kid if they really wanted it, he could make him into a capable hockey player. But he said, *they've gotta want it!* That's the thing."

Tommy Taylor laughs when told the story. "I remember Nobles, I got two goals my first game at the Four Seasons, I think we were playing Milton. I was lucky, I had Dennis and Kenny when I was a sophomore. There was Rusty and Peter Oberlander, Richie Graham, there were a lot of good guys, really hard workers. These guys didn't come up through any programs at all."

"I only started skating in eighth grade," Ken Reddick concurred. "Only skated with Mr. Clifford, on Donovan's rink, and out at the creek. I went out for basketball in eighth grade! Reverend Dan Young asked me if I skated, if I wanted to go out for the freshman team, and I said sure. Dan Young was everything to me. Had the crewcut, I had him for Church youth group, Sunday nights at seven. Dad loved him! And then I did everything I could to improve, skated every chance I got, spent hours in the garage shooting pucks.

"I remember freshman hockey, we played all our games at Tabor Rink in Needham. And we'd play Needham, who was loaded. Connie Schmidt, Eddie Barry, Bruce Dumart—three sons of former Bruins—Scott Godfrey...and I remember one game, it meant the world to me. We played the game, and as I was coming off the ice there was Milt Schmidt—*Milt Schmidt!* —and as I passed him, he patted me on the shoulder and said, 'Good game, kid.' I was thrilled! It meant the world to me!

"The '67 team had only five seniors—myself, Pete Oberlander, Rusty Tobin, Kevin Murphy and Richie "Mouse" Graham," Ken Reddick continued. "Don Wheeler often ran his teams like a college program, more sophomores and juniors than seniors. And he would cut seniors, even if they had played before, if they were not going to be regulars. In addition to the five seniors, we also had the two best juniors at their positions in the state—defenseman Jack Cronin and goalie Neil Higgins. Both are in the Norwood Sports Hall of Fame; both went on to play at BC and those two have remained life-long best friends ever since. I was pretty lucky, I got to play with Hall of Famers Rich Hebner and Blaine Maus in '65 and Hall of Famers Jack and Neil in '67. Not bad company.

"Everyone knows of course how great Neil was, but Neil would be the first to tell you that he owed a lot of that success to Jack's presence in front of him. Jack just owned the crease, couldn't be moved, and was impossible to beat one-on-one. Norwood's best defenseman of the decade. So we had a pretty good start to our team with those two guys. A pretty good team, Oberlander, Graham and Tommy Shea—another Hall of Famer, but in football, not hockey—on one line, myself, Denny Hebner and Tommy Taylor on a line, with Leo McInerney and Johnny Ranalli taking shifts every game. Rusty Tobin, a great guy and friend, and Bob Begley rounded out the defensemen."

Walpole star Paul Giandomenico described the 1967 Bay State League hockey environment for Jerry Kelleher's film, *Banner Years of Hockey*: "Every Saturday night my whole family, aunts, uncles, cousins all went to the Boston Arena to watch Walpole play Bay State League Hockey. It was something."

"The league was strong that year," said Ken Reddick. "There were real good players at most schools, Paul Giandomenico at Walpole, Kevin Kimball at Framingham, Billy Munroe at Wellesley, Al McKinnon at Dedham. But the Needham team was just loaded. Boston Bruins' sons Connie Schmidt, Eddie Barry and Bruce Dumart along with excellent players like Scott Godfrey, Dave Jones and a great goalie in Dan Eberly."

Newspaper reporting of the opening day 4-1 win over Wellesley indicated jitters as well as presaged performances to come. Jack Rutledge wrote in the *Patriot Ledger*, "'Neil Higgins was a little worried before the game,' revealed Norwood coach Don Wheeler. 'He was concerned whether or not he could repeat the great job he did last year. But after Wellesley got that first goal, he quit worrying and just played hockey the way he knew he could.'"

Coinciding with the departure of Richie Hebner, whose 69 goals over the previous four seasons had defined Norwood hockey, was the emergence of *The Fray*. After the opening night win, Frank Wall reported, "The crowd was almost all Norwood with one side of the arena jammed with Norwood fans. When the Locals came onto the ice, a deafening roar went up...Russ Tobin did a fine job, and Denny Hebner, playing in his first varsity game, handled himself well...Hebner came onto the ice for the first time and immediately stopped Steve Marchetti with a resounding check...John Marchetti tried a rush but Denny Hebner decked him at the blue line..."

Frank Wall wrote of an ensuing Norwood-Walpole clash, "Higgins made a diving save and had the puck smothered but he was being whacked at by four Walpole players who thought the puck wasn't frozen. Denny Hebner came roaring into the pile and send Giondeminico[20] sprawling but he went to the box for charging... Hebner came out of the box and threw a hard check on Wayne Kole as the action and contact picked up..."

Like neighborhood and playground before, Dennis Hebner projected a dominant physical presence on Bay State League ice, and like his brother, mustered whatever it is that "money players" muster, and

---

[20] Frank Wall out-did himself, making *three* errors in one attempt to spell Paul Giandomenico's name!

performed. Under bold headlines, *Hebner, Oberlander Goals Sink Walpole,* Frank Wall wrote in his post-game chatter,

> It was Hebner's third goal of the season and all three have been critical. He scored against South, Needham and Walpole at clutch situations in the games...the entire Norwood bench emptied and swarmed onto the ice and mobbed Hebner. When the announcement went up, "goal by Hebner," a thunderous ovation came from the Norwood fans.
>
> The two teams were all fired up for the game and it was pitted as the battle of goalies. That is just what it turned out to be. Both were superb. Before the game most Walpole fans had conceded defeat but with a goalie like Kevin Woods around, Walpole will never be out of any game. The parking lot at Four Seasons was closed at 7:30, two hours before game time...immediately after the final whistle Kevin Woods skated over to the Norwood bench and was met by Neil Higgins in a fine gesture by the two top goalies in the state.

Another game of note was the 3-0 win over Framingham South, in which Ken Reddick notched Norwood's only hat-trick of the season. The game featured a notable opponent. Frank Wall wrote of the game, "Norwood checked South's first line of Kevin Kimball, Don Anderson, and Ned Dowd...South's fine scorer Ned Dowd had clean breakaways in on Higgins and couldn't light the red lamp..." The future Ogie Oglethorpe was on his own path to hockey immortality.

Reminiscing '67 players agreed on the regular season's most memorable contest.

"The next game was the Needham game; they were supposed to blow us out!" Tommy Taylor recalled. "We went down to Braintree to play Needham; at that time the locker rooms were under the stands. You could hear the noise under the stands! We blew out Needham 4-1, and I met Skippy Barry years later and he said who was this guy in my back pocket the whole game? That was good hockey."

"So, the game of the year came midway through the season," Ken Reddick agreed. "Needham was 8-0 and we were 6-1-1 and we had a great game at Ridge Arena on a Saturday afternoon. Kind of shockingly to some, we crushed them 4-1 with Tommy, Dennis and myself each getting a goal. And it started with Pete Oberlander shocking everyone by scoring fourteen seconds into the first period. Still remember it fondly."

Frank Wall's column,

> 'We won, we won!' shouted Norwood High Hockey Coach Don Wheeler as he dove into the jubilant Norwood dressing room after his team had upset previously undefeated Needham, 4-1, before a howling crowd of over 4,000 spectators at Ridge Arena, Braintree, Saturday afternoon. 'It was a team effort all the way,' shouted the popular Norwood High mentor, who plotted the defeat of the defending state champs, regarded previously by many as unbeatable. Norwood wanted this game badly…when the game was over the Norwood fans swarmed onto the iced in congratulating their heroes. The dressing room was bedlam for this was the biggest win this year on the Norwood High sports scene…Norwood had the largest crowd of the teams and when they went on the ice a deafening roar went up.

Wall's game notes included, "Jack Cronin and Russ Tobin played their best hockey of the season…this pair of Norwood defensemen should be rated with any pair in the state, and that Higgins is just too much…" and, "There was no Richie Hebner on the team this season but there was a Hebner by the name of Dennis who blasted the fourth tally into the cage and Norwood had the four-goal lead which cemented the victory."

"I don't know if Jack told you the story," Leo McInerney said. "In '67 we were very, very lucky when Hingham knocked off Needham in the tournament. They were loaded, absolutely loaded. They had Eddie Barry, Dumart, and Connie Schmidt on the first line, and Don decided that he was gonna, for the first time play some strategy and he put Tommy on Eddie Barry. And Jack actually played in a tournament later with Eddie Barry, and Barry said to him, 'Who the hell was that ape that covered me in that game?' He goes, *that guy was gruntin' and groanin' at me, every time I touched the puck that guy was right in my face!* Tommy Shea! And Pete had Dumart."

"When we beat Needham," Dennis Hebner recalled, "that game we played Needham down at Ridge Arena and Needham was loaded, they were so much better than us and we beat 'em 4-1. That was one of the best games we ever played, I think." Dickie Donovan, sophomore transfer from CM yet to join the team, remembered the impressive win. "I went to one of those games, Norwood was playing Needham in their first game of the season. Norwood beat 'em 4-1 down at Ridge Arena. Neil virtually shut 'em out. Fabulous. Neil was a player; Neil was as good as anybody I ever played with. I mean, just a wonderful guy to be around, and I said I don't believe how good this team is."

Ken Reddick continued the narrative: "Needham beat us the second time around and won the title with a 17-1 record. We finished 14-2-2 for the second year in a row but I think everyone was pretty happy with our season. So on to the tournament. We certainly were not underdogs—Norwood never is—finishing second in the Bay State league, but I don't think anyone thought we'd go as far as we did.

"After beating BC High and Auburn at Boston Arena it was on to the Boston Garden for the quarterfinals. Playing at the old Boston Garden was a huge thrill—even though we had been there in '65 and '66 it never got old. Skating across the spoked "B" at center ice gave me chills. It was also pretty intimidating and a little nerve-wracking. The place was packed—you know the number—for every game.

"To those who were there," Ken Reddick continued, "the quarterfinal game against Marblehead and the great Toot Cahoon was so memorable. We beat them 4-3 with Tommy Shea getting two goals, including the game winner late in the third period. I can still see Tommy dancing on tiptoes with the biggest smile you ever saw. Jim Gormley still tells the story of bumping into Toot years later and ragging on him about that game and Toot just shakes his head and says, 'we were beaten by a guy who could hardly bleapin' skate.' It was the highlight of Tommy's season.

"So then we beat Malden Catholic 1-0 in the semi-final with Richie Graham coming up big with the game winner and Neil as usual spectacular in the net. Richie had been good during the season, but he was great in the tournament. So on to the final against Arlington High."

Three years prior, Arlington had produced one of the greatest seasons in Massachusetts high school hockey history when they won the Greater Boston League title with a 17-2-1 record, then thumped Marblehead 5-1 in Boston Garden to win the state championship. Though led by co-captains Bobby Carr and Buddy Clarke, it was goalie Billy Langone who garnered headlines as he posted a record twelve shutouts, encapsulating a season of sustained excellence which produced this remarkable statistic: the 1964 Arlington team had allowed one goal or less in seventeen of twenty games.

The following two seasons the juggernaut was poised to equal their upperclassmen when they won the Greater Boston League for the third and fourth consecutive years with a combined 32-2-1 record. Their tournament losses were both to Bay State League teams, the 1965 a heart-breaking, 1-0 semifinal whitewashing of Charlie "Toz" Toczylowski and fellow Spy Ponders by Walpole's freshman goalie sensation Kevin Woods; the second a stunning 3-1 upset by Dedham in the quarterfinal, behind Joe Keaveny's hat trick. This '66 team had been led by goalie Dom Apprille, and had hammered opponents with 91 goals for, and only 7 against all season, resulting in the first undefeated season in GBL history.

Arlington had earned status as *the* powerhouse of Massachusetts hockey. They entered the 1966-67 season with momentum, a great coach named Eddie Burns, and a slew of hungry, talented skaters eager to avenge tournament losses of the previous two seasons
. For the second straight year the team went undefeated in league play. During the season Lynn English's "Tippy" Johnson's state scoring record was eclipsed by *two* Spy Ponders, Steve Donnelly and Bobby Havern. Norwood was particularly concerned with Havern, who had caught fire during the tournament. Days earlier he had notched six goals and two assists against Hudson.

"I met Bobby walking around Scituate Street back in the late fifties," Arlington co-captain Bob Bartholomew remembered. "He was sittin' on the front porch and he said hey, do you wanna play football? So we played football in the street. And he would call me Bart, the first kid to ever call me Bart. His father was such a great guy, and his mother, such a great family. Mr. Havern would take us into the Arena, but one thing about Mr. Havern was, if you wanted to go with him, we had to shine our shoes in the kitchen. He was a Marine. So he brought out the liquid Kiwi, and we had to shine our shoes before we'd go with him.

"Bobby was great, he was good at everything he did. We went to St. Agnes[21] together. He was great at baseball, running back, punt returner, kickoff returner in football, he was fast, nobody was shiftier, and he brought all of that onto the ice. Bobby was *really* good, good team player, had a ton of friends, I knew him *forevah*. Bobby was like, right around the corner. Great neighbor, great parents, we would play in the driveway. We built a hockey net, two by fours and chicken wire, and we took his old Davy Crockett tent, ripped that apart, put that over the chicken wire, shoot tennis balls or whatever at each other.

"And then we'd go up Robbins Farm every day in the summer and play baseball, football, street hockey, whatever. Great guy to be around, a great teammate, and let me tell ya, when he was in one-on-one with the goalie, it was all over. His father would tell him, come in, throw a little deke, and it's true, you can see it now a-days, he never lifted the puck. A lot of his goals he never lifted the puck. He'd just slide it through the five-hole. He broke Tippy Johnson's record, Bobby got 66 points in fourteen games, 66 points!"

"Bobby Havern was another skilled player, his stickhandling ability was terrific," Joe Bertagna remembered. "Both he and Billy Corkery weren't that big. If you looked at 'em from today's standards, they'd look out of place. But Bobby had set the state scoring record in Arlington before Ftorek broke it. The big thing with Burns was he had a series of breakouts that made us very regimented in how we would get out of the zone. He had a theory, we only played ten-minute periods and if you could get the puck out of your end, your never gonna have a really bad game.

"Two of his breakouts would result in breakaways. One is if the defenseman pinched, somebody would yell 'flip out,' and flip the puck off the boards. So without even looking, if you got the puck, you could bank it off the boards, and the center would break behind the defenseman. And the other one he called 'deep flip,' was if you noticed the two defensemen on the blueline were wide the center would just take off up the middle, and the defenseman coming around the net and somebody would yell 'deep flip!' and he'd look up and see this wide space and the center breaking, and Bobby Havern got a lot of breakaways from these two breakouts and getting behind the defense."

---

21 St. Agnes was Arlington's equivalent of Norwood's St. Catherine's, providing K-8 elementary Catholic school curriculum.

"This was the first of the four Norwood-Arlington games played in the late '60s and early '70s," Ken Reddick continued. "Who knew what was to come? Arlington had some great players, Bobby Havern, Billy and Brian Corkery, Jack Byrne, Bob Bartholomew and others and were heavily favored by most."

"I got hurt bad in practice," Rusty Tobin related. "It turned out my kneecap got cracked. There was fluid, Doctor Lydon was my doctor along with the team doctor. I was warned not to play and I had it drained, and I told my mother, they basically left it up to me. The doctor said you're not gonna change his mind, Anna, he said you might limp for the rest of your life. (laughs) He said I'll take care of you and he did. I went to school, you had to go or you couldn't play, and I sat in Piccirilli's office all that morning and people came by, *are you playing?*"

"That whole day we're all just daydreaming, it was that kind of a day, right?" Ken Reddick recalled. "I'm pretty sure it was math and I sat in the front row. Dino Fiorio was my math teacher, and I'm sitting there kinda oblivious and I hear voices in the background, I'm sitting there and I hear more voices then suddenly the whole room starts laughing and he gets up and comes over to me and says, *Ken!* And I jumped out of this stupor I must have been in, apparently, I didn't even know it, he must have called on me three or four times in a row to answer a question and I ignored him, just staring blankly at the wall, and all the kids in the class were laughing."

"I got it drained that afternoon," Rusty Tobin continued. "I had to keep ice on it the whole time, the ride in, I don't remember the ride in. I was on crutches, and Gormley took the crutches away, well we went in the back way so no one saw us. It was drained before the game, and I think before the third period. I played most the whole game, I just switched sides, Begley would come on and I would switch to the left side. At that time, I don't know why but he had faith in me, I guess. I was in good shape.

"I don't remember a lot, truthfully. I remember the first face-off, we had it planned. Havern would always poke the puck through, films that Wheeler watched and we watched a little of it, every time would poke the puck through the opposing centers legs and go around the opposing center, and in those days, it probably worked most times. But we knew it and our plan was for us to step up, and I remember he mentioned it years later, and Jackie would step up, or the wing. I don't remember much after. It really did go by fast. And all you can hear, you can't hear anybody, as you know. We're used to crowds so that wasn't a factor for our team, it's just noise, you know, you played in those conditions, it's just static. Like I mentioned before, it was our training, we just relied on that, and of course we were good because of that. In games like that, you do best what you know best."

"What I remember about that game, other than them running onto the ice—there's no way we thought we had an easy game," Bob Bartholomew recollected. "Norwood scored first on a mistake by me, I stopped going toward the boards and Norwood came out and scored, but we could not beat Higgins. Norwood went ahead and Norwood was good, but we were a senior-laden team, and they were younger. We were older, we dominated the game, but Higgins was awesome.

"Our first goal was scored by Dennis Sullivan because someone had come down, one of Eddie's scouts, and said what you want to do to beat him is you wanna try to wrap the puck around the net but go up two steps and beat him at the far side, so Dennis Sullivan he did that and scored the first goal."

"What do I remember about the state final game?" Ken Reddick considered. "The crowd was so loud, non-stop screaming every time someone would get the puck. You couldn't hear anything; the game went by so fast. During the season our line had a play where Tommy or a defenseman would move the puck up to Dennis who would try to hit me with a pass up the right wing. This play worked in the first period and I remember trying to beat Bartholomew and the next thing I knew he had the puck and I remember thinking, hmm, these guys are pretty good... And then as time was winding down Dennis got a severe cut on his forehead after colliding, I think with an Arlington player's helmet, not sure, and he got led off the ice bleeding like crazy, about a dozen stitches, as I recall."

"We played Arlington, and we lost 2-1," Neil Higgins recalled. "They actually dominated us; the puck was in our zone quite a bit of the time. Apparently, I did okay and they bestowed me MVP of the tournament and I cherish that, because being the losing goaltender and to get that really meant a lot. That was something. That was a highlight.

"I think it was a rebound, I think I had made two saves in a row, and then the rebound, I think it was either Bobby Havern or Billy Corkery who scored it. Prior to that, Bobby Havern—Arlington's M.O. that year, for quite a few years—Eddie Burns was the coach—was he would send his center, and it was always Bobby Havern, up center ice and split both the defensemen or go to the boards, and all the Arlington people would do is slap the puck up to center ice so Havern could have a breakaway, and I can remember stopping him three times on breakaways. He was the best scorer in the state that year, so that felt good. But losing...if we coulda won I'd rather give up all of that, to give our team a state championship, but it wasn't to be."

It was junior winger Billy Corkery who stepped up and took his first shot at becoming a Massachusetts hockey legend. "My brother Billy didn't make the varsity till the end of his junior year," Maurie Corkery, class of '72, recalled. "He got brought up at the end of his junior year. He wasn't a big fan of Burns. He was sixteen and a half when he graduated from Arlington. Yeah, he was young."

"I sent it in to Billy Corkery," Bob Bartholomew remembered. "He ended up taking a shot, Billy was awesome. You know that name Corkery? Billy got the winner. During that tournament, he got the winner against Gloucester, he got a goal and an assist against Canton, two against Hingham, and he got the winner against Norwood, and he didn't even make the all-tournament team!

"Oh yeah, we were on the ice. Prior to that, Dennis Hebner got hurt, he got cut bad, he hit John Allison, they collided, and J. A. who was sort of a head-down hockey player with a lot of strength, Hebner came in to hit him and J. A. lifted his head and cut Dennis over the eye pretty bad. It stopped the game I forget for how long; he was bleeding pretty bad. It kind of just changed the tempo of the game, and I think we had the puck down their end for quite a while and the buzzer went off, and that was it. It was a great, great feeling, so exciting to finally win it after seeing it happen in '64 and getting kissed in '65 and '66. We were certainly blessed with great athletes."

"Anyway, the time winds down and we can't get that last goal and we end up losing 2-1 to a pretty darn good team," Ken Reddick concluded. "I remember watching the old huge Garden clock, which you could hardly read, as the time disappeared and then watching the Arlington players jumping all over themselves at center ice, with fans streaming onto the ice, as we stood watching in a kind of stupor. Nothing feels worse to a seventeen-year-old than to be watching the other team and their fans celebrate a state championship."

Despite the loss, two state final appearances in three years had ensconced Norwood in Massachusetts hockey elite. At a Norwood hockey reunion in 1992 at Aho's on New Pond, Don Wheeler recalled the season. "The '67 team was my favorite team," the coach said. "They went the furthest with the least." When I related the comment to my brother in his living room on Florence Ave., he gently pushed back.

"I don't know how you can say that, we had two of the greatest players of the '60s, Neil and Jackie, on that team..." Over a half-century later Ken Reddick sighed, leaned back in his chair and softly mused.

"I don't know if that's a compliment or not..."

THE GAME

Let a few men with sticks and a ball make their appearance and begin to knock the ball about. Very soon others will join in, a side will be picked up, and the game will not only have been started but also established; for whoever has once tasted the delights of hockey becomes soon its devoted slave to the end of his active existence.

— C. G. Tebbutt, *Skating*, 1892

How much fun can this be? How can an investigation into hockey's origins reveal an almost divine climatic intervention, a wonderful Boston irony, or correlate famed violin-maker Antonio Stradivari with the sport?

The history of a given sport, like the history of a town or cultural tradition, is often obscured by the mist of time. Metaphorical mist forms under disparate conditions; once deemed necessary by baseball's elite was the mythification of its origin involving Union General Abner Doubleday and the pastoral village of Cooperstown, New York. Hockey's mist proves more naturally enshrouding, involving not only distant lands, but a climatic aberration. But if one stares long enough, mist sometimes dissipates, revealing the most elusive clues.

The very vernacular of hockey suggests a timeline for its emergence in present form, as well as an indication of the sports' ancient relationship to village, tribe, and country. From Olde English we learn, for instance, that "score" meant, "a notch, scratch, or incision," and "a notch or mark for keeping an account, or record."

"We won" is defined as archaic, meaning "to dwell, abide, stay." To "lose" meant "a state of bewilderment, uncertainty, destruction, breaking up," and more telling, "to perish." "Team" in Olde English connotated "child-bearing, brood," but the most recognizable translation in the sport's descent from British timelessness is the word "goelan," today's "goalie," whose original expression meant, "to hinder, impede."

Fragments survive ages to indicate growing interest in winter sporting activities. Writing in the 1170s, William Fitzstephen records from London, England, "When that great fen that washes Moorfields at the north wall of the city is frozen over, great companies of young men go to sport on the ice, some striding as wide as they may do slide swiftly, some better practiced to the ice bind to their feet bones as the legs of some beasts and hold stakes in their hands headed with sharp iron which sometimes they strike against the ice. These men go as swiftly as doth a bird in the air or a bolt from a cross bow."

"Canada has never had a major civil war," former MLB pitcher Jim Brosnan once said. "After hockey, Canadians would probably have found it dull." What Canadians don't find dull are arguments about the origin of hockey, some of which verge on civil war. Indebted we are to Society for International Hockey Research members Carl Giden, Patrick Houda, and Jean-Patrice Martel, co-authors of *On the Origin of Hockey*, whose work overturned a Canadian tempest in a teapot, dousing our northern neighbor's familial squabbling as to the location of hockey's Eden. For years books, papers, and even a commission argued merits of particularly Kingston, Ontario vs. Halifax-Dartmouth, Nova Scotia as hockey's birthplace, assuming presumptive pride that the sport so beloved by Canadians could only be home-grown. The authors' 2013 book illuminated the game's relationship to European pastimes of shinny, hurling, bandy, and shinty, as well as identified the swath of countryside whose history, climate, and culture provided an environment conducive to the germination of a blossoming pastime.

The Fenlands is a region roughly twice the size of Massachusetts in England's eastern midlands, fronting the North Sea. Incorporating parts of Lincolnshire, Cambridgeshire, and Norfolk Counties, it surrounds a bay called The Wash. The coastal plain derives its name from the ancient English word "fen," which the Collins English dictionary defines as, "a low and marshy or frequently flooded area of land," and whose definition of "Fenlands" is, "flat, low-lying area of East England, consisting of marshes until reclaimed in the 17th to 19th centuries." And it was during this reclamation, involving construction of myriad dikes, pumps, and canals allowing sectioned areas to be flooded and replenished, that soil fertile enough to provide half of England's "grade one" agricultural land was created. Worked during warmer months, the land, with thousands of sheets of ice crisscrossed by hundreds of miles of frozen canals, lay vacant and beckoning during winters.

As we are indebted to authors Giden, Houda, and Martel, they in turn are indebted to the Tebbutt family of Bluntisham village, whose five brothers during the latter half of the 19th century were considered among the best hockey players of the area, and whose literary efforts provide insight into hockey's burgeoning popularity. Patriarch Charles Prentice Tebbutt had been born into a farming family in 1824, captained the Bury Fen Club in the 1850s, and played into the '70s, by which time his five sons and one daughter were scurrying across ice.

"The game of Bandy, or, as it is so often called Hockey on the ice, is one of our oldest games, though it is only of comparatively recent years that it has attained any general popularity," co-authors C.J. and Arnold Tebbutt wrote in *Skating*, 1892. "In a small district, however, of which the Bury Fen Club is the centre, records of the game date back to 1814, and there is little doubt that it was played long before that date.

"Concurrently with skating races, bandy matches have long been held in the fens. It is certain that during the last century the game was played and even matches were held on Bury Fen, and the local tradition that the Bury Fenners had not been defeated for a century may not be an idle boast. But it was not until the great frost of 1813-14 that tradition gives way to certainty."

The Tebbutts wrote of Bluntisham and sister village Earlith, describing the game as ancient within a "17-mile radius of Bury Fen. The names of these towns and villages are as follows: Huntingdon, Godmanchester, St. Ives, Chatteris, March, Sutton, Over-Swavesey, Somersham, Cottenham, Willingham, and Mepal."

Their 1896 book, *A Handbook of Bandy; or, Hockey on the Ice*, begins, "The game of Bandy, or, as it is often called, 'Hockey on the Ice,' is not of modern origin, although until within the last fifteen or twenty years it had, perhaps, never been systematically played elsewhere than in the eastern counties, and few persons outside that district had ever seen it or, indeed, heard of its existence." Contrary evidence, however, is contained in a letter written by a British icon born and raised in the west midlands' village of Shrewsbury, on the other side of England against the Welsh border:

"Georgy (referring to a younger son) has learnt to slide and enjoys it very much, and goes down by himself to the village-pond," Charles Darwin wrote his son William in 1853. "But this day's heavy snow will stop sliding and your skating. Have you got a pretty good pond to skate on? I used to be very fond of playing at Hocky on the ice in skates..."

Researchers have indirectly discovered hints of hockey's British breadth, such as this notice in the *Aberdeen Journal* of February 9, 1803, reporting a village tragedy outside Glasgow, Scotland: "On Saturday a most melancholy accident happened in the neighbourhood of Paisley—Two boys of about 14 years of age, the one named Ritchie, and the other Macallum were playing at shinty on the ice, at that part of the Cart called the High Lin, when the ice gave way with them, and they fell in, to the depth of 10 or 12 feet."

The notion was further dispelled in an 1898 book entitled, *The House on Sport,* "...hockey, or Bandy as we shall hence forth call it, is one of the very best of games, both from a scientific and from an athletic point of view. Bandy, as perhaps everybody is not aware, is the name given to 'Hockey on the ice'—rather a mouthful—by the skaters of the Fen districts, who we may consider are the great enthusiasts at the game...various names have been given to hockey in different parts of the British Isles, of which hurley, bandy, and shinty are the best known. Its Scotch designation is shinty, hurley its Irish, and bandy its Welsh."

Concurrent with the centuries-long evolution of ice games, from binding bone-to-shoe to the creation of London hockey associations in the 1880-90s, was the establishment of European colonies in the New World. At the same time that Englishmen began constructing systems of dikes, pumps, and canals in the Fenlands, intrepid British subjects were arriving at Jamestown, Plymouth, and the Shawmut peninsula. Eventual English dominance of the continent and its ensuing flood of settlers brought English taste, practice, and custom to flourishing villages, cultural traits particularly characteristic of the "lower classes" who comprised the majority of emigrants.

Staring, mist dissipates: The first mention in print of both skating and ice hockey in the New World is found in letters written by Sir John Franklin, the British explorer who himself would one day disappear forever in arctic fog. Franklin wrote letters home during his 1825-27 expedition to present day Nunavut and Northwest Territories. In October of '25 he described efforts to keep his men occupied during stagnant, frozen-in months. "We endeavor to keep ourselves in good humour, health, and spirits by an agreeable variety of useful occupation and variety. Till the snow fell, the game of hockey, played on the ice, was the morning's sport." Later that month he wrote of a snowstorm that had "put an end to the skating, and the games on the ice, which had been our evening amusement for the preceding week." Weeks later, Franklin wrote that their routine had resumed, and that "since the ice has set in they have been kept in full exercise by the game of hockey..." Sir John Franklin was born in Spilsby, Lincolnshire, and schooled in St. Ives, Huntingdonshire and Louth, all within the Fenlands, St. Ives and Huntingdonshire, as mentioned, within the Bury Fen Club radius of acute hockey interest.

Determining a timeline of hockey's spread in the New World can be roughly inferred from newspaper articles. The *Boston Evening Gazette* of November 5, 1859, described a game called rickets observed in Nova Scotia: "A good player—and to be a good player he must be a good skater—will take the ball at the point of his hurley and carry it around the pond and through the crowd which surrounds him trying to take it from him, until he works it near his opponent's ricket, and 'then comes the tug of war,' both sides striving for mastery. Whenever the ball is put through the ricket the shout 'game ho!' resounds from shore to shore and dies away in the hundreds of echoes through the hills. Ricket is the most exciting game that is played on the ice...It might be well if some of our agile skaters would introduce this game. It would be a fine addition to our winter sports, and give a new zest to the delightful exercise of skating. We have sent down for a set of hurleys preparatory to its introduction."

Sixteen years later Montreal's *The Gazette* reported on a famous hockey match, considered by many "the birthplace of organized, or modern, hockey." The article read, "At the rink last night a very large audience gathered to witness a novel contest on the ice. *The game of hockey, though much in vogue on the ice in New England and other parts of the United States, is not much known here* (italics mine), and in consequence the game of last evening was looked forward to with great interest."

Within a decade, the sport had spread like pumped water over a fen across all Canada, enthralling all classes. In 1892 Lord Stanley of Preston, London-born 16th Earl of Derby and Governor General of Canada, commissioned the Dominion Hockey Challenge Cup, donating the chalice to be awarded the amateur ice hockey champion of Canada. Lord Stanley wrote the Preface for George Meagher's 1900 book *Skating*, in which Meagher described the spread. "It would be difficult to conceive a wilder, more madly fascinating, and gloriously exciting game than hockey," Meagher wrote. "We have just to look about us to see how intensely popular this sport has become in Canada. I may say that every Club—to say nothing of churches—and almost every large business concern throughout the Dominion, has its Hockey Club, and there is every reason for it, as a more manly or scientific game has yet to be invented. It embodies all the good points of most games, such as football, lacrosse, baseball, etc., and has more additional requisites in which general athletic knowledge and ability may be displayed than any field game extant."

Hockey's formative years clearly occurred across the sea in 19th century England. For the next century Canadian hockey, with its Stanley Cup, fully developed, defined and dominated the sport. All of which seems a tidy story, but lays bare one curious question: how did skating and hockey develop in a land whose winter temperatures average 46 degrees Fahrenheit?

Despite a Fenlands latitude similar to Edmonton and Moscow, the eastern midlands, indeed the entire British Isles, enjoys a temperate climate. Governed by the Atlantic Ocean's Gulf Stream, the effect elevates average temperatures approximately eleven degrees above corresponding latitudes. Palm trees grow in Ireland, especially along Kerry and Cork coastlines. How did a sport conducted on ice, which freezes at thirty-two degrees Fahrenheit, thrive in such an atmosphere?

Historians, aided by paleo-climatologists, answer with an explanation of the Little Ice Age. Wending way not through mist but clinging fog, without written records and relying on imperfect and circumstantial evidence, scientists believe a cold spell existed in the Northern Hemisphere from medieval times into the 19th century. The Baltic Sea froze twice in the early 1300s, the south of the Bosphorus in 1622. British Isle waterways often froze enough to support skating and encourage new winter festivals. Once again C. G. Tebbutt in *Skating* describes a common experience: "When the army of Napoleon, retreating from Moscow, were starved and frozen to death by the thousands, when, at home, Prof. Sedgwick had to burn his gun-case and chairs to keep himself warm; when the scarcity of coal at Cambridge was so great that the trees within the grounds of St. John's College were cut down for fuel, and in all the colleges, we are told, the men sat in their rooms two and three together for warmth; then the hearty watermen, gunners, and labourers were quickening their circulation by playing bandy on Bury Fen."

David Calderwood, Scottish theologian born 1575, commented on the severity of winter 1605-06, as well as the resulting games on sea ice in his book, *The Historie of the Kirk of Scotland*: "A vehement frost continued from Martinmas (St. Martin's Day, November 11) till the 20th of February. The sea freized so farre as it ebbed, and sindrie went into shippes upon yee, and played at the chamiare (Scottish for "shinty") a myle within the seamark. Sindrie passed over the Firth above Alloway and Airth, to the great admiration of aged men, who had never seene the like in their dayes."

Across the Irish Sea, a 1740 newspaper reported similar conditions. "Accounts from Nenagh under date of Jan. 5th say: 'The Shannon is frozen over, and a hurling match has taken place upon it; and Mr. Parker had a sheep roast whole on the ice, with which he regaled the company who had assembled to witness the hurling match...'"

New York harbor froze in 1780, enabling a walk from Manhattan to Staten Island. "The ground between the Collect and Broadway rose gradually from its margin to the height of one hundred feet," contemporary William Alexander Duer wrote, "and nothing can exceed in brilliancy and animation the prospect it presented on a fine winter day, when the icy surface was alive with skaters darting in every direction with the swiftness of the wind, or bearing down in a body of pursuit of the ball driven before them by their hurlies."

That Massachusetts was similarly affected, experiencing deeper cold than today over a period of years, can be extrapolated from Henry David Thoreau's journals.

Jan. 29, 1854. A very cold morning. Thermometer, or mercury 18 degrees below zero.

Feb. 6, 1855. The coldest morning this winter. Our thermometer stands at -14 degrees at 9 a.m. There are no loiterers in the street, and the wheels of wood wagons squeak as they have not for a long time, actually shriek. Frostwork keeps its place on the window within three feet of the stove *all day* in my chamber.

Jan. 7, 1856. At breakfast time the thermometer stood at -12 degrees. Earlier it was probably much lower. Smith's was at -24 degrees early this morning.

The gradual easing of the Little Ice Age and the British Isles' return to temperate clime was indicated by *The Standard* of London. On December 29, 1873 they printed, "There is no ice at present, so that hockey, one of the best games imaginable on skates, has had no trial this year. In the fen country, when there is frost of any duration, skating races and handicaps are of frequent occurrence...Unluckily for this our winters are so uncertain and short that skating will never be able to take its proper place among our sports unless the Yankees cut through the Isthmus of Panama in a fit of spite and divert the Gulf Stream into the Pacific; then we might get some winters like they have at Moscow."

Thus, during a relatively brief historical timespan and concurrent with British colonizing of the New World, did hockey in varied and primitive form emerge on the Old Continent, then spread and flourish in the New.

The wonderful Boston irony being that the original English village of Boston, from which came many original settlers of Massachusetts Bay Colony and for which they named their new settlement, lies fifty-seven miles north of the Tebbutt's village of Bluntisham, amidst the fens of Lincolnshire. The founders of Boston, Massachusetts referred to reed-bound, back bay marshland of their new town as "the fens," likely applying familiar vernacular than in any homage to their roots. In the latter part of the 19th century these back bay fens were filled, creating the Fenway neighborhood. Thus, in 1912 when Boston Red Sox owner John I. Taylor purchased land in this neighborhood and began building a new baseball stadium, he was laying the foundation of irony, that today's oldest and dearest iconic baseball landmark, Fenway Park, was named after a swath of English countryside from which emerged the sport of hockey.

The correlation between Antonio Stradivari and hockey? The artist crafted violins during the Little Ice Age, from 1680 to 1725, and which today can sell, depending upon condition, for tens of millions of dollars. His instruments are renown for impeccable craftsmanship and what is considered their unique tone. Posited by some is that this rare sound is produced by denser wood grown only during the Little Ice Age. And what a wonderful correlation that is! That from a shared climatic aberration should the graceful flow of a brand-new Stradivari violin accompany our sometimes dainty, sometimes dangerous, developing dance on ice.

As a kid I was struck by hockey's innate fairness. The sport does not require a physical attribute as a primary asset as, for instance, height in basketball, or overall strength and size in football, but more resembles baseball in that anyone, of any size, can not only play, but excel. It allowed a 5' 7", 160-pound Henri Richard to win eleven Stanley Cups and be elected to the Hockey Hall of Fame, soon to be joined by 6' 9", 250-pound Zdeno Chara. That strength and size aren't prerequisite is born out at every level.

"I heard of McGee as a marvel and was ready for a savage looking player," a Canadian sportswriter noted of legendary Frank McGee in 1905. "I was fooled; McGee pushed open the little side door of Dey's famous rink in Ottawa and stepped on the ice—a regular dude. His golden hair was parted exactly in the center, his hockey pants were snow white and actually creased. His boots, I believe, were actually polished. I was never more surprised in my life. I asked Bob Shillington if that was really the famous McGee and he only nodded."

"First time I ever met Gretzky in person was in the dressing room after a Canada Cup game in '87," the late Canadian sportswriter Earl McRae once said. "Had a towel around his waist. Surrounded by reporters. All I did was stand there thinking, I don't get it. He's small, he's skinny, he's pale, he's frail-looking, he has no muscle tone. He looks like every wimp you ever saw on the beach. How is it this nothing-looking guy standing before me is the greatest effin hockey player who ever lived? I don't get it!"[22] Whether it was the early amateur game, the matured professional game, or Massachusetts high school hockey, the observation is verified; sophomore sensation Robbie Ftorek weighed 135 pounds.

---

[22] A challenge in this book's narration is sometimes leaving quoted minor errors, or faulty opinion, alone. But some instances are too egregious to ignore. Bobby Orr was the greatest effin hockey player who ever lived.

Hockey's scorecard also indicates an egalitarian bent. That both a goal and an assist are accorded equal value in scoring impresses, as it recognizes and rewards teamwork. That a second assist is recorded in equal measure accentuates the recognition, affirming, for instance, that Stan Mikita's playmaking ability in center ice was every bit as valuable as Bobby Hull's slapshot inside the blueline.

But before any 1960s ruminations was the sport's coalescence with Massachusetts culture. The return of "normal" climate in the northern hemisphere restricted hockey to areas conducive to winter skating. Though technology to create artificial ice was developed in the 1870s, it was decades before this critical improvement was financially viable for most communities, leaving Minnesota, Michigan, and New England natural centers of U.S. interest.

Much of that interest emerged in universities. Harvard's hockey team was founded in 1898, their first intercollegiate game played against Brown University on an out-door rink at Mattapan's Franklin Field. Over the next decade most northern colleges and universities fielded teams, only to see dozens cancel seasons and suspend programs due to lack of reliable ice. In 1876 the first artificial ice-skating venue was built, unsurprisingly, in London. New York's Madison Square Garden followed in 1879, but early refrigeration technology, though essentially the same as used today, was hampered by the primitive state of newly devised and constantly improving electrical technology. As a result of, and subject to, these conditions, Boston Arena was built in 1912, becoming the focus of Massachusetts hockey for the next half century.

Area high schools in the 1920s and '30s struggled with a host of athletic issues, not least of which were primitive playing conditions. Noted in Arthur Early's 1937 *Tiot* yearbook is this football game,

> Norwood's first game was with Hudson High, a little cornpatch town in the western part of the state. Played under very unfavorable conditions, the game proved disastrous. Nine of the Hudson players were veterans, and they knew where the stumps and mounds of their field were located; whereas, the Norwood boys, green to begin with, had difficulty in keeping from tripping

in the briar patches. The partiality of the officials might further explain the score of 27-0.[23]

"Vinnie didn't play sports much in the spring, summer, and fall because there were always chores or jobs that might help out the family, but in the winter when chores and work let up, he could play hockey. He was a member of Walpole High School's first hockey team and played on the team for its first three years."

John Martin's remarkable folder on Vinnie Fitzpatrick provided an early glimpse of hockey's primitive conditions in the Norwood-Walpole area.

"At the time, hockey games were somewhat less formerly scheduled events," Vinnie told John. "First, because they were played on ponds, the weather decided whether games might be possible, and consequently, schedules were uncertain. Second, partly because of this uncertainty but also because opponents were few and far between, hockey was unlike more established sports. At times, when snow covered the ponds, the player might be excused from classes early to clear the ice. They also had to prepare the rink prior to games by placing wooden boards to set the rink bounds. Then after games, the boards had to be stored for future use, because a storm or thaw might entrap the boards in or below the ice."

The *Walpole Times* article included in the folder continued the hockey narrative of the 1929 Walpole High graduate.

> "Doc Gordon started it in Walpole in 1927," said Fitzpatrick. "It was informal in the first year and we played on Allen's Pond. The first official team was in 1928, and we had snowbanks for the outside of the rink. John Allen donated the wood for the boards and we had 30 or 40 10-foot sections of boards and supports. We had to take them off when we were done because if there was a night thaw, they'd sink.
>
> "The coach would call up a team, Norwood, Stoughton, and find a school available," said Fitzpatrick. "We'd play wherever there was ice and if there was a snowstorm, that didn't stop us.

---

23 While field conditions were no-doubt primitive, this drips with condescension for the "western little corn-patch town" of Hudson, located, as it is, within today's Rt. 495 beltway. It is a litany of excuses, inexperience, field conditions, officials. In other words, Norwood got its ass kicked.

We would send a notice around the school for anyone to clean the ice and get off school early. The team would clean and put the boards up and that was our warmups. If there was ice, you'd play a game. We used to get tired with no subs, so I would tell the umpire my glasses were fogged up. That would give us a little rest when I went and cleaned them off. I would get booed because they would know what I was doing."

"I can't believe you're talking about Vinnie Fitzpatrick," Joe Morgan exclaimed. "Holy mackerel!"

Best known for exploits on grass, Joe Morgan also starred on ice in his youth, which spanned formative years of local high school hockey. "I thought of Fitzy a million times, I go by his house about five times a week. Let me ask you this, did it say anything about the racing dogs they had? They had a racing pit in back of their house and ran greyhounds and Raynham a little bit. I'm surprised that wasn't in there. I think I remember seeing him walking to work, yeah. He was a big, tall guy, wasn't he? I think he was. Big, tall guy, he had glasses when I knew him. I even talked to him, he knew who I was, but I never knew what the hell he exactly did. Did he go to Walpole High at all?

"I knew who he was, and I met him. And I knew he went to Dartmouth. I'm assuming Vinnie played at Dartmouth at the end of the '20s or early '30s. He lived on East Street only about a half mile from me or less. But I heard people talking about him that he went to Dartmouth, but I never knew how good he was. Was he a defenseman? In those days, Dartmouth had guys around who would interview potential prospects. So I went down Norwood to this guy named Barr, he was a Dartmouth grad and he interviewed me, and he must have put in a lot of the interview because they didn't accept me at Dartmouth. So I went to BC and beat the crap out of them in baseball and hockey for four years!

"In Walpole when we were kids, there were ponds everywhere, and we always had some place to skate," Joe Morgan continued. "My first day on a pond was November 20th, 1936. I remember it because my mother bought me some heavy stockings to put inside of a pair of skates that a doctor gave me, and they were three sizes too big for me. And I skated on this little pond out back of my, it wasn't a pond, it was just a little ditch. So that's the day. Remembered it. Because my birthday's the nineteenth, and the next day all that happened. How 'bout that, fans!

"I can tell you this, there were times when we skated two weeks in a row without the ice leaving us, it got so chopped up it wasn't worth skating on. But in these days, once the ice gets hard, within a day or two you get some kind of rain or snow or something, so one day I saw Tricky Dick Albert, you know him? Former weatherman. Okay. I asked him, why in the heck does it snow and rain so much? I told him when we were kids, we could skate two weeks in a row. He had a good answer. You know what he said? He said, when you were growing up, there were far less automobiles, far less homes, and now there's a ton of moisture in the air, and it's gotta go somewhere. Pretty good answer, I thought!

"Well anyway, I loved hockey. I couldn't wait for the ice. Many a day I was on a pond for an hour in the morning, the only one there, waiting for the rest of the troops to show up. In high school we played with a guy named Stan Mueller who went to Clarkson, and before that we played quite a bit on the ponds with Harold Songin and Wally Songin and Cliff Harrison, all those guys, they were all good players. I saw Richie Hebner play only twice, but he was a good skater and he was strong, and when he shot the puck, he hit the net. Scored a lot of goals, too, I suppose. By the way, I was his manager his first year in pro ball, Raleigh, North Carolina.

"Hockey to me was much easier to play than baseball. Baseball was way harder.[24] I would put it this way. When I was in hockey, I could definitely make a difference in that game. When I was playing baseball, I was just another guy in the pineapple fields. That's the story. Hockey was more fun. You know why? Cuz when you went on the ice, it was up to you to find the action, you didn't have to wait for it to come to you. Baseball, you could play shortstop for a double header and never have a ball hit to you.

"I played center, where all great players play! You know why it's good to play center? Because you really show anyone what you can do, because the puck comes your way more than often, and you can skate all over the place, you don't have to stay on the wing. Who do you think I'd say was the best

---

[24] Dennis Hebner concurred with this assessment. "It's the toughest game to play," Dennis said. "In baseball, you get up to bat and strike out every time, you *suck*. You know it, everyone knows it. You can't hide in baseball. Every other sport you can hide a little bit. Baseball is the only sport where you cannot hide. I've said that all along."

hockey player I saw, all around? From the '40s up to the ones I saw a lot, from the '40s to the '80s? Who do you think it was? In the big leagues? *Milt Schmidt.* He was *dynamite!* He did everything, skate, score, shoot, backcheck, forecheck, good in the corners, was a great hip checker, team player, stickhandler—number one! I would say Gordie Howe was number two in them days, Jean Beliveau might'a been number three with me.

"The Bay State League I think started in '37, and Walpole came in next to last, then won the thing in '38. Then up to 1950, we were pretty good. We ran second three years in a row when I was in high school. Walpole didn't have a team until 'round '38 or something like that, and that's when they started to play good. Because then a few years later the Songins came, all three of them, and we were great then, and when I was there, we were pretty good. The Songins were big, the Harrisons were big, there were six of those total, and there were many other good players that came out of Walpole. I graduated at Walpole in '49.

"When I was playing against Norwood, they didn't have very good teams. Naw. We beat 'em 10-0 on New Year's Day one year. Believe it or not, the record for most points in a game was seven. I had seven points and the coach threw this little kid on the ice name, Charlie Gould? He was a freshman, he let him play, and I gave him a pass and he scored a goal! Right in front of the net, and the referee did not put my name in. Everyone was laughing, who's that water boy out there! So unofficially, I tied the guy, whoever had seven. (laughs) We didn't make an issue out of it.

"We played in Boston Arena, we used to play Friday night or Saturday afternoon. The Arena was good, but those boards were hard as concrete. When you hit 'em you weren't going anywhere but down, or backwards, oh yeah. To me the rinks today, though, are way too small. These guys are so big and so fast, they can't do much, and the way they hit and smash people today, it kind of takes the enjoyment out of the game for me to watch it. I would think the rinks should be about fifteen feet wider. It's long enough, but not wide enough. That's why they can't stickhandle or play-make, they gotta get rid of the puck. When we played, you couldn't check anywhere but behind your own blueline. You knew that, didn't ya? So what a difference, you could skate and stickhandle, you had a picnic skating through center ice! Christ, it was a *picnic* all the way to the goal!

"Vinnie talked about the boards on the ponds? I remember the boards they had. Here's one thing about the boards. They had them on Memorial Pond one year and the ice got a little soft and the boards, the ice caved-in and the boards got so waterlogged, after a while they sunk to the bottom. How 'bout that for apples!"

In 1967 Frank Wall wrote in his column,

> Where did it all start? Well Norwood came into the Bay State League in 1942 when Quincy dropped out. There were 50 Norwood fans in the Boston Arena when Norwood took the ice against Watertown on Saturday, December 19th. With just 13 seconds gone in the game, Al Billingham took a pass from John Carroll and fired the puck into the cage. Norwood won the game 3-2 with the players for that opener including Ed Chandler in the nets, Ray Martin and Ed Praino at the points, and a first wave of Al Billingham, John Carroll and Bob Stanton. The second wave had Fred Carroll, Fran Harrington and Russ Mattson.

Frank Wall wrote, "The first years in this sport were pretty lean, but they were the players who started it all and there were some great ones." Our scribe noted that Norwood won its first "hockey crown" in 1957 under coach George Ronan, and that "hockey really started an upward trend in the years '58-'64 with another championship being attained." Bobby Dempsey noted the fervor with which the sport caught hold during that period.

"My aunt and uncle from Walpole got my mom and dad to go to some of the Bay State games way back in the early '60s when Walpole had some of those great, great teams. And then Richie Hebner came along and it was the place you had to be twice a week, to be at a Norwood game, if you were lucky enough to get in, because back then, they knocked 'em out. I remember my dad came back from Europe one time and he wanted to see the Norwood-Walpole game. He got up to the Four Seasons and he couldn't get in, but he knew Nick Abraham and he got in, he had his luggage with him! It was taken that seriously, where you wanted to be there. If it was an afternoon game at Loring, you were there. Didn't matter. You had to get there early, like an hour, just to get a seat. Which is kinda sad now where you might have a couple hundred people, we had a couple thousand. So we kinda lived a dream."

George Ronan, having won Norwood's first Bay State League title with captain Hank Valentinas, retired as coach and was replaced by former player John Monbouquette. When John Monbouquette stepped down before the 1962-63 season, another former player stepped forward, who secured Norwood's second Bay State League title the following season. When filmed by Jerry Kelleher over fifty years later, Don Wheeler could not contain long-held grievance at the school committee's parting admonition at his hiring. "Just don't embarrass us, they said," the coach seethed.

And thus had arrived Norwood, in the Time of Hockey.

BASEBALL

Each one of us, then, should speak of his roads, his crossroads, his roadside benches; each one of us should make a surveyor's map of his lost fields and meadows.
— Gaston Bachelard, *The Poetics of Space,* 1958

When Jerry Kelleher and Brendon King were filming *Banner Years,* their documentary on Massachusetts hockey, they invited me, along with Ed King and Peter Brown, to Billy Clifford's house. We took turns ruminating on various topics in front of klieg lights and camera, and my interview went fine until Jerry asked, "Was hockey the major sport in Norwood?"

I immediately and emphatically answered, "Yes."

I was wrong.

"We had the best baseball town in Massachusetts growing up," Paul Angelo affirmed. "You're talking hockey? Baseball was number one! Because of Minty, Frank Wall, all those guys. No one ever talks about it. You talk about hockey; baseball was number one."

The popularity of individual sports is influenced by accessibility. Today soccer enjoys a huge following because it can be played by kids anywhere, of any economic strata, in any weather, with simply a ball. Dispelling the proverb that familiarity breeds contempt, familiarity in sports breeds ardent, life-long passion. 3.5 billion people viewed at least a portion of the 2018 FIFA World Cup, its final game viewed live by a full 1.12 billion souls. Likewise, by simply adding bat to ball, baseball and its derivative forms of softball, flies and grounders, scrub, workup, stickball, whiffle ball, backstop, engages the masses. Ice hockey has always been less accessible.

Ice only forms naturally in northern climates, and for only a season. Artificial ice, whose technology evolved during the last decades of the 19th century, solves this problem, but historically artificial ice rinks only sprouted where the sport had already taken hold, only recently expanding into warmer climes. Further restricting is that unlike running, learning to skate is challenging.

"Like many other things, skating ought to be learned in youth, when one has not far to fall, nor much dignity to lose," C. G. Tebbutt wrote in his 1921 book, *Skating*. "To children there is nothing formidable about it; the motion once learned is almost as easy as walking, but at first there are some difficulties to overcome. The young beginner feels terribly nervous when he finds himself on the ice in a perpendicular position."

Winston Churchill learned to skate, while others struggled. Famed investor Warren Buffett "tried skating, but his ankles wobbled..." In 1969 Rhodes Scholar Bill Clinton, on a mainland trip during his time at Oxford, sent a postcard home: "Have been in Bavaria for a week seeing churches, castles, landmarks. Staying in a little village outside Munich. Sunday I went ice skating for the first time."

We have no further scouting reports on Bill's success, but Carlos D'Este wrote about the efforts of an adolescent General George Patton. "During the Christmas holidays of 1904 he decided to make the best of winter and took up skating, but his early attempts brought about frequent contact between his posterior and the ice, leaving him assured that his future as an outdoor sportsman lay elsewhere. Acknowledging to (wife) Beatrice that he had, 'just gotten to the stage where I look upon anyone who can stand up on the nasty things, with feelings near to worship...'"

Locally, Charles Fanning confessed his own struggles in his book *Mapping Norwood*: "And then there was hockey—to me, the most exciting of games. I played with friends on local ponds and listened to the Bruins on the radio, but there was a problem—I couldn't skate. I hadn't started young enough and had never seen the inside of a rink, so my ankles remained weak and wobbly, there was much leaning on my stick, and skating backward was an unattainable skill."

More positive was the educator's recollection of Norwood baseball: "In one of these playground games, I had my shining moment at the plate. Norwood's most famous athlete in those years was Richie Hebner, a boy so talented at both hockey and baseball that he could have played either sport professionally. He chose baseball and went on to a creditable, seventeen-year career (with a lifetime batting average of .277) as an infielder with the Pittsburgh Pirates and the Philadelphia Phillies. He was at third base when the Pirates won the World Series against the Baltimore Orioles in 1971. Richie loved to play baseball, anytime, anywhere, including in the Playground League, where he participated (without a scrap of condescension) on his neighborhood's team, Father MacAleer's. Richie was five years younger than I, but I'm still proud to let the record show that one morning in July I hit a triple off his pitching in an Intermediate game between my team, the High School Playground, and Father Mac's."

Richie Hebner was not the only Norwood kid who loved to play baseball anytime, anywhere.

"It's just what we did as kids," Barry Sullivan related. "I would leave my house on Marion Ave., probably at, I don't know, quarter of eight in the morning, eight o'clock, somewhere in there, and I'd know there was a midget game at Father Mac's, there's an intermediate game at Shattuck, and there's another baseball game down at Balch. So I'd get on my bike, put my baseball glove on the handlebars, you know what I mean? And I'd go to game one, game one, nine o'clock, Father Mac's, and play that game.

"Then, I was too young to be an intermediate, I was only like nine or ten whatever, but I'd go down to the intermediate games which was Babe Ruth League age, thirteen to fifteen, and hope, hope, hope that they only had eight players so I could be the ninth. And sure enough, more often than not, I'd be the ninth player playing right field, batting ninth. With kids seven years older than me. And ah, it was fun. I used to take my bike to every single playground in order to play baseball. To see if they needed a player.

"Who'd I play with? Well…know who was good at Father Mac's? Joey Jenkins. Never played sports in high school. Him and Jackie Cronin were the best two baseball players. It was fun playing with the Drummeys and Chris Dixon. They were all so damn good that they all used to bat lefty instead of righty. If you were too good, you were made to bat lefty. Dixon was a fucking star. He was. He was a star. I always measured myself against Chris Dixon. Swear to God. Because he was so good. I was like, I'm gonna be as good, I'm gonna be *better* than him. That was hard! It was very hard to do, you know what I mean? To be better than him, because he was *good*. But I put my mind, I'm gonna be better. He was a very driving force in my eleven, twelve, thirteen, fourteen, fifteen-year-old psyche, because he was better than I was, and I didn't think *anyone* could be better than I was. Yup, yup. Shattuck, six, seventh, eighth grade. They didn't make *me* bat lefty, you know what I mean? You know what I'm talking—right? But they made *him* bat lefty."[25] (laughs)

"We get up at seven o'clock in the morning and go play baseball and come home when it got dark," Paul Angelo concurred. "And we were playing intermediate when we were eight. Intermediates were twelve and over, okay? Minty, there'd be fifteen guys in Minty's car going from one playground to the next. Great players, Richie, Mike Carney, Dave Hardy, all those kids. Ricky Falcone, unbelievable, he had so much talent. The camaraderie! Everyone grew up on the playgrounds. When you got to the high school, you knew everybody! Today they go to their school, they don't know anyone. Right? Now kids want to pay ten thousand dollars to go play hockey. It's bullshit. These kids should not be out of high school. I mean, this is how you're growing up. You need to make friends. You made friends, I'm still in contact with my friends."

In the 1950s and '60s, virtually every Norwood kid interested in athletics—and some that weren't—played Little League baseball. Skip Lockwood described the experience in his book *Insight Pitch*:

> Little League tryouts...On this overcast spring day, Little League tryouts were proceeding in a chaotic manner. Boys of all ages, sizes, abilities and attitudes nervously assembled along neighborhood lines on the patchwork field of grass and mud. They were wandering around in baggy shirts, asking questions like, "When is this going to start? When am I going to get a chance to hit?" Some of the boys had already lost their caps and misplaced their new gloves. A few were aimlessly crowding into small groups in various parts of the field, bored because, for some, their parents had made them come. By now many just wanted to go home. One little boy, awkwardly shifting weight from one foot to the other, was trying to find a coach. He had to pee badly.

---

[25] Forcing an older, or much better opponent to bat lefty was common across Norwood's playgrounds and fields, which led to a humorous incident in "the first field" behind Crestwood Circle. Their reputation at a very young age already widespread, the Hebner brothers were required to bat lefty in their first appearances there...

Indeed, decades later many carry memories of Little League. "Mike Martin was a good Little League player, played baseball with Sails, was a Brave," Peter Brown related. "I was a Yankee, *go Yankees.* Rosy was a Yankee; Thornton was a Tiger. The way we classify anyone we run into now is what Little League team they played on. Chris Dixon, Indians, Eddie Hickey, White Sox..."

Driving past the Pleasant Street baseball field, Ken Reddick recalled, "Opening day, 1961, we were the opening day game. We walked through town, the Little League parade, the whole thing, and we were the opening day game. Indians versus the Red Sox, Norman Johnson was on the Indians, I was on the Red Sox. 1961, the year Maris hit sixty-one home runs, Norm Cash hit forty-one, and Norman Johnson threw a no-hitter against us on Norwood Little League opening day!"

The flowering of any culture germinates from a variety of seeds. Technological advances, like those that fostered development of artificial ice, contributed to the loss of regional accents via mass audio-visual media. Cultural transitions accelerate during and after wartime, as, for instance, an easing of traditional religious animosities occurred after World Wars I & II, where Universalists and Methodists fought alongside Roman Catholics and Episcopalians, who shared fox holes with Jews. Worthington noted the effect in his 1827 history of Dedham when he wrote, "when the ever-memorable events of the revolution agitated the community, we may perceive considerable changes in the manners and habits of the people since that time..." Strides in race relations occurred after Dover and Norwood men fought alongside Roxbury and Dorchester men, who all developed admiration for Gurkhas. It was no coincidence that Jackie Robinson made his MLB appearance in 1947, or that Harry Truman desegregated U.S. armed forces by executive order in 1948.

The Civil War was a homogenizing event in American baseball. The sudden and intimate association of thousands of men and boys rural and urban, northern and southern, wealthy and poor, created conditions dooming the silly rule or odd habit of dissimilar, far-flung baseball derivations, engendering a formal norm, a standardization. Baseball's rise in popularity during the decade between Appomattox and the first, fledgling professional leagues is indicated in historical records. Members of

George Armstrong Custer's 7th Calvary "played ball" during their 1874 Black Hills expedition, Custer's brother-in-law James Calhoun recording in his diary, "The men played the popular game of Base Ball."

A fine account of this amalgamation of baseball rules and regulations, coalescing with its post-Civil War spread, comes from one of Norwood's own. In Win Everett's *Tales From Old Tiot*, a collection of early 1930s columns penned for *The Norwood Messenger*, appears an interview with John Kiley, "for many years town clerk of Norwood, a popular merchant of shoes and now, in his seventies, a machinist living in his charming home at 14 George Street."

John Kiley's on-line professional baseball synopsis reads, "John Frederick Kiley (July 1, 1859-December 18,1940) was a Major League Baseball outfielder and pitcher, born in Dedham, Massachusetts, who played parts of two seasons in the majors. In 1884 he played 14 games in the outfield for the Washington Nationals of the American Association. He did not appear again in the majors until 1891, when he started one game for the Boston Beaneaters, which he lost. He died in Norwood, Massachusetts."

Norwood, of course, was Dedham's South Parish in 1859, which makes the left-handed hitting and pitching Mr. Kiley Norwood's first professional athlete. In a remarkable interview, worthy of any account of baseball's origins, John Kiley told Win Everett,

> The years between 1869 and '73 were indeed the formative period of baseball in Norwood and the country over. But what is hard for you young fellows to understand is the way the older people in those days ignored all such games. They were just 'boy's games,' a noisy mysterious thing the kids did after school. Or some men playing a game on which they are probably BETTING! There was not the slightest respect for or interest in sport or baseball as we understand it today among the adult population. Men and women worked ten or more hours a day. They took no vacations and few days off.
>
> "For some years before 1869 boys and men played 'round ball,' sometimes called 'Massachusetts Ball', or 'plug ball.' Three posts six feet high and three feet in the ground were set up in a big triangle. The team was scattered in the field and one man pitched to a batter who used a flat bat much like a cricket bat.

He could hit the ball in any direction front to back or side. The one who caught or got it could throw or 'plug' it at the running batter who made for one of the posts and swung himself around if he got there before being hit. If hit, he was out. He made the next post on the next hit and so on, home. A simple, rough tough game I assure you.[26]

"I was a kid about eight when the first baseball game was played in Norwood, probably around 1868. It happened like this: A group of South Dedham men somehow learned to play a new game called 'baseball.' They invited another group from West Dedham (Westwood, formerly The Clapboardtrees or Third Parish) to come over and learn it. They did so—and this initial game of instruction was the first game of baseball ever played in this town. I was only a little shaver, and I remember the names of all the Norwood men who took part in this historic game."

Thus ends Everett's account, frustratingly premature for one researching Norwood's baseball roots. Who were these South Dedham (Norwood) men who "somehow learned to play a new game," their names still remembered? Were they among the Dedham volunteers of the Grand Army of the Republic, a mere three years released from service and having learned baseball once immersed in sudden and intimate association with thousands of men and boys, rural and urban, northern and southern, wealthy and poor?

On deck was Marty Callaghan. Born in Norwood on June 9, 1900, and a 1916 graduate of the high school, the left-handed hitting outfielder played two seasons for Worchester of the Eastern League before opening with the Chicago Cubs in the spring of 1922. He tripled off Dolf Luque in his first game but played only sporadically over three seasons before returning to the minor leagues. For the next eight seasons he hammered minor league pitching, garnering over 200 hits thrice, and batting over .350 twice. This earned him a cup of coffee with the Cincinnati Reds in both 1928 and 1930, but it was back to the minors for four more years,

---

26 This is virtually an exact description of the English past time of Rounders, as described in William Clarke's 1828 London-published as well as, significantly, its 1829 Boston-published edition of *The Boy's Own Book*. Ken Burns would have been thrilled to find this first-hand quote for his epic *Baseball* documentary.

before returning to Norwood and finding work at Plimpton Press. His baseball career, undoubtedly rewarding as experience, tempered his view on the sport as a career.

"Marty Callaghan was my Babe Ruth League coach," Jim Gormley recalled. "I had great respect for him. He told me to get my education first, then think about baseball if I was still interested. I was playing for the Norwood Nitros in 1959, and some scout said something to me after a game. Marty waited till that man left and he asked, someone filling your head with dreams? He said, you are a good little ballplayer. There are hundreds like you. Someone might offer you a tryout or even a minor league contract. They will send you to someplace out west and you will play class D league where the lights are terrible and you will have trouble seeing the ball and if you do okay there you will go to the South and next year there will be a dozen guys fighting for the spot you want and the mosquitoes will make playing night games impossible, and you will be back here working in the Press with me. Get your education first."

Marty Callaghan spent half a lifetime chasing a boyhood dream. Teammate to Grover Cleveland Alexander and Gabby Hartnett in Chicago and later Harry Heilmann and Leo Durocher in Cincinnati, he experienced major league baseball during its roaring '20s, and curiously shares a major league record. He is one of just over a dozen men to have had three at-bats in one inning, which he experienced in the fourth inning on August 25, 1922, against the Philadelphia Phillies. Callaghan stroked two singles and stuck out, bettering one co-sharer of the record named Ted Williams, who remains the only man in baseball history to bat three times in an inning without getting a base hit.

Disparate seeds of a flowering national pastime: Electric trolleys and cable cars expanded access to local venues, formerly accessible only by foot, thus increasing attendance and its subsequent groundswell of interest. The proliferation of trains during the second half of the 19th century allowed distant cities to organize into national leagues. The telegraph and telephone enabled expanding daily newspaper coverage of local teams, but it was technological advances in radio, and then TV, which allowed every individual in the country to participate, solidifying baseball as a true, trans-national pastime.

"I listened to the World Series baseball game over the radio," a Nebraska farmer named Don Hartwell wrote in his 1934 diary. "The N.Y. Yankees beat the N.Y. Giants 18 to 4. One can hear the ballgame in N.Y. City from the radio (wireless transmission) in his own home. You can hear the crack of the bat and the ball hit the catcher's glove. Who would have thought it possible 25 years ago!"

The flourishing sport entered the war years, when not only social norms were challenged and often altered, but also players' personal circumstances.

"I didn't turn from a pitcher to an outfielder overnight, as some people seem to think," Babe Ruth wrote in his autobiography. "It was a gradual sort of thing, and I guess the old German Kaiser deserves an assist in my conversion. (Red Sox manager Eddie) Barrow probably would have been committed someplace if he had worked a 23-game winner in the outfield when he still had such players as Duffy Lewis, Chick Shorten and Jimmy Walsh on his team. But 1918 was one of those makeshift seasons. It was like 1944 and 1945 during the last war, when a manager had to make the best of the material he had left on his hands."

"The last full season that Lloyd and I played together on the Pirates was 1940," Paul Waner told Lawrence Ritter for his classic, *The Glory of Their Times*. "That was my fifteenth year with Pittsburgh, and Lloyd's fourteenth. Heck, I was thirty-seven by then, and Lloyd was thirty-four. Of course, we hung on in the Big Leagues with various teams for about five more years, but that was only on account of the war. With the war and all, they couldn't get young players, so I played until I was forty-two, and then my legs just wouldn't carry me anymore."

Waner is noted for an incident during those last five seasons when, on June 17, 1942, in quest of his 3000th hit, he hit a ground ball that shortstop Eddie Joost knocked down but could not make a play on. Waner was awarded a hit but convinced the official scorer to change the ruling so that his historic entry into one of sports' most exclusive clubs be inarguably legitimate. Two days later he lined a single off Pirate pitcher Rip Sewell to accomplish the feat. Overlooked is that had World War II not created the dearth of younger players, Waner never would have achieved 3000 hits at all.

The war years saw Norwood's Ray Martin and Charley Bowles make the big leagues. "I grew up on Mylod Street, Mylod and Washington on the corner white house, my grandmother and grandfather's house, that's where I lived," Bucky Sexton, nephew of Charley Bowles related. "My grandfather was David Bowles. I'm in the same mode, my dad was alcoholic, I grew up mostly with my grandparents. My mother passed in 1966 when I was twelve, which caused me to miss the Little League championship. In '66 we beat the Phillies with Joe Porcello. Another tremendous ballplayer, Joe Porcello. He had a tough senior year, he didn't have anyone hitting in front of him or behind him, and as far as putting a ball from centerfield, he was the best I ever seen.

"In the summer every morning I went to Endean playground and we had baseball games every morning, nine o'clock sharp. The Saads—everyone was different, we had Syrians and Portuguese and Irish, we had everything. David Saad was a really good, good baseball player, and that's how we learned. And I would play—the bigger kids would play at eleven, and I'd want to play with them too, I wanted to play with the older kids. Peter Trusevitch was older, Barry Dyke—remember Barry Dyke? Barry and his brother Kevin played. I played every day, two or three games. I'm gonna tell ya, if we didn't have enough guys to play, we'd play against the backstop. If you hit the ball to the lower—they had three levels of chain—actually four. If you hit the ball to the lower section of chain, it was a single. The second rung of chain was a double, third a triple, and top level was a home run. If you hit it over the backstop, everybody out, automatic, everyone was out. If you hit, say, a triple, and someone caught it falling, you were out. There was a skill level to it, placing it. So you'd try to find a spot for it. Sounds a little crazy, but it was great for hand-eye coordination, which is baseball.

"My grandfather pitched for Bird & Son, remember Bird & Sons? My grandfather David pitched, and this goes to 1914, 1915, somewhere in there. David was by far the best baseball player at the time. Franny, Francis Bowles, was the first son—there were six sons—he played third base for the mills. My grandfather was still pitching even then. Franny was killed during the Second World War; he was pushed off a troop train in Richmond and drowned. They found his wallet on the train. He was murdered, probably a robbery.

"Now comes Charley. Now, Charley grew up with my grandfather pitching for the mill,[27] and he learns everything about pitching. My grandfather had the longest fingers I ever saw, and Charley had 'em too. You can throw a curve ball better with longer fingers. Now he goes onto Norwood High in 1931, I believe it is. He goes on to his high school career until his senior year, nobody could hit him, gets the records for strikeouts with ninety-nine in nine games. Before he graduates, he goes to Braves field and pitches to Babe Ruth. When Babe Ruth was playing for the Braves. They brought him to an exhibition to see who wanted to sign him. Said Babe Ruth was nothing but a big kid, trying to tell him where to pitch it, where he wanted it pitched.

"He worked for the Philadelphia A's in the tail-end of '43, and in '44 he was in the minors, I think. In '45 he's brought up again. He ended up with a 1-4 record for that year. After '45 he came back to Norwood and they were gonna have an exhibition game at the Civic, and he hurts his arm in the exhibition game. Today he'd have Tommy John surgery, they didn't have that back then. Then he became a player-manager for a number of years, across the South. Atlanta Crackers. He said a lot of the things you see in *Bull Durham*, the movie, happens all the time. In fact, that was his favorite movie.

"My teacher was Snuffy Bowles. Snuffy was the fifth of six boys in that family. They all played baseball, they all pitched for Norwood High. He was my godfather, too. He taught baseball, everything you needed to know. Now, Snuffy played with Dickie Bunker, they were teammates. Dickie was a year ahead of him, they had a great pitching staff. That would be '53, '54, that era. Snuffy still holds the record, he struck out twenty-three in two consecutive games. That's the record, *has* to be. Course, no one keeps records anymore after Frank Wall is gone."

An examination of Charlie Bowles' career statistics reveals an astonishing example of one who refused to relinquish his baseball dream. Spanning eighteen seasons, he played for twenty-two teams in fifteen leagues, from the Welch Minors of the Mountain State League, to the Atlanta Crackers of the Southern Association, to the infamous Durham Bulls of the Piedmont League, to the Toledo Mudhens of the American Association, as well as two brief stints in the majors, both in Philadelphia

---

27 My father John Reddick worked at Bird & Son his entire career. In any discussion of work, the roofing plant on Pleasant Street was always referred to as, "the mill."

of the American League. His statistical reward for a lifetime of effort? Six hits, 51 innings pitched, and one win in The Show.

Batting cleanup is a Bowles' contemporary, of whom it could be asserted that World War II hindered as well as helped his baseball career. Jim Gormley wrote a chapter on Ray Martin for the publication, *Spahn, Sain, and Teddy Ballgame, Boston's almost Perfect Baseball Summer of 1948*, in which he describes the life and times of the star pitcher.

"Raymond Joseph Martin was born in Norwood, Massachusetts, on March 13, 1925," Gormley wrote. "His father was a house painter and later a night watchman at the Charlestown Navy Yard. His mother was a secretary at the Plimpton Press in Norwood. Ray was an only child.

"Martin lived across the street from a large field known as White Mike's,[28] named for the owner, white-haired Mike Curran. It was there that Ray developed his athletic skills, as his dad would hit fungos to the neighborhood kids... Each of the playgrounds in the community had a ball team, and Ray and the other young players rode their bikes or walked to all parts of Norwood for regular games umpired by the playground instructors. Many of these instructors were themselves former high school athletes.

"Opportunity abounded. There was a strong twilight league for boys up to 21 years of age, and there were playground teams for 'midgets' and 'intermediates.' There was also junior high baseball during the school year; the St. Catherine's school Ray attended, which went through grade nine, had a strong spring team as well as a summer CYO squad. Many of the other churches sponsored uniformed teams, as did various social clubs. Norwood was clearly a good place to grow up if you liked to play ball..."

Described in the article is Martin's outstanding tournament performance in which Norwood High School captured the 1943 state baseball championship. In the deciding game against Dalton in Fenway Park,[29] Martin struck out twelve in the nine-inning, six-hit, game-winning effort. Scouted by several teams, Martin signed with the Boston Braves on June 21, 1943. Once again, the dearth of younger players due to the

---

28 Fields referred to as White Mike's were the precursor to Father MacAleer playground, commonly referred to as Father Mac's.

29 Of note is that Crestwood Circle's Ed Praino, "whose induction into the Navy was delayed one week so he could play in the tourney," stroked the winning hit. Louis Parker's father Charley was also on the team.

war allowed players like Martin to prematurely stride onto a major league baseball diamond.

Ray Martin "actually did get into two games for Boston in 1943," Gormley wrote. "He relieved in the ninth with the Braves losing to the Cubs, 7-1, on July 2, and retired Lennie Merullo, Claude Passeau, and life-time .300 hitter Stan Hack on seven pitches. In his one other appearance, he pitched two innings and gave up three hits, a walk, and three earned runs."

The same winds that lifted the older Waner boys, however, blew ominous for any healthy youngster in 1943. But before the phenom's August Army induction he, too, brushed against baseball royalty.

"The eighteen-year-old Martin got to pitch to Babe Ruth that summer," Gormley wrote. "The Braves held an exhibition game for the war effort and Ruth, who retired as a Brave in 1935, pinch hit. A nervous Ray's first pitch was in the dirt. The second went to the backstop. 'Phil Masi, the catcher, called time after The Babe said something to him, and walked out to the mound,' said Martin. 'I asked what Ruth said. Masi said Ruth told him to remind me that nobody came to see me and to just throw one where he could get a good swing. I threw one belt high, and Ruth hit a long fly to the warning track for an out. As I passed the clubhouse after the game, I saw Ruth changing and heard him yell out, 'Hey Kid, nice pitch!' as he raised a beer bottle in salute.'

"He was shipped out to Europe in January 1945 with the Ninth Infantry," Gormley continued. "His unit marched across Germany, finally meeting the Russians at the German border eight days after the war was over. Martin's most intense battle experience came in March at the Remagen Bridge over the Rhine, where 50,000 Germans were attempting to retreat. 'We were under heavy artillery fire and only had about a minute and a half between shelling to get our troops across the bridge,' he recalled."

At age twenty-one, Ray Martin had already pitched in the major leagues and fought in World War II. But when discharged from the service, almost three of the most important developmental years for a professional baseball player had elapsed and he found himself in the minor leagues. Struggling through two losing seasons with ERAs closer to five than four, the Norwood native was brought up to the majors toward the end of the 1947 season. The callup, coming as it was post-war when major leagues were again flush with the best players in America, indicates Ray Martin's true talent. Jim Gormley describes the result.

"On September 27, 1947, Martin won his first and only big-league game, a 2-1 victory over the Brooklyn Dodgers at Braves Field. The Dodgers had already clinched the National League pennant, but still played Eddie Stanky, Jackie Robinson, Pete Reiser, Spider Jorgenson, Stan Rojek, and Duke Snider that day. Martin, number 24, gave up seven hits, walked four, and struck out two in the complete game." Ray Martin appeared in one MLB game the following season, before running out his career over three more minor league seasons. Despite the baseball-young age of twenty-six, he decided to retire.

"'I really hated the minor league bus rides and I did not want to hang around the minors waiting for another shot at the majors,'" he told Gormley. "'I basically lost interest. I figured that since I did not have a college education, I should take a job with good training. I went to work for General Electric…After a couple of years I went to Picker X-Ray and stayed with them more than 30 years as a sales manager, calling on doctors and hospitals throughout the Northeast."

Martin's MLB statistics include 14.2 innings pitched, 3 strikeouts, and 1 win. Like Marty Callaghan, Ray Martin's career contains an asterisk for the unusual. His is perhaps the most unusual ending to a pitching career in professional baseball history, mirrored by only one hitter.

Joe Pignatano was a .234-hitting backup catcher, whose eight-year career included only a few hundred at bats and a handful of home runs. On September 30, 1962, against the Chicago Cubs, in the last at-bat of his career, Pignatano came to the plate with Mets teammates Richie Ashburn on first and Sammy Drake on second. The catcher promptly lined into a triple play, becoming the only hitter in MLB history to end his career thus. Ray Martin, playing his last professional contest in Atlanta, was called into the game in the ninth inning with the bases loaded and no outs. His first pitch was fielded by the second baseman, the resulting action making him the only pitcher in baseball history to end a career with a triple play.

Norwood was thus represented at baseball's highest level throughout baseball history, but the best was yet to come.

On the evening of April 23, 1965, before 9,812 fans in Cleveland Stadium, Kansas City Athletics manager Mel McGaha pinch-hit in the top of the 7th inning for pitcher Jim Dickson. Up to the plate strode eighteen-year-old "Bonus Baby" third baseman Claude "Skip" Lockwood. The Ridgewood Drive kid was walked by Luis Tiant, and left stranded on first base at inning's end, concluding his MLB debut.

On September 23, 1968, in the bottom of the 6th inning in a game against the Cincinnati Reds, Pittsburgh Pirates manager Larry Shepard pinch-hit for Manny Jiminez. Up to the plate strode a raw, lean, left-handed-hitting third baseman named Richie Hebner.

"That's a good story," the Nahatan Street kid recalled. "It was a guy, a Latin guy, was up, called strike said something to the umpire, next pitch another close pitch called strike, guy gets thrown out of the game. It's in Forbes Field against Cincinnati, Jim Maloney's pitching, he's got about twelve strikeouts. Jim Maloney was a good pitcher. Patek on first. Larry Shepard's the manager, looks down, says Hebner get a bat. I says *oh shit*, I'm getting up there oh and two with Jim Maloney pitching. Two outs, I get in the box and Johnny Bench says hey howya doin' kid and I says *aaallll right Johnny*. Maloney takes a stretch; the first pitch is a pitchout and Patek gets thrown out at second. I walked back to the dugout and said the son-of-a-bitch didn't strike *me* out, did he! That's a true story! I don't think that's ever happened to anybody. It wasn't an official at-bat, but it was my first time stepping into the batter's box in the major leagues."

About this time in a local rink, I walked with my father out of the arena after watching my brother Gordon play in a CYO hockey game. In the nets that day for St. Catherine's was a lanky kid who did not exactly impress with his goalie skills. Frankly, he had played very poorly. Typically a man of few words and impeccably mannered, my father spoke up as we passed the goalie's father and namesake, Sgt. Bill Travers.

"It's a good thing he can pitch," my father said.

For most of the following decade, Norwood fans followed major league box scores that included three native sons who had simultaneously emerged from a golden era of Norwood athletics. Of note is that despite one renown as The Legend, it was left-hander Billy Travers who was the first and only Norwood kid selected to an MLB all-star team. Skip Lockwood retired after the 1980 season with arm trouble. Billy Travers retired after the 1983 season with arm trouble. Richie Hebner retired in 1985, having completed a playing career in which he was described by one baseball writer as "one of the best players in major league history never to have been selected for an all-star team."

Perhaps this chapter on baseball, inserted amidst a hockey narrative, tarries a bit after closing time. But its relevance is symmetry opposite that legion of Norwood youngsters who in the 1960s ventured onto the creek, or Froggies, or Pettee's, or Ellis Pond, or, if fortunate enough, Boston Garden ice, the words of philosopher Jacques Barzun an appropriate summation: "Whoever wants to know the heart and mind of America better learn baseball."

That's how the writer in me ends this chapter. This is how the Norwood boy in me ends the chapter: Hey, what do Norman Johnson and Bob Feller have in common? *They both threw no-hitters on opening day!*

THE COACH

Listen, son, goddamit. Let me tell you something and don't ever forget it. You play games to win, not lose. And you fight wars to win! That's spelled W-I-N! And every good player in the game and every good commander in a war, and I mean really good player or good commander, every damn one of them has to have some sonofabitch in him. If he doesn't, he isn't a good player or commander. And he will never be a good commander...games and war aren't won by gentlemen. They're won by men who can be first-class sonsabitches when they have to be. It's as simple as that. No sonofabitch, no commander.

— WW II General Lucien K. Truscott, to his son

Deliberate of speech but with a twinkle in his eyes...a hockey man through and through.

— Don Wheeler's *TioT* yearbook description, 1952

Perhaps no Norwood personality of the past hundred years engendered more fear, more awe, and more passion than the kid from Cypress Street. Recently—and almost a half century after having played for the man—I attended the wake of a former coach's wife at Gillooly's Funeral Home. Upon arrival and before entering, I was informed by *two* different people, "Don Wheeler's inside!"

There were players, very good hockey players, who could not play for the man, who simply folded under his brutal gaze. Others would not play for him. Stories of his demeanor are relayed in barrooms, at reunions, and on social media to this day. One tells of the long bus ride home after a tournament loss in the mid '70s. "We get home, but he doesn't get up from his seat. You know, he always sat in the front, behind the driver. When he doesn't get up, none of us get up either. We're waiting...and after what seemed like an hour he finally rises, turns to us and says, 'Well, I guess you can't turn chicken shit into chicken salad.'" Another '70s player chimed in on Facebook:

"Insight into why I am the way I am: As I was showering this morning, I remembered this quote from my Norwood High School hockey coach: 'I hate losing. When I play cards with my wife and lose, I tear the cards up and throw them in her face.' I am going to suggest to Bartlett's that it be added to its 'Famous Quotations' volume along with my own personal favorite: 'What are you so happy about? My grandmother in a wheelchair could have scored that goal!' (I subsequently used similar lines to instill confidence in my sons when they were 15 years old, since it worked so well with me) Last year this coach was inducted into the NHS Sports Hall of Fame. Go figure."

Jim Gormley was assistant varsity coach at Norwood from 1963 to 1970. He explained how he came to be involved with Norwood hockey and Don Wheeler.

"Dan Young had joined the program with Don," Gormley related. "Dan and I had played on the Nitros, the semi-pro baseball team, and Dan was second baseman and I was the shortstop, and Dan had played up at Bates. He had played for Burrillville in high school, so he had very good coaching. He had Eccleston as a coach. Don came to me and he said, would you be interested in being freshman coach? This was '63-'64, and I said I'd love to. It paid $300, and that was probably a good portion of my tuition as a day student at BC. I couldn't believe it. I remember getting the check and giving it to my mother, I think it was $250 a semester. I honestly don't know if there was a freshman team before this.

"So I became the freshman coach, and I was also the assistant varsity coach. And they didn't have anyone to work with the goalies, so I got drills from books and other places. I'd go to watch BU, and watched a lot of BC practices, Northeastern, and BU when they were playing at the Boston Arena. I'd watch some of their practices, and so I'd pick up ideas. I remember Don, Dan Young, and I went down to Burrillville for an all-day conference, it was a coaching clinic. It was all his drills, too. Tom Eccleston had been the football, hockey, and baseball coach at Burrillville High School, and Dan Young was a very good X's and O's guy, and as Frank Wall said, Don Wheeler was the drill instructor!

"This is the way you wanna do it, this is the way you wanna do it. That's the way Don was. He wrote every practice out in ten-minute blocks. And I never forgot that. As long as I coached, I would write out what my practice was gonna be and put it up with a piece of tape right at the door where they were going out so everyone knew what we were gonna do, and it just saved a lot of time and explanation. And they knew the drills, so it just made it a lot easier. Dan and Don and I used to meet regularly and we would go over strategy, and who should be playing where, this sort of stuff. And Don to his credit just gave me the freshman team and said, you coach them. He said, I can't be there, I may come to watch now and then but the varsity's my thing.

"The first practice I had at Norwood High was at ten at night, and the bus left at eight o'clock. And I said come dressed, that's always the thing, you come dressed, so all you have to do is put on your skates. It was Tabor, or Noble & Greenough. Those were the two places basically where the JVs practiced. And once Walpole opened, we'd get some ice up there, but it was cheaper at Tabor, or Noble & Greenough. It forced me to learn to take control and try and teach them the system Don was using. And I stayed with Don through the 1970 season.

"Don was very organized, very structured, and everything had a purpose. And he believed in breaking down, he'd say to me or to Dan Young, go down and work with the forwards, you've got fifteen minutes, and he'd be working with defensemen. And he'd also give me time with goalies. And we usually had three goalies, we'd want all the goalies to know all the goalie drills. I coached the freshmen for two years until Dan Young transferred. He got into counseling, I think. I'd often take kids from varsity practice over to a JV practice and go through drills. Put 'em in the car, and take 'em over to Nobles, or Tabor, places where we primarily had ice. And I enjoyed it.

"I think part of it was the Marines. He was a Marine officer in the '50s. It was absolutely a big part of his life. He was a good coach. He wasn't afraid to make a decision, either. I remember the time I caught Richie Graham parking. Bobby Donahue called me. He was making the calls that night and he said, coach everybody checked except Richie

Graham. I said okay. I said, Bobby, do you have any idea where he could be? And he said they have a dance at St. Catherine's, I said to Judy—we were watching TV—I said I'm going to go out for a bit, I got a problem with one of the hockey players.

"So I picked up Bobby, went down to the dance and Skipper Connolly's mother was chaperoning. Have you seen Richie Graham tonight? She said, checking on the boys? I said yep. Oh yeah, he left a little while ago, but he didn't go home, and he left with a girl. So I looked at Donahue, and I said where has he gone? And he said, don't ever tell anyone I told you this, but probably FM road, Factory Mutual Road. Cuts through Pleasant Street to 1A, that's where they go parking. I picked him up and said, we're gonna go find him. We were playing Walpole the next night. So we go down there and he said, I think it's his car. So I said Bobby we gotta be sure, so we swung by his house. He lived on 6th Street, or 1st Street, 6th Street I think it was. We went by and his car wasn't there.

"So we pulled up, you couldn't see anything. We flicked the lights and I said oh my God, it's Richie. I said, get your ass home *now!* Just then, a cop car pulled by. I forget who the cop was, but he recognized me, said what are you doing down here? He said who's that with you? I said Bobby Donahue. I said we have a hockey player in the car over there.

"He said sunnafabitch! I have a bet with a Walpole cop on tomorrow night's game! He said you get the hell out of here, I'm gonna clean up the whole street. It was Keystone Cops, there were snowbanks like this high, there were a number of cars there. And Bobby says to me, Coach, get out of here! If it ever gets out that I was with you when the cops chased everybody out, I'll be dead in school! I said okay, but let's make sure first.

"So we waited, and the car didn't start. The cop comes up to me, he said what do you want me to do? I said that car there. Has one of my hockey players in it. We're playing Walpole tomorrow. He said I *know;* I have a bet with a Walpole cop on the game! He said, I'll clear 'em all out! Bobby said, get outta here! If I ever get identified as the guy who shut down FM on a Friday night...

"So we played, and we won. And Monday we had practice over at Harvard, a scrimmage against Melrose, and I came over from BC and Don said, why didn't you tell me? I said Don, if I told you, I know what you would have done. I said he was humiliated; you do what you have to do now. He broke the rule. And I said if I had told you, I know what you would have done. So I kept it quiet until now. He didn't criticize me; I did what I thought was best for the team. Go ahead. So he suspended him. He was suspended for the next game, which I think was Framingham North. A little easier game. (laughs)

"He was always trying to learn. He was open to talking about drills. He and Dan Young and I used to sit together all the time and talk about it. One thing I learned from him is that defense comes first. If you're strong in goal and strong with your defensemen, no matter what else you have, you'll be in some games you shouldn't be, and you'll win a lot of them.

"The '72 team? Hey, you have a team like that, you have to take off your hat to the head coach. He had standards, and you met the standards. That's all he wanted. He figured, you play guys who really wanted it. He could take any kid if they really wanted it, he could make him into a capable hockey player. But he said, *they've gotta want it!*

"That's the thing."

Caution is warranted in drawing any definitive conclusions about Don Wheeler. Opinions of the man are so varied and so strongly held, that all deserve consideration. Perhaps the fairest way to assess is simply to convey the words of his players, and let conclusions fall where they may.

Bucky Sexton: "I'm gonna tell you, for me, people say I'm crazy, but I played baseball for Wheeler on that JV team and I think he was the best coach I ever had. He didn't have the baseball knowledge, he wasn't a baseball man, he was a hockey man. But he had field command of *everything*. He treated everybody exactly the same, everyone."

Charlie Donahue: "Don Wheeler was fair, he treated everyone the same. He treated *everyone* like shit. I didn't know anyone who ever played for him that didn't respect him in the end. He cut seniors so sophomores could play."

Rusty Tobin: "I remember the great players, well, very good players that got cut because they wouldn't fit into Wheeler's, the way he wanted to play. Two off the top of my head are Jimmy Scott and Billy Turner. Both were very, very good. And I think Mike Falcone would have played at Norwood, but he also was an individual. I know he got cut and then didn't go out after.

"That happened to a lot of people, I think. Billy won't tell you, but he butted heads with Wheeler the whole time, well I can do it my way, you know, that type of thing, and Jimmy was like that too. He was on the team one year and then got cut. Jimmy Scott. He's FBI now, I think. Billy did all right too, Fire Marshall. But they butted heads. Jimmy was very skilled, but whatever Wheeler said he'd almost do the opposite. I played with Jimmy in leagues after, on teams after, he always regretted it. Yeah, he did. He said that is one regret, I should have listened to him."

Leo McInerney: "In '64, he cut a whole bunch of kids. And you know what? They went and played on the CYO team and went undefeated and won the whole thing. It was Billy Kelley and Tony O'Day, Gary Crowell, Jeff Story, there was a whole bunch of them, good players. He always cut a senior, he cut Petrovek our senior year, I think just as a message. Pebbles was another one that got cut as a senior! And Pebbles was a decent forward, not a stud, but a decent forward. Him and Billy Pender. Billy was a defenseman, Pebbles was on that '65 team that went to the state finals, and he got cut as a senior. I remember the Ranalli boys, I think he cut Pudgy, Mario, I think he's another one he cut in '66. I think he was just sending a message. I said to Jimmy Gormley one time, I said I was afraid he was gonna cut *me* my senior year! And he goes nah, he wouldn't cut you, and I'm like, yeah, he would cut *anybody!* If he thought it was gonna send a message, he'd do it!"

Peter Brown: "I remember Don stepping on Davey Katchpole's stick, cuz it was curved. Davey's junior year, and he cut him his senior year. That thing about Don that I always had a problem with? Was that. Davey Katchpole should have been on our team. That was Don's thing, you had to be able to take the heat. Normal people can't! You're a normal person, we go in we're like normal, you're smiling—*don't smile!*—and it changes ya! Don taught us how to win, he didn't teach us how to lose. And if you never lose and never learn how to lose, losing can throw ya. And it's an acquired skill to be able to lose and come back the next day without carrying the piano of loss on your back. In the long run it keeps with the theme of accept no excuses, but in life you're gonna experience loss. And not teaching us how to lose—which was his point, *I'm not gonna teach you how to lose, it doesn't even exist*—but for normal people, normal people couldn't. Wouldn't have hurt anything to keep those guys, would have made a big difference in their lives. That's a bitch I have. Our junior year, guys that were getting cut could play on any team. Borderline guys he would shitcan. They all would have played!

"That's the side of Don that's hard to reconcile. That he would take no prisoners. That was pretty dramatic. I think my senior year I knew I was gonna make the team. (laughs) Don Wheeler couldn't exist today. The self-entitlement? He'd be incarcerated. But clearly, the overarching theme with Don is he took hungry, tough kids, that's what he wanted, and when he had us, he still wanted that. Maybe like five years after us, he was used to more talented players, but he wasn't like oh good, let's pass the puck around, I'm glad you're very skilled players, I'm glad you can skate, I'm glad you're good hockey players, you can pass the puck, but you guys, you're not Timmy Twomey! I'm glad you can pass the puck, I'm glad you're a good hockey player, you're not ah, Tom Shea, or whoever.

"We're nine and oh, we beat Dedham," Peter Brown continued. "On Monday, he skated our balls off because they got two goals in the third period. He went off a few times. For some reason, if we had beat 'em ten to nothing he would have found something to bitch about. Does that excuse it? Not really, because it sucked. I got a few more of those that I chock up as a bad experience. And in a family growing up, are you gonna have bad experiences? Yeah. But overall was it good? Yeah. But overall, would I have wanted to play for Wheeler? Yeah, absolutely. Would I have had him be a different person? Yeah. Do we all have some stuff we gotta work out? Yeah. But overall, were we better off coming through that family? Yeah."

Richie Hebner: "He was all right, he was in the Marines, tough guy. I did a banquet where they honored Don, and I said Don, you could have a birthday party in a phone booth with all the friends you've got, and he broke up, he broke up! He was tough, I mean, we had drills, I don't know what the high school kids do now, but we'd push nets. We'd leave practice and we'd say this guy's a complete asshole. But he got the most out of everybody, they produced."

Paul Angelo: "Don was very fortunate, because the kids could handle discipline. He would have been a *loser* if he kept on coaching, because you can't discipline kids today. Now you can't even yell at them. He was tough, but kids respected him. They came from houses where you couldn't go home and tell your parents you screwed up, they'd give you a backhander. Today you go home and say the teacher did something and you have the police and the lawyers and everyone else...

"You were always terrified of making a mistake with Wheeler. It was stifling. That's the only thing I can criticize him for. That's the only thing I can ever say. Charlie Cinto won a state championship because those guys were loosey-goosey. Don taught you how to work hard, he taught you how to play hockey, he taught you discipline. Everything. He was a DI, and don't forget, he played club hockey in college. He traveled everywhere to play; he loved the game. Oh! He loved it! I think he loved the game more than he loved anything in the whole world."

Billy Sullivan: "I thought he kind of tensed me up a lot. I played a lot better when I was out of high school. He just got me all wound up. Some guys flourished with that. I don't know. I have no hard feelings about it, that's the way it was. But he got the best out of us, that's for sure."

Rusty Tobin: "I mean Norwood wasn't easy on your practice, I mean, if you were easy, you'd go sit down. You know how Wheeler was, he'd go Tobin you're up, one-on-one, send two guys in, and you'd hustle back and give Wheeler the puck, and he'd go Tobin again, you know? I got so mad once I shot the puck at him. I think he said something, he made me sit down, and said something like I'm glad you don't have a very good shot. Not in front of everybody, he was skating by when I was sitting on the bench.

"I didn't think he thought much of me. Well, he didn't like me. He didn't like anybody. He wasn't a pat-on-the-back coach. I heard he became that later over at Xaverian, but he certainly wasn't with us. But we would skate through the boards for him. So he had my respect, but I probably didn't like him very much. I wouldn't hang around with him, let me put it that way."

Ken Reddick: "I had the best game of my career against Mount St. Charles. It was a regular scheduled game, it wasn't the Bay State League, but it was treated like a regular season game, and I scored five goals. Best game I ever had, and the next day I was in the dressing room with Rusty I think, and for some reason everyone else was out on the ice except the two of us, and I was laughing and Wheeler comes in. He gets right in my face, *you think you're hot stuff? You think you're special? Get out there!* And then he got in Rusty's face. I don't have anything bad to say about Don Wheeler, I mean, he was a task-master, but he always treated me fairly."

Dennis Hebner: "Well, Wheeler had his favorites. I mean, Jackie and Neil were his favorites. And I thought Rusty Tobin was as good a defenseman as Jackie Cronin. I thought he was, but he was kind of a fuck-off, and Wheeler didn't like that, so he never really praised him. Rusty hardly ever made a mistake, I thought. I thought he was a *great* defenseman. But Wheeler just stayed with Jackie and Neil. Who else, even Begley, Bobby Begley, he never gave him credit either and he was a pretty good defenseman. Everything was Jackie. I mean Jackie was definitely good, but shit you can't do it alone, you gotta have other guys to help ya."

Jack Cronin: "As you compile, you realized that no one said anything good about Don Wheeler, give me a call, all right? I can give you some good stories about Don. I was fortunate. I had some place to go after Norwood High School. My career didn't end at Norwood High School. So anything negative that transpired at Norwood, I had the opportunity to, at least internally, improve on. So I mean if my career ended at Norwood, my hockey career, yeah, I might feel differently.

"One of my best friends who you would benefit talking to is Leo McInerney. Leo was actually a very skilled hockey player and Wheeler didn't cut him, but Wheeler wouldn't play him. And Leo carries that with him, he can't stand Wheeler, he'd be someone who could fill in a lot of blanks. He was there, he knew all the guys, and he, truthfully, when I talked about being blessed, I mean, I was blessed because I had the support of a lot of people in town, but I for whatever reason was able to play hockey and I was treated, I'd like to say I was treated like everybody else, but I wasn't. Leo would be the first to say Wheeler would yell at you, Wheeler would yell at me, but he'd do it in a different way. He wasn't damaging my ego when he yelled at me. At least it didn't feel like he was. A lot of other guys, I guess you'd say they were abused.

"But there was also the type of player, and I can name two, that did flourish with him, and one was Tommy Shea, and another one was Kevin Murphy. Neither of them had high skills, but they both worked their ass off and Wheeler... It was almost like if you worked hard, he'd overlook your mistakes. And if he thought you weren't willing to give, to spill your guts, he didn't care how good you were."

Neil Higgins: "He also, when things were going real good for me, he'd say you can do better. Yeah. Yeah. And here I'd get a little angry, and then I'd say, he's right. I *can* do better, I can do better, I need to work harder in practice. That's what he taught me. And like I said to you before, he had us ready. For the ones who understood it, that bought into it, he had us ready for every single team we played. He told us what they were gonna do, he told us, you wingers you backcheck half-way, or backcheck all the way, because they're gonna do this. They're gonna do that. Defensemen, they are not gonna dump it in like we are. What you wanna do is play them toward the boards. Other defensemen, you go to the center net, cuz they're gonna spring someone center net. But once again, we were young boys. Our attention span back in those days was a good thirty seconds, and twenty-nine of those seconds was thinking about girls. So it, when we let it sink in, it worked. Nobody can say anything bad about the coach, in my eyes. I know people who'd say, well, he was good to me. Yes, he was. If I goofed off in practice, he would take me aside and read me the riot act. Same as my dad would. So, you know, did he call me out a couple times? Yes, he did. Did I want to get called out again? No I didn't. Why? Because he was right, and I was wrong."

Tommy Taylor: "Wheeler doesn't know how lucky he was. You know how you told how Gormley brought me up, I think it was after the fifth game? Gormley took me aside, go to Jimmy Scott's house and get his uniform. At that time, we were best friends. Do you know how hard it was for me to do that? He never played Norwood hockey again. Certain guys could play for Wheeler and some guys couldn't. I have to say this about Jimmy Scott, he handled it really well. If you were gonna go to college, he did nothing for anybody. I played for him for three years, and when it was over, he didn't say a word to me. Didn't come over and thank me, nothing. Dickie Donovan loved him. Dickie thinks he was the best thing since sliced bread."

Jerry Drummey: "I hated practice, and I was lazy. I played varsity my sophomore year for six or seven games then got hurt, didn't inform the coach I was hurt, and then the next thing I know there was a knock on my door and your neighbor Gary Sortevik who says, coach wants me to take your shirt. (laughs) That's how I got cut. I get it. I didn't put the time in, you know? I loved playing the games, but I wouldn't put the time in for the practice end of it, in the off-season. I got what I deserved. Jimbo Scott and I got axed the same day. It was a terrible thing, I mean I was home in bed with a concussion, and I never informed the coach that I had it, and Sortevik, I wasn't playing well, so I deserved to be replaced. But it was just the way he went about the thing, you know? Kind of, what the fuck are you doing here? I mean Gary saw the look on my face and he said sorry, the coach told me to come down and get it. Don gave me a fair shake. He was fair to me, as fair as can be. I didn't deserve to be there and I accepted that, but it was just the way he went about the thing."

Ken Reddick: "The same thing happened to me. When I was a sophomore, they made me go up to Timmy Armour's house and get his shirt."

Dickie Donovan: "We had arguments, you know, but not all the time. I realized I got to skate in Boston Gardens, you know, a little kid from Crestwood Circle, and I'm skating in front of 13,000 people and I'm in awe of the whole situation. And we wouldn't be there without coach Wheeler. A lotta people still got some negative thoughts about Don, but we wouldn't have been there all the time. Don forced you to do one hundred and ten percent of what you even thought you could, and I appreciate that now. When I got to college, I appreciated what he had done. All the other kids at Bowdoin College, they were good players, but they didn't have the work ethic, you know, I saw this in high school.

"Tommy Taylor was a good player. Tommy and I scored ninety-nine points between us in 1969, more than any other tandem in the history of our school, by far. I say Tommy, without him pushing us, there's no way we'd a-done it, no way. Well, playing hockey in front of that many people was the most, it was thrilling. To succeed on that level with thousands of people watching you, year after year we would win fifteen games a year, that's a sign of success. That's why I say Don Wheeler was a heck of a coach. He pushed everybody to be better than they probably thought they could be."

Bobby Rosata: "Someone told me recently Dickie Donovan liked him. I was surprised by that, because I thought he tortured Dickie Donovan, but maybe I'm wrong. Don was, Don would be arrested today, right? (laughs) Don never had that soft side. I mean maybe a little when you went to his house in Dover, but even that was all business, look at this guy, take your shoes off, he didn't have that soft side. He was yelling and screaming, I remember pushing that net and him standing on top of me screaming at me, you pussy, whatever, and digging his skates in to hold back and puking in middle bucket, I mean, the guy was a certified crazy. I think because I had older siblings, I think I was a little more worldly in high school than my friends, and that's why I think that senior year, screw this guy, he's out of his mind. I'm just gonna enjoy hockey and play well, and I felt like I did that. It wasn't easy playing for him. He didn't talk to us! He talked to maybe Bobby because he was captain, Arvidson did his talking. Any message from Wheeler to me was from Arvidson."

Outside eyes had both negative and supportive views.

Catholic Memorial's Ray D'Arcy: "We heard that about that (that Don didn't help get guys into college), but mostly when I used to watch Norwood High hockey I'd watch and go, gee, all they're doing is throwing the puck in the zone, and Joe Quinn would almost not allow you, unless you were changing lines, to throw the puck in the zone. He'd say, you gotta make a play at the blueline. He goes, your most important area on the ice is five feet before the blue line and five feet after the blue line. Don't give the puck up to the other team, do something with it, make a play with it, and that was one of the big differences I thought between the style of hockey we played, and what I observed Norwood High playing.

"Course certainly there were guys like Dickie Donovan, you know, Dickie could handle the puck with anybody. But by and large the wingers that Norwood had, Wheeler would have them just throw it in the corners and chase it, bang in the corners and not learn any skills, and that's the skills that we learned at CM.

"Tommy Shea, there's a guy," Ray D'Arcy continued. "I was trying to think of the epitome of Don Wheeler players, it was Tommy Shea! (laughs) Yeah, Tommy Taylor, they were all in great shape, they worked really hard. They won a championship, but at the end of the day, for me, and I'm sure Zeke Doyle will say the same thing, it was more about high school hockey. It's more about the college hockey level, and particularly the Division One hockey level, where Joe had and still does probably has the reputation for putting more kids not just into college hockey, but Division One college hockey."

Arlington's Joe Bertagna discussed coach Eddie Burns' role in college admissions, the logic of which was readily applicable to Don

Wheeler. "I don't actually recall him playing a major role in that, and I don't mean that as a criticism as much as just an actual memory, I think most people were on their own. The program had a good reputation and because you also played so deep in the schedule, and you got those headlines and you played with the big crowds, if anything, the success he fostered in the end put you on a stage where you were gonna get attention. So it wasn't necessarily him sitting down and writing letters and making calls and I don't know if he did that, I wasn't aware of it. But he still gets credit for creating the success that by definition put you in front of a lot of people."

Alex Skene: "As I got older, watched, played more hockey and played with different players, played with and against some guys who would play Division One and even some pro hockey, you begin to realize there are some subtleties to the game we weren't being shown, or were not being impressed upon us. I mean, like, Mikey Martin, but Mikey was on a different level. He could do things, he had that sense of how to, I mean you don't have to go full speed and run through walls all the time. The ability to change speeds, and know exactly when to move the puck, the sense of *exactly* when to move the puck, and where. The timing, you know, none of that was taught, but we all had more skills because we played a lot more hockey than some of his previous teams."

Mike Lydon: "I told you the story about what he said to my mother! My mother was worried about it, she thought we were drinking out at the cabin, of course she was right. So she went to a PTA meeting, first one she ever went to in her life I think to check up on me, and Don Wheeler's my Earth Science teacher. So she's sitting there and Mr. Wheeler comes by and she goes hi I'm Anne Lydon, Michael Lydon's mother, and he goes *God damn it Mrs. Lydon he has to be more aggressive on the ice!* She goes, *I'm not here about his hockey, I'm here about his schoolwork!* Goes, oh...

"I didn't like him mainly for what he did to Mark Flaherty. Mark was a close friend. Mark was playing on the varsity since he was a sophomore, and he hurt his ankle and he went to my father and my father taped it, put him on crutches and told him not to skate for two weeks. Mark went to practice and was in the stands, he's sitting up there with his crutches. Wheeler told him go in put on your uniform and get out and skate and he ruined his ankle for the year and couldn't skate again. I said fuck that, I'm not playing for this guy. My father was pissed too about that because he told him not to play. Don Wheeler right now, he'd be in jail! He'd be like the nuns at St. Catherine's! Sister Alvera and Don Wheeler in the same cell! My money'd be on Alvera!"

"What I got from playing for Don, it wasn't about Don," Phil Nolfi said. "Because I can remember him yelling at the referees, *you're ruining it for these kids!* He never got in a fight about his ego, or what he wanted to do. He, wanted, Norwood, to, win. I think he wanted to beat Arlington.

"But you know, looking back, it was great. We were lucky to live through it. People don't experience shit like that, it was unbelievable! The hockey thing was such a big thing back then, there was so much stuff going on. The CYO team won two or three championships. The junior varsity was undefeated, our freshman teams, I think we were like 16-1. Something like that. Your freshman team was undefeated. Norwood just had tremendous hockey players. But to get to Don one more time, the guy was just successful. And I used to hear complaining about him, I started dating Donna and I can remember telling her at the time a lotta guys don't like the coach. But I remember saying you like skating in Boston Garden though, don't ya? Because he keeps getting you there.

"One thing that I learned, even as an eighth grader playing for the freshman team, don't take it personal. Cuz Don's gonna yell at everybody. He's not gonna pick you out of the crowd. I was scared shit of him when I'm in eighth grade, I was thinking I'm not gonna play for this guy, I won't be able to make it! Then I started looking around, he's yelling at him, he's yelling at him, he's yelling at him, he's yelling at *him!* So if he yells at me, so what? Maybe I should be honored! Because if he didn't like me, he wouldn't be talking to me at all!"

Frank Baglione: "Paul Riley also couldn't play for Don. Paul was a damn good skater but couldn't get along with Don. He had a girlfriend and she was damned good-looking, I don't blame him... He ruined Paul, but Paul didn't need Don. Even at a young age, Paul was a very intelligent guy. Paul said fuck this."

Peter Tamulionis: "I *loved* Leo McInerney. As a matter of fact, when he graduated, I took number three because Leo wore it. And I think, honest to God, and I think Wheeler hated Leo. I don't think he liked Leo at all. I don't think he liked him. He hated Eddie Graham, I know he hated

Eddie Graham, did Eddie Graham end up quitting him? Did he ever finish playing hockey at Norwood High? I can't remember. I can't remember. But Leo and Eddie were two of a kind.

"Leo was a good hockey player, I'm tellin' ya. He was a hot shit and he laughed a lot, but he was a hell of a hockey player. I know he was, and Don didn't play him, he didn't play him. I never understood it, I've never understood it. Who are we to question? Leo was a hell of a hockey player, and I'll never take that away from him, he could skate and he could play. Oh my God, oh my God! Wheeler just never freakin' smiled. *Never.* He's just a, you think about it now, he's just a pissed-off man. You know, I'd still be afraid to go talk to him! Honest to God, I mean, we're grown men, but I still think it would be a little nerve-wracking to talk to him!"

Bobby Thornton: "The Donahues were very close with him, and they would invite him every year up to Walpole to the Friends of St. Patrick, every St. Patrick's Day. And he would go up there and he would be there at the table, I'd talk to him, and we'd wind up going to the Barleycorn afterward. And I wanna tell you what, so we're sitting down there and it's funny. If you had told me I'd be sitting there with this fucken guy at the Barleycorn…and what did we have in common? We both were drinking the Green Hornets! Don Wheeler loved Heineken! We're both drinking Heineken. Next thing he's up there getting fucking rounds, I'm going, what the…and you know what? He just wanted to talk!

"I think his thing was, he was Mr. Discipline when we played for him, obviously, to an extreme, you know, passionate, to an extreme, but teaching you about the work ethic. It's my view, if you look at his numbers which are silly, you know they're stupid, the percentage of games he lost was like ten percent. It was stupid, but I think what he realized, back when we first started, there was some talent there, but they weren't deep. I think what he said was, look, I think for us to establish ourselves here, you know there were ten-minute periods, we had to come out like buzz saws. I gotta get these kids in shape and just run through walls, and if I can find people that will do that for me, there'll be some talent, but what we're lacking in talent we'll make up with desire. *Dee-sire*, that was his big word. And he designed a system that would allow for whatever you had to maybe succeed in that limited amount of time.

"Nobody was more pissed at him ever than me," Bobby Thornton continued. "We all had that in common. It was sort of a strategy. There's a name for it, I forget what it is, where the drill sergeant—it's like a common hatred you get for the CO, commanding officer. The guy that trains everybody, *everybody hates his guts!* So, it makes them come together. We have a common bond, and what is it? It's hatred of this bastard, right? I was not immune from that whatsoever. I think I told you how he started, day one –*day one!* —fourteen years old. It was not abusive to me, but he challenged me to the max. My thing was, he put me in there throwing the puck in the corner against Hebner and Shea, Hebner and Shea, the two biggest eighteen-year-olds on the team, and I'm fourteen-years-old, a freshman, and they're eighteen and seniors and big dudes, and I hadn't totally matured yet. And I'd do it and come out, and do it again and come out, and do it again, but then I had to get sick, legit. I started skating off with my head between my legs, and I don't know if he thought it wasn't legit, but then he said if you're gonna get sick, get sick right here. And I said sure, no problem, and I got sick and I said okay, got back in line. The thing is, not that I hated him for that, but he wanted to see if you had intestinal fortitude, those were his two big words. I didn't know what was inside of me as most of us didn't, and he had a good way of bringing it out. And part of that was getting in your face. Could some people have thought that could be seen as being abusive sometimes? Because he wasn't warm and fuzzy? Maybe.

"This guy brought it to a new level, that's the truth. And you know what? I have friends who started way above me and a bunch of other people, and they went away because they didn't want to pay the price or didn't like it. He challenged your limits. And this guy said, for me to do what I think I have to do to turn this into a winning formula, is get these kids in shape and just run through walls. And if I can find people that will do that for me, we'll succeed."

Alex Skene: "Playing for Don, you know, I always find it amusing, whenever I look back at team pictures, nobody's ever smiling. He pretty much skated us until we were cross-eyed almost throwing up. I remember one practice before the tournament, maybe we'd had a couple days off, but he pretty much skated us until we were cross-eyed falling off. I remember throwing up on the ice, and that was late in the season. I'm not talking about the first practice or anything. I mean, that's fucking ridiculous. You've already skated three months, and he's beating on you like that, I mean what was the point? There was a lotta dread when you knew that kind of thing was coming. I remember leaving the ice at the end of a practice and being so, throwing up in the locker room and being almost *blind*, I mean, on the edge of something, some other *reality* from the beating he put on ya. No high school coach would get away with that now. Was it a good thing? I don't know. I don't think so. I don't see if that accomplished anything. I don't really see what that accomplished. I mean, that doesn't really help. It doesn't get you into another level of shape. We were in good shape. You didn't need to throw up on the ice."

"Without a doubt," Peter Brown said, "what Don taught us is how to win, what it takes to prepare as an athlete. And what we thought—first of all, kids will never support an agenda in their best interest. You know what I'm saying? You wanna train, or you wanna go down Father Mac's drinking? *We're goin' drinkin'!* Not in your best interest! What Don taught us, or gave us an opportunity to get, either through just the repetition, and it wasn't like it was theory, and he wouldn't just say the words. It was about the repetition, of every day in practice. I remember, every day in practice, *whaddaya mean, we have to work our asses off every day?* Every, fucking, day. Every, shift. And he taught us what it takes to prepare, not just to be a good athlete, but to win. The overall thing is that he really taught us what it takes to win. Without any of the nonsense. You gotta do this. However, could it have been tempered? I don't know. You know what I'm saying? Would we have got this; do you get *this* without *this?*

"So, Don really gave us that. It's funny, down the Colonial, after Don's induction into the Norwood Hall of Fame, I'm saying, *I went to BU, after my first workout, when are we gonna start working?* Bobby Clifford said *same thing,* and Paul Angelo said, *I said the same thing when I went to boot camp!* Right? So he gave us that.

"For what we did and the league we played in, to be successful, his agenda was to be successful as a team, not have it so Mikey Martin or whoever gets seventy-five points this year. You know? And that's a gift. That's a gift. But it came at a cost of trauma. Do you get the gain without the trauma? So Don taught us really how to prepare, what you gotta do to win. There's no excuse. You don't give yourself an excuse, you push yourself beyond your physical... When I started, my first day as a freshman, I never thought I could skate four years every day in practice like this. If you asked me, is this what it's gonna be like? I'm like, *what? No...* This is what you have to do for four years? Well, I might play basketball... But that was a gift."

"I'll tell you a crazy thing, this just happened last week," Leo McInerney said. "I got up and I said to my wife, you're not gonna believe the crazy dream I had. And she goes, what? And I said I dreamt that I pulled a groin and I'm like, oh shit, Don's gonna find out I pulled a groin! I said if he finds out I pulled my groin I'm gonna be on the green line! And she says, Leo, *you're seventy. Years. Old!*

"That's the effect he had on people."

SPORT SLANTS

THE HIGGINS MASK

Norwood sings with the sound of stories. Don Kent, well-known WBZ weather reporter, once skidded during a snowstorm into the Andy Jewelers store downtown. Arthur Early told of playing third base at the Civic Center in the mid-1930s with Red Rolfe of the New York Yankees in attendance, who, after hearing it called across the field, inquired as to his nickname, *Bananas*. Reggie Smith moving to a house on New Pond and subsequent sightings around town were front page *Norwood Messenger* news in 1967. A photo of Senator John Kennedy, posing with Norwood firefighters, hangs upstairs in Paul Angelo's Olde Colonial Café. Debbie Dray, class of '68, tells of serving Alabama's George Wallace in Dandy Donuts during his third-party Presidential campaign in 1968. But no story is more bizarre than the night Red Sox first baseman Dick "Dr. Strange Glove" Stuart was introduced to a '72 classmate—in his Sycamore Street bedroom!

"I remember it quite well," Bobby Mulcahy recalled. "January 1st, 1964. My parents had dinner reservations for New Year's Eve at the Iron Horse on Rt. 1. He did something to piss her off so was told to take a hike, at which point he went there alone and bumped into Jack Mulvehill—he was my Godfather, Teddy's Uncle—my father and Jack Mulvehill were buddies. My father would talk to anybody, and they run into Dick Stuart and somehow convinced him to come back to the house! And then he had the gall—or lack of brains—to return after midnight, half in the wrapper with Stuart and Mulvehill, his partner in crime. Next thing I know, in the middle of the night, Dick Stuart is at the foot of my bed and my mother is going—let's just say she was not real happy. My mother could be tough...

"Stuart lived in Dedham right near Mary Hartigan's restaurant. What my sister Susan remembers most is my mom getting upset, which led to this 'congregation' being very brief. Mid-'60s, I was a Little League kid. It was still very cool as me and Susan were big Sox fans.

"My sister tells me that my mother was awakened, as we all were, by the commotion and said the following, paraphrasing, 'I don't care *who* you brought home you goddam fools! Get the hell out of here you bums!' Mom then proceeded to chase them out of the house. So then Mulvehill took Stuart to *his* house down the street to meet *his* two kids, Diane and Tommy... A lot of fun that night in the Mulcahy household! My mother ended up throwing them out! All my dad was thinking about was giving his kids a thrill...wish someone held on to his autographs!"

Crestwood Circle kids, unaware, of course, that a future baseball celebrity already walked amongst us, had their first sports celebrity encounter in 1961 when we heard that my next-door neighbor Mrs. Terrangio's cousin was visiting. All of seven years old, I had no idea who he was, but followed the "big kids" as we retrieved pencils and paper and approached en mass the Terrangio back door. After waiting turn on the steps, I entered the kitchen in which sat the grinning, accommodating gentleman. After leaving, I lifted my paper, looked down and read, "Jim Kaat."[30]

A handful of years later we again fell in line, this time to take turns peering in a cellar window of the Higgins house. The hush-hush, forefinger-to-lips demeanor of Dickie Donovan and Gary Sortevik suggested something nefarious. When my turn came, I peered into the cellar to see Mr. Higgins, his pipe hung from the corner of his mouth, grinning up at me before turning to a man lying on his back. Little did Crestwood Circle kids realize what we were witnessing would one day be featured in the Hockey Hall of Fame.

"We'd be in Neil's yard," Dickie Donovan recalled, "and Eddie Johnston's pulling up in a car. And an hour later Gerry Cheevers. Ernie made the first mask! We'd sneak in, we'd look down in the cellar, and they'd be lying on the pool table. We'd be on the driveway, they'd go walking up, I mean, a *real Bruin!* On Crestwood Circle! It was unbelievable!"

"There were quite a few people in the greater Boston and Norwood area that mysteriously needed hockey gloves, and mysteriously they got a package on their front door of brand-new hockey gloves," Neil Higgins remembered. "Some kids needed skates, mysteriously they got brand-new

---

[30] Jim Kaat was pitching for the Minnesota Twins in the first full season of a 25-year career that totaled 283 wins. He told my father that his dream was to play for the New York Yankees, which he did, 19 years later.

skates. He was notorious for that. There were, I think I might have been a freshman at BC, or I might still have been at Norwood High School as a senior, it was one of the first tragic shootings of a Boston police officer and he passed. He had a little boy named Johnny and Johnny and his mother were over at the Boston Skating Club, and the little boy could hardly stand up, and the mother was crying. Ernie found out who she was, and of course it was in all the newspapers and on TV, and he couldn't skate, and she couldn't understand why he couldn't skate. And Dad said, ah, it's a skate problem, don't worry about it. Next day there was a brand-new pair of sharpened skates that Dad said he found at a job site in Boston. Those were some of the things Ernie did that nobody knew about. I don't mind telling people about it now, Ernie would be upset with me that I did, but…you talk to Jimmy Gormley. Jimmy Gormley will say, one day Jimmy was a struggling schoolteacher back then, and a brand-new pair of hockey gloves appears, the palms were out of Jimmy Gormley's, I can go on and on about that."

Neighborhood kids were fortunate to gain insight beyond the plumber's largesse. Behind glasses and pipe was an earnest interest in developing responsibility in our young lives. One of my first memories of Ernie Higgins is at Tabor rink, lined up with several other six or seven-year-olds as Ernie went down the line, tying our skates. This went on for several weeks until one morning I heard Ernie saying, as he tied the kid's skates next to me, "You've got to learn how to tie your own skates like Donny Reddick, here," signaling, of course, that it was high time Donny Reddick tied his *own* skates. I immediately bent over and began. No one has tied them for me since. Recently I told my brother this story.

"I remember riding my bicycle by his house one day," Ken Reddick remembered. "It still had those training wheels on, even though I didn't need them, and Ernie yelled at me to get rid of the training wheels, that I was too old for them. I took them off that night!"

"He was always working," Neil Higgins continued. "When he wasn't working, I don't know where he found the energy, because he was a union plumber by day. We didn't have a whole lot, not many people on Crestwood Circle did. We didn't know we didn't have a whole lot, but we got an electric train set for Christmas because he went into housing projects in Boston during Christmas, the winter months, and all of their toilets and their water lines were all freezing up, and he would do that, overtime, and try to help people out. And somehow people would give him, they gave him a set of Lionel trains, and somebody gave him a piece of plywood and he made two-by-fours and made us a train set out of it, that was like the greatest Christmas present ever! He would work overtime, he went into Baker Chocolate, and they were big chocolatiers, and because he kept their equipment running and unfroze the lines, where they were busted, he repaired them, and this was after his job on the freezing high-rise, the open high-rise buildings in Boston. I remember him coming home with a great big block of chocolate, it was incredible! (laughs) But he was always working. He worked Saturdays and some evenings at Norwood Buick as a salesperson, just to make sure we had hockey equipment and a baseball glove and baseball bat. He was the one who made out of two-by-fours the nets that we had, with chicken wire for our street hockey games. All that stuff he said he found at the job site or was given to him at the job site. He was always doing something for everybody."

When his son became a goalie, he looked toward what he could do for him. A goalie's safety has always been of concern. "I remember during practice once I shot way too high," Ken Reddick remembered. "Didn't hit Neil in the head, but he had to jump up and it glanced off his shoulder. He came charging out at me! I told him it was just a mistake, but he was *pissed!*" Watching his son under fire no doubt prodded Ernie Higgins' imagination.

"I've always been interested in hockey having been born in Canada, and in my later years having a son of my own that was a goalie," Ernie Higgins explained in an early interview. "At that time when he was twelve years old, I had tried three different types of masks I had bought. I couldn't find a mask that suited me, and I decided to try to make one. I had tried many different types of materials and many forms, and I think I have the best product. It is a total impact mask. It sits like on an outer skin on the person. If the puck hits, the shock is distributed completely all over the face. And it fits so tight, that the eye holes can be cut to a minimum, and yet give perfect vision."

After creating for Neil a home-made mask, word quickly spread through the hockey community. It reached the professional level when

Neil attended a hockey school and former Bruin Ed Chadwick noticed his mask. He asked where he got it. "My dad made it," he was told, and Chadwick soon had one made for himself. Marcel Faille and Ross Brooks of the Providence Reds were fitted, as well as BU's Jack Ferreira and BC's Jeff Cohen. And in the era during which Stan Mikita introduced the curved stick and teammate Bobby Hull made it sing, goalies at the highest level began to take notice.

"I remember when Glenn Hall put on a mask," Gerry Cheevers told the *Boston Globe's* Dan Shaughnessy. "He had played way over five hundred straight games without one. We were playing at the Boston Garden, and he was at one end and I was at the other and Bobby (Orr) let a shot go and it went through a screen, and Hall had his catching mitt over his face and his stick mitt over his crotch and it hit the glass. And he put on a mask the next game.

"It got to a point where you just couldn't play anymore without a mask. My attitude was, if I can't find a mask, I'm never going to play. The first mask I had was developed by a trainer for the Detroit Red Wings. But if you got hit on the cheekbone, it would shift the whole mask and wreck your face, so when I was with the Bruins, Ernie Higgins and I got together and worked on one. We decided we needed a sponge inside." Cheevers played his first NHL game with a mask on Oct 11, 1967.

Boston Bruins teammate Eddie Johnston explained to documentary filmmaker Jerry Kelleher his impetus for acquiring what was then a novel piece of equipment, not yet mandated by the NHL.

"Well, when I got hurt in Detroit and was in the hospital for six weeks in a coma, I was forced to wear it," Johnston related. "Ernie Higgins name came up, and so I talked to him about it and he's the one that made the mask for me and thank God...I remember in goal in Chicago, and Bobby Hull got a semi-breakaway and Teddy Green give him like sort of a spear in the back, he let the puck go and it hit me off my forehead and it went through the press box. Ted Green says to Bill Friday, *outside!* Bill Friday says go look at E. J.'s head and tell me where... It took the skin right off. It went right through the press box, and Lynn Patrick was up there, our GM at the time, and missed him by about an inch, went right by his head. It ricocheted right off my head, and this much more and it would have killed me...no stitches, just took the skin off!"

"I guess I'd never be designing these things if it weren't for my son's interest in hockey and being a goalie, of course," said Ernie Higgins, whose sidelight admittedly keeps him so busy he "sometimes doesn't have time to breathe." Somehow the plumber with two jobs found time to perfect the process.

A consultation explained the preparation and fabrication of the molded mask. The client would lie down, face-up. A shirt box with an oval opening was placed on the goalie's face. A nylon stocking was placed over the hair. Vaseline was applied to the face and exposed skin. Cloth pads were placed over the eyes, with Vaseline sealing the edges. Straws were placed in the mouth to allow breathing. Ernie then mixed plaster of Paris and filled the box over the face. After the plaster had solidified it was removed, providing a negative mold of the goalie's face. Once a positive mold was created by pouring more plaster into the negative cavity, Ernie then began building layers of fiberglass cloth and resins, creating the mask. Ventilation and eye holes were perfected, and the finished product coated with a smooth resin.

"Some people get real nervous about the breathing." Higgins explained. "Then I don't plaster around the mouth until near the end." Billy Pieri recalled what many clients considered something of an ordeal.

"It was a process where you put the plaster of Paris over your face and you'd breath out of two straws, which I guess some people used to freak out when they did that. And they had it sit on your face to create a mold. And with that mold he would then do his fiberglass process of pouring the fiberglass into the mold and create different designs and stuff and go back to his office and get everything on your face. I thought it was a great mask. I got hit many times, sometimes you get hit and go down like you were hurt, you're like no, I'm not hurt, it was just really loud!"

"I was one of those early-on customers, I went up to Crestwood Circle," Norwood native and Harvard All-American goalie Brian Petrovek recalled. "I can remember the first time he put that Vaseline on my face, put that junk on me, put the straw—I was scared to death! That was pretty exciting, I remember my dad was there the first time I got it. He was afraid I was gonna freak out with all that stuff on my face. I didn't know what he was gonna do. I didn't know how long he was gonna keep that on me.

"Neil was probably the first one, but I was one of the early ones. I can remember Neil always had the best equipment; I can remember watching him play. And so I wore his mask through when I stopped playing, I never wore anything but. And Ernie would always give me abuse because I'd always cut open the eyes (laughs) and I can remember at one point he might have seen a picture of me playing at Harvard and I had a crimson-colored mask and I got some message through a third party that 'you're risking your eyes' or something like that. I think I had three masks made over the course of those eight years, and when I went to the L. A. Kings' camp, he made another for me as a backup."

"If I'm gonna make it, if I'm gonna have a career in the NHL, I gotta get a mask," Gerry Cheevers recalled in an interview. "Finally, I found Ernie Higgins and we made this mask. Ernie Higgins was quite a character. He came into the next practice, and he was all concerned about the reaction to me getting hit right in the nose. And I said, 'Well, we have to do something about the chips getting in my defensemen's eyes.' He thought I was serious!"

The most famous mask in hockey history, crisscrossed with magic-marker stitches to represent cuts the goalie would have endured without it, is a Higgins mask. It hangs today—to the chagrin of the Hockey Hall of Fame—on the bedroom wall of Gerry Cheevers' grandson. Doug Favell's mask, the first ever to be painted, and which was loaned to the Hall of Fame, is a Higgins mask. The last goaltender to play without a mask was Andy Brown, whose last NHL game was in '74, and last WHA game was in '77. By then it is estimated that Ernie Higgins had provided masks to two-thirds of NHL goalies, many of whom had trekked to Crestwood Circle. But the core of the restless plumber with the huge heart was unsatisfied with merely improving hockey equipment.

Self-acquired skill at molding casts allowed Ernie Higgins to branch off into the field of specialized orthopedics. He retired as a plumber in 1967 at the age of fifty-four, stating "I just decided I wanted to use my hobby as my business." While continuing to provide goalie masks, he developed specialty casts for those needing long-term recovery, including children with severe head injuries. He fashioned a lightweight, removable cast for Ken Harrelson's leg, and when Wayne Maki crushed Ted Green's skull, he made the special helmet used by Green the rest of his career. And Norwood sings with the song of stories.

"That was funny, I used to go to all the games," Mike Lydon recalled. "Dad brought me to the games. I knew all the Bruins, and I was a nut, and I remember after Teddy Green got Wayne Maki's stick off the head, and I knew Ernie Higgins was making masks and working with Green. Anyway, Teddy Green comes into Shurfine with his two kids they were getting an ice cream, and I'm starstruck. And he takes off, and I go running down to Henry McEwen, Henry you wouldn't believe who just came in the store! And he goes who? And I said Teddy Green! He blanches and he goes up and turns the lights off and locks the door, I go what's the matter? He goes you said Teddy Green was in here and I says he was, I didn't know there was a Teddy Green bank robber at the time! A notorious bank robber back then, and he thought he was getting robbed!"[31]

"A couple of years after high school," Ed King remembered, "I was helping out at a summer hockey camp at Four Seasons Arena. I noticed this one kid who pressed his stick with his upper hand against his abdomen when he shot the puck. When I spoke with him and explained how best to hold a stick while shooting, he took off his glove and showed me that he did not have a hand. He explained that a birth defect had left him with a functioning wrist, but with a truncated hand that terminated about an inch from the wrist joint.

"After practice I waited for him, his brother of about the same age, and his father in the lobby and told him about Ernie Higgins, the goalie mask maker from Norwood. I explained that Ernie might be able come up with a creative solution in the form of a prosthetic hand using the same techniques he used to create masks. I called Ernie and told him of the boy's situation, and he immediately agreed to help and felt confident that he could come up with a solution.

"Ernie made a mold of his brother's hand while holding a hockey stick and created a prosthetic that strapped to the boy's wrist in a clamshell design. This allowed him to manipulate the stick while shooting in a more natural motion.

---

31 Theodore "Teddy" Green was a Jamaica Plain native and bank robber, who had been released from prison in 1967. In 1970, when Ernie Higgins would have been working with the hockey-playing Teddy Green, the bank-robbing Teddy Green was selling cars in Boston, assuring customers, "Fords are reliable and have great pickup, which is why I chose them when stealing getaway cars."

"Needless to say, the boy and especially the father were overjoyed with Ernie's expertise and willingness to help. I remember the father crying with happiness when I met him again at the rink. I don't believe Ernie ever charged him for his services and just explained that he was happy to help and that the hockey community consists of a lot of good people."

"This is what I like to do," Ernie Higgins said to an interviewer. "It gives you a tremendous amount of satisfaction helping people with injuries."

In 1991, while researching *Dawson City Seven*, my novel about the historic 1905 Yukon team that traveled to Ottawa to compete for the Stanley Cup, I sat down with Ken Forrest, grandson of Dawson City's goalie Albert Forrest. During our discussion Ken mentioned, "We didn't know how big the story would become. You won't believe this, but we just threw Albert's skates out about five years ago. They'd been hanging down cellar forever, and we just threw them out." Those skates were Hall of Fame-worthy, their loss a mini-tragedy of hockey history. Never in imagination did I think a similar situation would occur two houses from mine.

"I didn't get my Higgins mask until after high school," Arlington's Joe Bertagna recalled. "First it was at his house, second time he had a studio on Rt. 1 in Norwood. He was kind of a character, and in his studio he had molds of the famous goalies that he had done. He would basically build a bust of your face and lay the fiberglass fabric over that, so he had this kind of ghoulish looking gallery of the goalies he'd made."

"I save all the molds of the pro and college players at home," Ernie Higgins stated in an old interview. "I don't bother saving the ones I've taken of high school goalies because their facial features change while they're growing."

When the Costello family purchased the Higgins house, much of the ghoulish gallery of goalie molds, the molded face casts, had been left in the cellar. I inquired as to their fate.

"Wow! I remember the masks now, hockey masks, right?" Nancy Costello responded. "That brings back memories. I lived there from when I was in elementary school till 1981. I think it was 34 Crestwood Circle, the yellow Cape Cod house with the two-car garage not attached to the house. Next to the Connors."

And what had become of the ghoulish gallery?

"My grandfather got rid of them," Nancy recalled. "I'm not sure where they went. Probably to the dump. Wish I could be more help."

1968

*I can't get no, satisfaction,
'Cause I try, and I try, and I try...*
— The Rolling Stones,
(I Can't Get No) Satisfaction, 1965

It became personal in 1968. Tables had seemingly turned when Arlington's five-year run of Greater Boston League titles was ceded to a strong Brookline team, and Norwood's substantial talent matured. Led by super-star seniors Neil Higgins, Jack Cronin and the sheer athleticism of Dennis Hebner, seasoned with the '67 state final run as well as emerging star Dickie Donovan, the talented, experienced, and yes, *ravenous* sextet was the best Norwood hockey team ever assembled. This team was strong, as described in the '68 *Tiot* yearbook:

> Under the leadership of Captain Jack Cronin were some of the best icemen in the state; All-Star goalie Neil Higgins, whose brilliant net-tending saved many a game and earned him 32 shutouts in 3 years, as well as the respect of all opponents; All-Star forward Dennis Hebner, a terror on skates, whose gargantuan frame made opponents think twice before they got in his path and whose clutch goals were a big reason that Norwood went to the State Finals; Bob Begley whose checking on defense and slapshot on offense provided back-up for Higgins and Hebner; Tom Shea whose hustle, desire, and speed was matched only by his strength and fore-checking. And of course All-Star defenseman Jack Cronin himself—one of the best players to pass through Norwood High in years. He proved to be a great all-round player, who knew how to combine thinking and instinct. His hustling, along with that of Hebner, earned them places on the Tournament All-Star team. Leo McInerney, Dick Donovan,

Tom Taylor, John Ranalli, and Gary Sortevik rounded out this fine team.

Leo McInerney discussed the dreaded process of making the Norwood varsity roster:

"I don't know how he did it with you guys, but you'd have to go downstairs down by the shop by the gym in the old school, and he'd have the list up there, these are the kids that are coming to practice tomorrow. You'd check out the list, and you'd hope, shit I hope, I brought my bag, I...and no explanation. At tryouts he'd skate you till somebody threw up!"

"Oh, I remember when we had the workout for the hockey team with Wheeler," Dennis Hebner recalled. "He'd work our balls off! Kids would be throwing up, and I'd get home and be so fucking tired, it was only like an hour and fifteen-minute practice, but you never stopped."

"With Wheeler the coach, it was almost like, if you want to be here, you're gonna pay," Jack Cronin said. "I can tell you a funny story. When I was a senior, Bobby Thornton as a freshman played, and at the time it was Begley and me, I forget who the other defenseman was. And I can remember him coming to his first practice. The season had already started, but they brought him up so it was somewhat of a big deal. And Wheeler's practices, he would always separate the forwards and defensemen, and he would, excuse my French, but he would always beat the shit out of us. He was incredible. But anyway, Bobby Thornton now was with the group. I didn't say anything, it wasn't my style, I just wanted to see how he reacted, and he reacted really, really well. But what I remember is him leaning over the boards and puking his brains out during the practice. That was like a badge of honor, and in my mind at that point, he made the team. He made the cut. There were a lot of kids that would find an excuse not to do this, because they were challenged so much by Don Wheeler. I don't think I ever even said that to Bobby. He went on to be a great player. He had what it took at that point, he just had to mature."

"You remember pushing the nets?" Leo McInerney asked. "If he didn't think you played well? Brutal. And if he was really mad at ya, he'd stand on the net? And if he was *really* mad at ya, he'd make you push Tommy Shea! He never let up. Shea outweighed us by thirty pounds. Today you'd be in jail, completely different world. It wasn't all great, it wasn't all horrible, it was what it was. We built a lot of tradition, though, and it's too bad what has happened to it. I remember when I went to college people were like, you played hockey at Norwood? *Jesus*, that's a hockey factory! The takeaway for me was we were really a great defensive team. It's really hard to come up with offensive players because of Don's influence, because Don's influence was on defense. If you keep the puck out of the net, you win games. Don knew defense was the name of the game.

"Don liked the throw-it-in and go-get-it guys," Leo McInerney continued. "He *loved* Tommy Shea. Loved him. Oh, yeah, just thought Tommy was everything that he wanted in a player. And I give Tommy all the credit in the world, he was the hardest working kid that I ever saw as a hockey player, but he wasn't, not to say anything bad about him, but he wasn't the most skilled guy I ever played with. That's the only thing he knew. That was the way he lived his life. Great shape, great shape. I mean, next to Richie, he was probably the most of a man-child I ever saw. Tommy was a great baseball player, too. Great baseball player. But he wouldn't play because they wouldn't put him on the varsity as a freshman. *I don't play JVs*, a little bit of an ego."

"Tell you who was a good guy," Tommy Taylor said, "Jackie Cronin. He was good to a lot of the guys; he was good to me. *Tommy, this is what it's all about, this is how to do this*, or if you were gonna get in trouble, he'd say start to toe the line a little. He was ahead of his time; he was just a special guy. Jackie Cronin is one of the nicest guys you'd ever meet."

"Like many games that I played in during that era, I don't remember the details," Jack Cronin reminisced. "I played as much as I physically could. I didn't come off the ice, and that was a different era, that's what they did in those days. And so in front of the net it was like hand-to-hand combat all the time, it was a real physical event for me playing, you know, getting the puck out, you know my responsibility which was explained to me a thousand times by Wheeler a zillion times, was cover in front of the net, and move the puck out of our end. It wasn't like you gotta score a goal, or you gotta do this or that, although in the state final game he did grab me, he grabbed me by my shirt and he was basically saying you gotta put the puck in the net and get this thing over with, which I wasn't able to do, but that's another issue. Arlington was a well-coached team that was hungry. And they were like the antithesis of Norwood. The Norwood team that I was playing on...they played I think because they loved the coach, and they were enjoying themselves, whereas—and this is just an opinion, I have no evidence other than anecdotal—that a lot of kids for Norwood thought they might lose their job if they didn't play well, or the coach would yell at them if they didn't play well, and it was almost like we were playing not to lose, rather than playing to win. That's a kind of strong thing to say, but I think that was a prevalent attitude."

"I used the same stick the whole fucking year," Dennis Hebner recalled. "I think it cost me five dollars and fifty cents back then. And the heal of the stick was always separating so every couple days I'd have to go down cellar, Elmer's Glue, put it in the vice, go down the next day and get it and it was nice and tight. Until it loosened up again. Used the stick the whole fucking year. The blade started like this, and was down to *this*.

"Did I get along with Don? No. No. Did anyone get along with Don? Oh, Jackie probably did. Don benched me one game. One of the games when Kenny was on the team, we were playing over at Loring Arena when I was on defense, and I just fucked up, I fucked up a play. I tried to go in and pinch the puck, and the kid went around and he fucking scored. We were ahead 6-0 at the time, and this is the second period I think, and Wheeler comes in after the period and starts yelling at me. *Hebner do you realize what you did? Neil lost his shutout!* I said yeah, but we're winning the game. *You're on the bench!* That's what I said to him, I said we're up 6-0, I said the main thing was winning. That's all he thought of. I felt bad for Neil, what he have, twelve or thirteen shutouts?"

"Your brother probably doesn't say much about this," Tommy Taylor said, "but the most underrated hockey player that ever came out of Norwood was Dennis Hebner. Dennis came from being a goalie, to a defenseman, to a forward, and he scored big goals, he'd go down and block shots. To come after his brother... I don't think Wheeler gave him enough credit."

"I think Bobby Begley got overshadowed," Neil Higgins said. "He was a good defenseman with a good slapshot, but he was overshadowed by Jack's prominence in the game. Dennis, I think everyone wanted Dennis to be Richie. Well, Dennis was a very good hockey player, but Richie was an unbelievable hockey player. On any other town or team, Dennis would have been a standout. But having Richie, no matter what Dennis did, even as great as Dennis was, nobody could live up to Richie. Richie was one of a kind."

"Let me tell you," Jimmy Gormley said, "Dennis Hebner was one heck of a hockey player for a guy who wasn't a good skater. I remember he was a goalie, Richie used to shoot on him all the time. But he wasn't a good skater and the thing that was going to hurt him as a goalie—I suggested to him you're not gonna beat out Neil Higgins. You can learn to play another position and be very good at it. I said I'm gonna play you at defense for now, you've got size and you can handle the puck pretty well, but you've got to work on your skating. And then the next year we turned him into a forward. And he scored some big goals for Norwood in '67 and '68. And he was like a third defenseman.

"In Don's system, the center would come down low and play fifteen feet in front of the net, and I said Dennis all you have to do is basically go from faceoff arc to faceoff arc and play the body at the top of the triangle. We called that the triangle, and there was no time to be worrying about sticks in there, there were stick on stick, body on body, and just keep tapping 'em, tapping 'em, don't trip them, don't knock them down, but letting them know you're right there. And he was excellent, because he would block shots. He was a tough kid. He was fearless. And he had a great shot. I'll tell ya, he...he was never a great skater, but he was a competitor. He could compete. It was the same in baseball too. I mean, he could hit a ball! I have tremendous respect for him as a player. And I have tremendous respect for him now."

"He was good, he was good," Dennis Hebner said of Neil Higgins. "He was trained to be a goalie; he was like a robot. He loved hockey, his father loved hockey, so his father probably knew he couldn't skate that well, he says I'm gonna make you a goalie, and he made him a goalie. He was like artificial intelligence. Really. I mean he was a *great* goalie, I mean, he was the whole backbone of our team."

Rusty Tobin had seen chafing develop in previous years. "I can imagine what Dennis said about some people. Dennis and Neil didn't get along great. Fact, as you know the hierarchy of the, the older you get you sit in the back of the bus, and Dennis sat more with us than he did with the juniors. And Jackie always sat with Neil, they were best friends. Neil and Jackie got a lot more accolades than Dennis, and Dennis deserved them.

And truthfully, Dennis was one of the best hockey players around, he was terrific. And of course, Richie squashed any comparisons, but he shouldn't have, Dennis held up the Hebner name. And he was a great teammate, he really was. And people look at Dennis, and Dennis put on the act too, *he's lazy*, but he wasn't at all. He worked his butt off."

"Once we were coming home from practice and it was snowing out," Dickie Donovan recalled. "Don says okay, when you drive—we didn't take a bus that day, so the seniors drove. I jumped in the car with Denny Hebner, and I'm with Johnny Ranalli and Denny Hebner. Don says drive home real careful. So it's snowing out, so we take the exit going onto Dean Street and it turns pretty sharp to the left, Denny goes right over the snowbank! Who comes along two cars later, it's Don, *Dennis I told you be careful*, and Denny starts going, *if I was Jackie Cronin you wouldn't be yelling at me!* True story!"

"Dennis and I have had a bumpy relationship," Jack Cronin acknowledged. "I love the guy now, now I can sit down and talk to him, he's a nice guy. But Dennis, he liked to do things the hard way. I think he may have changed a little now, but when you talk about rough around the edges, that describes Dennis.

"Dennis was a phenomenal athlete. He was a goalie, and then he became a forward, and in many ways, he was a man among boys physically. He couldn't skate and he couldn't run, if he could run and skate, who knows what could happen. But he had great hands, great hand-eye coordination, but he wasn't dedicated to, I don't know psychologically, who knows. Maybe because he was in the shadows of his brothers—plural—but yeah, he and I, he was one of these guys, I was the captain my senior year and he was one of these guys that would make remarks. And as a captain you want to make sure particularly the younger guys are buying off on things, and he was one of these guys... Who knows, under his breath, so I basically, when I say bumpy road—we had it out. We both went into the locker room, and I'll never say what went on, but we both went in the locker room alone. And we ironed out our differences. And he was fine, he was fine after that. He was good... Sometimes he just needed to understand what the hell he was doing. But I have a lot of respect for him, he's a friend and teammate. We're all a product of our, I guess our parents, our upbringing, and I think the Hebner boys—and I can only speak from what I've observed—their dad was tough on them, I think. He expected them to be world-class in whatever they were doing. He was surrounded by all his brothers who were great.

"Even back in high school I saw some maturing, although he's so funny, he's the crudest son-of-a-bitch, excuse my French, some of the stories...but I love him. It's who he is. You know he was the kid that scored the two goals in the state final that could have been the... You know what he said to me? This is typical Dennis. He said you know I would have scored *three* goals if I hadn't passed the puck! That says it all."

Tying the Needham Rockets for the Bay State League title was no indication of weakness. Needham was a powerhouse, considered the best team in the state, led by established stars Scott Godfrey and Larry Anderson, but thrust firmly into Massachusetts hockey elite by sophomore sensation Robbie Ftorek.

"We tied for the Bay State title my senior year," Dennis Hebner remembered. "cuz that Needham game was unbelievable. Four Seasons, they had to chain the doors closed. They had to close the place, there were so many people in there, cars were parked up on Route 1, they were parked on the driving range up there, they were parked all over the place. Close to five thousand people, I don't know what it holds, they were standing... We had trouble getting the bus down there, cuz we got there like forty minutes before the game, the place was already packed! The bus had trouble getting into the parking lot!

"I loved it. I mean, I played baseball too, but baseball didn't have the glory or the, I mean, the baseball you go there and there might be ten people watching the game and they're all parents. But the hockey I just loved!"

Arlington was unseeded in the 1968 state tournament. They had come in second to Brookline, interrupting their string of five consecutive GBI League titles, and had lost ten seniors from their state championship team, notably Bobby Havern, who had established the new state scoring record. Needham was the pre-tournament favorite, seeded number one and followed, in order, by Brookline, Melrose, and Needham's co-champions of the Bay State League, Norwood.

"We were bursting with confidence," Arlington goalie Joe Bertagna remembered. "I mean, we went into this tournament without people expecting much. We finished second to Brookline, we didn't have great expectations, and the first game we won 9-3 but they weren't very good, and we beat Christopher Columbus 4-0, and that was a nice win, and then we get to the Garden and we knock off Melrose, and it's like *woe*, we got something going here! And now we play Ftorek and Needham and win 1-0, so we're like we just played two of the best teams in the state and only allowed one goal, we were pretty full of ourselves. Now we go into Norwood and we beat them the year before, and we still had Billy Corkery and a few guys from that team. What's wrong with that, why shouldn't we be full of ourselves?"

Norwood opened with a 4-1 dispatch of Lynnfield, then faced Xaverian in a game of great interest to our townsfolk, particularly those from Crestwood Circle. The *Patriot Ledger*:

> It's neighbor against neighbor tonight at Boston Arena where Norwood and Xaverian clash in the Eastern Mass hockey Tournament. Norwood's all scholastic goalie Neil Higgins lives across the street from his Xaverian counterpart, Brian Moloney. They grew up together. In fact, the mask Moloney wears against Norwood was designed and constructed by Neil Higgins' father Ernie. Xaverian, winner of the Catholic League, has seven Norwood residents on its squad. Moloney, a junior, starts in the nets while Bob Murphy centers the first line. Tom Rodgers figures to see plenty of action. Coaches Al Whitty and head coach Bob Richards are both from Norwood, Whitty a member of the '64 Bay State League championship team, and Richards coached at Norwood.

"We've been friends ever since I can remember," Neil Higgins told the *Ledger* at the time. "We learned to play hockey together. I used to take shots at Brian in the back yard." A half century later he adds, "Brian Moloney and I were very close friends, we were. We didn't go out of our way *not* to see each other; we just didn't see each other before the game. But we're talking on the ice, the only friends I had was my team. After the game I gave him a big hug and told him you're still my best friend, my neighbor, and I love you, and the game could have gone either way.

That was Brian and myself. But nope, nope, nope. A Wheeler-ism was you could be friends, but get your game face on, the task at hand..."

"Against Xaverian," Bobby Thornton recalled, "the two goalies who played incredibly well were our Neil Higgins and their Brian Moloney. What are the odds that these two kids were next door neighbors living on a tiny little street in Norwood called Crestwood Circle, alongside other Norwood players and neighbors Dickie Donovan, Gee Sortevik and Denny Hebner? An amazing, but true story."

Frank Wall described the action,

> The spark for the Hawks was goalie Brian Moloney who came up with 18 saves during the night and many were ticketed for what looked like sure goals. Donovan scored at 8:54 of 3rd period to nail it. 'I knew we needed one more to ensure the win and I just fired it from in front on Moloney,' Dickie told the Norwood scribe in the locker room. "'That has to be the sweetest goal I have ever scored.'

"Xaverian almost fucking beat us," Dennis Hebner recalled. "The Arena was a weird fucking place. We went in there thinking these Catholic kids... We only beat 'em like 3-1. They gave us a good game. Tom Rodgers played for them, Jimmy Serbo from Walpole, few other kids, they were pretty good."

Falmouth fell next 4-0, before Dick Donovan came through in the clutch, notching Norwood's only goal in their 1-0 semifinal encounter with Hingham.

"Neil was amazing!" Dickie Donovan recalled. "One of the goals I remember that I scored, we beat Hingham, and they could fly, they were faster than we were, they were faster than Needham. We played them in the Garden, there were 13,000 people on a Saturday afternoon, and I beat—Tommy Hutchinson was playing in the net for Hingham, and funny, he went on to Bowdoin College and the first thing he says to me was Donovan, I double-clutched, and I said *get outta here*, I beat you so cleanly it was ridiculous! But I can remember looking up in the stands, all the people were gone, and my mother and Mrs. Higgins were hugging each other, because it was me and Neil on the ice getting a picture taken. We were on the front page of the sporting sections in all the papers in Boston the next morning, me and Neil, arm-in-arm. It was unbelievable, it was fabulous."

The Hingham win set the stage for a Norwood-Arlington rematch. The game, which would enter the realm of legend for both towns, was played on Boston Garden ice on Monday evening, March 18, 1968. Nerves were on edge, from superstar seniors to a fourth-line freshman wing.

"I came out and saw all those people, I said holy shit, I wanna go back in the locker room!" Phil Nolfi recalled. "Sitting on the bench and marveling at the guys that played and how much talent was out there. There was no way I was getting called out there. I didn't want to go out on the ice. Shit. Look at all those people, holy *shit!* I'll go back in the bus, let me know how we make out!"

"It was anybody's game," Neil Higgins remembered. "They weren't better than us, I think we were very even with them. We played them really good, and it was an unseasonable warm day and the ice was slow, and it was wet. And we truly felt that was to our advantage because we were conditioned, no question about it. Coach Wheeler had us conditioned. We would do wind sprints, Canadian wind sprints, Russian wind sprints, that really leveled the playing field and made us actually faster or as good as their skaters."

Arlington sophomore Tom Deveaux scored two quick goals in the first minutes of play, but Norwood fought back, with a Bob Begley shot deflecting off Arlington defenseman Mark Noonan's stick and past Joe Bertagna, the first period ending 2-1. Billy Corkery, hero of Arlington's '67 state final, scored for Arlington in the second period, and Norwood struggled to cut the lead for the entire second period, and most of the third. Down 3-1 with 2:18 remaining in the game, Don Wheeler pulled Neil Higgins for a sixth skater, setting up the most harrowing three minutes in Norwood hockey history.

"Well, the first one the Arlington kid put it in," Dennis Hebner recalled of Arlington defenseman Mark Noonan's mistake. "I just kinda went after him and he got so nervous he turned around, he thought he was firing it behind the net and he hit the corner perfect!" (laughs)

"And then Noonan's goal," Bertagna remembered. "I've played more hockey with Mark than anyone else in my life. We were teammates in the Belmont bantams when we were both defensemen, we were teammates at Arlington, we were teammates at Harvard, we were teammates on a couple of senior teams, and I played with him a month ago. He lived two streets away from me growing up, and we've played almost non-stop together for fifty years.

"Mark Noonan comes around the net, he can't get out of the zone on the left, and he tries to fire it behind the net to his partner, and he just beats me. It went off my left hip, between the post on the left side and my hip, and went in. I was told that Burns told one of his subsequent teams that I should have had the short side! I should have had that covered! But anyway, it was still 3-2 and we still felt pretty good, and then Dennis ties it up. My recollection was a hard, high shot that broke off my glove. Noonan claims, now Mark you have to understand is a bit of a character, he likes to shock with one liners and things, he claims he got *all three* goals. I said what do you mean all three goals, he says the other two deflected off my stick. I have no memory of Dennis' shot deflecting off anything. I thought he just had a really good, hard shot and broke off the end of my glove."

"The last one," Dennis Hebner recalled, "I didn't think I could shoot like that, tell you the truth! It was the adrenaline; you were so pumped up. The puck was near the net or something, and all of a sudden it came out and Tommy Taylor was going after the puck, *I got it!* I yelled at him, cuz I could see it was right on my stick, and I yelled at him to get the fuck out of my way, and I just shot it and the fucking thing went in. At least thirty feet... Fourteen seconds left in the game. Biggest goal in Norwood history at that time, where would the statue be?" (laughs)

"Dennis, Dennis, somebody woke the bear, right?" Leo McInerney said. "I mean two goals in two minutes is pretty awesome. Fourteen seconds. Yeah, fourteen seconds, and he to this day says he had an opportunity to get a third one, and unlike any of the Hebners, he decided to pass! (laughs) There's probably a lesson there for everybody, don't pass, and *shoot* the damn thing!"

The goal ignited an explosion of dancing delirium that rocked Boston Garden. "I still remember that '68 game," Bobby Rosata said. "When

Hebner tied it up, Skip Connolly almost threw me off the balcony! We were on that third balcony standing, and you're hanging over, and when Hebner scored that goal Skip's like *yaaaaahhhhh!* and he pushes me and I'm like *whoooooaaaaa!* That's how exciting that was! I remember that, oh God I remember that!"

Dennis Hebner had scored the biggest goal in Norwood history under mythical circumstances. With his two goals scored in the last two minutes of play after pulling Neil Higgins from goal, the tying goal with just fourteen seconds left in the game, Norwood retired to their locker room at the end of regulation time.

"We came in the locker room after Dennis had tied it," Leo McInerney recalled. "I'll never forget this as long as I live. We were in the locker room, and it was bedlam, it was bedlam, people were hootin' and hollerin' and just out of their minds! And Don came in and says, *Shut the fuck up, you guys stunk the place up for three periods!* Imagine saying that? It was like he stuck a pin in a balloon!"

"McInerney was right," Dennis Hebner agreed. "Wheeler tried to calm everyone down, he probably thought everyone would get too hyped up and not play the way they should. I don't know, he had a reason, but he couldn't let us enjoy the moment."

"Wheeler came into the locker room," Tommy Taylor remembered, "we were jumping all around, and he told us we stunk the place out for two periods and you're lucky you're going into overtime. I can remember he put me out there with Shea and Dennis, Dennis scored with like thirty-five seconds to go in the game. He took me and Dennis aside...he tried to blame Begley for some strange reason. He was just a miserable man; he didn't appreciate how lucky he was. You know something? If you look back, if this guy had common sense and patted you on the back, he'd have won more."

"It was heartbreaking, it was heartbreaking," sophomore third-liner Pete Tamulionis recalled. "And to this day I say freakin' Don Wheeler lost it. We were so pumped up in that locker room, I mean Jackie Cronin was a quiet guy, basically quiet, but when he spoke, everybody listened. Every. Body. Listened. And when we came into that locker room and he was *fired up*, and we were yelling and screaming, you know how it used to be, yelling and screaming and Don comes walking in and he says sit down and shut up, you sucked out there, and all of a sudden everybody's just sitting down. It was demoralizing. You don't think of being demoralized then, but years later I'm thinkin', Jesus Christ, if he just let us go on, let Jackie keep on talking, it might have been a different outcome."

Overtime in Boston Garden in a state final contest; the building shook with sounds and furies, you could not hear yourself scream. Not a soul in the crowd was sitting and all momentum was Norwood's. But unfortunately for the Mustangs, one of the kids returning to the ice was Billy Corkery.

"Billy's family came from Cambridge," Joe Bertagna said. "A lot of Arlington came from Cambridge and Somerville. He was a clutch player, he had a little bit of Cambridge street smarts in him, very talented with the puck, smart hockey player. And just kind of ice water as far as never being nervous, and certainly rising to the occasion of the moment."

"Billy Corkery was a great little athlete," Bob Bartholomew agreed, "not big in size, but he could play. Street hockey, ice hockey, so smooth, great hands. A perfect gentleman, smart as a whip, Billy could do everything. Really good guy, he could play softball, baseball, like I said, everything. A really good team player, and a hot ticket!"

Referee Billy Cleary stood astride Dennis Hebner and Billy Corkery amidst a cacophony of emotion literally shaking the old building and dropped the puck. Frantic anticipation reached a zenith when during the first minute of play, Arlington wing Bernie Quinlan was called for hooking, putting Norwood on a power play. And just as suddenly—and in most brutal fashion—the music died.

"I do remember the last play, which I'll never forget," Jack Cronin related. "I think it was Corkery, comes down the ice—as a young hockey player they teach you to keep the player in front of you and look at his belly button, cuz that's the thing he can't move. And I played, in my mind and people can argue this point, but I played him perfectly. I picked him up just inside the blue line, he was in front of me, I know he shot the puck and I poke-checked and I didn't get my stick on his stick, but I was in position where I made the play. Ninety-nine percent of the time, that play would be enough to…Neil will be the first to tell you that if some kid's shooting inside the blue line, he's gonna save it ninety-nine times. And I don't know what happened, to this day I've never seen the film, I don't know how it went in. And I don't care to dwell on it, because I know a lot of people pointed the finger at Neil which was totally—the reason we were there, the reason we excelled is because Neil was that good. He certainly has the, he certainly can get away with not making a good play, if that was the case. And as far as I'm concerned, as far as I know, I made the right play."

"I don't remember any of the goals except for the one in overtime," Neil Higgins recalled. "It came in from about the blue line and it was a knuckle ball, and I tried to move out into it and get my body into it, and it hit the ice and took a freak right-hand turn, the puck was going to my left and went over my shoulder, and in. And you heard football players, baseball players, all sorts of athletes say, it was like all the air went out of the Boston Garden, and all the air first was pushed on me, and it all left. And I said *uhf*...I didn't know what to say or do. I've played it over in my mind a thousand times, I couldn't have played it any differently, all I tried to do was get my body, as much of my body in front of a bouncing puck as I could. It musta hit, I guess—only a guess—it must have hit one of the ruts in the watery ice and knocked it back in another direction. That's all I can say."

Bertagna watched events unfold from the opposite end. "We go in the locker room, we come out and Bernie gets the penalty. We're short-handed, but I still don't have any recollection of panic or anything. I'm sure we were concerned we had to kill off the penalty, and then Billy takes this slapshot that bounces, and, you know, Burns never wanted our players to take slapshots, it was one of his rules. His theory was we played the Arena that had very shallow corners, it was almost like egg-shaped, and Burns' theory was if you missed the net in the Arena, the puck would come out of the zone fast and some lazy guy not back-checking gets a breakaway. So you watch Arlington play and it looks so foolish when a defenseman gets the puck sixty feet from the goal and takes this old-fashioned sweep shot cuz he didn't want us to take slapshots. So it was somewhat ironic that at this big moment of the season that Billy breaks the coach's rule and unloads a slapshot, and then it bounces. I think one of the newspapers, maybe the *Herald*, had a picture of the goal where they superimposed an arrow going over Neil's right leg, beat him on the stick side which probably makes more sense than the glove side, and that was it. It was kind of a surprising ending to that game."

"It's history now, there's probably a lot of opinions out there," Jack Cronin continued. "Neil has said that to me, you know we don't get together and talk about that. Neil's my best friend. Neil and I talk all the time, but that's one of those things. He's not, it's funny, obviously I talk a lot, I talk about this stuff. For some reason he doesn't have the same level of interest, although he will, he'll open up."

Fifty-three years later, Neil Higgins is philosophical about what can only be viewed as a cruel ending to a brilliant Norwood career. "It wasn't meant to be, and more than likely it made me a better person and helped me in my business career. What doesn't kill you, makes you stronger. I think it makes you stronger and a better person. You know, many people, if you don't learn defeat, you can never truly enjoy a victory." Others were less philosophical.

"I blame—we lost that game for one reason, and it was because of Don Wheeler," Leo McInerney declared. "Back then—it would never work today—but back then he was the be-all, end-all of Norwood hockey. With Sails playing him up and Joe Curran always supporting him from the school perspective, that guy had the reins, and he wasn't letting go. That was the dumbest move, that was absolutely the dumbest move, just really stupid. That was really, really dumb.

"After in the locker room it was silence, the bus ride home I don't even remember anyone saying anything. We were flat when we went out, I mean after that it was... Oh, poor Neil. Yup. Billy Corkery. Yup, yup. He was throwing it in, too. That's what everyone remembers, too. Bar guys—not the hockey players, but our friends—they'll still bring it up to him to this day. What the hell were you doing on that shot? And he just kinda goes, I don't know, it hit a bump or something, I don't know... He was throwing it in to change up, cuz Cronin was right on him, and being the hockey player he was, he was on-net with it, and it kind of rolled up the stick and up the sleeve..."

The '68 players are almost unanimous that their coach had erred in his bedside, locker room manner. A couple of voices, however, took a broader view.

"I know the guys that didn't like him—they were boys," Neil Higgins maintained. "We were all boys. We weren't men, we were boys. And adolescent boys are, we are cocky, we are aggressive, we think we know it all, even to our parents. So another authority figure, meaning the hockey coach, it would be easier to take it out on, or easier to be more upset with than a Jack Reddick, or Roger Sortevik, or Bob Donovan. It's very easy for people to find fault with that person. I always respected him so, and he always treated me with respect and dignity, and treated me like a *man*, not a boy. Nobody can say anything bad about the coach, in my eyes."

Dennis Hebner holds a considered opinion.

"I'll say one thing, my senior year, the state finals, Don Wheeler blew that game. Have you heard it before? Well, we tied it up and we went into overtime. Twenty seconds into overtime they get a penalty. They took us off the fucking ice. Every goal that Arlington scored was off the second line. They didn't score any goals against the first line. And he took us off the ice and they scored twenty seconds later, scored at forty seconds of overtime on a shit shot that Neil—I can't blame Neil, if it wasn't for him, we wouldn't have got that far, but it was a shot he would have stopped ninety-nine percent of the time, it kinda bounced. Wheeler fucked that up. We were high as a kite, we had tied the game up, we had a power play, and he took us off the ice. I said, *what the fuck is he doing?* I was pissed, I was really *pissed*. I think, I don't know..."

"How do you argue with success?" Phil Nolfi countered. "I mean, the guy made the best choices that he could. I understand Dennis being mad and of course, they just made the biggest comeback in high school hockey history. Against a pretty good team! Arlington, you weren't playing a bunch of bums, there was a reason they were there for the state championship, too. Don gave it his best guess. Because who did he put out instead of Dennis Hebner, Dickie Donovan? Not like you're putting out a freshman that weighed 135 pounds, you're putting out a damn good hockey player. And then for the goal, cuz I was sitting on the bench and I saw it happen, and it was like watching a movie. Did that *really* happen? I mean, it was just a *fluke!* It wasn't as if Neil didn't get the shot or the guy picked his corner. Ba-dink, ba-dink, ba-dink, and it went in. That was quite a game."

Dennis Hebner's voice trailed off, reminiscing of events over a half-century removed. The goal had cost Norwood its third shot in four years at winning a state championship, and also handed tourney MVP honors to Billy Corkery instead of either Dennis, Dickie, or Neil, and certainly cost Neil's place on the All-Tourney Team, which went to Joe Bertagna. The heart-breaking defeat ended the careers of three Norwood hockey legends in a fashion as unkind as Richie Hebner's broken skate. As we concluded our interview at a picnic table in front of Norwood Cinema, Dennis turned back to me.

"He used to piss me off, he didn't really like me, I don't think. He talked to me when they had the film here, Kelleher's film. Ftorek didn't show up, something came up. After the thing was over and people were milling around, I went over to Don to shake his hand and he finally praised me, after fifty years. Maybe he was bullshitting me, but he said Dennis, that game there was probably the greatest goal I've ever seen in my life coaching hockey. That's what he said." Dennis Hebner turned away and stared across Norwood common.

Where would the statue be?

TRAGEDY

You don't know a goddamn thing, do you. You don't know a goddamn thing about tragedy. Tragedy's a bad, bad thing. And it don't just happen. It only happens after a whole lot of good things happen, otherwise it ain't no tragedy, just bad luck, or tough luck. What makes a tragedy is when you lose something you've already got. Losing your seeding with a spring washout ain't no tragedy, losing it harvest eve to sudden frost, when the corn is full and high, is a tragedy. Having first Freddy die at six months ain't no tragedy, having second Freddy die at eighteen or nineteen was...

— Don Reddick, *Victory Faust*

Sometimes a mood of depression falls over me, and home seems so far away...

— Lance Corporal Dick Murphy, USMC
May 23, 1968, letter from Vietnam
to Father Paul McManus

Great change swept America during the 1960s. The decade began with crewcuts, dress codes, and the innocence of song lyrics such as, "I want to be Bobby's girl," and ended with disheveled hair and beards, open campus, and the despair of, "We gotta get out of this place, if it's the last thing we ever do."

The decade began with school kids standing and reciting the Pledge of Allegiance, and ended in Woodstock with the crying, chaotic chords of Jimi Hendrix's, *The Star-Spangled Banner*. The decade began with idealistic calls to serve in Vista and the Peace Corps, and ended in disillusioned, endemic draft evasion and fragging. With the assassinations of the Kennedys and Martin Luther King, Chicago's Democratic convention, violent race riots across the nation, with four dead in Ohio at the hands of our own National Guardsmen mirrored by napalm, agent orange, and far-off cries of, "we had to destroy the village in order to save it," the decade was one of transcendent and tragic turmoil, home and abroad.

The decade began with the optimism and grace of the youngest President in history whose iconic mantra was, "Ask not what your country can do for you, ask what you can do for your country," and ended with the election of the first president to leave office disgraced and forever quoted, "I am not a crook." It began with unbounded enthusiasm and confidence of The Greatest Generation, and ended with unimaginable savagery in Charles Manson, the atrocity of Mai Lai, and over 50,000 heartbroken families.

Even the soundtrack of our lives was changing; *I Wanna Hold Your Hand* had become *Lucy in the Sky With Diamonds*...

Popular culture reflected change. Its lead actor described *The Dick Van Dyke Show* as "Kind, gentle, compassionate, empathetic and wise"; indeed, the decade began with TV shows such as *My Three Sons, Leave it to Beaver,* and *Bonanza* that were essentially sermons, each episode conveying a wholesome lesson to a coalesced country, and ended with fragmented, counter-culture alienation of *Easy Rider*, anti-hero protagonists in *Butch Cassidy and the Sundance Kid*, and Dustin Hoffman, of whom in his role as Benjamin Braddock in *The Graduate* historian Doris Kearns Goodwin wrote, "came to epitomize the unknown everyman who was the hero of the late sixties, uncertain, alienated, and, by any traditional standards, a loser."

Goodwin described the generational collision these changes effected in her book on President Lyndon Johnson,

> "How in the hell can that creepy guy be a hero to you?" Johnson asked me after we saw *The Graduate* in the movie theater on his ranch. "All I needed was to see ten minutes of that guy, floating like a big lump in a pool, moving like an elephant in that woman's bed, riding up and down the California coast polluting the atmosphere, to know that I wouldn't trust him for one minute with anything that really mattered to me. And if that's an example of what love seems like to your generation, then we're all in big trouble."

Within this great change, our awareness seemed parochial, and itself subject to change. What understanding eleven-year-old kids growing up in Norwood had in 1965 when American troops were first committed en masse into Vietnam contrasted with what understanding we had at seventeen or eighteen in 1972, and subject to the draft. For kids graduating in the mid '60s, Vietnam was often a sudden and largely unexpected intrusion into their lives. Peter Oberlander, playing in what he considered the biggest game of his life against Arlington in March of '67, was fighting for that very life on the Mekong River less than a year later.

For those of us graduating in 1972, Vietnam had essentially entailed our entire conscious lives. Active U.S. participation in the war began in the early sixties, when we were ages seven or eight and would not end until three years after our graduation. Beginning in 1965, the war led the nightly news, so that throughout the '60s it was as much a part of our lives as the wallpaper in our living rooms. And not all of us particularly paid attention to the wallpaper in our living rooms. As time passed, a more concrete narrative formed, yet reactions varied. Many, such as Ray Johnson and Nahatan Street's Paul Coughlin and Glen Cutler, volunteered. Teddy Mulvehill joined, while two of his '72 classmates formed an agreement to move to Canada if drafted, while still others drifted toward a bell-bottomed, tie-dyed opposition.

Complicating further was an obscure facet of the generational collision, addressed by Doris Kearns Goodwin in her Johnson book.

> The values of any new generation do not spring full blown from their heads; they are already there, inherent if not clearly articulated in the older generation. The generation gap is just another way of saying that the younger generation makes overt what is covert in the older generation; the child expresses openly what the parent represses.

While history has idolized our fathers, anointing them "the Greatest Generation" for their performance in World War II, an underlying reality, seamlessly meshed with that generation's reticence, existed. We had heard rumors of a teammate's father's nightmares of horrors experienced in the South Pacific. We knew that shell-shocked individuals swept floors and emptied trash barrels in town jobs provided for those with war-related, psychological wounds. We knew the VA hospital in West Roxbury held victims of war for their entire remaining lives, so that while some parents were staunch supporters of the Vietnam war, others were more reserved, restrained in view and voice. As bright-eyed school children we were taught the great victories of our fathers but saw, alongside fierce and warranted pride, eyes also subtly reflecting the enormous cost. Bernie Cooper saw this reflection in his father's eyes.

"He only talked about the war once," the late assistant town manager related. "The only thing he would tell me is he had shrapnel in his leg. I was twenty years old before I knew what happened."

Otis Cooper and his father Jacob were proprietors of Town Square Hardware when the war broke out. After joining the army, Otis was part of General George Patton's army which swept through France in 1944.

"My sister Marianne asked him about it in 1968 shortly before he died, and he talked. He had landed at Normandy a week after the invasion, and he told us that coming ashore he was shocked at how they could have taken that beach. He was wounded in Luxembourg in September, or October. They had bivouacked in a vacant farmhouse and put a sentry out on the front porch and a mortar shell—a lot had dysentery, and the guy out front started throwing up, and my father went to help him, and a mortar shell hit close by and they were both wounded, the other guy more seriously. He walked five or six miles before a jeep picked him up and delivered him to a field hospital, and he was evacuated to England. I remember asking him, do you ever see these guys, ever talk to them? I remember asking him what had happened to the guys in your unit, not understanding that he barely got to know most of them. He was thirty-three and already a father, and most of the men in his unit were kids, and there was constant turnover... Other than that, he never talked about the war."

"My father served in the Army for the 26th Division infantry," Billy Pieri recalled. "He was wounded in Nancy, France when the jeep he was passenger in ran over a land mine in 1945. He was like a jeep mechanic guy, always doing cars and all that stuff. The jeep he was in ran over a mine, and all the shrapnel, he was never the same after that. He didn't have a spleen I don't think, my mother changed his bandages every day, big bandages, the size like a foot by six inches. In and out of the hospital, I remember going to the VA hospital three times a week. You know, I was born in '54 and he died in '62, that's all I remember. I remember my mother would drive in to the hospital and myself and my brother were left in the car. She'd go in for an hour, forty-five minutes, and she'd come out and we'd be in the car. You had to do it. I guess the big thing was the spleen, I guess nowadays it wouldn't be such a big issue, but then it kinda was. He spent practically the rest of his life in and out of the VA hospital in Boston and died in 1962. So he never really fully recovered from that."

"My father was in a tank someplace in Africa, I think," Bobby Dempsey said. "When he started out, he goes, what do I have to do not to walk? Well, you can get in a tank, so he said get me in a tank. It mighta been BS, but that was his story and he was sticking to it. Past history. He was in Italy for a long time, Africa, whatever, guys in those days did what they had to do. Guys don't talk about that, really, my brother in Vietnam, they don't talk about that."

With this backdrop, kids growing up on Crestwood Circle, our lives emanating outward first from street, then neighborhood, town, and country, saw tragedy encroach.

"We were playing street hockey on Higgins's driveway when Henry Baker pulled into his driveway," Ken Reddick recalled. "He walked over and told Ernie Higgins that his wife had just died, and it was awful, he was weeping and repeating over and over, 'What am I going to do now? What am I going to do now?'" Mrs. Baker had succumbed to cancer, leaving her husband and five children. The street saw tragedy repeated when Eddie Praino, hero of Norwood's 1943 State Championship baseball team, succumbed to a heart attack in 1968, leaving his thirty-five-year-old wife Shirley with *their* five children.

The neighborhood suffered every mother's nightmare and re-enforced every mother's admonition to "look both ways before you cross the street" when in 1960 five-year-old Paul Gearty was hit by a car.

"Oh my God, yeah," Dennis Hebner recalled. "I still remember almost right to the second what happened. I don't even know how old I was at the time, I think Paul was in kindergarten, so I was in the fourth grade, I guess. Something like that, and I was always friendly with the family, used to go over there and almost like babysit and take care of him, play games with them. I saw Paul walking ahead of me, cuz I was getting out of St. Catherine's and I think he was in Shattuck cuz St. Catherine's didn't have kindergarten. So I caught up to him and I was talking to him and we had just crossed Silver Street and we were on my side of the street, his house was on the other side of the street, and I said to him when we get up to near your house I'm gonna help you cross the street, and all of a sudden he just took off. I don't know if he didn't hear me say the whole thing, or he just heard 'cross the street,' I really don't know, and all of a sudden, he got hit. I can still hear the sounds the car made when it hit him, it was just disgusting. And I ran to his mother's house to tell her, and in the meantime, I think Mrs. Kinsman called the ambulance…I could hear the brakes screeching, and him getting thrown, I think he got thrown a hundred and five feet, he got thrown on the other side of Silver Street, and we were already crossed over Silver Street on the sidewalk.

"Mrs. Gearty screamed all the way. From the time she left the door of her house to the time she got to the street she was screaming; I don't even know what she was screaming. She was screaming the whole time, and they didn't expect him to live and I think he was in a coma for a hundred and three days, something like that. He was in Boston. And they used to bring him home, and they'd ask me to come over when he was sitting at the table and talk to him and try to get him out of his… I still think of that. Probably sixty years ago for me."[32]

But it is loss of life to country and its subsequent memorialization in stone and gilded letter that wounds a tight-knit community forever. This pageantry of loss will last as long as a lone bugle sounds "taps" across Highland Cemetery every Memorial Day, every Veteran's Day, and in the hearts of their families, *every* day.

John Concannon of the 101st Airborne Division was first to fall. On May 4, 1966, he had volunteered to assist a friend, a Roman Catholic Priest, conduct a Mass for a remote unit about to deploy. The helicopter in which they were riding, along with twenty other paratroopers and officers, crashed in a non-hostile incident in jungle north-west of Saigon. There were no survivors. John Concannon, former Roosevelt

---

[32] Paul Gearty was in a coma for five months before a case of chicken pox brought him out of it. A Nahatan Street kid as tough as they come, Paul had to relearn how to walk and went on to work thirty-eight years as a custodian at Blue Hills Regional Technical High School. I attended his retirement party at Lewis', in 2018.

Ave. resident and 1958 Norwood High graduating classmate of Henry Valentinas, was buried in Arlington National Cemetery in Virginia.

On a Saturday morning in June of 1967, Marietta Mitchell answered the door of her Andrus Place home in South Norwood to find Captain Harold Kless, his U.S. Army dress cap in hand. The Army officer informed that her husband and father of their two young children had been Killed in Action in Quang Ngai Province, South Vietnam. Sgt. Lawrence Mitchell, also a member of the 101st Airborne, was riding in a helicopter felled by enemy fire on June 16th. Larry, after attending Balch elementary school and Norwood Junior High School, had left Norwood High to work at Kendall Mills in Walpole, where he undoubtably crossed paths with Vinnie Fitzpatrick. Twenty-six-year-old Larry Mitchell was buried in Highland Cemetery.

These deaths were a shocking revelation of the true cost of the nation's deepening involvement in Vietnam. But it was during the spring of 1968 that Vietnam's brutal legacy was indelibly embossed upon Norwood's consciousness.

On January 29, 1968, the Tet offensive was launched by North Vietnam, triggering a descent into madness that touched every nook and cranny of America, as well as Vietnam. From February to June, American combat deaths exceeded 8,000, with over 50,000 additional wounded requiring hospitalization.

The timeline represents an escalating horror: on February 1st General Nguyen Ngoc Loan was filmed summarily executing a bound Viet Cong prisoner on a Saigon street, the Pulitzer Prize-winning photograph enraging a growing anti-war movement. The week of February 11-17 recorded the most U.S. casualties of any week of the war with 543 killed, 2,547 wounded. Two days before Billy Corkery broke Norwood's heart in Boston Garden on March 18, American soldiers walked into the village of My Lai, mirroring the Phong Nhi and Phong Nhat massacres the previous month by South Korean allies.

In a national address on the evening of March 31, President Lyndon Johnson, distraught with escalating impotence over controlling our Vietnam involvement, threw American politics into chaos by declaring, "I shall not seek, and I will not accept, the nomination of my party for another term as your president," providing the opening for Bobby Kennedy's campaign for the Democratic Party nomination. Martin

Luther King was assassinated on April 4th, in Memphis, Tennessee, enraging yet another segment of American society already enflamed within the Civil Rights movement.

On the morning of June 5th, the second-floor scholars of 57 Crestwood Circle were awakened by my mother with these words, hollered up the staircase: *"Wake up! They've shot Kennedy."*

These events proved prominent entries in U.S. history books, but it was the front page of the *Norwood Messenger* that conveyed local pain and suffering. Charlie Drake, Walpole High School's 1966 class president and captain of both their football and basketball teams, was killed on the first day of the Tet offensive. Headlines on April 3rd announced Norwood's descent into sadness.

> *Vietnam War Claims 4th Norwood Victim.* One of Norwood's native sons, Pfc Patrick K. Burke, 20, eldest son of Mr. and Mrs. George T. Burke of 377 Nahatan Street, paid the supreme sacrifice near Da Nang Saturday noon." Pat Burke, a member of the Army's 9th Infantry Division, had been Killed in Action by "multiple fragmentation wounds."

The *Messenger* covered his funeral a week later, noting the young man was a graduate of both St. Catherine's and Norwood High School, his pallbearers "all close friends of Cpl. Burke: Joseph Goodwin, Terry Buckley, Paul Kelly, Joseph Baldwin, John Stanovich, and James Perry." The article's final paragraph proved a sad footnote.

> Pfc. Donald Perry of 401 Nahatan Street, also stationed in Vietnam, was granted 15 days leave by the Army as a personal friend of Corporal Burke and was assigned to accompany the body to the United States but missed plane connections. He arrived in California late Wednesday night hours after the funeral was over...he has been wounded in action and is the recipient of the Purple Heart and Bronze Star.

Childhood friends, Donnie Perry, the kid that had battled Jay Dixon on Shattuck School steps, had grown up on Nahatan Street, five houses from Patrick Burke.

I delivered the *Patriot Ledger* newspaper as a fourteen-year-old in 1968. Collecting one afternoon in mid-April, I stepped into the foyer of the Fitzgerald house on North Ave. As Mrs. Fitzgerald fumbled with her coin purse, I glanced into a darkened living room. With lights out and shades drawn, the room's focus was the fireplace mantelpiece upon which was placed the formal portrait of a helicopter pilot in Army dress uniform, framed by lighted candles, religious cards, and rosary beads. Staring at the memorial in the darkness, silent and immobile in his armchair, was Mr. Fitzgerald.

Johnny Fitzgerald was Killed in Action two days after Patrick Burke's funeral, his *Messenger* headline reading, *Norwood Copter Pilot Is Killed in Vietnam*. The article read,

> The son of Mr. and Mrs. Joseph Fitzgerald of 54 North Avenue W/O Fitzgerald was twice decorated for bravery under fire. Holder of the Distinguished Flying Cross, as well as the Medal for Gallantry presented by the South Vietnam government, he was shot down twice on the same day last August. He was shot down again April 12 while piloting an Army helicopter over enemy territory…the only child of Joseph and Sandra Fitzgerald, he was educated at St. Catherine's School, Catholic Memorial High School, and Lowell Tech.

Thirty years later, a 1998 *Norwood Bulletin* article profiled Mr. Fitzgerald. He described working as a custodian for thirty-two years at the Prescott School, where Army officers had arrived to deliver brutal news in 1968. "'It was the longest day of my life,' the eighty-one-year-old related. 'But I had to stay strong. For my wife. I came home and told her to sit down. I said I had some bad news about John…'"

North Ave., of course, is off Nahatan Street, next to Shurfine Market. It is a two-minute walk to the Perry and Burke households, by the corner of Prospect and Nahatan. From this corner—where my mother was a crossing guard for twenty years for kids walking to Oldham School (and the Shattuck School crossing at Fulton and Nahatan one block toward town manned by Mrs. Burke)—it was but a five-minute walk up Prospect Street to Vernon Street where lived Norwood's Chief of Police, who had represented the town at both recent funerals, and who also had a son serving in Vietnam.

"My family settled in South Dedham the year before it became Norwood," Brian Murphy, son of police Chief James Murphy, related. "They had been in the U.S. for four years, New York City to Fall River to Boston, to South Dedham. They lived in a house on the tannery property. If you remember when we were kids, behind the gas pumps there, behind them were two gray houses, in 1876 my grandfather was born in one of them. Lyman Place, named after Lyman Smith, the owner of the tannery. Because of the tannery it was called Stink Alley, because of the smell.

"My grandfather was a policeman for a bit, he worked at the Press. My grandmother, she was Italian, they kind of had to run away to get married, mixed marriages back then, and they came back. My father looked more Irish than Italian, his brother John looked more Italian. So my grandfather referred to the kids as Gaelic and Garlic. You're talking 1914 or so, 1915. They lived in the Ward, a two-family house, 877 and 879 Washington Street. It's gone now, they knocked it down. My father grew up there, they lived there when they had their first seven kids and moved to Vernon Street when they had me.

"My father enlisted the day after Pearl Harbor. The afternoon of Pearl Harbor they found out, and my Dad and John D'Espinosa went to the recruiting office and it was closed, so they went back on December 8th to the Marines, and in 1943 the Marine Corps reactivated the Woman's Reserve and my mom was one of the first batch from Albany, New York. She was in Marine Aviation and they assigned her to Miramar in California—this is before they married—she was there from 1943 to November of '44. My father returned in November of '44 from the South Pacific. They'd bring them back and retrain them for the invasion of Japan. He was an airplane mechanic and tail gunner on a Grumman Avenger. It's a torpedo bomber, it's the plane that George Bush 41 was flying when he got shot down. The next target I think was Iwo Jima, I think Tarawa was '43. My father was in Guadalcanal.

"The story I was told is that my father went into the PX to buy a card for his fiancé and met my mother. My father was training to go back for the invasion. When the bombs dropped and the surrender came in the beginning of September, my father was out of the Marine Corps by October. That's how fast they demobilized. My mom got out in February of '46 and they were married in May.

"Dickie was the second-oldest. My brother Jimmy was born on my parent's first anniversary. Dickie was born eleven months later. Kevin—you know Kevin? He played hockey for Norwood. He was born eleven months after that. My brother Bill was born twelve, thirteen months after that. Four boys in four years. Dickie was the biggest of them, the ones at the ass-end of the family were bigger than them. By then my mother probably gave up on the broccoli.

"Dickie was big, he was confident, he loved baseball. My father took Dickie out of the Junior High School to go into Fenway to see Ted Williams' last game. There was only 10,000 people there and they were two of them. He was a huge Red Sox fan and they sucked all his life, and you remember in '67 when they came back from that road trip when they won ten in a row? When the Sox were finally getting good, Dickie left for boot camp four days later.

"He had friends all over the place, probably his best friend was from Dedham. He had this girl from Walpole, another from Westwood, he had about five dates a week. But he never got too close to anyone. I have the list he had in Vietnam, the list of those he'd write to, girls he'd gone out with, girls he hoped to go out with. He had a girlfriend in Vietnam. In one village he'd see her, meet the family. He joked he wanted to 'squeeze information out of her.' And he'd write to Kevin, he wrote a lot of letters to a lot of people, some have come back to me. Dickie Joseph, Vito DiCicco. I've got a lot of the letters that he wrote. He was a special kid.

"He sent letters home to us to the house which were pretty much okay to be read by everybody. And there were other letters he sent to the station, to my dad, darker stuff. Now my mother was a Marine so she could handle stuff, but he really worried about her. And so I think some of the grittier stuff, the bigger questions—after the battle he was wounded in, when he lost his Lieutenant, he lost several buddies, was a very dark period. All he wanted to do was go back and kill as many as he could, pay them back for what they did to all of them. But at the same time questioning, is it wrong? Is it wrong to wanna do this, am I a bad Christian? And deep into it, his letters at the end of March when LBJ announced he wasn't gonna run and he was halting the bombing, he was angry, everybody was angry, saying we're gonna get the shit kicked out of us now. Because the bombing that was directed at the North was not only to get them to give it up, but strategic bombing to slow the supplies of equipment and personnel down the Ho Chi Minh trail. He knew that the shit's gonna come down unimpeded now, we're gonna get the shit kicked out of us. And April, May, June and July of '68 were the four worst months of the entire thing, particularly for the Marine Corps up in I Corps, up in the northern part. And they did, they went from battle to battle to battle, and they did get the shit kicked out of them. They lost I think sixteen Marines and two Corpsmen the day that Dick was killed, and three days later they lost twenty-one."

In a letter dated May 23, 1968, to Father McManus, Dick Murphy wrote, "The time in Vietnam is passing, sometimes fast, sometimes slow, but the clock keeps right on ticking. As much as we all hate war, we know this war must be fought. Many have died already and if peace talks don't get off the ground soon, many more will die. Sometimes a mood of depression falls over me and home seems so far away..."

Brian Murphy, in life-long passion to keep the memory of his brother alive, has met men at Marine reunions who were with Dick on June 15th, 1968.

"They knocked the piss out of them... The battle of Mike's Hill where he was wounded in January and the battle of Phou Nhoi where he was killed, the Marines have the high ground. They're on a hill, and the NVA—these are all North Vietnamese regulars, not Viet Cong. In the villages everywhere there were people playing both sides depending on the time of day, you know, they're your buddy during the day but coming after you at night. It's interesting that they would call it a human wave considering in some respects they didn't consider them human, just like Japan, you know, they were smaller, they would do things we wouldn't do, the savagery and stuff, the way they treated prisoners and stuff, they just sent—and these are all like fifteen to twenty-five, most of the old men are long dead—and they just kept sending them up. I mean, if we lost eighteen, we've killed one hundred and forty. Maybe some of the body counts are exaggerated or padded, but it was still overwhelming, maybe six or seven, eight to one, and so that's what those battles were like. And then they'd go out on ambushes, they'd set up an ambush where you'd send eight or ten guys out there and they'd set up and they'd stay up all night and hopefully someone would be awake and wait for movement that either they could report back or if small enough to take 'em out, and sometimes they'd walk into ambushes. It was not the type of war that we'd fought...

"There was a battle in the morning, they could hear shit down below, and they knew there was a lot of movement down there. At the break of dawn, they were attacked, and we lost some guys during that battle, maybe ten or so. It went on all morning from like dawn to like eleven o'clock or something. After a lull of a couple of hours, the order came down from above to go and perform a sweep. They were supposed to go down and look for wounded, any of our wounded that might be down there and still laying low, the enemy wounded, recover weapons, and count bodies, and so Dick was chosen to go with his fire-team. A fire-team team would be four guys, they had a Corpsman with them, and so they're going down, and Dick was so—the more I look at it, the more I learn. Dick was such a squared-away Marine. He carried himself with confidence. I mean you could probably look and see the guy who got here yesterday, you see the guy who's been here for six months, and Dick was the first one hit by a sniper. Dick was shot through the chest. And that makes sense, because what they wanna do is put him down and make somebody come to him. I know this from the physician from Phoenix, he had a diary.

"And he heard this kid named Thibault from New Jersey, who had just been there for a month or so—this guy's name is Candalaria—he's with another Marine and a Corpsman helping a guy who had been down on the side of the hill with a leg wound or something. You get something like that, if you're relatively safe, you just shut up and stay there, you know, maybe take aggressive action only if you see someone going up the hill. Meanwhile Dick and the fire-team are down below in some kind of hedge row, it's very thick jungle, and Candalaria hears the first round from the sniper, and this guy from New Jersey said, 'Oh my God, Murphy's hit!' And then there's another shot and the guy's yelling that he's hit, he says something like my arm, my arm, and then a third shot silences him. And so the Corpsman goes down to Dick, and no sooner does he get there— I have another account where the guy heard the Corpsman say, 'He's dead'—then *he's* hit, he's hit in the head. Thibault's hit in the head, the Corpsman's hit in the head, and the firing continues and the radio operator is a kid from Phoenix, he is named Lopez, he's killed, hit in the head.

"And the Corpsman that's with Candalaria and another Marine helping the other Marine, he hears Dick had been hit and he sees that the other two Marines can get this guy up and he says I gotta go, he says Murphy's my friend. So he goes, and he's actually, I don't know how close he gets to Dick, but he's trying to get in to where the sniper is, and he calls to this other Marine to throw him a grenade. Now, this guy's name is Cruse, and he's from Paducah, Kentucky. So he's trying to get a grenade from somebody, and *he* gets hit in the back of the head. So meanwhile they figure out where the sniper is, and by that time they have what they call LAWS, Light Anti-Tank Weapons or something, like bazookas, and they send like twenty of these into the trees, and that's the end of it. If you were able to interview the sniper, you might find out he picked out the squared-away Marine."

"I was in fifth grade in Shattuck School, Mrs. Walker's class, and it was the last day of class. We were in the front room, second floor on the ballfield side, and we were due to get our report cards and having punch or Kool-Aid or something, a cupcake, and you go across the room to 6th grade, Mrs. Gavin. And so before that happened, probably even before my cupcake, Mr. Fox—if you remember Bob Fox, I don't know how big he was but to us he was huge, glasses, like you never saw his eyeballs, you just saw a reflection. He was very quiet and he had those big orthopedic shoes, they were like love seats and he was at the door. There was no intercom there, I remember seeing him come to the door when I was in first grade, because he would come to the door to bring the checks around, so you'd see him on a Thursday or Friday, but in first grade the teacher turned around crying and just said everybody go home. That was day that President Kennedy was assassinated. He's up there and she's up there, and they turn, she turns and she focusses on me, and she tells me to go see Mr. Fox up at the doorway and he tells me to collect my brother and go right home. I was almost home before I figured it out. There's a spot on Vernon Street where it got to me, we must have been discussing why we were sent home. Dick had been wounded at the end of January, we were in school and we weren't called home or anything, and then the last, roughly about a block, the rest of down to Prospect Street...

"You could see cars all over the place and you could hear the crying inside because a lot of them had gotten home. The call went out and a dragnet went out for my mother, she was out shopping someplace and she had the baby with her, Paul, who was four and a half, not in school yet. So she was—they have all the cruisers out looking for her, somebody's checking A & P, Star Market and First National, she could be at Sparks, she could be at Mal's, she could be at Ann and Hope saving twelve cents on a box of Kleenex... When I got in there, it was me and Jack and I think Dad had just told somebody else and he was crying, even if you compose yourself, you're gonna lose it when you tell the next one. It was a little sad bonus, when he could tell the two of us at once.

"The older ones were smarter, they knew. Picture yourself at seventeen or nineteen if you were told to get right home and you know you have a brother in combat. Sheila says *I knew*, Tommy says *I knew*, Maureen was in junior high, the end of March Sheila had seen Peggy Burke pulled from class, Sheila was close with Peggy Burke, Pat Burke's younger sister. Still are.

"I came home and everyone's crying, and my father said, 'Dickie's had it, he's had it,' and I'm there thinking, what do you mean he's had it, what do you mean *he's had it?* I figured out right away, or already knew... It was just a phrase you'd see in World War II movies and stuff.

"My father found out at the station. Joey Jenkins, Johnny Jenkins, remember them? Their father was a Colonel in the Marine Corps, and he was local,[33] I don't know if he was in Weymouth or at the Naval Air Station or somewhere in Boston, but the casualty list and the notification list comes across, and I think he decided to do it himself and came out here. I don't know who the Priest was, but he grabbed a Priest and they went to the station and they filled my father's doorway, and he knew. When the Marines went without a Priest, when Dick was wounded... They got better at giving notifications during Vietnam, better than World War II when they just sent a telegram.

"Your whole life changes right at that minute. It's like no other duty for a Marine to climb those stairs knowing once the door opens everybody inside and hundreds of people around, their lives are gonna be changed forever. My father, he pretty much knew where everybody was, you think sometimes you gotta remind him that it's your birthday or something, but

---

33 Col. Jenkins lived in Norwood, having purchased 36 Harrow Road from my future in-laws, Bud and Jorita Symington, in August of 1967.

he knew what schools we were all in, and how to reach everybody else. Jimmy at work down at the highway, Kevin painting the Polito's house, and wherever Billy was, two weeks out of high school. He might have been at Clark's, he worked there too, but really not knowing where the hell my mother was, because she was out shopping…

"He went home to receive everybody, and one by one everyone was told to go home. People tell you where they were when they heard…Vernon Street was, with downtown and Father Mac's up the street, there was a never-ending, I mean you could sit on my front porch and just look at the girls go by, you know that old girl-watching song. They had their transistor radios up to their ears, you're hearing *Hang on Sloopy* or *Crystal Blue Persuasion*, I mean all the music of the '60s, some of them found out that way. One of Dickie's girlfriends and sometimes date Barbara Halloran, lived up by Spruce Road I think—she was pretty—and I remember her walking up and just seeing somebody tell her and her expression changed and her falling apart…there are just so many people around in Norwood, there were sixty-five kids between diapers and diplomas just on Vernon Street.

"My mother avoided the whole dragnet and she was the last to come home. She came up Vernon Street and saw the cars everywhere, certainly too much activity, and my father went out and met her in the driveway, and I was watching from inside and it was just horrible, falling down…it was their worst fear…

"Dick was killed the 15th, we were notified the 19th and within a day or two there was another telegram that he'd arrive at Logan on the 27th, on such and such a flight. They sent all the particulars, this would be paid for, this would be paid for, and so we, I don't remember, between that time, between the 19th and the 27th, the house was just full of people most of the time. One of my father's friends sent in a crew for a couple of days in the middle of it and just painted and papered, the dining room, the kitchen. And there was always food being sent up, Chinese food from Bing Chin over in Islington and big, huge things of coffee and stuff, and they sent us around, us kids, we were shuttled around a little bit. We ended up at one of my father's cousin's house, but we still got to our Little League games and stuff, I had my birthday two days after we were notified."

"I was sitting there in the store," Bernie Cooper recalled, "and I remember John Cooke coming down and sticking his head in, saying Chief Murphy's son was killed in Vietnam, you knew him, right? My father gave Cooke an office above the hardware store for his newspaper, and he came down and told us. I was just stunned, disbelief, Jimmy was in my class, Dickie a year behind...we were in Boy Scouts together...the only other thing I remember is the cars outside of St. Catherine's at the funeral, two, three deep, just incredible. It's one of the only times in my life that I cried."

"I remember it was a sunny day, I remember the silence," Debbie Dray, shortly to become Mrs. Kenneth Reddick, remembered. On the day of the funeral, she worked at Dandy Donuts, across the street from St. Catherine's. "We had just graduated, so we didn't hear about it at school, but what I remember the most is the enormous amount of people that showed up. They double-parked, nobody came in while we were here to be served, it was an enormous amount of people, the enormity of it. Everyone was solemn, just taken aback that it had happened, after Patrick Burke and Fitzgerald..."

"I first met the Murphys actually walking back and forth to Father Mac's," Billy Sherman recalled of the day that changed his life. "You walk by the house and everybody would say hey that's Chief Murphy's house, there was always some Murphy kids around somewhere. You kept at arms-length because they were the Chief of Police's kids, I didn't necessarily grow up in that neighborhood. I had an arms-length relationship with the Murphys for a long time, and then the day of that funeral I had heard about it, I don't know from who, but I had to go up. So I got on my bike with the banana seat and the long handlebars and drove up town and I was shocked. I remember being shocked at all the people lining the streets. To me it was like *wow*, all these people to see the chief's son who died in Vietnam, you know, and of course you see the procession with the horses and the carriage drawn with the flag over it, and the Marines marching and the police and all that. What struck me more than anything was the look in people's faces, you know, it was a mixture of pride and sadness. Proud of one of their Norwood boys which has a rich tradition, as I'm sure you're aware of, of military service, and also a rich tradition of Marine Corps service in that time.

"I saw all the people's faces and it just shocked me, but it also gave me a sort of a reverent feeling. It was like *wow,* this is something, this is something I need to tap into. I don't know, maybe it was a hero complex I had in me, my dad was gone, I needed a direction, I didn't know it at the time, but it was what was going to point me in the right direction in life.

"I drove up there and saw the whole thing at the cemetery, the very solemn twenty-one-gun salute, very solemn day. But what got me was all the people from Norwood that turned out for that despite, you gotta remember, at this time you had the anti-war protests but none of that stuff was in Norwood at that time that I was aware of. I was only fourteen at the time that this happened, and so I guess to make a long story short, what got me the most was the look on the people's faces. I wanted them to look at me the same way. I wanted them to notice *me*, I wanted them to be proud of *me*, and I wanted to be brave, you know? And to me that was all the elements of being a man, and I was looking for that. I didn't have a father, and I was searching."

Brian Murphy slides the front-page *Record American* photograph toward me. If a picture is worth a thousand words, this commands a dictionary. It shows Mrs. Murphy, face buried in hands and her head leaning against Dick's coffin on the tarmac at Logan Airport. Chief Murphy's arm is around her shoulder, the couple surrounded by seven sons and two daughters, and assorted friends.

"That's my father with his arm on my mother... This is my grandmother, that's my uncle John, XL's father, that's my brother Jack, my sister Sheila, she graduated two years later in '70, that's me, I'm being held by my brother Jimmy, he's the oldest, he's the class of '65, there's Billy, he'd just graduated a couple of weeks before, class of '68. That's his girlfriend Claire Jones—they got married—she graduated '69, from Jefferson Drive. Brother Bobby, that's Father Rocco, I'm not sure who this guy is, he might be from the funeral home, Kevin behind my father, that's Maureen, she was being helped by Kevin, that's his future wife Roberta Polito, she graduated in '70. That's Arthur Groh and his wife, that's Billy D'Espinosa, Dickie's friend, Nose's cousin, that's my brother Tommy, that might be Barry McKinnon, even in the picture there's another heading to Vietnam, Billy D'Espinosa. He was a photographer in the Army.

"The saddest sight I ever saw was Mom learning Dick had died," Brian Murphy told me. Dick Murphy's letter to Father McManus had ended, *"Please say an extra prayer for my mother. I know my being in Vietnam is hard on her. I worry about her. I didn't have to leave home to know I had the best father and mother in the world. God bless them..."*

Brian's eyes remain fixed on the photograph, his voice firm and low, steeled after a half-century of grieving. "My dad told Dick when he brought him to the airport, that we'll all be here when you come home."

THE OTHER TOWN

Needham and Norwood put up a fight. Give it to Corkery and say, "Goodnight!" "Hey, Dad," my son said, "When you were in school I heard you guys were good—that Arlington ruled. So, what's the real deal? Were your teams always that good? Did you ever give up? Did you give all that you could?" I stopped and smiled...and thought of the lesson learned. "No...we couldn't give up...we played for Eddie Burns!"
— Ed Mulcahy, class of '67, poem for Eddie Burns' commemorative banquet

The gut-punch 1968 overtime loss, the first overtime in a state final game since 1944, put Arlington in Norwood's collective head. After the exuberance of a first-time appearance in a state final game in '65 and consecutive one goal Arlington losses in '67 and '68, a rivalry had formed. Norwood had emerged a super-power in high school hockey, but inevitable comparisons to the reigning champions proved nettlesome.

Norwood was proud of three final appearances in four years; Arlington, after '68, had *won* the championship a record five times.[34] When Norwood's sophomore sensation Neil Higgins tied the Massachusetts schoolboy record for shutouts in a season with 12, it was only to equal Spy Ponder Bill Langone's mark. The state scoring record was held by Bobby Havern with 66 regular-league points; the most any Norwood player had scored was Richie Hebner's 45.

---

34 1968 was the first year that champions of Eastern, Central, and Western Massachusetts were determined. The Central and Western champions played-off for the right to play the Eastern champions for the state title. Arlington, after its dramatic overtime win over Norwood, lost the first East-West match for the "State Title" to Auburn, a cautionary tale for Eastern teams going forward not to be over-confident against traditionally inferior teams. For years under this system, the Eastern Mass. finals was still considered the defining game.

Further comparisons indicated Arlington always a step ahead, or notch above. For colonial-minded Massachusetts, Arlington's genesis began in 1635, a year before Dedham's, and a full forty before Norwood proper. While Norwood venerates Aaron Guild for leaving his plow to rush toward the fighting of April 19, 1775—and whose record remains hazy as to whether he even reached the running battle in time to participate—Menotomy, Arlington's colonial name, saw more bloodshed on its roads and in its houses that day than skirmishes at Lexington and Concord combined.

Comparisons reveal much in common. Both early villages thrived with the development of mills along workable waterways, Norwood on the Neponset River, and Arlington on Mill Brook. Both towns supported thriving pond-ice production, Norwood on Ellis Pond, Arlington on Spy Pond. And both towns experienced burgeoning populations after the turn of the last century as workers flowed toward newly created manufacturing jobs, rendering the '60s offspring of both municipalities predominantly sons of blue-collar workers. Like Norwood's Tiot, the Algonquin translation of Menotomy is disputed by local historians.

Coincidentally, both became incorporated townships in 1872, Menotomy evolving through West Cambridge before taking the name Arlington, in honor of recently fallen Civil War veterans interred in Arlington National Cemetery, while Norwood evolved through Tiot and South Dedham. As the 20th century progressed and Arlington became enmeshed in the expanding Boston metropolitan area, one last difference emerged as a minor, if noticeable divide in this clash of civilizations: Arlington boys we considered city boys in their leather jackets; Norwood boys they considered country bumkins.

The Arlington hockey experience mirrored Norwood's. Maurie Corkery, class of '72, related that kids "went to Arlington, and it was just tradition to play there. It was inbred in Arlington that you played hockey. We had JV teams that could beat a lot of varsity teams. A lot of kids got cut, I know a lot of them, some of them got cut when they were seniors. Burns was kinda tough on that stuff, he'd bring a kid in as a sophomore and if he didn't pan out by his junior year, he was gone. Yeah, a lot of kids, you kept them around for two years, and they come to their senior year, and you cut 'em. Well, obviously they didn't improve. There was a couple of guys he could have kept who were pretty good players and ended up being pretty good players elsewhere."

"The old man told me, he goes you weren't gonna be tall enough for basketball," Jay Shaughnessy remembered. "In those days we used to go over to the Arena and you'd get the broken sticks, that's how we got our sticks. It was pretty much hand me down skates for a lot of Arlington boys. Burns the coach, his family grew up right behind us, we were on Park Avenue they were on Hillside, we used to play a lot of street hockey on the driveway over there. I used to always walk down to Menotomy during the week, and during the weekends we'd walk down to Spy, drop you off early morning pick you up late afternoon. That's pretty much how we got into it.

"My heroes? Right off the bat, Buddy Clarke. My brother played goalie behind Billy Langone on the '64 team, they won the states but lost the New Englands. But Bubby Clarke was really, really good, I think he was All-American over at BC. He was a nice guy, funny guy, I always looked up to him, played like he played. He was very good. And Charlie Toz was good, and who else was on that team, Richie DiCaprio, like I say, down at Menotomy, we'd go down there, we had games down there, a lotta times the bigger kids were playing, a lotta times the smaller kids would jump in and play with them and I think that was a big thing, because we noticed a speed difference, so much faster and stuff. Menotomy was Hills Pond. Joey Bertagna lived across the street from us. The first set of goalie pads he had he bought when he was a freshman in high school, he bought off my brother Tom. Bertagna had an incredible tournament. He always rose to the occasion, he played against you guys, he played really well. He was clutch, plus he was one of the smartest guys you'd ever wanna meet.

"Myself and Kevin Carr made the varsity when we were sophomores. In '71 I think I might have been one of the only single captains in the history of Arlington hockey, there wasn't too many single captains that I can remember. I'm going back to like the '50s, and it wasn't so much that they wanted me, it's just that there were seven seniors on the team, and they were all, they voted for me because they knew I'd be out drinking with them on Friday nights after curfew! That's how I got it."

"Arlington population was roughly 50,000 people when I grew up," '68 goaltender Joe Bertagna related. "I have nothing but good memories of growing up in the town, it was a very attractive town, the school system was good. Looking back with the awareness I have now, it wasn't a very particularly diverse town, not many minorities at all. When Kennedy ran for President, there was a national story about a Catholic running, those of us in Arlington were like, what's the big deal, isn't everybody Catholic?

It was a town of heavily Irish and Italian Catholics. There were, let's see, one, two, three Catholic Churches I think in town at the time, and a fourth just over the line in Winchester.

"The people that bought my family house in 1973 still live there, and I've not been shy about going back and knocking on the door and just walking in and I've become friends with them. The address was 101 Brantwood Road. We used to play street hockey in front of the house but more importantly within sight of the house, if you looked down the street there was a pond, not Spy Pond, the big pond that Arlington sports teams got their nickname from, but a small pond called Hill's Pond. It was one of those places I have it in my book[35] that at the end of the day in grammar school, they have the PA system announcements and they would tell you if they had safe skating and was tested by the town and Spy Pond was so big they'd never say it froze to the point they would say it's safe because there were too many places where it wasn't. But they would say safe skating at Hill's Pond, and you'd have a big smile and go home and get your stuff and go over and skate."

"I grew up on Newport Street and I still live in the house I grew up in since 1948," '67 captain Bob Bartholomew remembered. "We played everything in the street, up the Farm, but I got introduced to hockey at Rt. 2 which was an outdoor rink. They had a youth hockey league run by the recreation department on Saturday mornings. But prior to that I met a good friend up on the next street, Bobby Havern, are you familiar with that name? Bobby led the state in scoring as a senior with 66 points and then went on a tear in the tournament.

"Mr. Havern asked me if I'd like to go in to Boston Arena on a Friday night to watch high school hockey, and I'd never been to a game. It was the old GBI League,[36] I wanna say circa 1957, and I just could not believe what I was watching. It was just awesome. A team would play a period, then another team would play a period, then the first team would play

---

35 Arlington High and Harvard graduate Joe Bertagna served 23 years as commissioner of Hockey East. He was the first coach of Harvard's women's hockey team, Boston Bruins' goalie coach for seven seasons, as well as assisting Team USA in the 1991 Canada Cup and the 1994 Olympics in that capacity. He graciously allowed free use of his work in progress, Late in the Third, his reminiscence of a lifetime in hockey, for this book.

36 Arlington played in the GBI League, technically the Greater Boston Industrial League. It was often referred to as the Greater Boston League, and eventually came to officially use that name.

their second period, and then they'd clean the ice. I think Arlington played Stoneham that night and we were just there for four games, and like I said it was a Friday night and I was just like stunned and then we followed them on a regular basis, my dad would bring me into the Arena.

"In 1959 Arlington had played Melrose twice during the season, and they were playing Melrose for the state championship game. And I sat next to Joe Hogue, who was the athletic director and the football coach at Melrose High School. It was a great game, Arlington scored early, Charley Chisholm got the goal, but the Arena turned three thousand people away. They're already in the neighborhood, so they all went to watch those kids play and that really got me involved. I was there with Bob Havern and Bobby Havern, Jr., and we just fell in love with Arlington hockey. And then I was skating down at Spy Pond one day and my dad introduced me to Eddie Burns, and he said if you want to learn to play hockey, you wanna come to Arlington High School. Because we were all at St. Agnes, and we all couldn't wait to get out. (laughs) We were all there and couldn't wait to get to Arlington High School. We got there in the fall in 1963. But we were big on following Arlington hockey, football, baseball, all the sports, but hockey was King."

"I had a brother Bob who played for the high school," Joe Bertagna continued. "He was four years older than me, so we were never in school at the same time, but I'd watched him and how important playing for Arlington was. He went on to be a radiologist, but he'll tell you the most important thing, the most significant thing he ever did in his life was play hockey for Arlington. It was that important to him. And so, watching him and watching what it meant to him and how he lived and died with everything, it was the first idea in my head of a goal, something I wanted to do, I wanted to play for Arlington. And my older sister took me to games. Arlington was good all that time, so you grew up learning about how successful the team was, and the state tournament, and it was in the papers.

"So I was well versed in all of that, and so the desire to play for the high school became really important to the point I slipped from defense to goal, because even on my own I realized I wasn't gonna make it as a defenseman, or enough parents and friends told me, hey you're a pretty good goalie you ought to try that, which was probably their way saying...(laughs) The path to that was made available because Ed Walsh, who was the star goalie of our age, shifted from Arlington to Brown & Nichols prep school, and he went on to be an All-American at BU and backed up Dryden at Montreal. So he and Neil Higgins and Cap Raeder, who was a little bit younger, those were the goalies of our time that everyone looked up to, they were the gold standard. So when Eddie left, I had to scramble a week before tryouts my sophomore year to get goalie equipment, and I ended up being one of four or five guys who rotated as backup for the varsity and got to dress for the state tournament, the night that Arlington won in '67. I was less than a full year as a goalie, but I was on the bench.

"The following year I started off alternating, and by the time we got to the tournament, I split the first game with another guy, got a shutout the second game, and Burns decided to stay with me, and then we went to the Garden and beat Melrose, Needham, and Norwood."

"You couldn't get near the Arena for games," Bob Bartholomew said. "And then, like I'd go in, the Junior Suburban League at six, then the Greater Boston League would come in at 12:30 and we'd hide everywhere just so we wouldn't have to pay again, and then we'd watch the Greater Boston League and hide again, and then watch the Bay State League, and then make it home by eleven o'clock.

"I was never the best. I did a lot of raw, high stuff. We did a lot of street hockey and stuff, and I'd be always shooting pucks, we had no plaster left on the house, the plaster was gone. Football was the game I wanted to play, but then when Bobby Havern and me went into the Boston Arena, that didn't change things, but then hockey came on the horizon, too. Like I said, I was never the best. So there were a lot of good players and I looked up to them.

"My heroes were a kid named Harry Howell, graduated in '59, went to Harvard, he never came off the ice for Arlington. There was him, there was a great line, this is '59, Aiken, Allen, and Chisholm, the kid I really liked was a kid named Allan Kierstead, number 11. Ended up going to BC. He could skate like the wind and shoot the puck, great two-way player, and that's why I took the number 11 in high school. We would practice at BC at McHugh Forum on Monday's and Wednesdays at 7:15, and a lot of times we'd get there early and BC would be on the ice practicing, and you'd get to watch him. All of them. They were a tremendous club; they were all Massachusetts kids at the time. Buddy Clarke I liked and Charlie Toz and Dick DiCaprio, and Eddie Roland, I mean we were all good friends and everything, but those were the guys you watched play, and then you'd tried to idolize them.

"I was a good listener; I'd do everything I could possibly to get better at the game. I had the strongest desire to play for Arlington High. In eighth grade when I couldn't skate backwards, that sent a message. And I went to Snooks Kelley's hockey school, every Sunday in the fall, and Red Martin was there, Billy Daley was there, Snooks Kelley was there, Jimmy Logue, Jackie Cunniff, all these great former BC players, Stucco was there, and that was a great clinic. And I knew I was getting better when I was in the eighth grade, maybe, or ninth grade. I was in the B group and the older kids would come on, and they'd come up and ask me, can you stay for the next hour? And so I'd have to ask my father, yeah, you can stay. So I got to play with the older kids. And I just kept working at it. Working, working, shooting pucks down the high school, I had a paper route. When I was in high school, I'd deliver, my dad would drive around, I had five Sunday routes, so that was my conditioning. I could sit on the back of the station wagon and I'd walk from house to house to house. And that kept me going. And when Eddie talked to me at Spy Pond and Bobby's dad brought us into the Arena, that was it. We actually made a pact in 1959 that we were gonna go to Arlington High School and win a state title, me and Bobby Havern. Ten years old at that Melrose game. While we were eating the French fries!"

Sportswriter Ralph Wheeler recognized an emerging legend in a January 2, 1961, *Boston Herald* article. Under the headline *Scouting Key to Arlington Hockey Success,* he emphasized the preparation of a former Marine, writing,

> Arlington High's amazing success in hockey is attributed to the most comprehensive scouting system in schoolboy sports, in addition to the sound fundamentalist in veteran coach Eddie Burns. Assistant coach John Byrne and one or two former Arlington

High stars sit up in the press box during the entire three periods of every game which the Red and Gray plays at the Arena. "They take notes on everything worthwhile during those three periods," said Coach Burns. "They dissect the weakness of our team as well as the opposition, chart the shooting, list the back-checking, errant passing, and keep tabs on the players who wander out of their lanes.

"Making our first liners skate their lanes is one of our big problems this season, in as much as the three boys all played center in previous years. Incidentally, we check our scouting reports after the first and second periods. We also go over these reports from one to two hours every afternoon during the week. We practice twice a week from 7 to 8 at the McHugh Forum at Boston College."

Burns also appreciated his assistants. "If they had a better idea, I would go with it," he once said. "I always took notes when scouting other teams and I asked my assistants to do the same. And I read all the books written by the great coaches and learned from them."

Edward Patrick Burns was born in Lexington on November 20, 1920. His family moved to the next town over, where he became a football and hockey star at Arlington High School. After a year of prep school, Burns attended Boston College where a stellar athletic career was interrupted, as were so many, by World War II. Assigned to a Marine artillery unit at Villanova University, he played football during the fall of 1942 before shipping out to Guam in the South Pacific. Burns returned from the war and to Boston College, where he competed in both football and hockey during the 1946-47 season, his prowess rewarded with draft selections by the Pittsburgh Steelers in football and the Philadelphia Phillies in baseball.

Arlington hockey, meanwhile, had made its mark with 7-0, 1947 state championship win over Boston Tech. When coach Charlie Downs decided to go out on top, Eddie Burns applied for and was accepted as the new head hockey coach of Arlington High School. On December 16, 1947, Arlington defeated Rindge 7-0 for the rookie mentor's first victory.

"Always Mr. Burns, there was a tremendous amount of respect for him," Tony Lyons, class of '67 said. "You know, there was a little bit of fear, ah, because he had that, he was an old Marine, and he brought that out all the time. And expected you to be a little bit of a Marine. And if you go back and talk to anyone who played for him, there's always that ethic, that kind of Marine Corps ethic, never leave anyone behind, and always, always come home as a winner."

"He had a lucky hat," son Brian Burns explained. "He smoked cigars back then and he'd come in the locker room every time and he'd stick it in the shower or hide it somewhere and everybody knew he did it. If we won like a really big game, like we beat Norwood or something, one of the seniors would grab it and light it up!"

"Eddie Burns was probably in his forties when he coached us," Joe Bertagna related. "He got out of BC in the late forties, and then we're there in the late sixties. So, he wasn't an old guy, but when you're fifteen or whatever he seemed like this old, wise guy. They had a sportsman's club in Arlington that raised money to run dinners for teams and give awards out to championship teams, there were about twelve adults and my parents were both on it with Eddie, so they were friendly with him. So I knew him through the family, but I mentioned someplace, he was like a father figure. Sometimes they refer to somebody who didn't have a father and they latched on to an older gentleman who acted like their father, but those of us who had good, strong father figures had a second one in Eddie. And we had this unquestioned respect of him. He had us have meetings, after school we had to meet for a half hour, we had to keep notebooks, and I remember watching my brother's notebooks. My brother was very illustrative, drawing the breakout plays, and I kept a notebook as a goalie of every goal I allowed, what I did, what I could have done, notes about the rink, if the boards were lively. Those days the rinks weren't very uniform, some had glass, some had chain-link fence, some had better lighting than others, so you could find different features of a rink and I was just organized, and I'm sure that came from how organized Eddie was.

"We just respected the hell out of him," Joe Bertagna continued. "The fact that he kept winning was part of it, but he had a presence to him, kind of a gravelly voice that we all did our impressions of him, but not in front of him, we had too much respect for that. Had the cigar, it's funny now because you can't smoke in any of the buildings. He'd actually come in the locker room, he'd have his cigar and he'd put it up above at the Arena, some of the walls didn't go up to the ceiling, so he could reach up and leave his cigar on top of the thing, and God knows how dirty it was, but he'd go out, we'd play a period, he'd come back in and reach up and get his cigar and puff on it. One time we had a teammate who moved it about three feet so when he went up to reach for it, he had to search for it, pawing at it and he finally found it, and we just grimaced, oh my God how filthy it must be up there!

"He was organized, we had our breakout plays, we had all these names, the defensemen at the points he had generic names, so if you were in the corner digging for the puck, someone would yell *Mike! Mike! Mike!* It wasn't because that guy's name was Mike, it meant the middle point guy was open, and if you yelled *Pete!* the point along the boards was open. So you had Mike and Pete, yelling those names, and the opponent might have been thinking those were guys' names were Mike and Pete, but it was really Burns' names for the points, and allowed you to know what was open without turning around and looking to see, so he had that level of organization. You know, they always counted shots, how many on, how many off. Had little decals, they called them Chevrons. I don't know what the origin of that word is, but that's what they called them. The star player might have twenty decals on his helmet for accomplishment. He brought the system to hockey and he gave out little stickers for guys to put on their helmets, and not necessarily for scoring goals, for other things he wanted them to do."

Despite the fealty induced in his players, Eddie Burns was not immune from working-class whispers among his subjects. "Burns won, and he won often," Joe Bertagna wrote in *Late in the Third*. "He wasn't perfect. And we had fun with that. He might start a story with, 'Ninety-nine times out of ten...' The capacity crowd of 13,909 at the old Boston Garden might come out as, 'Thirteen thousand nine-oh-thousand.' Before taking on a major rival, his pre-game talk frequently included some politically incorrect motivation. 'Nervous? Why, there are fifty million Chinamen who don't even know you're playing.' His wardrobe made even me look like a GQ model. And we all tried to mimic that gravelly voice. But never in front of him."

"His nickname in the '60s was 'the Bun,' Maurie Corkery said. "Bun. Burns and Bun sound alike. Then the Bun found out about it, and they changed it to 'the Nub'. Why the Nub? Well, that was just the Bun spelled backwards!"

Eddie Burns coached Arlington hockey for 50 seasons, as well as coached varsity football for 21. He left behind a set of numbers—notably 695 hockey victories—so long and impressive they blur the totality of his accomplishments. But it is his bequeathing a tradition, a work ethic, a *direction* to his players that is truly incalculable.

"Hockey was a central factor in my life," Joe Bertagna said. "First of all, and I've said this in different ways, playing in the state tournament took you from playing on a small stage to a big stage. You start out playing in your back yard, down the street at a park, and then you play your league games so that was a bigger stage cuz you get to play in the Boston Arena. But then you get to play under the bright lights and the tournament and the media coverage and all of a sudden, you're going from unknown person in your neighborhood to, you know, stardom with a small "s", we'll put it that way, celebrity with a small "c". People know who you are, here we are talking about this fifty years later, and you have a chance to either succeed or fail and fortunately in that first opportunity I succeeded, which led to Harvard. Could I have got into Harvard without hockey? I don't know. The reason why I say I don't know is maybe if I didn't play hockey maybe I'd do something else. Maybe I could have been good at something else. But I wasn't gonna get in just on my grades, so it had to be my grades and something else. And the way it turned out back then, that something else was hockey.

"For better for worse, I'm still referred to as 'former Harvard goalie Joe Bertagna.' For better or worse, it's something you have, and I've always thought a group of people made a decision about you based on your life's work as a sixteen-year-old. You get this benefit; you get this asset that stays with you your whole life. And then I was able to make a whole living on hockey and play it, and make friends, and I met my wife because she was working at Harvard Sports Information covering the hockey team. Her father had played for the high school, she had two uncles who'd played for the high school, her mother had been a cheerleader at the high school. (laughs) So hockey carries over to your social life, and so your self-esteem, your friends, in my case your marriage, your family, made a living out of coaching, and playing and paid to play, paid to coach, paid to administer, and still, just from this conversation you can tell how much it has been and still is a part of my life.

"I'll be seventy on my next birthday and I'm still working for a National Coach's Association, I'll be on the ice coaching goalies tonight. I'm still working with the Eastern Hockey League, so it's never left me. It would be really hard to believe if I didn't have this kind of awareness of what it's done for my life. It's also allowed me to travel and see the world. I played in Italy, I've gone to Belfast with this tournament that's been interrupted by Covid, I've made twelve trips to Northern Ireland because of this hockey tournament. I've made ten trips to Cortina since I've played, so there's not much in my life it hasn't touched."

"I had a great love for the game," Bob Bartholomew concluded. "I loved playing outside. We would practice at Belmont Hill outside, on Rt. 2 outside, first time I ever got to play inside was at the Skating Club. Listening to the Bruins on radio, listening to the Red Sox, whatever, you know, black and white, you'd have to whack the TV, but for the game itself, I just liked the competition. I also liked meeting a lot of great guys like Vinnie Shanley who was a captain at BC, Richie Umile at Melrose, Bobby Harrison Melrose, just all the great friendships you made, the list is enormous. Billy Munroe who played at Wellesley, you never realized how good these guys were because a lot of those teams didn't make the tournament. They had some really good hockey players, and we became great friends on and off the ice. The competition level was good, the friendships were lifelong, that's what I would have to say, just great friendships.

"And then seeing their kids develop, and getting to coach their kids in high school. Teaching their kids in middle school or high school, that's definitely important, and then to see them grow up and then have families of their own. That's what Eddie would always tell us. That his love for the game was because he wanted to see what his players become, go to college, or to serve in the military, use their skills and then come back and raise a great family. That would be one of your goals, to make you successful. That's what Eddie Burns would tell us."

THE ICE ADONIS

No man is a hero to his valet.
— Medieval European proverb

And then something happened to Bay State League hockey. Leo McInerney relates the awe with which the phenomenon was first observed:

"I can remember we opened up our senior year against Framingham North at North, and Dennis and I each had a goal and an assist in that game, and so we were having breakfast. We went to church, I think we went to church, we were supposed to go to church, and we went down to McManus' to have breakfast and of course we brought the *Record* to look at ourselves in the box scores. And there was a kid named Ftorek—this is '68 now, the kid would have been a sophomore—Needham opened up against Braintree and they won 16-0. And this kid we never heard of in our lives named Ftorek had eleven points. *Eleven points!* Un-freaking-believable! We're like, who the hell, what the hell is this Ftorek thing, what the hell is *this?* I mean you could go a whole season without getting eleven points in that league!"

Like many working-class towns, Norwood has produced an array of individual achievement. Its sons and daughters more than filled its quota of professional athletes, actors, professional baseball umpires, Judges, All-American hockey players, and writers. South Norwood's John Chervokus, grandson of early Lithuanian immigrants, created the 1960s' famous, "Please don't squeeze the Charmin!" marketing slogan. Prospect Street's Tom Shillue is an accomplished stand-up comedian, actor, and commentator on Fox News. Sycamore Street's Dickie Barrett is a rock star, lead singer of The Mighty Mighty Bosstones.

A Nichols Street kid became a writer for *The Boston Globe*, which published the following 2001 piece wonderfully describing the *Norwood, in the Time of Hockey* era, specifically Norwood's breach in hockey dominance and its principal nemesis.

BRIAN MacQUARRIE

Gallons of ink have been used to chronicle the past and present of local legend Robbie Ftorek, new coach of the championship-starved Boston Bruins. Undersized but tenacious, the Needham native is rightly regarded as the greatest high school hockey player in Massachusetts history. Two state championships, three state scoring records in three years, 54 goals in 23 games as a senior—Ftorek's numbers are stunning.

But this guy, as wondrous as his numbers were, transcended data. Just ask my class of 1970 at Norwood High School, where our last three years coincided with his time at rival Needham High.

In our town, in those days, hockey was king. Forget football, basketball, and even baseball. Hockey was the thing, and Ftorek's magical talents stoked a passionate mixture of envy and wonder. Just as Bobby Orr mesmerized us on the professional level, Ftorek brought an almost supernatural presence to the high school game that made every Norwood-Needham contest a nearly unbearable blend of anxiety, hope, and dumb-struck awe.

For a high school kid, it didn't get any better than that. And, for me, the Red Sox pennant drive in 1967 remains the only sporting event in this sports-crazy region to match the excitement of those winter nights. Ftorek looks fairly ordinary now, although his coiled intensity and athletic trim belie the fact that he's one year shy of a half-century. But when I look at him, I don't see the Bruins. I still see those high school games, Homeric epics staged twice a season before standing-room crowds crammed into primitive ice rinks like the old Four Seasons Arena in Walpole.

I see classmates bundled up against the cold, standing in line for popcorn and hot dogs at too-small concession stands, their breath turning into hazy clouds around their scarves and woolen hats. I see cigarette smoke rising from the spectators jammed together on frozen bleacher seats, and the late arrivals leaning against the grimy concrete walls behind them. And I see an expectation in my neighbors' eyes of something wondrous about to happen, an unscripted athletic spectacle played out amid hand-wringing hope that Norwood somehow could topple the great Ftorek and his starry supporting cast.

I rarely expected Norwood to beat Needham in my high school years, when the Needham Rockets blasted their way to two state championships. But when Norwood's skaters lost, they seemed to fall in grudging defeat to a superior team with a juggernaut's combination of strength, depth, finesse, and the ultimate X factor in Ftorek.

That's what I remember, anyway. And the glow of watching something extraordinary while cheering, in simple Andy Hardy fashion, for my school and my town. I suppose I learned—mostly from defeat—that striving can be victory in itself, that the good effort is its own reward, and that great satisfaction can be gleaned from fiercely held loyalty to a simple, noble cause. Those memories also help reconnect me to the elemental vitality that pure sport—waged solely for competition, among one's neighbors and friends—can bring to the soul.

More than 30 years have passed since I last saw Ftorek skate for Needham, but his image still floods me with thoughts of a simpler time, and a smaller universe, and a reminder that when teenagers grow to adults, they need not leave their dreams behind.

"Ftorek was a better high school hockey player than Richie," Dennis Hebner acknowledged. "Yeah, he was..."

"I was his class, yes," Mike Lydon recalled. "When we first started skating, we played over at Tabor with Mr. Clifford, early Saturday mornings, the original Norwood Hockey Club in its infancy, its early years, and Ftorek was often over there skating. We only played against him a few times, but he was just—not fair to have him on the ice with kids his age. Even in high school, he was playing a different game. When we were freshmen, we had a good freshman team, most of our freshmen didn't play for Wheeler after the junior year, but we were the only team that beat Ftorek. They won every other game they had cuz Ftorek as a freshman couldn't play varsity, the rules were such then, I guess he wasn't eligible to, something to do with junior highs, I don't know. But we beat them because their coach took the team off the ice because the refs weren't calling penalties on Norwood for hitting Ftorek. Christ, it's the only way to slow him down! Catch him! Forfeit, yeah. But he was playing a different game than we were, he was something."

"Ftorek was good," Dennis Hebner continued, "he was just, he was the kind of kid you couldn't get a good piece of. He would always finesse around ya, do the right kind of pass, get a pass right on a stick. He was good, he was probably the best finesse hockey player in high school when I was playing, that whole era. Light on his feet, you just, you couldn't hit him. I did hit him once; I got a penalty! I couldn't stand playing against him, I *had* to hit him!"

"Norwood and Needham had a long rivalry leading into the 1967-68 season and this year would be no different," Bobby Thornton recalled. "This year marked the appearance of the best player to ever play Massachusetts high school hockey, Needham's Robbie Ftorek. I will never forget hearing about this kid in the locker room after the first game of our season. We were all celebrating our first win of the year against Natick, when there was an audible buzz in the room about something. Even then, before the advent of cellphones or computers, we had received word that Needham had *crushed* Braintree that night by an unheard-of hockey score of 16-0. But the bigger news was that this rookie with a funny name had made his debut by scoring *ten* points in the game! I had the misfortune of playing against this great one for all three seasons of his high school career. Aside from this season—where we were even with them—I can honestly say that the next two years were the only time in my life where we went into a game *knowing* we were going to lose, because of *him*. He was that good. In each of Robbie's three years playing for Needham, he wound up breaking the State scoring records. He was so dominating by the end of this year that his Bay State League-leading scoring title of 62 points was exactly twice as many points that the second-leading scorer had from Framingham South."

"My senior year we were totally outclassed," Dickie Donovan recalled. "They just beat us 5-1, I think, and 4-1. We couldn't stay with them. But in 1968 we tied Needham for the Bay State championship, and Needham and Norwood were seeded like one and two in the state tournament. There was a game, Needham was ahead of us, we had a game in February at the Four Seasons. The rink was filled an hour before the game, and the cars were parked on Rt. 1 all the way back to Norwood and people were walking up in the snow. And the fire department from Walpole finally had to come up and told Nick Abraham you got to shut the doors, we can't allow anymore in. There was four thousand people already in, and they said can't do it. Norwood-Needham was, I mean...you were there, you were there. 2-2, yeah, we tied 2-2. Dennis Hebner and I scored the Norwood goals, and Ftorek got the, we were up 2-1 going into the third period and Ftorek got the tying goal.

"Best player I ever played against. By far. And I played in college against good guys, he was better than all of them. I mean, he used to play in the summer leagues, like in high school, and they'd go up against teams with all the BU defensemen on it, and he'd just turn 'em. I mean, he was the trickiest son-of-a-bitch I ever saw in my life. Easily. Best player I ever saw. I had fifty-five points my senior year, I averaged over three points a game. Ftorek averaged over *four* points a game. I finished second in the state, to him. And I said I'm not even that close, and I wasn't."

"I always compare him to Muhammed Ali," Bobby Rosata recalled. "Muhammed Ali in his prime, when someone would go to hit him, you couldn't hit the guy, right? Ftorek was the same way. We would hunt him down, there'd be two of us going to hit him, and he'd just, we'd end up crashing into the boards. He was just so elusive yet could hold onto the puck. I always called Hebner a man playing with boys, the way he could hold people off, but Ftorek was just much more skilled than the rest of us and saw the ice, and you couldn't get him. I had to take some faceoffs against him a little bit, his hands were unbelievable. He could go into a crowd, there'd be two guys checking him, but he's gonna come out with the puck. Every single time, no matter what you did! And he had good teammates, too. He actually was a team player; it wasn't just him. Like Hebner was just a man playing with boys, and he's gonna shoot that backhander harder than we shoot it forehand, but Ftorek made his whole team better."

"I went to the game, the state final, Needham was playing Melrose," Dickie Donovan continued. "I sat in the Melrose section and I bet a dollar with the Melrose people. Needham came on the ice they said, *well look at these kids, they're so small, look at that Ftorek,* and I said well, you wanna dollar bet on it? So he bets. Needham went down 1-0 on a fluke goal, then they scored five straight goals in the first period. The fifth goal, Ftorek held-off a big kid from Melrose—he went to BU—Ftorek held him off with one arm and with the other he one-handed it into the top of the net. Even the Melrose people, *oh my God*, he was unstoppable. He was, too. His sophomore year he had 60-something points, his junior year he had 74, and his senior year he had like 87, in the Bay State League, and that's not even counting tournament scoring. Best talent I ever saw."

"Without question, the best high school hockey player in Massachusetts, maybe ever," Bobby Dempsey concurred. "Was he big? Nope. Did he skate the fastest? Nope, although great skater. Did he have the hardest shot? Nope, although an incredibly accurate shot. But he could pass the puck, he was Gretzky. He was that good. Did he have talent around him? He did. Like Dagdigian, Parlato, Chucka Lambert, the goaltenders, but he brought them up to a different level, because he was able to feed the puck *so* well, *so* smoothly, so his records, his points per game, nobody could touch him. In the Bay State League in that era, nobody could come close to him, he was that dynamic. And the closest you can get is certainly Gretzky. Same situation. Fastest skater? No. Big guy? No. But boy, could he pass the puck. His vision, 365, 360, he got it, he was there. He could do it."

"Ftorek had set the state scoring record," Bobby Thornton said. "He beat his own record every year. So it went from 60 points, to 70 to 80 or something, and Paul O'Neil tied him our senior year from Malden Catholic, but it was in twenty games. He wounded up getting 223 points in three years! Ftorek! It's the only time in my lifetime, right up through four years of college, that I ever entered a game knowing I was gonna lose. I never said it to anyone. I just said, keep it respectable, playing against Ftorek. The only time, because he was that fucking good."

Arrival of the Ice Adonis coincided with two difficult years for Norwood hockey. 1969 was a season of disappointment with an epic quarterfinal, two-day, five-overtime loss to Marblehead; 1970 a fallow season most notable for the seeding of seven sophomores.

Town and team carried expectations with its confirmed acceptance into Massachusetts' hockey elite. The team had fought its way to three state final appearances in the preceding four years, the '69 edition led by superstar center Dickie Donovan. The maturing of the Crestwood Circle kid represented incremental advancement for Norwood hockey; if Richie Hebner's athleticism was blunt force trauma, Dickie's represented a refinement of accelerated skills.

"Oh, Dickie Donovan had it all around, I mean every year," Peter Tamulionis, captain of the 1970 team, recalled. "I think he was a little shy his sophomore and junior year, he didn't want to say too much. Now again, he was like a Jackie Cronin, he was a quiet kid, he was quiet. He was a quiet kid, but once the blood starts flowing and you start playing, he was one of the best hockey players I've ever seen. I mean, Dickie was, he was one of the best hockey players I've ever seen. He really was. He was *great*, he was *great*. Very, very smart man. Yes, he is. You guys had 'em all up there, Hebners up on Nahatan Street and you had the Donovans, the Higgins, the Reddicks all growing up back there on Crestwood Circle."

"Dickie, the laser focus on this kid, and what epitomizes was a game no one was at," Bobby Thornton recalled. "I remember watching him, his eyes were like a laser, he was just not gonna lose. That game—people remember the last thing you do? I will take that game to my grave. We were losing two-zip, and they were terrible. Three goals in 39 seconds, and it's called the '39 second miracle' with the headlines. Dickie was on the ice, I was on the ice, never came off. Each one of his guys on his line got the goals, McTernan, Taylor, Donovan. And for some strange reason, I was involved giving them a pass in each one. Don pulled Gump, Artie Harris with a little over a minute left to go because the faceoff was in their end. Ballsy move, no one had done it much back then. And we were hoping like, can we get a tie here? But we won, in regulation! In 39 seconds! And here's what I will take to my grave. He was like a laser, Dick Donovan. His eyes? I mean, he was *just on the puck, we're gonna win this thing*, and I think he figured in all three goals. The only time the puck came out of their zone was for a faceoff after we scored! Think about it!"

Bobby Thornton discussed the makeup of the '69 team. "Tommy Taylor, the closeness that we had, I was a young pup, he's my brother Michael's age, but they took me under their wing. We were like besties, and Gee, I saw Taylor about a year ago. This was one crazy bastard. You see pictures in these scrapbooks—his eyes were on fire. He ended up being fifth or sixth in the state his senior year in scoring.

"Gee Sortevik. Good shit. We were partners, and then Don pared me up with Peter after a while, Gee was a swingman but good, good shit. And that year, the other guys who were good teammates, Johnny Ranalli. He was very talented, he kind of bit the bullet for Don his senior year and played on the second line. The first line got two-thirds of our goals that year, Dickie, Taylor, and McTernan. Johnny Ranalli took one for the team. Johnny, I love Johnny, great teammate. Instead of getting all the glory—at one point, we were getting ready for the tourney and the season was over, he wasn't happy at this point. The season was over, he took a slapshot at Don. It was in practice, at the end of practice, and Don was being Don and he vented on Johnny, and Johnny had kind of had it up to here. Didn't hit him, *boom*! Took a slapshot!"

"You know who no one mentions? Who no one talks about?" Tommy Taylor said. "Gerry McTernan. He scored six goals in one game." But the ending to the '69 season all remember.

"The Marblehead Marathon and how *not* to get up the next day," Bobby Thornton wrote in an email. "After disposing of Catholic League powerhouse Matignon 5-0 in our first game of the state tourney, we wound up facing a perennially strong Marblehead team in our next game at Boston Arena. Marblehead had finished their North Shore League season with a record of 14-1-1. There were 6,000 screaming fans in attendance when we first faced-off on a Monday evening. There were four of the state's best hockey teams playing at the Arena that evening, Norwood vs. Marblehead and Needham vs. Melrose. The old barn was really rocking and our game gave all of the fans something to cheer about as we battled each other evenly, up and down the ice. Norwood was actually leading the Headers in this cliff-hanger with a minute left in regulation when Marblehead pulled their goalie for an extra attacker. They wound up tying us up with 44 seconds to play and the teams battled on into overtime. But after three regulation periods and two overtimes, the game had to be halted late that Monday evening because of state regulations. We were told we had to come back to the Arena right after school the very next day to complete the game."

"We had to win," Dickie Donovan recalled. "I can remember telling my mother the night before after we came home, I said, man I'm so tired, I got beat up tonight. They had no corners there, I used to be able to maneuver better, but there was no room in there. So the big defensemen were clocking me against the boards and I said I don't feel good about tomorrow, ma, I don't feel good. And sure enough, we played in front of nobody, there was nobody there, and we lost 3-2. I think we played three overtimes the night before, big crowd for that game, huge."

Bobby Thornton continued the narrative. "Because of the roller-coaster of emotions from playing in front of a raucous, full-house crowd in a thriller of a game on Monday night, to arriving at a nearly empty Arena to play it out on Tuesday, another tactical mistake might have been made. Although this decision made a lot of sense in theory, it kind of backfired a little for some of us. Because we were all kind of hungover from the night before and because we knew that this could end just like *that* with a quick goal, someone had an unusual idea of how to get our adrenaline going before the Tuesday matinee game.

"They brought blocking dummy pads, used by the football team to prevent injury in hitting drills, into the locker room before the game. We were each handed the blocking pad and told to pair off with a teammate. And then, pair by pair, we would kind of attack each other to simulate a fight without hurting the other guy. Well, the good news is that it made some sense and achieved the intended objective of elevating the adrenaline levels. The bad news was that we did this exercise in our skates right before we left the old locker room to go out onto the ice. Because of the terrible condition of the old linoleum-type locker room floors in the bowels of the old Arena, several of our players lost the edges on our skate blades. Several players fell to the ice when we went out for warmups. And, of course, there was no skate sharpening service available in the old Arena for an early Tuesday afternoon matinee with sudden death on the line. Still have nightmares occasionally about this one!

"Well, it didn't end well for the locals. In an eerily quiet and sparsely attended Arena the next day, Norwood simply did not have enough left in the tank. At 3:18 mark of the *fourth* overtime period, Marblehead scored the winner. The next day headlines in the Boston papers read, 'Lack of scoring beats Norwood.' Over a combined three regulation periods and four overtime periods, Norwood had 77 shots but only scored 2 goals. What an ugly and depressing ride home!"

Peter Tamulionis had hit the post during one of the Tuesday overtimes, before a kid named Herbie Pearl batted a puck out of mid-air past Arthur Harris for the winning goal. Frank Wall's column the next day was openly despondent, but noted Dickie Donovan's stellar performance, setting a Norwood scoring record with 55 points, and also acknowledged the end of another Crestwood Circle kid's career,

> Gary Sortevik also had some big shoes to fill, and in the tourney, there wasn't a better defenseman. Gary had it when it counted, and when the last big games came he seemed to rise to the occasion. If he had had a little more experience he could have been on everybody's all-star team. He should be a fine college player.

The 1969 team, with the matured skills of Dickie Donovan, the inexhaustible hustle of Tommy Taylor, and the unheralded talent of goalie Arthur Harris, had rivaled the '68 team. But like so many quality Norwood teams before them, they endured one last, long, quiet bus ride home from Boston.

"There was a cartoon in the *Boston Herald* about the Norwood High hockey team," Jerry Drummey recalled. "I think it was from '72. It showed a wave of three or four lines just coming over, it was a great cartoon and it said this is what Norwood had, they just keep coming line after line. Cuz most teams had two lines, but Norwood has four lines and they keep coming *atcha*, coming *atcha*, coming *atcha*. It was a great cartoon.

"The whole area was hockey nuts. Every yard had a hockey net in it. You played up at Father Mac's pool, street hockey games everywhere; once that pool was empty, up we go to play pool hockey. It was just a love of the game. It was a hockey world. There was no cable, no playing games on computers and stuff, it's what we did."

"Yeah, that was a big part of Norwood hockey," Bobby Dempsey said. "It was almost impossible to get on the varsity back then, the talent was so deep, and the CYO team was so good as a result. The CYO could have literally played in many leagues and done decently. Frankie Eppich in goal? Hello? Pretty special right there, turned into an All-Scholastic. I didn't get on the varsity until 1969, I played on the '68 CYO team, on the '67 team. Bob Donovan was the coach, one of your neighbors, of course.

"It's an addendum to a couple of good high school classes. '68, '69, '70, oh yeah. They were all good classes, and these kids just didn't have enough to get onto the varsity. They were all good players, real good players. It was freewheeling, it was a lotta fun."

"One game," Billy Sullivan recalled, "we kind of dominated everything, and Jerry Drummey was a junior or senior, and one game he took the puck from behind our net—it was like him playing pond hockey— Jerry skated all the way up, went behind their net and came all the way back and took a shot on our goalie! You know how Jerry was, ah, trying to think who our goalie was, mighta been Frank Eppich."

St. Catherine's Catholic Youth Organization hockey team won championships in both 1968 and '69. "The first one," Jerry Drummey continued, "my junior year would have been '67-'68, that's Bob Donovan's last year. We won the championship because of Frank Eppich. The team outshot us 2-1, but Frank just stoned them the whole way. In the middle of the game, he started laughing at them! He was a great, great goalie, I think the best Norwood had. Frank was All-Scholastic in the *Herald* the year they didn't make the tournament. We played St. Patrick's of Stoneham and we won, 1-0. I got the goal."

How good was this CYO team? It included Captain Jerry Drummey, Bobby Dempsey, Bob Rosata, Teddy Curtis, Mike Lowey, Frank Eppich, Johnnie Lawrie, Billy Sullivan, and Jackie Clifford, all of whom had, or would play varsity hockey for Norwood High School, as well as Crestwood Circle's Bobby Connor. The following year the team was as talented.

"We had a good CYO team," Mike Lydon said of the '69 team. "Jerry Gotovich played on that; he wouldn't play for Wheeler. The CYO team was good, but we snuck a few ringers in from the varsity, Johnnie Ranalli. Richie Lovell was our coach, Tony O'Day was his assistant. That was a great time. Playing over at McHugh Forum over at BC, we even had cheerleaders! Mark Flaherty, Fred Ravens, Eddie Letts mighta been with us, he was a good, solid defenseman."

"In '69 it was St. Theresa's in West Roxbury, it was 2-1," Captain Drummey recalled of the championship game. "Sully got the first one, I came in on a breakaway and I had the goalie down and out and the puck slipped off my stick and I'm like, *what the fuck!* and the goalie started laughing, but coming right down the slot was Moxie Sullivan… And they tied it up, and then it went to overtime. On a change-up, my brother Mark pulled one of those Carol Vadnais things, flipped the puck up in the air, lets it bounce right in front of the goalie, and in it went."

"Myself, Rosy, and Sully was one line. The other line was my brother Mark, Johnnie Lawrie, Mike Lowey and defensemen were Mace Clark, Tommy and Mike Lydon, and I think Eddie Letts. Eddie Letts was one of those guys that Wheeler brought up, I think he may have been our fourth defenseman. Gerry Gotovich was the other one. And Billy Pieri and Louis Parker were the goalies. This is '68-'69. The next year Billy Travers may have tried out for goalie when he was a senior. Stanley Bonham was actually the starting goalie."

"It was nice to be able to compete," Jerry Drummey summed up. "A lot of places you go to, you get cut from the team and that's it, there's nothing else to do. But in Norwood you got to go to CYO. And there were some quality teams there and it was fun. It's a good way to vent the steam, instead of, you know, what am I gonna do this winter? So this way you could get off your ass and do something and have fun doing it."

The 1969-70 season was a year of turmoil for Norwood High hockey. Two of the best hockey players in town were attending Catholic Memorial. Some players decided they simply could not play for Don Wheeler, Johnny Ranalli's slapshot evidence of growing resentment toward the coach. There was a hangover atmosphere of lost opportunities, *too* many lost opportunities. And there was a melding of ages, those from the old school who had come of age in Boston Arena joining graduates of Norwood's now-thriving youth hockey programs. The season is now looked upon as a rebuilding year with seven sophomore seedlings, but in truth it was a hard-fought effort that only saw the Good Guys eliminated from tourney eligibility in the second-to-last game of the season. Any rationalizations, however, were lost on Don Wheeler, who after the eliminating game rendered his most infamous post-game rant.

The team was led by fiery Pete Tamulionis, who sang a familiar song. "The biggest thing was those Saturdays," the captain recalled. "For fifty cents my father would take me into Boston Arena on St. Botolph

Street and we'd watch all the Bay State League games, all day long. We'd watch the greatest high school hockey you could ever think of. It was unbelievable. I'll *never* forget those days, they were *great!* Always remember me and my dad going in there and him paying a buck, fifty cents for him, fifty cents for me, you know, I'd eat there. You'd get a hot dog for a quarter and a coke, and oh my God, I just fell in love with the guys, the Hasenfuses, Billy Hasenfus played, Blaine and Dana Maus, Timmy Twomey, you know, guys like that. Rusty Tobin. You walk around the Arena, you see these guys, the Cliffords, the Hebners, I mean Tommy Smelstor, and Norwood High had some great goalies, great goalies coming all through the system, all the time they had a great goalie. It was just something else, and I remember I was in the eighth grade and Norwood and Walpole met up for the state championship. Do you remember that? We couldn't make it and I'm listening to it on my father's car radio, and we lost, 1-0. It was unbelievable, it was heart-breaking.

"I always thought very highly of Blaine Maus. I always thought he was the fastest, I thought he was like Yvan Cournoyer, I thought he could *fly*. I just thought he was unbelievable. I mean, Jackie Cronin was only a couple of years older than me, but I always thought very, very highly of Jackie. Kenny was a hell of a—oh God. You know, he had to live next to Richie Hebner, but Kenny Reddick was a hell of a hockey player, one hell of a hockey player. He had a great reach; I remember his reach. He was number 15! I'll never forget him, Kenny Reddick was good, very good, and Rusty Tobin, loved those guys. Mousie Graham, Richie Graham, those guys were unbelievable with a puck on the end of their stick. Richie Graham, he could stickhandle, he was like Mikey Martin could do it. Dickie Donovan was unbelievable. Oh, God! I could go on! Peter Oberlander. I just thought Rusty was just as tough as they come.

"Sophomore year, me and Guy Marzullo got called up. We practiced with them, we played with them, we got on the ice every now and then and it was something else. I mean you're looking at Denny Hebner, and Jackie and Neil, and Bobby Begley. When we were practicing with them when I was a sophomore, Bobby Begley would try to ram me into the boards and I knew he was trying to get me, and he was always a nice guy afterwards, but he could be vicious! He could be vicious! But ah, it was ah, it was unbelievable. You're walking on clouds. You're on the Norwood High varsity hockey team and you're just walking on clouds. You didn't care if you got on the ice, you were *there!*"

Despite opening with four shutout wins, the season regressed badly, the first season in seven that a Don Wheeler team missed the tourney. The deciding blow came in the second-to-last game of the season, an incomprehensible turn of events to a coach who felt motivation alone should win any hockey match. Every single skater present remembers Wheeler's post-game tirade, which ended with the now infamous, *"You will rue the day I was your coach!"*

"Dedham beat us to knock us out of the state tourney," Bobby Thornton recalled, "and we had one game left. So, first time in Don's history we didn't make the playoffs, maybe since his first year. It was *rue*, r-u-e, *you will rue the day I was ever named your coach!* I remember going, it was bad enough without…it was at Ridge Arena, it was at fucking Ridge Arena, and so from that game to the last whistle, we never saw a puck in practice again."

"Do you remember the practice?" Billy Clifford recalled. "He put us all down one end with pucks, blew a whistle, and had everyone skate around crashing into everyone, we only had fifty-minute practices, we must have done it for forty-five minutes, just kept going and going and going. People crashing into…*You'll rue the day I coached Norwood High hockey!*"

"Funny anecdote," Bobby Rosata said, "it still rings in my head. My junior year, tough year, and there was a lot of puking, and I'll always remember we'd be riding into practice on the bus, and I always had this song I'd sing to myself, *don't it make you wanna go home, now, don't it make you wanna go home*, (laughs) cuz I didn't want to go to practice! I still remember singing that, because we knew we were gonna get *killed*."

"Only one time in four years in playing did I know it was gonna be our last practice," Peter Brown remembered. "We had lost to Walpole to knock us out, but we also tied our last game, Dedham, 4-4. *You'll rue the day*. What the fuck does 'rue' mean? That was a bad year. Don wasn't a good loser. Missing the tournament by one game when it was seventy-five percent winning percentage, that's like going oh and five hundred, right?"

In fact, until the end of the '70 season, we rued the day. *Don't it make you wanna go home, now, don't it make you wanna go home...*

But as with any burnished image of schoolboy stardom, is its initial forging. Oft quoted is German philosopher Georg Wilhelm Friedrich Hegel's rendition of the medieval European proverb, "No man is a hero to his valet," its usage normally conveying the more common, "familiarity breeds contempt." Mike Lydon's testimony suggests the genesis of necessary countermeasures taken by a 140-pound superstar in a high school era of no fighting, which roughly translates in hockey to, "no protection."

"Well one thing, the SOB gave me six stitches over my right eye at Braintree Ridge Arena," Peter Tamulionis recalled of a '70 season Needham contest. "They were just annihilating every team they played and we lost to them at Ridge Arena, 2-0. Do you remember that game? I swear to God I scored two goals in that game; I swear to God I scored two goals in that game. To this day—the light guy, turns the light on for goals, he never put it on. I could be wrong, it was Cap Raeder, that's his name, right? Cap Raeder? Wasn't he the Needham goalie? Another hell of a goalie, let's face it. I probably didn't score them, but in my mind, I swear to God the puck crossed the red line and his glove got it later and we should have tied them. But we lost to them, 2-0. And we really played hard. And then we lost to them at Four Seasons that year too, and it was a close game."

It could have been closer. The captain had asked during our interview if I remembered that game, and in truth I would never forget it, for it was the first time I stepped onto the ice for Norwood. The scene in the dressing room prior the third period was no doubt influenced by Wheeler's successful attempt to fire up Norwood's first line in '65s' Milton game by sitting the first line, which had resulted in historic goal-scoring. After haranguing the troops and on his way out the door Wheeler had whirled and declared, *"Third line starts the period!"* I sat there and suddenly realized...holy *shit*... Tamulionis or Marzullo jumped up. "The third line's not starting! *We're* starting!" But when the coach returned, he was adamant.

I remember gliding past Ftorek, already leaning down at center, to line up at my left-wing position aside Steve Dagdigian. And I remember twenty seconds into the shift crossing the Needham blue line, and suddenly, almost inexplicably, seeing the puck virtually still on the ice thirty feet out. My head down and without any awareness other than that puck, I *snapped* it—and rung it off the post to Cap Raeder's left![37]

But our captain's six stitches paled with the incident in the second 1970 Norwood-Needham game.

"I was out, I couldn't play," Peter Tamulionis remembered. "I was on the bench because I hurt my Achilles heel, and I'll never forget Robbie Ftorek took his stick and he brought it up in between Pete Brown's, young Pete Brown's legs into his balls, and brought him to the ice. I was flipping out on the bench, Wheeler was holding me back, because I was heading to the penalty box to beat the shit out of Robbie Ftorek. I wanted to freakin' kill him. He hurt him bad, he hurt him bad."

"And of course, Robbie Ftorek," Phil Nolfi recalled. "I chased him since I was in eighth grade, but I couldn't catch him. I made the freshman team as an eighth grader, so I got the chance to chase Mr. Ftorek then because he was one year ahead of me. Talented hockey player. Piss you off, boy, cuz you couldn't hit him, you think you had him lined up, and all of a sudden he's gone, where did he go? Really talented guy, love him or hate him, he was really talented. I think I got two penalties in playing hockey for Norwood, and one of them was he speared Peter in one of the games, and I tried to take Ftorek's head off. But again, I couldn't get him. I got called for cross-checking, but I wanted to kill him. I wanted to behead him. We were a group. We were a group, you hurt one, you hurt 'em all. I didn't give a shit if Ftorek was all-star material or what, you don't do that. You wanna hit, you wanna hit clean, and I got hit clean plenty of times. But you don't go spearing somebody, there's no need for that."

"One thing about Ftorek, if you stayed after him, he was gonna spear you," Peter Brown remembered. "He was a dirty little fuck. Great player, great player, the best, but was a dirty little fuck. He butt-ended me in a game my freshman year. So yeah, okay, I already know this guy. This fucking guy, he's playing in a different league than I am. But you learn. So sophomore year, 2-0, really good game. Second period it was, it was just a regular play, it was 0-0 and he didn't have a goal, we were shutting him

---

[37] It was the inauspicious beginning of my scoring threat as a Norwood Mustang. If brother Ken, in Jim Gormley's parlance, "could bury the biscuit," I couldn't hit the Mystic River from the Rusty Tobin Bridge.

down. So he was frustrated not getting his fucking points, the little dink, right? But it was also being a competitor, right? I was simply covering him on the back post, he was trying to sneak in behind me on the back post. Don always preached 'back post coverage!' I turned and picked him up and bang—he speared me right in the balls. He got me, he got me *real* good! You know when you're sick to your stomach, he got me good. He got a five-minute major. He should have been kicked out! If anyone else had done that, they would have been kicked out! He got a five-minute major. Now, Tappy might not have been playing, Tappy was on the bench and went after him, they had to restrain him. Tappy was injured, and he went after him."

"When I look back at it, when I look back at it, he was very apologetic," Peter Tamulionis continued. "He came up to Don after the game, he saw me, and he really apologized and felt very bad, and I just looked at him and Don said, Robbie, you're a better hockey player than that. There's no need for that. And again, Ftorek apologized. But he came over by his self to apologize. I'll never forget that. I'll never forget that, either. He took two hands and right in between Pete's legs, and just ripped his stick up and knocked him out. It wasn't pretty."

The first game was the closest score experienced by the undefeated Needham juggernaut of the '69 and '70 seasons. "It was 2-0 we lost to them," Pete Tamulionis said, "and we gave them a game and a half. I mean, we were pumped. I don't believe in moral victories, you either win or you lose. We played hard, we played hard."

Norwood's '69 and '70 teams couldn't beat Needham, but a couple of other teams were eager to take them on.

"We were always looking for Needham, because we were starting to grow as a team," Mike Milbury said of his '70 Walpole team. "Unfortunately, we lost in a quarterfinal game in overtime, I wish we could play over again, I think, you know, Malden Catholic, Paul O'Neil, Mike Fidler, pretty good players, too. The damn referee who didn't call the hooking penalty when I had an open net, was about to tuck it in for the winning goal and I got hooked, these days the guy would have been in jail for freakin' ten years. Anyway, I digress. Oh yeah, it hurts, it hurts. We wanted Needham in the worst way. We didn't look past Malden Catholic, we just had trouble finding the back of the net. Give them credit. In the end that was the year Needham won 11-1 in the finals, that's the game we should have been playing."

A couple of other Norwood kids also wanted their shot at the Rockets. Jimmy "Zeke" Doyle and Ray D'Arcy, two Winter Street kids, skated on the formidable Catholic Memorial team.

"In some of the spring leagues over at the Boston Skating Club over in Brighton we'd go up against Ftorek," Ray D'Arcy recalled, "but in high school we never played Needham head-on. They had a great team, and the only team that could have beaten them was us. We were pretty confident that we had the type of team that could beat them.

"Buddy Powers was from Hyde Park and so he and I and Zeke formed a line as freshman, and we stayed that way for the entire four years at CM. I was maybe 124, 130 pounds, Zeke was the only big kid, he was at least six-foot-one. Me and Buddy were the same size, but we could skate. Zeke was a terrific goal scorer. Just as an aside, few people knew back then the *Boston Globe* and the *Boston Herald* use to have their All-Scholastic teams, and they'd only pick six guys for their paper. Now they pick twenty or forty guys, but back in those days in our senior year the only two players who made both the *Globe* All-Scholastic and the *Herald* All-Scholastic was Zeke Doyle and Robbie Ftorek. So that's the level Zeke was at.

"So anyway, the three of us played together for four years there. Senior year the Catholic League was formed and that year we went undefeated. Needham was ranked number one, they had the Ftorek, Dagdigian and Tommy Parlato line with Chuck Lambert on defense, Cap Raeder in the goal, and so the seedings were lined up so that them and us would end up in the state finals.

"They were undefeated, we were undefeated, so in the second round we had to play Brookline. (laughs) We had played Brookline in scrimmages two other times during the season, and we had beat them, 15-0 and 11-0. Then comes the state tournament. We ended up, they had five shots on our net and four of them went in and their goalie had like fifty saves. I'll never forget his name, Richie Diamond. And our goaltender had a real off night. One of the goals was an icing and it hit his stick and went in the net. It was a sad way to end, and we ended up losing 4-3 to Brookline, and that was the end of our undefeated season."

Yes, a familiar quote from an old German philosopher. Less remembered, however, is Hegel's entire rendition of the ancient proverb, expressing its normal usage but adding nuance. "No man is a hero to his valet," the philosopher wrote, but added, "This is not because the hero is not a hero, but because the valet is a valet." For three seasons the Bay State League merely dressed the Ice Adonis, polished his shoes and pressed his pants, brushed his jacket and straightened his tie, preparing his debut in the greater hockey world. His journey took him to magnificent destinations, notably Most Valuable Player of the WHA in 1977. Perspective of his high school talent comes from the second-most talented player of 1969.

"My senior year we went out to play Needham and we were down like 3-1, 3-0, in the first period," Dickie Donovan remembered. "And Don came in the room. He says, Donovan, three of those goals were your fault. And I got *bullshit,* the whole team went on edge. I said who do you think I am, *God?* He's the best player I've ever seen! I tried, but he's *better* than me! *All right?* Don said you're a helluva player, and he just walked out. They were a better team than we were. Best team I ever saw, by far.

"Best player I ever played against. By far."

OUR TOWN

I was in a bar in Fredericksburg. A little man was talkin' about Houston. 'Ever been to Houston?' I said. He said, 'Naw, I ain't never been to Houston.' And he said, 'It never will 'mount to nuthin' anyway.' And I asked him, 'Why?' And he said, 'Too far.' Now that's great! I love that! But other people don't enjoy it like I do because I heard it first-hand. Right off the top of a beer.

— Hondo Crouch

A lover of stories appreciates however they arrive, and in whatever form. There are majestic Rocky Mountains of stories, such as Tolstoy's *War and Peace*, or Melville's *Moby Dick*, thousands of pages culminating in almost inaccessible, historic works of art, and often viewed only from afar. More common are Appalachian affairs, standard 80,000-word efforts such as Steinbeck's *The Grapes of Wrath* or Kerouac's *On the Road* which, if conquered, still leaves one breathless. Then there are more accessible Green or White Mountains of short stories, compelling in simple, truncated form, such as London's *To Build a Fire*, or Hemingway's The *Snows of Kilimanjaro*. Less distinct but most common are gentle footpaths through woodlands and meadows of everyday vignettes.

One description of a short story is, "Within the space of a few pages, an author must weave a story that's compelling, create characters readers care about and drive the story to its ultimate conclusion—a feat that can be difficult to accomplish even with a great degree of savvy." Mr. Webster's dictionary describes "vignette" as, "a short, graceful literary sketch; a brief, quietly touching or appealing scene or episode in a play, movie, or the like."

It occurs that this attempt to describe a town allows neither time nor space for challenging expeditions, or even a brief side-trip to Quechee Gorge, or the Kancamagus Highway. An overview, like flying over the

Grand Canyon at 30,000 feet, does not do justice to the array of color below, the varied shades, the slanting lights, the quiet whispers only revealed up close. It occurs that perhaps the best way to describe a town during a specific period of time is to introduce characters readers care about, illuminating their graceful, touching or appealing scenes, their array of color and quiet whispers, simply by trodding short stories and vignettes on well-worn Norwood streets.

One of the earliest first-person accounts of colonial Dedham is the account of Mary Knight, from *Madam Knight's Journal, A Woman Travels to New York, 1704.* Her journal begins,

> MONDAY, October the second, 1704. About three o'clock afternoon I began my journey from Boston to New Haven, being about two hundred miles. My kinsman, Capt. Robert Luist, waited on me as far as Dedham, where I was to meet the western post.
>
> I visited the Reverend Mr. Belcher, the minister of the town, and tarried there till evening, in hopes the post would come along. But he not coming, I resolved to go to Billings's where he used to lodge, being 12 miles farther. But being ignorant of the way, madam Belcher, seeing no persuasions of her good spouse's or her's could prevail with me to lodge there that night, they kindly went with me to the tavern, where I hoped to get my guide, and desired the hostess to inquire of her guests whether any of them would go with me. But they *being tied by the lips to a pewter engine*, scarcely allowed themselves time to say what clownish-

The original journal at this point is missing the next half-page, depriving denizens of social history further description of what clownish behavior men in a Dedham tavern exhibited to Madam Knight, their lips tied to pewter engines, in 1704.

In his 1887 *The Clapboard Trees Parish* history of Dedham's third parish and future Westwood, George Willis Cook relates the following anecdote involving parish Reverend Thomas Thacher, circa 1790,

> There can be no doubt he would have thoroughly enjoyed the spirit of one event, which, says tradition, happened during his

ministry in the parish. One of his young men wished to marry a young woman who lived in Walpole, and he was very anxious to have Mr. Thacher perform the marriage service. The tradition says that the law did not permit a minister to go out of his own town to officiate on such occasions, and that the service must be performed in the town where the bride lived. To get over these difficulties, the parties concerned proceeded to Bubbling Brook, where the happy couple stood on the Walpole side, and Mr. Thacher on the Dedham side, and the marriage took place.[38]

The History of The Norwood Roofing Plant From 1904 To 2004, the first third written by George E. Smith, who began his career at Bird & Son in 1885, provides an anecdote of Bird's East Walpole location.

> Opposite this Tavern Building and our office stood an old barn which housed a few of the mill trucking horses and a lean-to attached was used as the first storehouse for the water-proof roofings and building papers. Some of the very first shipments were carted over the road by Lewis Holmes of North Sharon to the Boston hardware dealers and he brought back paper stock, mill supplies and groceries for John F. Freeze, the general store-keeper. Holmes was a great imbiber of hard liquors. One particular lot of Neponset Black was loaded on his team one afternoon for delivery the next A.M. There was one telephone in the office and I remember being called to learn that Holmes had not shown up, so we started a tracer on horseback and found him stranded on a woods road with a gallon of hard cider. After revival, he made delivery the next P.M. and the order was saved…

We are fortunate to know today of perhaps Norwood's greatest character, illuminated by an unlikely source, a man who never once set foot in our hometown. In 1907 Joe Mitchell was born on a tobacco farm in a

---

[38] Cooke writes of Thacher, "he possessed a high and delicate sense of honor…it is evident that Mr. Thacher was generous, sympathetic, hospitable, sociable, and a lover of wit and fun." The next page states he once "said of a woman in the parish, 'If the Lord should send for the greatest slut on earth, I should tremble for my neighbor's wife.'" I don't know who's more curious, Cooke or Thacher. Or the neighbor's wife.

rural, unincorporated area of North Carolina. The oldest of six siblings, his interests exceeded what he considered agricultural drudgery, and moved to New York City, where he found work with *The New Yorker* magazine. Mitchell "worked as a reporter for 'a newspaper whose editors believed that nothing brightened up a front page so much as a story about human suffering,' and it was through his contact with the disadvantaged, the down-trodden, and especially the bohemians, who fed Mitchell's fascination of New York's underbelly." Which is how he met Joe Gould, native of Norwood, Massachusetts.

"I was born at high noon on September 12, 1889, in a flat over Jim Hartshorn's meat market," Gould told Mitchell. "A year or so later, my father built a big house on Washington Street, the main street of Norwood. 486 Washington Street. Norwood is a good-sized old Yankee town about fifteen miles southwest of Boston. It's a residential suburb, and it also has some printing plants and some sheepskin tanneries and an ink factory and a glue works.

"At this juncture of my life, my father took it upon himself to find a job for me. He had a friend in Boston, a Mr. Pickett, who was the lawyer for an estate that owned several rows of dwelling houses in Norwood. These houses were rented by the week by people who worked in the tanneries and the glue works, and Mr. Pickett offered me the job of collecting the rents. My father was tired of what he called my shilly-shallying, and I knew it was either take this job or leave Norwood."

Joe Gould then provided some of the best first-person observations of Norwood at the turn of the 20th century, as told to Joe Mitchell.

"I was terribly mixed up in my feelings about Norwood. I really never had felt home in it, but there were things about it that I liked very much or had liked at one time. I used to like to walk beside a little river that winds along the eastern and southern edges of it, the Neponset. And I used to like to wander around in a weedy old tumbledown New England graveyard that was directly in back of our house on Washington Street. The weeds were waist-high, and you could lie down and hide in them. You could hide in them and speculate on the rows upon rows of skeletons lying on their backs in the dirt down below. And I used to like some of the old buildings downtown, the old wooden stores. And I used to like the smell from the tanneries, particularly on damp mornings. It was a musky, vinegary, rail-roady smell. It was a mixture of the smells of raw sheepskins and oakbark acid that they used in the tanning vats and coal smoke, and it was a characteristic of the town. And I used to like a good many of the people—they had some old-Yankee something about them that appealed to me..."

Joe Gould's family received indication of his path when, after graduating from Harvard College in 1911, his mother inquired of his intentions and he replied, "Stroll and ponder." The aspiring writer strolled to New York City and ponder he did. He realized a job would interfere with his writing, and so began a life of bumming. And he began to write. He produced essays such as, *Why I Am Unable To Adjust Myself To Civilization Such As It Is, or Do, Don't, Do, Don't, A Hell Of A Note* and, *The Bughouse Without Bars, or Descents By Day or Descents by Night Into the Intellectual Underworld of Our Time.*

The Norwood native learned to speak seagull, explaining to Mitchell, "I spent a great many Saturday afternoons sitting on T Wharf in Boston listening very carefully to seagulls, and finally they got through to me, and little by little I learned the seagull language. I can understand it better than I can speak it, but I can speak it a lot better than you might think. In fact, I have translated a number of famous American poems into sea gull."

Gould was known to doff shirt at trendy bohemian, Greenwich Village parties and demonstrate his seagull fluency, prancing about and squawking to varied bemusement and disgust of attendees. But what fascinated New Nork's literati was the coalescence of these essays into Joe Gould's life-long obsession, his writing of the longest book in history entitled, *An Oral History of Our Time.*

The Washington Street kid wrote the epic, which a New York newspaper of 1937 reported totaled nearly *nine million words*, in notebooks he stashed in various safe houses throughout lower Manhattan. Gould described the work to Mitchell as, "talk he had heard and had considered meaningful and had taken down, either verbatim or summarized—everything from a remark overheard in the street to the conversation of a roomful of people lasting for hours—and of essays commenting on this talk."

Gould defended his effort. "I can understand the significance of what people say, maybe I can read its inner meaning. *You* might listen to a conversation between two old men in a barroom or two old women on a park bench and think that it was the worst kind of bushwa, and *I* might listen to the same conversation and find deep historical meaning in it." Gould told Mitchell, "my manuscript books shall be collected from the various and sundry places in which they are stored and put on the scales and weighed, and two-thirds of them by weight shall be given to the Harvard Library and the other third shall be given to the library of the Smithsonian Institution."

Alas, upon Joe Gould's death in 1957, it was discovered that his epic life's work, that which for decades he had hounded New York publishing houses with, that which he had endlessly discussed with acquaintances, that which he had spent tens of thousands of hours writing and had accumulated into over nine million words, did not exist.

Cathie Sheehan, class of '68: "Omg! I still have nightmares. Sooo mean! My mom would help me with math and she was from Ireland and would say 'not' for zero. I knew the difference, but next day after an intense math lesson from mom I aloud said 'not' for zero!!! Omg, you would have thought I'd dropped the F bomb!!! Yeah, parochial's hook at St. Catherine's was great!!! NOT."

Julie Lajoie Drummey, class of '68: "I remember the nuns telling us we need to admit we're Catholic but the communists would probably stick bamboo shoots up under our fingernails… I never forgot that. Does anyone else remember that? I never forgot it."

Barry Sullivan, class of '72: "I got in trouble at St. Catherine's school, I was in the third grade, and, ah, they said I had to go to the principal's office, and they said you can't come back to school until your parents come down and see us and I said okay. And then I was walking home I found out John F. Kennedy the president was dead and I said perfect, *fucking perfect!* My parents won't have to come down to school! (laughs) They'll forget about it! Swear to God! It's a true…I was walking home in front of the Union Warren Savings Bank which is now Conrad's, and I was walking up that way with Kenny Cavanaugh and Chris Kelley, and I was like oh man, I'm *fucked*, and they go the president's been killed and I'm like, *excellent!* I might be able to get out of this!"

I grew up in Norwood, MA during a time when everyone treated each other with respect. We didn't eat fast food. We drank Kool-Aid, water, lemonade and we ate homemade food. We ate what was put on the table or we went without. Meatloaf, hamburgers, macaroni and cheese, peanut butter and jelly, and bologna sandwiches.

We grew up during a time when people would gather glass bottles to take to the store and use the deposit money to buy something special on Saturday. We cashed in Green Stamps for special things. We got to go to a store for penny candy (we even got a brown paper bag to put the candy in); You sure could get a lot for five cents.

We went outside to play games, ride bikes, play baseball in a field, hide and seek, jump rope, hula hoop, hopscotch, and raced against each other down the road. We went fishing. We heard about the drag races at Art Johnson's. There was no bottled water. We drank water from the sink, or the hose if we were outside. No microwave or cable. No cell phones! And no one got offended by things they didn't like. We dealt with it. We didn't cry and act like spoiled children because we didn't get our way. We watched TV only after our homework and chores were done! Sunday night was The Ed Sullivan Show and Wonderful World of Disney. If you were bad in school, you got in trouble there and when you got home your parents already knew and you got in trouble again. Prayers and paddling were allowed in school and you behaved. Our house was left unlocked. Windows were always open.

Gary Peterson, class of '75: "I went to Balch elementary and I can remember that for recess we used to get one of those small cartons of milk, which I think cost four cents, and two Ritz Crackers. It was always fun when the teacher picked you to hand out the crackers. To this day whenever I have a Ritz Cracker, I am reminded of those days."

Dave McGuire, class of '72: "CYO dance at St. Catherine's, 1968. It's the last song of the night. You didn't have the balls to ask her to dance all night but now you run around looking for her and hope she's not dancing with someone else. There she is alone. You ask her to dance and she says yes. For two minutes you're on top of the world. The song ends, you smile and say thanks. All the way home you're smiling and the only thing you remember about the entire night is the last two minutes."

Mike Lydon, class of '70: "You've heard the story about Skip Connolly and myself, and actually Denis Drummey was with us, too. We were walking home one night, of course throwing rocks at the streetlights, breaking lights. We're on Prospect Ave. breaking streetlights, next thing you know, *boomp!* every house on the street went blank! The blackout of '65! Now we think we caused it! We get home, the lights are out, the lights are out in the whole northeast, we think we probably did it! We broke a streetlight just as all the lights went out! Skip threw the rock, Skip threw it, but Denis Drummey and I were there too!"

> *We would ride our bikes for hours without a cell phone or electronic games. And you made sure you went home when the streetlights came on. Walking, running and biking was our way of transportation to visit friends. We LEARNED from our parents and grandparents instead of disrespecting them and treating them as if they knew nothing. What they said might as well have been the gospel.*
>
> *If someone had a fight, that's what it was, a fistfight and you were back to being friends afterward. Kids didn't have guns and never thought of taking a life, especially not their own. We heard the dull roar from Norwood Arena Speedway every Saturday night. You had to be close enough to home to hear your dad's whistle or your mom yelling to tell you it's time to come home for dinner. And we ate around the dinner table, ate what was put on the table and talked to each other without the TV!*

Don Reddick, class of '72: "I wrote my first 'book' at age twelve, entitled *Four Poor Boys*. All of thirty-six pages long, it was essentially a confession of delinquent deeds. Indicative of the developmental stage of my imagination was the fact I used all real names, the effort containing such gems as, 'we really 'hit the town' that day. When I reached home I was so tired I could just fall,' and, 'The next day I explained everything to Dave, Brad and Frankie in my bedroom. We had cigars, cigarettes and beer with us, so it wasn't all work.'

"I shared my Great American Novel with co-conspirators, loaning it to Dave Early. He passed it to others. Unbeknownst to me, one avid reader was Dennis Cochiarra's older brother. I was this little seventh grader and David Cochiarra this Big Eighth Grader. As fate decreed, we found ourselves side-by-side at urinals in the second-floor men's room in Norwood Junior High School. As David glanced down and I looked up, he said, 'Hey, are you the one that wrote that book?'

"My heart skipped a beat, to coin a phrase, interacting for the first time in my life with someone who had actually read something of mine. I looked up hopefully at David Cochiarra and meekly replied, 'Yeah.'

"'I read it…' the towering figure replied, then leaned down over my face for emphasis, '…and it *SUCKED*.'

"And thus received was my first review."

Janet Harish Bartony, class of '69: "My Mom worked at Art Johnson's Friday nights and for breakfast Saturday morning, we had fried clams, onion rings, and a few scallops mixed in. After Mom worked a Saturday night, well yes again, the works. In my days working there were the car shows, the car races still went on, but anyone says fried clams when they think of Art Johnson's. When someone says Art Johnson's, they remember the fried clams."

John Conley, Blue Hills Regional Technical School class of '79: "Grew up on Myrtle Street. The Kelleys grew up on Pine, a bunch of crazies! They'd shoot at you—'hey, I'll count to ten before I shoot you, one, two, nine, TEN!' and boom! They had 22s! Behind Oldham. They had bows and arrows, they'd shoot arrows at you! I remember one time they shot an arrow through the streetlight on Pine Street. The arrow got stuck on the metal shield. And when the town truck comes by, they go out and ask for their arrow back! The town guy goes, 'Okay, but tomorrow, do the same thing.' The same thing? they ask. Why would you want us to do the same thing again tomorrow?

"'Double time tomorrow!'"

School was MANDATORY. We stood for the Pledge of Allegiance with our hand over our hearts, sang our National Anthem, and listened to and respected our teachers. We watched what we said around our elders because we knew if we DISRESPECTED any grownup, we would get our behinds busted, it wasn't called abuse, it was discipline! We held doors, carried groceries, and gave up our seat without being asked to. We roller skated at Roll-Land!

You didn't hear curse words on the radio or TV, and IF you cursed you got your mouth washed out with soap. "Yes ma'am or sir," "please" and "thank you" were part of our daily dialogue! We said, "you're welcome" instead of "no problem." We were rarely bored. If our parents heard us say such a thing, guaranteed they would find something for us to do. We knew what an imagination was and we used it to create things to do.

Mike Thornton, class of '69: "Had a high school date with Suzanne in Boston, Thanksgiving night, 1968. Took the bus to Forest Hills, then the Orange Line to downtown. Saw the opening of *Camelot* at the Music Hall Theatre, which didn't end until about 11:00 PM. Torrential downpour that night. Missed the last bus out of Forest Hills. Found a cabbie willing to drive us back to Norwood, based on the predicament we were in, I offered him all the money I had left, which was probably around five bucks. The cabbie wouldn't take it. Told us to remember the night a stranger did something good for us. No problem... I'll take that story to my grave. I offered to wake up my dad when I was driven home. The cabbie wouldn't let me. Just laughed and told me to remember this night. No problem there. It was a different world."

Norwood Salaries, 1972

Phillip O. Coakley, school administration	$26,500.00
Walter Blasenak, town manager	$21,688.25
John Coughlin, fire chief	$17,909.30
James Murphy, police chief	$16,531.14
Arthur Gulla, teacher and football coach	$14,997.45
Donald Wheeler, teacher and hockey coach	$14,821.74
Skip Lockwood, major league baseball player	$13,500.00
Kenneth Nolet, teacher and basketball coach	$12,978.87

"Skipper Connolly gave me nicknames," Bobby Rosata remembered. "'Hong Kong Bob', all sorts of names. He gave Mike Lowey his name. First, he called him 'Pad', and then he changed it to 'Brillo Pad', and he's still 'Brillo' today."

In 1960s Norwood, younger siblings were often branded with a derivative of an elder brother's nickname. "Pebbles" Folan's older brother was nicknamed, "The Rock." "Lippy" LeBlanc's younger brother Mike was "Lower Lip." Pat "Bumper" Riley's younger brother Ben was "Fender." John "Dinga" Bell's younger brother was nicknamed "Ringa," and Johnny "Pipe" Lawrie's younger brother Bobby was "Tube."

Hockey skills influenced nicknames: Bobby Begley was "Bullet Bob", in recognition of his slapshot. Leo McInerney was "Yvan", in reference to Montreal Canadians' speedster Yvon Cournoyer. Ken Reddick's nicknames reflected hockey skills when he was called "Sniper", but also dubious baseball skills with his other moniker, "Boots." His younger brother was nicknamed "Grinder," his youngest brother "Big D", the appellation bequeathed by legendary football coach Jack Martinelli.

Lenny Sansone described his neighborhood's method of imposing nicknames. "We'd take the first letter of a guy's last name and swap it with his first name. So Jack Halloran became, 'Hack' Halloran."

Hockey heroes influenced nicknames. Billy Pieri, in homage to goaltending hero Rogatien Vachon, was "Rogie", or "Gaht"; Bobby Thornton was called "Doors" for his admiration of Toronto Maple Leafs' defenseman Jim Dorey.

"'Redbird' came from Tommy Songin," Billy Sullivan explained. "He was called 'Big Bird', so he called me 'Red Bird.' Tommy's grandmother married my grandfather, when they were in their sixties."

Peter Brown has been known as "Bronson" since the late '60s. "Junior High School, waiting for the bus," Peter explained. "I've got my watch cap and I pull it down like that. Joe Curran is there at the bus, he looks at me and says, '*ooohhh, Bronson!*' For the guy in the TV show, *Then Came Bronson*. That's Joe Curran, waiting for the bus. It stuck."

Some nicknames appear inexplicable, such as Mark O'Connell's "Photon," or Alex Skene's "Noid." Some were derived from physical attributes, or abilities. One seventy-year-old today is still called "Head", "Squash", or "Skull", because of his childhood appearance of a large head. Another is nicknamed "Fish", not for any dipsomaniac tendencies, but because he could fit the entire end of a beer can in his mouth.

In *Travelogues of America* a facet of Norwood's character had been addressed in a short story I wrote about Jack "Hack" Halloran. Here is the true story of Hack Halloran and the author:

> We'll call him "Jack," if only because that's his real name. His is a face from my youth; when my older brother Ken had a summer job as steward of Norwood's Civic Center playground, Jack played on his baseball team. I don't remember him as an athlete of note during high school, but he was always there, always around, and as years slipped away, he became a townie, one of those faces reliably *scene*, usually stopping in at the old corner Guild Variety store each morning, emerging with a *Boston Herald* folded and tucked under-arm.
>
> We're talking forty years now. Reliably seen in Lewis', Norwood's main town tavern, a bucket of Budweiser and a Lewis Burger in front of him on the bar, his eyes upcast following Sports Center, then back down to his sports page. The man has never once spoken to me. And I'm thinking: what makes a guy like that? How can a guy pass me by for forty years without a word? Is this what New Englanders are really like? It all seemed a sad waste, a forlorn measure of unlovely music, forced upon an unpleased ear.
>
> It struck me how small-town New England it was, for forty years this guy, who obviously knew who I was, had never once— not once! —spoken to me, had never once asked how the kids were or how the job was going, never once sat to reminisce of things Norwood past, never once did more than look me in the eye in passing, and nod. We would always acknowledge one another with a nod.
>
> Why wouldn't he talk to me? He knows who I am, he's seen me these last forty years walking the same streets, watching the same games, talking the same local politics. We both love sports,

we both drink beer in Lewis', we both know the same people, so why wouldn't he talk to me? Does he not like me? Did he not like my brother? Does he not like my friends? Why has he never uttered a single word to me?

Forty years later we're in Lewis' with a few others. Ed Hickey is bartending, known him forever. Played with Jack on the same playground baseball team for my brother all those years ago. Jack sits seven seats away, eating, reading his newspaper. When he passes behind me to retrieve a bottle of ketchup he says, "Hey, how's it going, Don?" "Great Jack, great, how you doin'?"

I was elated that he had spoken to me! Finally, after forty years, this Norwood relic had spoken to me, and I marveled at how truly New England Jack was, and how sad and destructive, if those aren't too harsh a description, the whole thing seemed. I was so happy he had spoken to me that when I passed behind him on my way back from the men's room, I clapped my hand on his shoulder, saying nothing. I sat back down. And then I laughed out loud, my hand on my bucket of Budweiser next to my emptied Lewis Burger plate next to my opened sports page of the *Boston Globe*, all morphing into revelatory truth: I'd never uttered a word to him, either.

Jim Leahy, Dorchester native to Cathy Curran, Henry O. Peabody class of '71: "Forty-eight years and counting. We met in Norwood at the 1967 4th of July parade while still marching with the Valiants. Didn't get her phone number or address, so the next logical thing to do was grab a phone book and start dialing all the Curran families in Norwood. Any idea how many Curran families lived in town back then? I do… Happy Anniversary Cathy, I luv you, it was just meant to be!"

Anonymous, class of '72: "In the early '70s cabbies would take an alcohol order and deliver it. It only had to be received by an adult. After the games every Saturday night during the 1972 season there was a party at the Praino's house on Crestwood Circle, and sometimes it lasted longer. We'd call the cabbie, order, and put a kid in the bathroom who'd turn on the shower. When the guy arrived, the kid answering the door would yell,

'Dad! Dad! Cab's here!' and the kid in the bathroom would shout, 'I'm in the shower! Give him the money on the kitchen table and tell him to just leave it there!' It actually worked. Once."

The scantest of vignettes are self-deprecating quotes: After driving through the Sumner Tunnel, one Norwood hockey player, after noting how close the side walls were to the lanes, asked, "Where do they put the snow after a storm?" I heard myself an underclassman on my football team discussing what to do if the police catch you with beer in your car: "Just tell them you stole the car, and the beer was in it." Another hockeyist, after jumping a fence and standing in a Westwood field with several others during a, ah, pause in their nightly cruise, is quoted, "Hey guys, that cow has antlers." Yet another hockey scholar, riding the team bus back to Norwood from Four Seasons Arena and staring out the back window, spied the "Entering Walpole" side of the sign and hollered, "Hey! We're going the wrong way!"

Another Norwood native (attributed to Joe Anello, class of '71, but he denied it, then attributed to cousin Joe Anello class of '72 and he denied it, then attributed to Teddy Mulvehill class of '72 and he denied it, so who knows?) was pulled over for speeding down south. When the cop came up to the window he drawled, "Son, nobody drives through Georgia that fast," to which was allegedly responded in Norwood's sharp New England accent, "Sherman did." The Norwood native was said to have been sent on his way, after enjoying the hospitality of the Georgia State Police for the weekend.

Today he looks remarkably like an aging David Crosby and admits to having once been asked for the rock star's autograph.

He gave it.

Mike Lydon is perhaps best known for a riotous reign as owner of Shurfine Market. The Nahatan Street store was built in 1912, its first proprietor Peter T. Flaherty, who sold it to Henry McEwen in 1949. McEwen and Mattie Folan weathered the following decades to become one of the last old-fashioned, local markets that delivered groceries, and extended credit. Mattie Folan himself was a character—when I was a kid, Shurfine was known to us as "Mattie's"—and the quintessential salesman.

"Matty had a great story about Charley Rheault's wife Eleanor," Mike Lydon related. "She comes down and she wanted a roasting chicken and Matty only had one left. So he brings it out and he says this is beautiful and she says well, yeah, I like it, but do you have any others? He goes yeah, let me check. He went in and moved it around, bent the head a little and brought it back out he goes yeah, we have one other one. She goes, that's lovely, I'll take them both. Oh no! I can't! I've already sold one to Mrs. Osborne. Mrs. Osborne bought more things than she ever knew about!"

Mike estimates that there are thousands of Budweiser bottle caps laying today in the overhead storage cubby-hole in the back room, but this is a mere taste of what went on downstairs in the basement, where for some time was run essentially the last illegal barroom in Norwood. A scene of story and song, each afternoon a trickle of occasional escapees merged with a stream of regulars into a river of laughter.

"Heyja hear Einstein was really killed by the mob? Yeah, he knew too much…"

"Hey Mike, you like baseball and country music, why is Chet Atkins fat, and Bernie Carbo thin?"

The place—and Mike in particular—functioned as what I have come to call the Norwood Irish Coconut Telegraph, news and rumors relayed or verified—and sometimes created! —the place where you'd get the straight dope on what really happened, who was really responsible, or whether it really mattered. The front counter is where Rusty Tobin discovered that he was in possession of a $7,000,000 winning lottery ticket.

"Yeah, those were the days," Richie Hebner recalled, "walk down Shurfine. It was funny, I was with the Phillies, I was gonna fly down to spring training and it was the blizzard of '78, and my plane got canceled with the snow and I said I'm glad I didn't miss this storm. I got down spring training two days later, someone said where were ya, I said where were ya, didn't you have the news on? We got forty inches of snow! A lot of guys were from Texas and Florida, I said you don't know what forty inches of snow looked like, buddy. I missed spring training for four or five days, but like I said I'm glad I was home. Just to see it! Who knows, that storm was a freak storm, we may never see it again. I mean, you walked down to Shurfine, I was in my twenties, walked down to Shurfine, and there's no more beer left!"

"We ran out of beer," Mike Lydon acknowledged, "only time we ever ran out of beer. The last case out was a case of Billy Beer! Remember Billy Beer, Jimmy Carter's brother? The only way we got rid of it!"

Hey Richie, you played professional baseball for eighteen years, world-class athletes, who was the toughest prick, the absolute toughest bastard you ever played with?[39]

Shurfine Market was the realm of miscellaneous information, irrational conjecture, infrequent argument, and off-color, working-class humor. "*J'know Vincent Van Gogh originally wanted to be a concert pianist, but he didn't have an ear for music...*"

It was a place where regulars were hailed as The Reverend, The Governor, and The Captain; as Bug, Beetle, and Beansie. Kibby was a regular, as was Skull, Goat, and Ronby. It was there I learned, after knowing him half a century, what Pebbles Folan's first name really was.

"Ja'hear Michael's mother brings him down to St. Catherine's, he goes into confession, tells the Priest, 'I've sinned with the fairer sex.' Priest says, was it Molly O'Brien? Nope. Was it Shannon O'Toole? Nope. Was it Mary Catherine McTeague? Nope. Okay, for your penance do nine Hail Marys, and two good deeds. Comes out, mother asks, what did you get, Michael? *Three good leads...*"

"Is it all right to talk about Shurfine?" Mike Lydon repeated. "Depends what we're talkin' about! Yeah, yeah, downstairs got so bad, one night about two-thirty, three in the morning I look and there's about thirty people down there. I'm going *Jesus*, couple of firemen over there, those guys are cops, this guy's a selectman, I go, this is it. If you went by, the

---

39 His answer: Kirk Gibson. "I played with Gibby, Gibby was an animal. When Gibby signed with the Tigers, he thought he still had a Michigan State fucken football uniform on. And I told Gibby one day, I said Gibby, this ain't football. We were around the cage one night in Chicago, we're taking batting practice and Tony LaRussa is behind our cage. Which is not kosha. And I'll never forget, Gibson went back and said hey Tony, get the *fuck* out of our cage, and go to your dugout. And Tony said something and Kirk said, I'm telling you now before I punch your fucken lights out. And Tony LaRussa walked away and went into their dugout. Of all the years playing I've never seen a visiting manager lean against the cage while we're taking batting practice. That's not kosha. But I saw Gibby go apeshit that night, and I'll tell you one thing, I mighta been digging a hole in Tiger Stadium cuz Gibson would have fucken destroyed him. Gibby's a good guy."

parking lot's *full*. You wouldn't get away with it now, so I said that's it. I took out the TV, unplugged the cable, I said I gotta get rid of this before I lose my license. I'm glad I did, but then it just ventured into the back room. But the downstairs is where it got out of hand. Chris Drummey, we had a sixteen-year-old bartender making twenty-five, thirty bucks an hour and he quit because he didn't want to take shit from the old farts. (laughs) We had a cable TV down there, we had swivel chairs, barber chairs, VCRs, cash registers, hot dog steamer, oh God, nothing but trouble.

"Bottle caps? The last estimate I had was forty, fifty thousand. I used to get twenty-seven cases a week of bar bottles just for the back room. Just for the back room! That's over five hundred bottle caps a week. God, I had to make sure I got both Bud and Bud Light, because there were Bud Light drinkers back then. Yeah, there were. It's all right to mention Shurfine. Seven years is up, they can't do anything now!" (laughs)

Renown as an owner of Shurfine Market on Nahatan Street, Mike Lydon was also good enough to skate with the '68-'69 hockey team, where he became the only kid in Norwood hockey history to blow-off a state tournament game. Or more accurately, *half* a state tournament game.

"That only happened once, but it's true," Mike Lydon recalled. "You know, they call up a player or two late in the season when you're going to the tournament, you get to practice with the team. You know you're never gonna play. But you practice with the team and go on the bus, so we were playing Marblehead, and it went into like the third overtime, so they had us stop the game and finish it the next day.

"The next day Skip Connolly calls me up and he goes hey Lydon, there's a light rain out there, I go yeah, so? Perfect street hockey weather. I'm saying we gotta finish the game against Marblehead, he goes you ain't gonna fucken play, I go I know that! Wouldn't you rather go out and play street hockey? And I thought, *yeah*, I *would!* And so I went and played street hockey. Jim Gormley covered my ass, cuz Wheeler said, where's Lydon! And Jim says apparently he didn't know he should come both days! (laughs) I still can't believe I did that, to go play street hockey."

Norwood's characters and characteristics, through the years. When Lawrence Ritter traveled the country in the early '60s interviewing old baseball stars for his quintessential oral history, *The Glory of Their Times*, he tracked down Hall of Famer Sam Crawford, living as a virtual recluse in California.

"No, I don't have a telephone," Crawford told Ritter. "If I had a lot of money, I wouldn't have one. I never was for telephones. Just don't like them, that's all. Anybody wants to talk to you, they can come to see you. I do have a television over there—it was a gift—but I never turn it on. I'd rather read a book…I like to do what I like to do, that's all. I'd rather read a book, or fix up the garden, or just take a walk with my wife, Mary, and see what's going on, you know?"

It reminded me of Mike Lydon who, when asked if he had a computer, responded in deadpan earnest, "I'll get a computer, you know, when they catch on." I heard that in the back room of Shurfine.

Right off the top of a beer.

1971

I can't get no, satisfaction
'Cause I try, and I try, and I try, AND I TRY...
— THE ROLLING STONES,
(I CAN'T GET NO) SATISFACTION, 1965

Bobby Thornton.

No one better exemplifies the Norwood High School hockey player of the era than Bobby Thornton. When apprised of this project and sent the 1968 chapter as an example, his responding email included, "What I have read so far has given me a tickle and reminded me that at the time it was crazy, and we didn't know how lucky we were; but looking back, *Jeezus* we were blessed! (signed) your teammate, Bobby T. #7. Then Captain, NHS '71, first Norwood team EVER to go UNDEFEATED in BSL and state tourney...oh yeah, until the LAST FRIGGEN GAME STATE FINALS, FRIGGEN ARLINGTON AGAIN! We chose a bad time to lose 50% of our "D" in the third period when my partner Pete Brown and Johnny Lawrie both went out of the game with knee injuries and a bad time to lose OUR ONLY GAME OF THE YEAR, DUDE! FIFTY FRIGGEN YEARS LATER AND YOU'D THINK THAT I WOULD BE OVER IT, RIGHT?

"*NEVER!*"

Bobby Thornton: "I am a fourteen-year-old freshman. I have received the highest honor one can receive—in my fourteen-year-old mind in 1967—receiving an invitation to try out for the Norwood High School varsity hockey team. Only Hebner and Cronin had ever played as freshmen until that time, so it was a big fucking deal.

"Somehow, I managed to get detention that day from Mr. Tom McDonough, my home room teacher. So, I'm sitting there in his room, located above the old cafeteria. I am absolutely quaking in my boots, muttering to myself that my life is over. *I blew it!* Suddenly, I am jarred from my detention seat by a banging on the door. Oh my God, it was coach Wheeler himself, his steely eyes piercing the quiet from the door's window. *Whoaaah!* He and Mr. McDonough had a conversation outside. Suddenly, I was told to pick up my stuff and go. I will never forget Coach saying, look, Mr. McDonough, Thornton is very sorry for what he did, and I guarantee you two things: one, he will never do this again and two, I will work him so hard in practice today that in about an hour from now, he will be wishing that he had stayed here with you. After following behind Coach as he stormed the corridors of Norwood High School past the girls' gym and up to the bus filled with angry upperclassmen, I think that I had my first panic attack.

"Always true to his word, Coach made me pay for my transgression at my first practice—big time! He had this maniacal 'competition drill' for special occasions. This was where there were only three participants at a time, a goalie, a defender, and a forward. You didn't stop 'competing' until either the forward scored a goal—against Neil freakin' Higgins, *not!* —or the defenseman *carried* the puck out of the zone. Coach made me participate as the defender against the team's biggest—and eighteen-year-old—forwards, seniors Denny Hebner and Tommy Shea. Suffice it to say, this fourteen-year-old had his lunch handed to him that day and I truly *was* wishing that I had stayed with Mr. McDonough! As I was trying to crawl off the ice to go get sick, I remember Coach screaming at me, look, Thornton, where do you think you're going? I blurted out, I am going to get sick, Coach! And when he commanded, well then, get sick right here, dammit! I obliged. I turned and absolutely heaved a disgusting puke that was so bright red that it stained the Four Season's center ice area for weeks. Because of the disgusting nature of my sin, Coach bellowed at me, What the hell did you eat today, Thornton? And when I whispered, the cafeteria pizza, Coach, he let us all know, serves you right for eating that rotgut, Thornton!

"When the dust finally settled, I had persevered and made this 1968 state championship-caliber team, as a baby freshman. There were fifteen very experienced upperclassmen returning from the 1967 team which had made it to the state finals, so this was just incredible to me. To get the opportunity of a lifetime as a fourteen-year-old to 'lace them up' every day with such icons as Hebner, Shea, Cronin, Higgins, McInerney, Donovan, Taylor and Ranalli was something I had only dreamed about.

"Rusty Tobin was one of my idols growing up. He's the guy I looked up to, we used to play at Dunn's Pond. Rusty had an edge, but he played on one leg a lot because he had to drain his knee before the game. I remember knowing him from Dunn's as a little kid, then seeing him in the Arena and following him playing. So Twomey, Tobin, the two 'T's,' both number 7, Twomey and Tobin were just tough hombres, and they both wore that number. I remember plotting it out one day because I knew his route, cuz he lived kind of near me behind Star Market, now Shaws, and I knew where he liked to hang, Town Square Diner, Diner Boys, so I says maybe I'll see him. I run up to see him, I didn't call him Mr. Tobin—I should have—I say hi Russ and he says hey Thornton, what are you doin'? Not much, but I have a favor to ask ya. Is it okay if I wear your number? He says oh my God, course! You're a Dunn's Pond man, of course! Twomey and Tobin were just tough hombres, and they both wore that number 7."

Bobby Thornton— "Doors" to those near and dear—was accompanied onto the varsity in the fall of 1967 by another freshman.

"Scared shit," Phil Nolfi remembered. "I mean just like everybody else. I'll never forget, my father tried to be tough. I'm laying in bed, now I'm a freshman, I'm gonna go to practice, and these guys, not to be corny, but these are the guys that you went and you watched, now you're gonna go play with them? Holy *shit*. I don't know...so I'm laying in bed, and I'm just getting ready to go to sleep, and I'm not gonna sleep anyway, the covers come down, the old man grabs me by the ankles, he drags me across the bed and flings me against the wall. I'm looking at him, of course you wouldn't say anything, and he says I don't think you're ready! I said, *for what?* But he wanted you, you gotta get toughened up, because it ain't gonna be easy. It was true.

"Remember Don had a part of the program where he dumps a puck in the corner, and two guys go and get it? I might have weighed 140 pounds. *Nolfi and Cronin, center ice!* Now, here's a refrigerator that skates like a figure skater. Jackie could skate like a figure skater, but just *solid!* Puck goes in, I'm sprinting, I was okay, I was pretty fast, I mean, there wasn't much to me. I get in and touch the puck first and I'm thinking this isn't gonna be so bad, and then *ba-BOOOM!* And I'm laying on the ice and I look back up toward center ice and there goes Jackie skating back with the puck. I'm thinking, *ahh, ahh, I don't know...* He waits a little bit then says, *Nolfi and Taylor!* I know Tommy, he grew up down the Flats and I'm thinking, Tommy is the Tasmanian Devil! I'm not gonna survive practice! He *wants* me to be hurt! Course we go into the corner and Tommy just lays me out. And I'm thinking, I can run pretty good, maybe winter track or something? I'm not too short for basketball...

"He used to hang a list when you walked up, and I just went up and I looked. Never listed who was *cut*, just who was to keep coming. He carried me. I didn't play as a freshman; I don't think I got into two games. But he always carried a fourth line. And of course I loved it, all I wanted to do was play hockey. It was something you wanted. Every kid wanted to wear that uniform."

The new wave of skaters personified the era's familial experience, one similar to the hardships of Walpole's Vinnie Fitzpatrick.

"My father Tom Rosata was born in Hyde Park in 1917," Bobby Rosata recalled. "In 1921 when he was four, his father got killed in a motorcycle accident. He left seven kids and the oldest was ten, and one was still in my grandmother's womb, and they had no money, they had zero. They had a house with this huge garden, like I remember asking my father and my uncle, what was the depression like? And they go, depression? We were *always* in depression! And I said how did you survive, and they started crying because they said their mother just had this huge garden and they grew their vegetables and the fruits and they canned it for the winter and they got help from the neighbors, and then the boys would go out and shine shoes and they'd work, and the girls would go sew somewhere and they just survived. And they cried, we're only here because of our mother with her ingenuity, you know?

"So they grew up pretty poor, but then they became successful in life and my father became an electrician. Worked in the shipyard during the war wiring the ships and stuff, but what cracked me up, they finally meet the woman of their dreams, an Irish woman, my mother—and that's another thing, they want to assimilate to be an American, so their name was Rosa-*to*, and when the kids all go to school, they changed it to Rosa-*ta*. I don't know why that sounds less Italian; I don't know! And supposedly my father didn't tell my mother he was Italian when he met her, but they got married in 1941. And then they brought four kids up in West Roxbury, and then my father had enough money to move to Norwood, and that was huge. So when I was one, we moved to Norwood, 1954.

"So what amazes me is little things like, I know *nothing* about gardening. We *never* grew a flower or a tomato because I'm sure it reminded him of his childhood. He probably knew *everything* about gardening, but the old saying, they want their kids to have a better life. That's what that generation did, they worked *hard*.

"I grew up at 17 Bellevue Ave., which is a dead-end street up near the high school with the cemetery in the backyard. And the Sweeneys grew up in the middle of the street and the Clearys at the top, and I met them when I was three, four years old. We're still friends today, which I don't think happens a lot. We're still best of friends, which pretty much amazes me. I think of growing up in Norwood and hanging out in Shattuck Park and building forts in the woods and building a fort in my back yard and playing Little League and then Mr. Clifford started hockey. My brother had played with Mr. Clifford and that kind of got me hooked, and I found out I could play a little.

"We were outdoors a lot. I still think so fondly of playing street hockey at Father Mac's pool. I mean, that's, I'm a pretty good stickhandler. I'm still playing at sixty-eight years old and I can still stickhandle. I swear it was from Father Mac's pool, because we played, Skipper Connolly and Mikey Lydon, and every afternoon we played there. In fact, my mother had a thing, we would get sick if it was raining and cold, I would sneak dry clothes in a bag and go and play street hockey and change into my dry clothes and try to fake her out when I came home. And when it rained in the pool, I don't know if you remember this, you could slide and block shots like Don Awrey, it doesn't get any better than that!

"And the summertime Father Mac's and the swamp in the back. In fact, I just went by the old Shattuck School. We played baseball there all summer long. I remember Jerry Drummey hitting me fly balls like forty yards one way and then forty yards the other way and I couldn't get enough of it. He always said he made me the ballplayer I was, *hit me more, hit me more!* He would hit me fly balls, ground balls, and I couldn't get enough, *hit me more! Hit me more!* Every day you had something to do. I never remember saying, what am I gonna do today? Pretty lucky, very lucky. And my family, I happen to be the baby of five and I came much later, so was kinda spoiled in my own family. But I received a lot of love, and that's a good thing.

"I got involved with hockey because I joined Mr. Clifford's group. I had siblings a lot older than me, and I used to go to games in 1959, 1960 when I was seven years old, eight years old. I used to go to dinners at the Hebner house when I was a little kid, my sister took me everywhere. When I started dating girls, I'd *never* take their little brother with me, but my sister is eleven years older than me, took me to the beach with Billy Hebner, took me to the Hebner house for parties, they were crazy! And I was a little kid. I used to actually go in to the Arena with the Hebners and sit with my sister and Billy. And they had the front row behind the net on the balcony. They would get in there about three hours early, Mr. and Mrs. Hebner and the uncles and aunts, and I would get a seat, it's how I got to watch all those games.

"My sister and Billy Hebner took me to all the games, and then Richie came along and I watched every game he played. So those two as far as hockey goes, Ted Casey and Richie Hebner, a Norwood High player. He was another man playing with boys, that guy Ted Casey. I'm not an expert on this stuff, but when I think of the best high school hockey players I think Ted Casey, I think Paul 'The Shot' Hurley, I think Robbie Ftorek and Richie Hebner. Those would be my top four, and I saw them all. I remember Ted Casey from Framingham, them carrying him around the ice when they won the state championship. When I saw him, that was the first guy that got me, I want to be a hockey player, because it was unbelievable! This guy was like a cult hero, and he won the states!"

"I wasn't born in Norwood," Phil Nolfi recalled. "My mother's family came from New Hampshire; my father's family was from Dedham. He worked for the old gravel yard across from where Art Johnson's used to be, the old gravel pit that was there. They never had a house, he had a first wedding that didn't work out, apparently it wasn't great, but he wouldn't desert his kids. So he never owned a house, we lived in apartments. So we had an apartment in Walpole, then we had another apartment in Walpole, then when I was in fourth grade, we moved down South Norwood.

"I didn't know anyone down there. I met the Saads, and I'll never forget after school, I didn't know how to swim. I went over the Hawes Pool, I'm the new kid in town. I go how you doing, good, do you know how to swim? No, I don't. They threw me in the pool! Welcome to South Norwood!

"But we've been friends forever and ever and ever. Richie Saad, all the Saads, we were like brothers, Steve Fitzgerald, Dennis Rosetski. Tommy Taylor came from South Norwood, it was a great neighborhood, it was a lot of fun. We had a diversity that they talk about. There was everybody down there. But everybody got together, we were all neighbors. There were neighborhood fights, sure you punched somebody in the nose and the next day you were buddies. That's the way it worked. That was just the way, I guess. It started when you were a kid, course it was the way you were brought up too, you don't speak back. Living in South Norwood, if you did something wrong and somebody else's parents saw you, they gave you a whack, *what you doing*, well I know your father'd give you a whack, he's not here so *I'll* give you a whack. And nobody said anything, you accepted it and moved on. And then we had the pond down there behind the swimming pool, and that was the rink. That was the South Norwood rink. You go over there in the morning and you had to go home when it got dark because there wasn't any light. Stayed there all day. It was great, it was the best time of my life.

"At the time, until we were in, fifth grade? Mikey Martin lived up on Pleasant Street, so he made the trek down. The Taylors would come over, Fitzy, South Norwood had some kids who were pretty good athletes but they never tried out for organized sports. There were the Trusevitch brothers, there was the Percellis, they were good athletes. Every one of the Saads, I always said if Richie could skate, he would have made the Bay State League all-stars, he could stickhandle better than anybody. But he didn't have the feet for it. We had a bunch of great guys. We just got up in the morning, hang out, and get up the next morning and do it again.

"My dad took me over, got my first pair of skates, I'll never forget it, Raymond's. Used to be a store in Dedham like a J.C. Penney, I guess, took me over, and taught me some moves. Dad was always a sports fan.

He never got a chance to play, cuz when he was a kid at that time he was working, keeping the house going. But he gave me a chance and he taught me and I loved it, it was my sport. I played baseball too, played baseball until freshman year and then I looked around and said I gotta make some money, can't get any place without money, so I went to work at King's Market. Couple nights a week and all-day Saturday.

"I knew Eddie King young, Eddie and I, yeah. See, you're not supposed to know this, back then, King's Market was one of the only stores that delivered, and they delivered to the housing for the elderly and to the families that could afford to have their groceries delivered. Mr. King was a nice guy. So I got my license before Eddie, so I drove the delivery van. And every Friday we'd have to get the van emptied because Mr. King would go into the Boston market, buy all the products, bring it to the store and unload it. And then we would take all the trash and we'd take it up to the dump and unload it. And I don't know how it happened, but every once in a while a case of beer would make it into the van. And then on Friday night we'd find that somebody hid it somewhere, and we'd find it. They were good times. Everybody just got along, there wasn't any trouble. It wasn't like today; we were just having fun. I don't think Eddie will admit to it, either—*sure he will!* It was his idea! Did he hang a rope out his second-floor window, pull up a six pack of beer occasionally and drink it in his room? Yes, he did. Well, I think it *might* have happened, how's that. I'm trying to be a politician. But I don't do it very well!"

High school athletics are like ocean waves; though water remains in place, energy moves forward, each wave inextricably linked, the splash at the end normally noted. As each wave crashes and inevitably recedes, the next carries forth, a transition of conflicting forces. Robbie Ftorek and Dickie Donovan depart; Mike Martin and Phil Nolfi arrive.

Norwood's ever-vigilant coach undoubtably noticed Eddie Burns seed a "rebuilding" year in 1965 with nine sophomores, culminating in an Arlington state championship two years later, at his expense. Don Wheeler had selected a host of sophomores for Norwood's "rebuilding" season of '70, kids named Brown, Skene, Martin, King, Clifford, Pieri, and Reddick, with other sophomores, Louie Parker, Gary Donovan, Dave Katchpole and Billy

Denehy on the periphery. This season they joined two three-year veterans, captain Bobby Thornton and Phil Nolfi, as well as solid skaters Bobby Rosata, Jackie Clifford, Johnny Lawrie, Billy Sullivan, and Teddy Curtis to form a solid, potentially formidable team.

Don Wheeler made two important decisions before the start of the season. He chose Billy Pieri over Louis Parker for starting goalie, and, interestingly, moved Peter Brown up to first line center from his defense position. Coach apparently felt a defense corps of Thornton, Lawrie, Curtis and juniors Skene and King on "D" strong enough to borrow the developing superstar to bolster the offence.

Norwood started strong, led by Bobby Rosata's six goals in the first four games. "Rosy was a great athlete, great guy," Phil Nolfi recalled. "Great ballplayer, great hockey player, very underrated. Six in the first four games? How many guys scored six goals in the Bay State League?" But success came neither easily, nor lasted long for the blossoming star.

"That senior year, I don't know why, I was just fed up with Don," Bobby Rosata recalled. "Everyone was required to play a fall sport. You played football, all the other guys that didn't even want to play a sport either went out for cross-country, Jackie Clifford played on the golf team, soccer, Mike Lowey, everyone played. And I said, screw him. My one season off. I had played Legion ball, and then I grew my hair long, believe it or not. I had the longest hair on the team. I just didn't care. But I must have been good enough because he ended up keeping me, and I played second line center.

"This is the part, I just decided I was gonna relax. I felt like I would play better. I made a conscious effort to enjoy myself. I said fuck him, I grew my hair long, I scored two goals the first game, two goals the second game I think, and I'm having a ball! I'm in practice giving it the pump, I get a call, *coach Arvidson wants to see you.* Coach Arvidson brings me into the locker room by ourself. Mr. Wheeler's not happy with you. I go, why? I just scored friggin' four goals! It's your *laissez faire* attitude, you're having too much fun, this is serious stuff. And I'm like, *what?* Honest to God! So then I had to fake it, that I really cared!"

...nor lasted long... Frank Wall reported, with a dash of his infamous hyperbole, on a tie game with our ancient foe,

> In the Walpole game last Saturday, Norwood forward Bob Rosata got decked midway through the first period. He went to the ice but came back and played the rest of the game. Later in the dressing room Bob complained of a sore shoulder. The net result was that he had a cracked rib and played the last two periods in pain. He didn't tell anyone for he had dreamed since he was a youngster of playing in a Norwood-Walpole game. That, brother, is guts.

"It was a Norwood-Walpole game," the diminutive center affirmed. "All of us had the flu, a bunch of players had the flu. It was hot up at Four Seasons, I had a fever, and I got a buddy pass up the middle and someone *walloped* me, and what I'll always remember being an idiot hockey player, I'm not a big kid or a strong kid, but I finished that game. And I remember a couple times crawling into the bench. Tell you how stupid we are, went home with my father and mother, my father and I both said I just bruised my ribs, I just bruised my ribs, I went to bed. They said goodnight and I woke up in the middle of the night and fainted, took me to the hospital and I had three cracked ribs."

The injury was not the first to affect this Norwood team. The previous season Bobby Thornton had dislocated his shoulder, an injury that would haunt him the rest of his career.

"I'm chasing after a loose puck kinda near center ice near the boards," the captain recalled of a Natick game. "So I'm facing into the boards going full speed and the next thing I know it was like the Bobby Orr goal in St. Louis where he goes flying. This guy takes my feet out, skates out from behind and I go flying through the air and I said *oh shit!* I held out my arm up high to brace for the impact and the rest of my body went down. The arm comes out of the socket. The thing I'll take to my grave, I'll never forget this, I go air-born and all of a sudden, I hear Don's voice screeching *get up Thornton!* because a Natick guy picks up the loose puck and goes in on Frankie Eppich, right? And of course I go *oh jeeze*. I didn't know what happened cuz I was in shock, he's yelling at me to get up, I see the guy going in on my goalie all alone, so I try to go to catch him, and this was not part of my body anymore. The ball comes out of the socket, and when you try doing this the arm's over *here*, I'm going *ooohhh!*

"My world turned upside down. I said, oh my God, it's all over. All the hard work, you care so much... Used to pop out in my sleep. I used to have to wear a harness to bed. My brother would say, what are you doing? They got me a harness-type contraption so I could still play. You put a clamp here with a hook, then you put a clamp here around your chest with a hook, and you hook 'em together. But it's skating with one fucking arm! The main thing is, you can't. Think about doing strides, try to block out in front of the net, try to turn, it sort of throws everything off. But I look at the end of the season, I was still there. We did okay, but I should have got the thing operated on right away. And, as for the 'passion' component...that is a common thread that we *all* had. If you didn't have passion, you were not in that room. Period. But here is where the passion got in the way of pragmatism and common sense."

"Bobby Thornton, he's a solid guy," assistant coach Jim Gormley recalled. "I used to tape his shoulder for him, and I used to take him over to Doc Linskey. He could barely shoot with it, and he couldn't lift it...I remember the troubles he had with that shoulder. Fact I think it was Charley Donahue that got him a brace, a special brace, leather, lot of rawhide in it and stuff, I don't know if it's rawhide still, but it was something."

The memorable game of the early season was the showdown between undefeated Norwood vs. undefeated Needham. The defending state champions carried their record 37-game winning streak into Walpole's Four Seasons Ice Arena. Before a raucous, standing room only crowd of 4,500 and led by Phil Nolfi's first of seven hat tricks, Norwood overwhelmed Rockets' goaltender Cap Raeder with 44 shots on goal, ending the Ftorek era once and for all with a resounding, 6-0 whitewashing. "It was a complete victory," Don Wheeler told Frank Wall. "We forechecked, we backchecked. And we've been doing something else this season we haven't done in a while—use some finesse as well as throw our weight around."

Mid-way through the Bay State League schedule Norwood remained undefeated and gaining attention. A stellar defense corps had allowed just 6 goals in 9 games. The *Boston Globe's* Kevin Walsh rated Arlington first in the state, just ahead of Norwood. Frank Wall, perhaps reflecting still-raw wounds, responded in print, "Arlington is loaded this year, and if you don't believe us, just look at the Boston media. They always have and always will get the headlines..."

"This is the best hockey team we have ever had talent wise," Wheeler told Walsh. "I just can't say how great the club is at this point. It's really too early to tell. I want to see what this group can do the second time around the Bay State League when everyone will be waiting to knock us off. I'll just say it's a good team. I can't say it's my best because I've had some very good teams." Walsh noted, "The present edition of Norwood hockey has added polish and finesse to the familiar go-go style clubs that always had plenty of size and strength. Wheeler praises junior center Mike Martin as 'the best passer I have ever had. He shows a new move every game.'"

Mike Martin, Sophomore of the Year in the Bay State League last season, was not just emerging, but dominating. The first line center scored 13 goals in the first 6 games of the season, then zoned in on the passing lane to his left, toward Phil Nolfi. Emerging also, however, was Mike's personality; Mike Martin's dance on ice—indeed his dance in life—was not merely to a different drummer, but to a percussionist's dream of drums, cymbals, xylophones, gongs, bells and rattles...

"Don wanted my job as a senior to sit with Mikey, to sort of maintain...peace," Phil Nolfi recounted. "Cuz Mikey would come out with a few things, and I think Mikey had a little respect for me. I could talk to Mikey; I could calm him down."

"This may sound weird," Bobby Thornton recalled, "but one of the hockey traditions that I could not wait to participate in was the pre-game silent 'prayer.' Try to imagine the total excitement of running out of the locker room to see 4,000 screaming fans—10,000 plus in the tournament! —the adrenalin raging. Then, right after warmups and the national anthem here is what happened. The starting six players would gather at their goal for a silent prayer. The six would get on their knees in a semicircle around the goal crease, join their gloved hands together and pray. The puck could *not* be dropped, and the battle could *not* begin until after the starters prayed together! It was, and still is, one of the coolest things that I ever participated in, especially considering some of the less than saint-like buddies that I used to 'pray' with!"

"I remember kneeling down by the net, and saying a special prayer," Phil Nolfi said, "and I remember there were a few characters around that net. Mikey Martin, you know, when you finished the Hail Mary's he'd say *let's go out and get these fucking guys!* C'mon *Mike*... (laughs) Lenny Ceglarski said Mikey Martin was the most talented natural hockey player he ever saw. And Lenny Ceglarski saw a lot of people.

"Dickie Donovan was a talented hockey player. Unbelievable. He was a little bit quicker than Mikey Martin; Dickie had a little more speed. Mike, super talented. But Mike, he didn't seem like he skated, he all of a sudden moved, and he was there. I mean, you'd see a guy pumping up and down, Mikey never had to do that. Dickie was a little faster on his skates, but I don't think one had more talent than the other. Head up, playmaker, Mike would stickhandle, and Don, *Mike Martin you're attracting a crowd*, and Mike would just look at me and smile. He loved it, because stickhandling, but that was Mikey's, *stop stickhandling you're attracting a crowd*, but that was Mikey's plan, to pull two guys from the other team on him, somebody's gonna be open, Billy Clifford, Peter back at the point..."

Or Phil Nolfi, flying down his left wing.

"He was just a natural sniper," Peter Brown recalled. "As a peewee, Phil Nolfi was getting goals off his shoulder, off his nose, shooting it in, know what I'm saying? And it wasn't luck, because it would happen three times a game. Not that Mike wouldn't use his backhand, the natural way to go is to your forehand. They were sympatico, Nolf wouldn't have had his year, and Mike wouldn't have had his year, you had Mike the great passer, the playmaker, and Nolf the kid who always scored, always scored."

When Phil Nolfi scored his sixth hat trick in the second Needham game—his sixth hat trick in eight games—newspapers began to take notice. With 26 goals, the winger was closing in on Richie Hebner's Norwood record of 29 goals in a season. Reporter Chuck MacFarlane also wrote of that Needham game, "The only injury sustained to Norwood was that to Bob Thornton, but for the defenseman, the injury was not something new. 'Bobby injured the shoulder last year (dislocation) and it was separated twice out there tonight,' said Wheeler. 'The injury is the same as the one that Johnny McKenzie has and will require surgery. But Bob wanted to play hockey this year so the surgery was put off. After the injuries tonight, he still did not want to quit. He just wouldn't get off the ice. He wanted to play,' Wheeler said."

A week later in a 9-1, second-to-last game of the season blowout of Framingham North, Phil Nolfi broke Hebner's record. Frank Wall,

> The big story on Wednesday was Nolfi. He scored his 29th of the season just 26 seconds after the opening whistle had blown. This goal tied him with Hebner. At 4:11 of the third period Nolfi broke the record. Mike Martin grabbed the puck behind the North net and circled out front. He fired a pass to Pete Brown at the points and Brown whistled a low shot which Nolfi got his stick on and tipped into the net. He was mobbed by his mates after the goal and grabbed the puck as a memento. The public address announcer George Delaney proclaimed the feat and Nolfi was given a thunderous ovation by the 2,000 fans at the game.
>
> Nolfi was elated over the feat. "You know, when I was a kid, I used to go to the Norwood High hockey games with one thing in mind. I wanted to watch Richie Hebner play hockey. He was sure something and I marveled at his every move. Just can't believe that it is me who is breaking his record. Just to be mentioned in the same breath with him is something. I have to say that the biggest thing that led me to this mark has been the play of my center, Mike Martin. He has set me up all season with perfect passes, and without him, I could never have done it.

"First two games I got nothing," Phil Nolfi reminisced, a half century later. "First two games I didn't score any and I thought oh shit, Don's gonna move me down, this isn't gonna work. I think we played Framingham North or Milton, and bang, bang, bang it went in, it started to go in. And I still kept practicing my shots, and I know it sounds corny, but I was more concerned with us winning, because I wanted to get back at Arlington. I really did. There was just something about it that, we wanted to keep them from saying they're always the best. And even though we got good numbers, everybody played like that. It was a team.

"I remember the first one was a rebound, second one I don't remember, and the third one Brownie fed me from the point. Peter was on the point, I was on the left side of the net, Peter sent me in a pass and I looked and said oh look, there's an opening, and it went right where it was supposed to go. Didn't always happen. And they announced it on the loudspeaker. It was an honor, it really was."

One hurdle remained for the aspiring hockey team, and hardly an easy one. In the season finale, Dedham had a state tournament berth on the line; they had to win or they were out. Norwood needed to win or tie to become the town's first undefeated team. And in a furious contest in which both teams had something huge on the line, Norwood defeated Dedham, 3-0.

"This is something that no one can take away from us," Don Wheeler gushed afterward. "To go through a league like this undefeated is doing something above and beyond anything normal. To go undefeated in this Bay State hockey league has to be one of the greatest athletic feats in the history of the town. These kids are just the greatest and they deserve the win. I can't say enough about each and every one of them. This year has to be the greatest, no matter what happens in the state tourney. We were thrilled by that gigantic parade and to the hundreds of people who lined the streets and participated in the parade and the huge crowd at the high school I offer my thanks." In his column, Frank Wall wrote, "Captain Bob Thornton was sitting in a far corner with his head in his hands slumped over. He was in tears. He was just so overwhelmed and happy that he had to sit and get the happy choked-up feeling out of his system."

"This is the best two-way team I've ever had at Norwood," Don Wheeler said. "They go real well, and they come back strong. I believe backchecking is a key to winning hockey." But after the bedlam of the locker room, after the fire engine ride through Norwood center, the next morning brought a sobering reality: the historic victory had come at a cost.

> At the midway point in the third period Martin lost his stick and dove feet first to keep the puck in the Dedham zone. As he dove, he twisted his body and Dedham defenseman John Murphy collided with him, with Murphy's skate opening a severe cut on Martin's back. The cut was between the waist and the left shoulder, and the Norwood High scorer lost a considerable amount of blood. Martin agreed that it was an accident and that Murphy couldn't help the collision. It is expected that he will not see

action in the all-star game this Saturday, and his playing in the state tourney is a question mark. He has been the scoring spark for the Mustangs all season.

I helped Don Wheeler lift Mike Martin's jersey on the bench to assess the damage. The best I can describe it is, it looked like a piece of steak that you'd drawn a sharp knife through, a vertical gaping, open wound. "It's a real bad cut" said Wheeler. "I don't know yet just how long it's going to take to heal, and we hope no infection sets in. It's only conjecture on my part, but I think he might be ready for the tournament."

The injury added to Rosata's slow recovery from broken ribs and Thornton's continuing shoulder issue. "I can remember one of the next to the last games," Phil Nolfi said, "Bobby got hit and he went down, and we were just looking over the boards, and his hand was turning blue because there was no circulation because that shoulder had been pinched. I don't know if Doc Lydon snapped and popped it back in, but Bobby, you couldn't keep him off the ice."

The brief interlude before the tourney gave time to assess the season. It was the hockey team's first undefeated season. The team set a record for goals with 98, allowing only 12, one more than the team record. Individually, Phil Nolfi had eclipsed Richie Hebner's single season goal-scoring record, and Mike Martin had come up just short of Dickie Donovan's record of 55 points.

Norwood prepared for the state tournament, key elements falling into place. Peter Brown, after thirteen games, had been put back on defense. "The experiment did not work out really well for anybody, in my view," Bobby Thornton recalled. "Although Pete did miss a few games due to illness—with pneumonia! —his usual scoring touch was limited to three goals, as he was bounced around to playing on several different lines and different linemates during this experiment. I was *so* happy when Don finally made the move to re-unite the defensive tandem of Thornton and Brown. It felt good to be back together." Eddie King, when Rosata had gone down, was lifted from the defense mix, and inserted on the second line where he immediately made an impact, scoring 11 goals in the last 11 games to cement his presence. "I was third line at the end of the season," Bobby

Rosata recalled. "In the tournament I was the second line with Eddie and Jackie Clifford, and then he made me the center in like the second tournament game. And we clicked, me and Eddie on the left, Jackie on the right. And that's the way that line should have been all along."

Don Wheeler prepared his team during the interlude as always, scrimmaging the best teams he could find. But this season, fate had yet to bestow its last decree.

"We scrimmaged Auburn and some kid took me out, and I sprained my ankle so bad they put me on crutches," Phil Nolfi recalled. "And I'll never forget, I was in a study hall and Don came in and he said I want you to think about sitting out the first game of the tourney. And I looked and I said Coach, I can't do that! This is what we worked for all year! So first two games I was out there but wasn't the same. Wasn't the same. And Mikey got hurt, he got cut, he took a skate across the back. Didn't Neil Higgins' dad make up a protective plate for him for his back? But again, Mikey like myself, you can't tell us we can't play! I second guess now, because I wasn't as effective, maybe if I had taken a game off, they didn't need me! Because we had enough talent, they didn't need me. We could have beaten anybody with me sitting on the bench." Reeling from this latest setback, Don Wheeler nevertheless performed his duties as head coach of Norwood High School hockey.

"Not a lot of people know this story," Phil Nolfi continued. "Sitting in study hall after the season getting ready for the tournament. And again, coach Wheeler comes in and he sits down, and he says I wanna talk to ya. I'm thinking you already asked me not to play, what's *next?* So he says, I wanna let you know I went to the meeting of the coaches to select all-star teams, and the coaches came up to me and said coach Wheeler your choice, who do you want for MVP? Just like that. And Don said because of his leadership and everything he did, I told them I wanted Bobby Thornton, and I wanted you to be first to know. And I said I wanted him, too. He deserved it. He played with one arm!"

Bay State League MVP, first defenseman in league history to win the award, and his number was 7: *Twomey and Tobin were just tough hombres, and they both wore that number...*Bobby Thornton fit the description to a "T".

An anonymous on-line fan recalls the era: "Hockey in that period, late 60's and early 70's was different than what I read about and get to see once in a great while today when I'm in the Boston area. Teams then could rarely skate three lines. Only Arlington and Norwood that I can remember could do so. But the sport was covered in the press far more than today. Sunday *Globe* would have two full pages in the back of the sport section on Saturday's results. If you made the Eastern Mass. tourney you played in the Garden for as far as you went. Regular season games had a large fan base anyway in the public schools. A game between Weymouth and Hingham in the old South Shore League would fill old Ridge Arena with 2,000 fans and a lot of police officers. The safest place would have been on the ice."

Norwood, of course, brimmed with anticipation as the tourney approached. Family and fans' typical concerns were obtaining tickets and arranging transportation. And there was the Norwood kid thing.

"I'm from Myrtle Street," John Conley related. "Used to be busses that picked us up at the end of the street to bring us to the games. I went to more than one. I was born in 1960, so I was ten, eleven years old. Parents thought nothing of letting their kids go into Boston at night on those busses. I remember waiting for one, it was late. So we get into a snowball fight, and you know, I'm from Myrtle Street, had four older brothers that tortured me, so you need a piece of ice, a road apple, in your snowball. And I remember hitting this kid with glasses on right in the head, broke his glasses... I didn't mean it. Don't be saying my name, I don't need him showing up today, saying, 'So *you're* the one...'"

The *Boston Globe* rated Norwood number one in the state, and Arlington second. The seeding for the tournament, however, listed Malden Catholic, Arlington, Norwood, and Canton, in that order. Despite lingering injuries to four key players, Norwood burst into the tournament, raining shots on goal as though on a mission. Before 6,000 fans in Boston Arena, Billerica fell 6-0 under an onslaught of 36 shots. Randolph fell next 6-1 under a barrage of 36 shots, enabling Norwood to skate on Boston Garden ice for the first time since the overtime final game of 1968. "We are heading to the Garden!" Peter Brown declared in a jubilant dressing room. Today the defenseman recalls the atmosphere of tournament.

"We're in the Arena, I think against Randolph or somebody, but Bobby and I were skating toward each other—*smash!* A beer bottle—*smash!* —explodes, and nobody even makes a big deal about it. Clean it up, right in the middle, right? Was it mentioned in the paper? Did anyone even bat an eye? People may have, but did you or I? Not really. They came out and cleaned up, but it was like, did it crush anybody's skull? No? Okay we're good."

Woburn fell next, the game marred by frustrated violence from the Middlesex League champions. Billy Clifford was knocked from the game in the second period with a shoulder injury, Teddy Curtis left in the third, his hip injured. Bobby Rosata was decked and took several minutes to rise from the ice. After Mike Martin scored his second of the game at 9:48 of the third period, the Woburn team descended into an embarrassment of cheap shots, six penalties called in that period alone, including a disgraceful shot from behind on Bobby Thornton's shoulder. A disciplined Norwood team kept a composure that didn't prevent Peter Brown, toward the end of the game, from gliding to the penalty box in which sat the Woburn captain, pointing to the scoreboard and winking.

The last obstacle to yet another state final appearance was Catholic Memorial, who had buried top seeded Malden Catholic, 6-3. Meanwhile, Arlington had kept pace, allowing just two goals in wins over Wakefield, Marblehead and Needham, joining Norwood and Malden Catholic for their own semifinal matchup against Archbishop Williams. And before over 10,000 fans in a raucous Boston Garden, Norwood defeated Malden Catholic 5-1 with Bobby Rosata scoring twice, and Arlington beat Archbishop Williams, 3-1. The Norwood win was its 20th of the season, a new Norwood record, but a fact missed by most in an emotional locker room whose collective psyche now focused on one last thing, *the mission.*

All roads led to Boston Garden on Monday evening, March 15, 1971. It was a classic heavyweight bout between towns that had developed a bitter rivalry. "Where we wanted to be all year," Don Wheeler told Boston papers. "In the back of everyone's mind, this is the game they've been waiting for," said Eddie Burns, echoing the sentiment. "Everyone picked Arlington and Norwood for the final during the season and it's come true. I never had any doubt about Norwood making the final, but I had to worry about us getting there. Now that we're here, it's a great relief. This is going to be one of the greatest games of tournament play. Both teams skate, and there'll be no holding back. It's the type of game the fans wanted."

"The schoolboy hockey game that has equaled the buildup of the Ali-Frazier heavyweight fight as the high school game of the year," the *Boston Globe's* Kevin Walsh wrote. The *Herald's* Bill Abramson recorded Wheeler alluding to the influence of the Norwood youth hockey programs. "This team seems more together. It's the first group we've had at Norwood to come up through the peewee programs as a unit. They've played against a lot of the Arlington boys in the past and we're cautious but confident. I'm really proud to be in the final. Those other three finals could have gone either way and this year we've got as good a chance as any other Norwood team." Burns expressed a shared coaching philosophy, "In a game like this one," he said, "the incentive to win is much more important than ability. We've beaten Norwood twice before in the finals and they've got enough incentive. That's what we're afraid of..."

"Having been there as a freshman," Bobby Thornton recalled, "and then as a sophomore we didn't make it to the Garden because we lost in two days to Marblehead. But having played in front of the big crowds at the Arena and the Garden several times, by the time we got to that game, we believed in ourselves so much. You know, first time it's ever been done, going undefeated, and the intensity in my head... People say you gotta be kidding me, in the Boston papers—Boston papers! —they said there was more than 14,000 there, but I just saw twelve people. Our six and Arlington's six. And I swear to God as my judge, when they dropped the puck, there were twelve people there, six and six. That's it. The intensity was so strong, all I remember was the maroon shirts and our blue and gold. We knew who they were, and they knew who we were.

"Talk about passion, I remember we're skating around the Garden ice, we come out with our hair on fire, and I remember skating around the pre-game warmups. First undefeated team in Norwood history and we're gonna be the first team to beat Arlington, right? And everyone's running out of that locker room and Mikey Martin was a *little bit* too juiced up. What does he do? He goes skating up to their *captain*, Jay Shaughnessy and *he's* a fucking wild man, red-headed, I got to know him afterwards, good shit—Martin skates up to their captain, just to show him how much disrespect he had for him, in the pre-game warmups he goes skating up behind him, takes his skates out, pushes his skates in behind him, and Jay goes right on his ass, into the corner! And I'm going, Mikey, you didn't just *do* that! I go what the fuck, man? And Mikey turns and screams back at me, *fuck him! fuck him, Doors! fuck him Doors!* And I'm going Mike, Mike, don't give them any extra edge, man! (laughs) That's a true story! What did I see in Mikey Martin? *Passion!*"

"Skating out onto the ice," Billy Pieri recalled, "I don't think many noticed this, but there were two kids on the bench for Arlington, and I think they threw a couple of pennies on the ice in front of me and I stepped on 'em. I fell and they laughed, yelling *you suck, you asshole,* and all this stuff."[40]

"Kevin Carr was an unbelievable goal scorer," Arlington's Maurie Corkery said. "He could shoot the puck. And he was probably, talent wise, the best player on the team. Jay Shaughnessy, if anyone was gonna go professionally, you thought it was Jay. Cuz Jay was kinda a showboat and kinda crazy. He was vice-president of his class. And I'll tell you right now, he couldn't spell cat if you spotted him the 'c' and the 't'. Brian Mulcahy was quiet, small, but a good defenseman. He could get the puck up, you know? And there was Robby Quinlan, and he was a senior too. He was quiet, never said anything. Very quiet. I ended up on a line with his brother Alan Quinlan."

"I remember us dominating the first period, and thought we outshot them 15-2," Bobby Rosata remembered. "It's not true. When you see the film, we out-shot 'em, we out-*zoned* them, but we weren't getting a lot of quality shots, Jackie Clifford had a couple of quality shots he coulda scored on..."

---

40 John Conley, a ten-year-old spectator at the game, had told me a story a couple of years before my interview with Billy Pieri. "I remember one of the Norwood players picked up a penny off the ice before the game, picked it up with his glove. Don't know how he did it, with his glove, but he skated over to the side—there was no glass—and he handed me the penny. I don't remember who it was—but years later I'm sitting in Mikey Lydon's house, and I tell that story. And this guy—I don't remember if it was Phil Nolfi or Bobby Thornton—but this guy goes, 'That was *you?* I hadn't thought of that in forty years!' We were the only two guys in the world who would remember that, and it came up in Mikey's house!"

"I think we realized, especially Bobby and I, this was our last chance, you're not coming back and doing it again," Phil Nolfi recalled. "You gotta win. I was pissed cuz I was hurt, and I knew I couldn't do as much as I could. I remember going down on a rush, and I didn't have the speed I should have had. I don't know who was playing goalie that night, it wasn't Bertagna, he had moved on—Cremens, right! —when he caught that first shot that I took and I'm thinking, that should have gone in. This is gonna be a long night, I just had this feeling, son-of-a-bitch, that was supposed to go in! I mean, even half the time Pierski couldn't stop that in practice! And when it didn't go in it was uh-oh, gonna be tougher than we thought."

Norwood outshot Arlington 11-3 in the first period. "An average team could have folded under that barrage," Burns said afterward. "But we're not an average team, and we didn't fold." Arlington came out strong in the second. "That was another difference between Wheeler and Burns," Bobby Rosata said. "We had a good first period, and then Burns adjusted. He changed something. I'm not sure what he changed, but we went from dominating the game to, ah, struggling."

"I remember being really nervous," Peter Brown recalled. "Not like scared nervous, but really intense. And I also remember being able to have time with the puck. Not when they dumped it in to pick it up, but once we got control. They played us different, they didn't force us, they were kinda like trapping us, in that, at some point Bob and I started moving it. What they did was instead of having a hard forecheck, what they did the first part of the game was take the wings. When I got the puck as a defenseman, the center and the wings were taken away, I'd have no one but my partner.

"Don did not adjust at all. I'm not faulting him; I'm just saying that's what happened. Eddie Burns? Want to talk about adjust, he was a coach that adjusted in those days. That was Don's limitation. I think because his development as a coach and the talent level that he was very successful with, kind of changed. With this against that, you needed to also develop the game, you also had to adjust the game. That adjustment, we didn't have to do that in the Bay State League. If you're really, really, really good at one thing, beat 'em that way. If that's your only way and you're successful? That's what you do, and that was Don."

"When I started playing with teammates from Arlington," Bobby Thornton recalled of his later college experience, "they told me the story about Eddie Burns figuring Don's formula out, and he said here's what you're gonna see, boys. They're gonna come out, it's sort of like being in a cage, and they're gonna come out and beat the livin' shit out of you like their hair's on fire. Stay with them for one period, they're gonna blow their wad. And you know what, I still think second period, it was still a 1-0 game at the end of the second, beginning of third, it was still 1-0 and then a couple people went off, got hurt, but he said hang with them, it'll be okay."

"In retrospect," Peter Brown asserted, "I guarantee Eddie Burns' coaching strategy wasn't to get outshot fifteen to something the first fucking period. That was not his game plan, okay? And if we get a goal off Cremens, who reminded me kinda of, oh my God, like Paul Skidmore in the Beanpot my senior year at BU—he had like 60-something saves to beat us in the Beanpot—Cremens was kinda doing that shit against us. He was making some saves I remember he shouldn't have."

"I got a story about that game," Jerry Drummey related. "It was after the first period when Norwood outshoots Arlington, 12-2? They're all over them, typical Norwood, right? I'm walking down by the locker rooms going the bathroom or whatever between the periods, and there's Eddie Burns standing outside. He's shooting the shit and he's high-fiving with people rah, rah, rah, like he's got a five-goal lead. I go down another hundred feet and there's Wheeler, his face is white as a ghost. He's sitting all by himself; he was talking to himself! Almost talking to himself instead of being in the locker room saying *great job, guys*, it was just the opposite. They went from such a high to such a low because he just sat there and panicked! You know? I couldn't believe what I was seeing!"

"Chuckie Cremens was the difference," Maurie Corkery concurred. "Midway through that season—Chuckie was my year, '72. We had a goalie named Frankie Logastino who started, he was a senior. This is another funny story. So we were at the Arena and Frankie was up at the food stand, he had a fucking hot dog before the game. So we're in the locker room, it's like half-way, three-quarters through the season and coach Burns comes in and goes, Frankie, was that you I saw eating a hot dog before the game? Yes, it was, coach. Okay, Chuckie, bring it home from here. Frankie never played again."

The game was 0-0 until 9:03 of the second period, when Brian Mulcahy scored on a power play. "I didn't want to shoot wild, so I fired the wrist shot," the Arlington defenseman said after the game. "I figured we had the extra man, and there might be a rebound if the shot was on net."

"Aaawww Gawd," Billy Clifford recalled. "I had the *best* view in the whole Garden for their first goal, their winning goal, game winning goal. I had gotten a penalty, the penalty was a trip, I believe it was, like Wheeler said, *you refused to backcheck*, right? And I busted my balls to get back to pick up the guy's stick, and he must have took a dive or whatever, but I ended up getting a penalty and off I go to the box. And I'm sitting there, and the puck comes over to Mulcahy the defenseman, and he winds up, and I had the *perfect* angle, as soon as that puck left his stick, I knew it was in the net. I mean, there wasn't a better seat in the house. I was right behind him, and I had the perfect angle. (laughs) That was the first goal. I'll never forget that. I can still picture the shot going in the net. After we dominated them in the first period. Wheeler blamed me for that one."

"And then when they scored that first goal..." Phil Nolfi said, his voice trailing off, inferring that oft-felt gut-punch of a team vastly outplaying another, only to see their opponent score first. "And I could tell Mikey wasn't himself, either. I think that cut on his back, he just wasn't Mikey. And they were fired up, they wanted to get us. There was no doubt about it."

"I just remember, and I guess it comes back to the whole flow of the hockey game," Ed King remembered. "We did not have control of the puck, and flow was not in our favor. To me a very disjointed game. We outshot them, but, you know, if you're not moving the puck and getting it into the kill zone, shots from outside, you know, there's a different way to play hockey and we weren't playing it. Hockey, for some reason, I don't understand it, is so emotional, revolving around who gets the first goal, and it doesn't intellectually, it doesn't make any sense. But you see it happen so often that it, I think it has more to do with injecting enthusiasm with the team that got it, than it does dejecting the team that got scored against. It doesn't make any sense. Maybe it's a little bit about confidence required, instead of just firing the puck when it hits your stick, maybe taking a look, that second to take a look, just drift it over to him, maybe that's part of it. Who knows?"

The game was 1-0 entering the third period, but fate added insult to injuries.

"They got a goal right off the bat, like at the forty-second mark I think it was. Corkery's little brother, I think," Bobby Thornton recalled. Corkery's little brother? *You know that name, Corkery?*

"I had a goal and an assist in that game," Maurie Corkery asserted. "I think it was like a two on one, and then we came in, I think it was Pieri that was the goalie, is that right? And I kind of lifted it over him, he kind of flopped and I put it over him, if I recall correctly. I assisted on the first one, that one I was in front of the net, I was trying to screen the goalie."

"And then that 2-on-0 happened," Bobby Thornton continued. "I think Peter collided with Teddy, and they went in all alone. Pierski didn't have a chance. And it was over. I remember Pete getting carted off when it was still 1-0, I believe, and Johnny Lawrie got hurt, and then kind of the roof fell in, and when it was over, later in the third period and they popped in a third goal, and we couldn't score on 'em! We just, we threw everything but the kitchen sink against them, we came out with our hair on fire, I think we out-shot them 19 to 3. But we couldn't put one by their goalie, and they hung with us. And I said oh boy and still we came back, we started getting tired and they hung with us. They were well-coached and we had our system, and the other thing I remember was that we just couldn't get it by the goalie. Rosy being sent down the wing and coming in and Jack Clifford, fast as a bastard, he had a great tournament that year. Phil Nolfi, you know, good scorers, we just couldn't get it by him. I saw it slipping away. Pete got carried off, I saw Johnnie Lawrie, God rest his soul, get hurt, and then when they finally got the third one in, I remember, the other visual I have is standing up, and because he wore a cage, Billy Pieri had tears running down his eyes. He goes I'm so sorry Doors, he says I let you down. And I grabbed him, in front of 14,000 or whatever it is, I remember grabbing him and telling him, don't you ever say that to me, *you're* sorry. *You're* sorry? Get it straight! We wouldn't *be* here without you! Get it straight! Are you *kidding* me! Oh my God!"

"It's an interesting game, in that Wheeler did a terrible job coaching!" Bobby Rosata assessed, long after. "Well, he only played three defensemen. Like all year he played Johnny Lawrie and Teddy Curtis and Pete with Alex Skene mixed in, yeah, but in the final, all he played was Thornton, Curtis, and Brown. Johnny Lawrie got only two shifts. Fact, we lose it in the second period, but in the third period when we tried to mount a comeback, Thornton and Brownie are just gassed. They had played, you wouldn't believe the minutes they played! Thornton played thirty-three minutes. He played way too much; Brownie played too much. Lawrie got like three shifts the whole game. It was pretty bad coaching on his part, I'm sorry to say."

"The way Norwood played in the first period might have tired out a team with no depth, but we have depth," Brian Mulcahy said after the game. "It was a pressure period on the defense, but they skated so hard the first twelve minutes I wonder if it didn't get them a little tired. We started beating them to the puck after that."

"Kevin Carr told Bob Thornton the Nub—what they called Eddie Burns, the Nub—said they're gonna come out with their hair on fire," Peter Brown said. "However, that worked out, they won the game, but in that hair on fire first period we get one goal? That might have been a 4-1 game, us. Who knows? So ten minutes into the second period, Mulcahy, little shit defenseman takes a floater with like a minute to go in the end of the second, they're 1-0. In other words, that's, so two periods it's 0-0. So if we get one bounce, I remember Nolf had a couple opportunities, I remember Jackie Clifford had a real good opportunity, we get that one goal..." The assessment was shared by Jay Shaughnessy.

"I didn't think you guys in '71 were gonna give us that good a game," the Spy Ponder captain said. "I don't think we got it out of our zone the first period, you guys were all over us. Cremens, I told ya, I fell down, it might have been Brown who took the shot, it was going right into the far corner, and a bunch of players in front of Cremens, I'm looking at it I said, shit, they're gonna score here, and outta nowhere Cremens' leg came out, kick save. That might have changed the pace of the whole game, I think. You guys scored then it might have been an avalanche the way you guys were pounding us. Brown said if you had scored in that first period it would have been 4-1? It's not far from the truth. If that one went in, we might have come back, who knows, but that first period we couldn't get past the red line."

One almost went in. "I think we coulda played better," Billy Sullivan recalled. "They were a good team. I do remember hitting the post in the first period. I think it did, I remember it in a dream, I thought I hit the right post, I haven't thought about that for fifty years. It was the right post, I know that. Low, too, because I couldn't lift the puck high. We were more corner players, Donny..." (laughs)

"Not to cry spilt milk," Phil Nolfi opined, "but I think if we were all healthy, it would have been a different game. Definitely would have been a different game. It's just something we couldn't do."

Ancient, embedded emotion surfaced with the time-less band-aid ripped off, the old wound examined. Phil Nolfi's voice cracks, he chokes up, after a half century. "I felt so bad when the game was over. It was a letdown, I never thought it would come to that. Welcome to real life. And then you realize it's just a game, but it was *so important*. I still have pictures of Norwood Nuggets and me and Bobby, Mikey Lydon, all that time, all these kids together. Didn't work out.

"I was emotional on the bus ride home. I didn't talk to anybody. I was on the verge of crying. But I felt like, for all those people that came to see us all those nights, it sounds corny, but I wanted them to win, too. Again, we would go to Wednesday night games and there would be 5,000 people! You couldn't believe it! So when we didn't win, I felt bad for all the people who went out on those cold nights, and we didn't win. And I've said to Donna if there was one day in my life I could take back, I would go back to that one, but be healthy. The goals, *bah*, I wanted to *win*. I wanted to be number one in the state. And it coulda happened. But it's the way it is. It's the way the ball goes. I felt bad for Don, because I think he wanted to win more than we did. It was just so disappointing. When you think of the talent we had..."

"I bawled my eyes out the day we lost to them," Billy Clifford recalled. "There was a party back at Thornton's, down in the cellar, there, when I got home, I was just fucking devastated. I thought...we should have won that game."

"I just remember Don telling us that he'd consider it a personal favor if we all went to school the next day," Billy Sullivan said. "So, we got beers out of Eddie King's store and Rosy, Mikey, me and Eddie drove around all day drinking. We never went to school!"

The game held a more sober element of emotion for Maurie Corkery. "Oh, I mean, that year was the year my mother passed away just before the tournament. February third, she died. A little heart-broken for that, but the championship picked up my father and my brothers and sisters. Well, it helped a little bit, anyways."

In the working manuscript of his book *Late in the Third*, Joe Bertagna describes Eddie Burns' developing relationship with an unnamed opponent.

> Burns was competitive. We never thought he placed too much emphasis on winning, but he wasn't afraid to make it clear how important it was. Once, after winning a state tournament game, he crossed the ice to shake the hand of the opposing coach. When he extended his hand, his vanquished foe ungraciously said, "Well, you're one up on me," and then turned and walked away. As fate would have it, the two teams met in the following year's championship game. Same result. As the post-game handshake was about to unfold and the losing coach feebly extended his hand, Eddie didn't wait. "Now I'm two up on you," he said with a smile.

One can only imagine how Norwood's coach processed that slight, and it remains unknown how Don Wheeler greeted Eddie Burns at mid-ice in Boston Garden after the '71 contest, with Burns and his Spy Ponders now *three* up on him. Clearly it did not go well. Animosity between two normally disciplined Marines, however, uncharacteristically leaked into the press after the game. *The Boston Globe* reported,

> Burns was apparently as enthused as the ball-throwing, confetti-tossing fans. He must have been because he let it be known afterwards that it was the third time Arlington had defeated Norwood in the finals. He also let it be known that he'd be glad to take Norwood on any time. He probably made that challenge because he doesn't think the Bay State League is

capable of providing a worthy opponent for his young gentlemen. He let that be known, too.

Another Boston sportswriter picked up on the exchange, noting,

> He must be pretty certain he can handle any future Bay State League teams he'll face in the tournament. He'll undoubtedly get a chance to stand behind those claims, and when he does, things may turn out differently.

Apprised of the Arlington legend's words, a steely-eyed Don Wheeler simply responded, "After losing three times to them, when we finally do win, it will be that much sweeter."

HISTORY, HOCKEY, AND IMAGINATION

"Had his genius been only contemplative, he had been fitted to his life, but with his energy and practical ability he seemed born for great enterprise and for command," Ralph Waldo Emerson read to Concord gathered, at Henry David Thoreau's 1862 funeral.

> Mr. Thoreau was equipped with a most adapted and serviceable body. He was of short stature, firmly built, of light complexion, with strong, serious blue eyes, and a grave aspect, his face covered in the late years with a becoming beard. His senses were acute, his frame well-knit and hardy, his hands strong and skillful in the use of tools. And there was a wonderful fitness of body and mind.
>
> He could pace sixteen rods more accurately than another man could measure them with rod and chain. He could find his path in the woods at night, he said, better by his feet than his eyes. He could estimate and measure a tree very well by his eyes; he could estimate the weight of a calf or a pig, like a dealer. From a box containing a bushel or more of loose pencils, he could take up with his hands fast enough just a dozen pencils at every grasp. He was a good swimmer, runner, skater...

Kenneth Roberts, through dialogue in his 1933 historical novel *Rabble in Arms*, described Benedict Arnold's physical presence,

> Nathaniel said to Cap: "If he feels that way about barbers, maybe he doesn't like gymnasts, either." The cart was empty, except for the Canadian driver; and with no gentle hand I helped Nathaniel up into it. Cap eyed him dubiously.
>
> "What was that? What is it he maybe doesn't like either?"
>
> "Gymnasts," I said dryly. "He means acrobats. Nathaniel heard that Arnold used to be a gymnast, but of course there's nothing in it."

"Oh, ain't there!" Cap cried. "Well I hope to die if there ain't! Even with a hole shot through one leg he's stronger'n quicker'n any other three men in the world! He's the only feller ever I see that could jump all the way over an ammunition wagon without touching a hand to it... This feller Arnold can *skate better than any Canadian that ever lived.*"

Long noted is a correlation between athletics and leadership. Qualities that draw eyes to generals are often exhibited on fields and ice of play. Perhaps it is ability and willingness to mount a stage, to perform, that mutually reinforces.

General Douglas MacArthur found baseball relevant to vision, preparation, and execution. Asked by journalist Clare Booth Luce his blueprint for offensive war in the Pacific, he invoked Wee Willie Keeler, "Did you ever hear the baseball expression, 'Hit 'em where they ain't?' That's my formula."

As Superintendent of West Point, MacArthur urged congressmen to appoint gifted athletes to the academy, and enacted compulsory intramural athletics for the entire corps. He penned and had carved in stone on the portals of the gymnasium:

Upon the fields of friendly strife
Are sown the seeds
That, upon other fields, on other days
Will bear the fruits of victory

Baseball captain Sep Johnson recalled MacArthur's college ability: "He was still a weak hitter and was barely adequate in right field. Yet he loved to play...he was far from brilliant, but somehow he could manage to get on first. He'd outfox the pitcher, draw a base on balls, or outrun a bunt, and there he'd be on first." Biographer William Manchester notes, "All his life he would be fiercely proud of his varsity 'A'. Aged seventy, he wore it on his bathrobe the night before the Inchon landing."

Robert Rogers, the scourge of French and Indian as leader of famed Rogers' Rangers, fit the mold. "Games of strength, speed, and cunning played fiercely prominent parts in the semi-annual Londonderry Fair, held on the common near the First Parish meetinghouse," John F. Ross wrote in *War on the Run*. "Small populations, dispersed over large areas, often spend their common time in trying to outdo one another, as one writer has said, 'out-running, out-licking, and out hollering one's neighbors...' The men lifted weights, pitched quoits, threw heavy pieces of iron, pulled sticks, and wrestled. By the time Robert entered his teens, he had grown into a powerful, athletic, and formidable competitor, a man 'with bark on'...even in that circle of hardy fighting men, Rogers stood out. His well-proportioned frame alone—pushing over six feet tall—was the equivalent today of a professional athlete...yet even more arresting was the catlike effortlessness of his movement... The grandson of his good friend John Stark asserted that Rogers never lost a match, an exaggeration certainly but one that acknowledged an already legendary physical prowess."

Ross describes events on Lakes Champlain and George in upstate New York, upon which Rogers introduced ice skates to warfare. "Strapped to their moccasins were rude iron skates, which had been fashioned by the garrison blacksmith out of quarter-inch-wide blades; they generally limited movement to skating head down and straight ahead. Grooved into a wooden, shoe-sized platform and pinned from the sides like a musket barrel, the blade reached only three-eighths of an inch deep, so the slightest pressure brought contact with the ice and stability. The men took short steps, half walking and half running across the frozen lake."

Both Abraham Lincoln and George Washington were formidable figures. Stephen Douglas once said, when "both comparatively boys, and both struggling with poverty in a strange land," that Lincoln "could beat any of the boys wrestling, or running a foot race, in pitching quoits or tossing a copper..."

Washington's physical size and strength was renown, his reputed athletic prowess gleaned from observations such as this, from David Hackett Fischer's *Washington's Crossing*, "Those who knew horses noticed that he rode with the easy grace of a natural rider, and a complete mastery of himself. He sat 'quiet,' as an equestrian would say, with his muscular legs extended...the animal and the man moved so fluently together that one observer was put in mind of a centaur. Another wrote that he was incomparably 'the best horseman of his age, and the most graceful figure that could be seen on horseback.' He was a big man, immaculate in dress, and of such charismatic presence that he filled the street even when he rode alone."

If the adage, "a woman loves a man in uniform," is applicable to both the Dress Blues of a United States Marine and the Adidas black and gold sweater of the Boston Bruins, then certainly these historic figures might have played a different game had they been born in the world they had bequeathed.

Today as I write this on Summit Avenue in Norwood, on the afternoon of June 12th, 2019, two teams are a handful of miles away preparing to play a seventh game of a Stanley Cup final series in Boston's TD Garden. You, the reader of these words, know the result, while I can only imagine. But as a writer of historical fiction, it is within the realm of artistic license, of imagination, to *not* see the afore-mentioned leaders as heroes—and villain—in roles of *yore*, but as *your* Boston Bruins:

Announcer Donny Brooks: "For the power play the Bruins bring out their top-scoring NEL line, their New England Line of Thoreau centering Arnold and Rogers, with the Twin Towers, Lincoln and Washington back on the blue. Thoreau and Rogers are both Concord boys, of course, Henry from Concord, Massachusetts and Bobby from Concord, New Hampshire, while Benny hails from Norwich, Connecticut. Washington was sorely missed these last couple of games..."

Color man Fitzy Cuffs: "Well, they don't call him 'The General' for naught. He's never been much of an offensive player, but his mere presence, his coolness under pressure, he's like a refrigerator that skates like a figure skater and he works so well with Lincoln, who's more willing to make the offensive foray. Abe struggled when he first arrived, but from what he's shown, TD Garden will be his signature address for some time to come..."

Alas, just as one finds time to return to finish one chapter, time relinquishes its hold on another.

The dressing room was solemn, interviews barely audible. Thoreau was philosophical about the loss. "Our truest life is when we are in our dreams awake..." he said, his voice trailing off. Others were less sanguine and seemed to brace for recriminations to come.

"When you ask for a frigate, they give you a raft," Arnold complained bitterly, apparently alluding to the Bruins' trading deadline effort, and seeming to deflect attention from his grave error. "Ask for sailors, they give you tavern waiters." Rogers, across the room, would have none of it.

"I've said it over and over," the wingman quietly said, leaning back against the wall in his sweat-drenched tee shirt. "If you oblige the enemy to retreat, be careful in your pursuit of them...prevent them from gaining eminences..."

But stolid force of the defensemen, Twin Tower stalwarts season-long, reined teammates with considered and measured words.

"It's better to offer no excuse, than a bad one," the General whispered. As though finishing his thought and reflecting the anguish of the entire organization and its family, fans and friends, Lincoln added, "I laugh because I must not cry. That is all. That is all."

In olde English, to "lose" meant a state of bewilderment, uncertainty, destruction, breaking up, and more telling, to perish. I saw General Bobby Thornton in a Boston Garden dressing room shower leaning, his face buried in his arms against the wall, weeping.

THE GREAT, "WHAT IF?"

Who on earth is Thomas Whall, born on another continent in a previous century, and how on earth could he have affected Norwood hockey? Frank Wall wrote the following in a 1965 Sports Slants column,

> In the very near future don't be surprised if the headlines read: "Lockwood Signs With Major League Team for Giant Bonus." The Lockwood is "Skip" Lockwood who is "Mr. Everything" at Catholic Memorial High School. Not only does Skip excel in baseball, but in track and basketball as well. At the graduation exercises at C.M. last Friday, he walked off with seven awards, including the outstanding athlete award. And the MVP honor. His four-year pitching record at C.M. was 22 wins and 2 losses, the latter both in his freshman year. He batted over .400 every year. You would think with all the honors bestowed on him and the biggest yet to come that Skip's ego would be slightly inflated, but this isn't the case. He is the same fine youngster that we knew in Little League eight years ago.

Claude "Skip" Lockwood, whose future held election to Catholic Memorial's Hall of Fame and a twelve-year MLB career, was perhaps the finest Norwood athlete "lost" to Catholic schools. Several star baseball players went to BC High, notably Mike Crimmins, but also Jimmy Symington and future Norwood assistant hockey coach Jimmy Gormley. Crimmins, a class of '65 Nichols Street kid, starred in football, hockey, and baseball in Dorchester, and in Norwood lore was also known for hitting one of the longest home runs against inmates in Norfolk State Prison.

"You started off at St. Catherine's, there was a good chance your parents would have had you go on to a Catholic high school," Mike Crimmins remembered. "That's the way most parents thought. They want you to continue the Catholic education. There's no snobbery involved in that, it was a segue to, you know, the kind of education you received at St. Catherine's, and so it was very similar at a Catholic high school. Course, everyone felt they fell from grace...I sort of kept with it. My blind faith stayed with me, thank God. And I'm happy about that. There's few and far between these days.

"Well, you know, not to sound like an idiot here, but there were traditional things back in those days. Everybody took the BC High test. If you got in, you went. It was an honor. It was the best. It was the dean of the Catholic schools. And those that didn't, went to CM. That's just the way it was in those days. There was a bus for Norwood kids going to CM every day. Picked you up at the donut shop down at Norwood center. I was one of maybe a handful that trudged off to the adventure of BC High. I liked the Jesuit form of education. I did like it. The Jesuits to me were the peak of the religious orders, they were very good teachers, I just liked conforming to their style of education, the Latin, Greek, languages, stuff like that. I was very comfortable there.

"Oh, I regretted it at first, I did, I did initially. I screamed and yelled, I said *nooo!* It was fear of the unknown when it got close to going to BC High. But that was quickly dispelled, I says all *right*. My mother was a strict Irish-Catholic and it would have broken her little heart. She was dying of cancer, so I didn't want to kick her in the teeth by going to Norwood High. Ultimately it wound up being the right choice."

Jay Dixon, who later starred at Boston University as a defensive end and was drafted by the Cleveland Browns, attended Xaverian Brothers High School class of '67, depriving Norwood High of one of the greatest football players the town had produced. Brother Chris, who later played basketball at Providence College, attended Xaverian class of '72, depriving Norwood of one of the greatest basketball players the town had produced. In the early sixties Robbie Hebner, a star pitcher, attended Catholic Memorial.

"Robert was a real smart one," Richie Hebner recalled. "He went to CM. He was the second class of CM, which I think was '65. CM now is like $22,000. My brother Robert went to CM the second year, what do you think CM cost? Two hundred and fifty bucks. I don't know why he went to CM, the other four went to Norwood."

While the town lost a slew of baseball talent—both Dixon brothers also starred in that sport—Allen Doyle and Freddie Kinsman were the first notable local hockey players to attend school elsewhere.

Doyle starred in multiple sports at the West Roxbury high school and became famous later for golfing achievements. Turning professional at age forty-six in 1995, Allen Doyle earned over $15 million in his golfing career, overshadowing another, more pertinent athletic accomplishment to denizens of Norwood hockey. The 1966 graduate was recognized by a Hall of Fame selection for his contribution on ice for the Catholic Memorial Knights. After his All-Scholastic performance, Doyle went on to Norwich University where he was ECAC golf champion, as well as the highest scoring defenseman in Norwich history. These accomplishments lifted Allen Doyle into the top tier of athletes comprising inaugural members of Norwich's Athletic Hall of Fame.

As for Kinsman, I recall in the early '60s the Hebner house being pointed out in recognition of the kid then dominating high school hockey, but also acknowledging the white cape three houses past.

Freddie Kinsman lives there!

After graduating from CM, Freddie Kinsman went on to play for Boston College and the semi-pro Braintree Hawks. He would not be the last Norwood skater to be educated in West Roxbury. The two most renown, in homage to their skills and potential repercussions of their absence, essentially became a Norwood expression: *Doyle and D'Arcy.*

The strain of assimilating disparate colors, cultures, and creeds indelibly scars American experience. The worthy metaphor implies healing, but nevertheless reminds whenever we look in a mirror. Today's scars were gaping wounds when Irish immigrants began arriving en mass in Massachusetts.

In 1845, Europe faced the emergence of a terrifying and unexplained catastrophic failure of potato crops that would last almost a decade. Two million people perished of starvation in The Great Hunger, full half of them in Ireland. They knew not what had hit them; many believed climate the cause, air pollution, static electricity, and excessive humidity other possibilities. Still others looked to recent scientific advances, perhaps smoke from steam locomotives or gasses from the newly developed sulfur match. Some noted recent volcanic activity and still others looked skyward, suspecting some ill-defined influence from above. Natural historian Edward Hitchcock of Amherst College perhaps summed up collective incomprehension best when he attributed the blight to "atmospheric agency, too subtle for the cognizance of our senses."

Whatever the cause,[41] the calamity induced mass Irish emigration, much of it destined for Boston, Massachusetts. The resulting influx of tens of thousands of predominantly Catholic peasanty into an historically Protestant bastion of New World wealth and power inevitably caused friction. New arrivals entered a land simmering in anti-Catholic sentiment, which had boiled over into violence with the '29 burning of Charlestown's (today's Somerville's) Ursuline Convent, demonstrating marked intolerance within an established Protestant hierarchy. When Irish immigration accelerated through the remaining 1840s and into the '50s, Boston's anti-Catholic sentiment peaked.

In a democratic republic in which each individual has an equal vote, "demography becomes destiny." Fear of shifting political power through the massive increase in immigrant population elevated this concern. The defensive backlash enabled the American Party, soon nicknamed the "Know Nothings", to obtain control of Massachusetts' legislature in 1854. Honoring campaign promises, the American Party, whose core values reflected their "Temperance, Liberty, and Protestantism" slogan, instituted a series of oppressive measures on the fast-growing Roman Catholic population. Prominent among a host of nauseating restrictions were various attempts to impede voting rights of newly arrived immigrants. Though the Know Nothings were thwarted in imposing their most egregious measures, and in fairness achieved enlightened advancements in other areas such as women's rights, their harsh impositions on public education particularly angered the Irish.

Boston public school students were required to sing Protestant hymns and repeat Protestant prayers. Compulsory daily readings from the Protestant King James version of the Bible were instituted. History books containing anti-Catholic and corollary anti-Irish sentiment were distributed. And it was mandated that each morning the Protestant, King James Bible version of the Ten Commandments be recited in each class. All of which led to a lad named Thomas Whall.

---

41 The 1840s potato blight was caused by microscopic mold called *Phytophthora infestans*. It is believed that its introduction into Europe was caused by its "hitch-hiking" in shipments of guano used for fertilizer, from Chile.

Born March 31, 1848, in Kilkenny, Ireland and washed ashore as a youngster in the flood of famine refugees, Thomas Whall attended the Elliot School in Boston's North End. Today the school is recognized as the longest continually operated public school in the city, catering to a varied, but predominantly Italian, neighborhood. In 1859 the school was surrounded by tenements teeming with newly arrived Irish poor.

The very name of the town from which the Whall family emigrated adds clarity to context of place and time. Kilkenny in Gaelic is *Cill Chainnigh*, or "church of Cainnech." It should not surprise that Thomas' father, with little to covet other than his pride and religion and in a town whose Concord neighbor had recently published *On the Duty of Civil Disobedience*,[42] urged his son to refuse to recite the King James version of the Ten Commandments during morning recitals. Called upon by his teacher to do so on Monday morning, March 7, 1859, Thomas dutifully declined.

News of the insubordination flashed through both religious communities. The following Sunday in the North End's St. Mary's Parish Sunday School, Father Bernardine Wiget urged hundreds of schoolchildren in attendance to resist reciting Protestant mantras, further warning that any child who did recite them would be identified from the pulpit. In school the next morning, Thomas Whall was singled out to recite the Ten Commandments and again refused to utter Protestant verses. This time the school administration was ready.

Assistant principal McLaurin Cooke was summoned, declaring, "Here's a boy that refuses to repeat the Ten Commandments, and I will whip him till he yields if that takes the whole forenoon." Cooke proceeded to beat Whall's hand with a rattan rod for a half hour, until the hand was bleeding.[43] Infuriated that Whall still refused to recite the verses, Cooke informed students that anyone intending to refuse the King James version

---

42 Henry David Thoreau's 1848 lecture at the Concord Lyceum was originally entitled, *The Rights and Duties of the Individual in Relation to Government*, and first published the following year under the title, *Resistance to Civil Government*. The famous essay's title only morphed into *On the Duty of Civil Disobedience* after Thoreau's death in 1862. I use that title because it commonly identifies the essay today.
43 This mode of corporal punishment existed still in the Shattuck School of the early 1960s. Punishment was always inflicted in "the cloak room," outside classroom view. When my turn inevitably came one fateful morn, the teacher, ruler in hand, led me into the cloak room, demanded I extend my hand, and then to tearful, frightened eyes, whispered, "Don't tell anyone," and led me back into the classroom.

was to leave school immediately. One hundred boys filed out and three hundred walked away the following day, comprising events now remembered as "the Elliot School Rebellion."

The resulting clamor, during which the school forbid re-admission of offending students as well as instigated a lawsuit filed by the Whalls (resulting in Cooke's acquittal), prompted St. Mary's Parish to create St. Mary's Institute, in which over eleven hundred Catholic boys enrolled the following 1859-60 school year.

These events caused a nation-wide debate on government's role in education in light of first amendment rights, culminating in a burgeoning of independent Catholic schools. Dorchester's Boston College High School, BC High, was opened in the immediate aftermath of the Elliot School Rebellion, in 1863. By 1917 Boston area Catholics had created twenty-nine elementary schools, four high schools, four academies, and Boston College. Though the 20th century would see a marked lessening of religious animosity, Catholic schools continued to be built.

Malden Catholic opened in 1936, while Cambridge saw Matignon founded in 1945. Westwood's Xaverian Brothers High School opened in 1963. Catholic Memorial High School in West Roxbury, commonly referred to simply as, "CM," was established in 1957, and immediately began luring area Catholic boys with the promise of a quality parochial education, and plenty of ice time.

"I grew up on Winter Street in Norwood across from the cemetery," Jimmy "Zeke" Doyle recalled. "My older brother played, Allen, he's four years older, so he started hockey a little before I did. My dad, he knew Tom Clifford pretty well. Clifford had a program that wasn't really affiliated with anything, because there wasn't really a Norwood program at the time, there wasn't an official Norwood peewees or bantams. So many of us started with Clifford, and we would do Saturday mornings over at Tabor, what is now the St. Sebastian's rink, but it was the Tabor rink back then.

"I think Norwood was a great town. To me it was a great town, it was, it was everything. Norwood meant a lot to me, you know, all my friends were from Norwood. Certainly, before I got to high school, I didn't know anything but Norwood. We played all sports. We used to play football, we used to play basketball, I mean, we played everything. We played baseball. In that sense it was idyllic. I love sports, and most of my friends did, too.

You obviously gravitate toward people you like, who like the same things that you do. I think it was an awesome town, it was just a neat place to grow up."

"I grew up on Winter Street," Ray D'Arcy said. "My next-door neighbor was the Doyles, and I lived at 305 Winter Street and the Doyles lived at 309 Winter Street, right across from the Highland Cemetery. We were next door neighbors, and besides Jim Doyle, he and I were the same age and friends, his brother Allen who's not only famous for his years in golf on the PGA and the Senior Tour, he's also an All-American hockey player at Norwich University and All-American golfer at Norwich University as well as Catholic Memorial.

"So we all got started playing hockey with Tom Clifford. We were probably, I don't know, maybe eight years old or so and we started up with what was called the Norwood Hockey Club, and we'd go over to Tabor arena, over in Needham there, very early in the morning, five or six o'clock in the morning, and the fathers, particularly Mr. Doyle, he would drive us over there and we'd play for an hour on the rink over there. With the weather being what it is around here the ponds used to freeze an awful lot more than it seems now, and we would head over to New Pond or Pettee's Pond and Tom Clifford would have already been over there shoveling the ice. We'd play for hours and hours out on the ice out there, and so that's how we got started. And then on to the Norwood Nuggets program and then on to CYO, then it was time to go to high school."

"Well, it wasn't a decision," Jimmy Doyle explained. "When I say that, I mean, my dad said I was going to CM. You know, probably one of the greatest decisions I *never* made, because most of my lifelong friends were CM kids, still are my friends, yes. Four or five of them pretty much are at the top of my friend list, including Ray D'Arcy. Ray and I are still very close, have been for sixty-some years, since we were three years old.

"Ray was a very, very good high school player. Last couple of years one of the top scorers in the league, real up and down grinder, small guy, maybe five, he got to be at BC maybe five-eight, 170 pounds, but again, good skater, pretty good with the puck. He was a pretty good college hockey player; he actually was captain at BC his senior year. He was a pretty good college hockey player and a very good high school player, obviously on the all-star team several years. Just a stick your nose in things, and a grinder."

"Did I have any heroes?" Ray D'Arcy repeated. "Probably Richie Hebner, and the Norwood High hockey team. We tried to get to their games when we could, but always fascinated with watching Hebner play in particular, and Blaine Maus, and Neil Higgins was a little bit older than me. But watching Norwood High School team play, those are the early days, you know, the guys that were fascinated by the game and got hooked even more on it by watching them. Then as time when on, we go over to—because my older brother went to Catholic Memorial, Allen Doyle went to Catholic Memorial, and so then we started making our way over to watch the Catholic Memorial hockey teams play. There were some great players on the CM team and that kind of got us hooked on, you know, when it came time to choose a high school, CM became the place we wanted to go.

"I would say, with me and I think you call him Jim Doyle, but his nickname was Zeke, Zeke Doyle, his older brother Allen, and an older brother Noel who was older than Allen, they both went to Catholic Memorial, my brother went to Catholic Memorial, so when it came time for us to pick a school, there was an awful lot of knowledge about the coach over at Catholic Memorial, Joe Quinn. And so we kind of followed in our brothers' footsteps to go to CM and you know also Joe Quinn had this incredible reputation of being able to coach kids in the way to play hockey in order to get them into and play college hockey. And so that was really important, particularly for me. I mean, my household there was no money for me to go to college, if I was gonna go to college, I had to get a hockey scholarship. (laughs)

"Don Wheeler, certainly all the guys who played for him have nothing but great things to say about him,[44] but we did notice that in terms of teaching kids how to actually play the game so that you could take it to the next level, it seemed to us from coaching my brother and Allen Doyle is that Joe Quinn teaches you more of the game to get you to play at the next level and so that was important. That's one of the reasons why I in particular reinforced following in my brother's footsteps and Zeke's footsteps. Course Zeke and I wanted to go to the same place. We played together since we were eight years old, we lived next door to each other. It was hard to get into Catholic Memorial, there was only seven of us in

---

[44] I had been warned that Ray D'Arcy was a master of tongue-in-cheek comments.

the whole town who went to Catholic Memorial, and there's no transportation, so we'd have to hook rides with any parent who happened to be working near West Roxbury who could drop us off. And sometimes that meant, some of the fathers had to get there at like, they'd have to be at work at seven-thirty, so we'd be dropped off at six-thirty in the morning and frankly the doors weren't open yet. So we had to knock on the windows where the Brothers were having church services to just let us in the door so that we could go to the gym until school started at eight o'clock.

"We had a really good team. And CM didn't have as many hockey players then as they do now, we only had fourteen kids on the team. So we were playing two lines and that was it, and three defensemen. So I tell you what, we got a lot of ice time, I'll put it that way."

The loss of great athletes to other high schools did not go unnoticed, nor was the loss restricted to Catholic schools. "The hockey was a lot better at Norwood, there is no doubt about it," Mike Crimmins recalled of his BC High experience. "We used to go to the Arena, you know, I'd go to a lot of the Norwood games on Saturday night, and I remember Jack Monbouquette was the coach at that time, and he used to talk to my father all of the time, and he'd, *oh, have Mike transfer back to Norwood, I'll guarantee he'll start* and all this, and I'm like Jesus, Mary and Joseph, what the *hell*...Tommy Smelstor couldn't have been too happy! (laughs) But it never transpired."

After the loss of Doyle and D'Arcy, Rita Lyons received a visitor. "Mr. Wheeler came over to the house," she recalled. "Mike was just entering high school. We had decided to send Mikey to Belmont Hill. My biggest fear of Norwood High School was that he wouldn't be pushed, that he might be just shoved along. He had a better education at Belmont Hill, it's a top private school. He had to study. I thought it was more important, I'm a stickler on education.

"He said he never promised anything in his life, but he promised if Mike came to Norwood, he'd give him a place on the varsity. Mr. Wheeler came and he was very cool, he was very polite. It was a very brief meeting, he sat in the living room for maybe ten minutes. He wasn't very happy with me. Tommy was playing for Wheeler at the time and we weren't going to go through that again. Let's see, it was 1970."

"Dickie Donovan had a great career afterward," Tommy Taylor said. "He went to CM and couldn't make the hockey team as a freshman, and came to Norwood and couldn't play anyway, he was a transfer. He practiced, but he wasn't on the team his sophomore year. He always talks about Doyle and D'Arcy. Dick and I would always say if they had gone to Norwood in '69 we probably would have gone further. They were the two guys we needed."

"They were good, *real* good," Dickie Donovan concurred. "I always told Jimmy Doyle, I said, if you and Raymonds went to Norwood High, we might have beat Ftorek. That's how loaded we would have been. We would have had two loaded lines, and Zeke could play defense, too. He was a good defenseman. Yeah, we didn't, I mean, Bobby Thornton and Peter Brown were starting my senior year and they were young, they weren't the great players they'd become yet. It would have given us a chance to be the best in the state. But we didn't have a second line, and the defense was so young, we needed some guys."

"Jack Cronin, he was another one," Leo McInerney recalled. "You talk about the guys playing in those days, Dickie started at CM and of course Zeke and Ray D'Arcy, Zeke Doyle and Ray D'Arcy were great players, and Jack was actually going to CM and his dad got sick. And he then had to go to the high school because of the money issue. There's a lot of good players, Petrovek, both of Brian's brothers played on the high school team…Allen Doyle went to CM, too."

Pete Tamulionis, captain of Norwood's '70 team, remembered well the implications. "Street hockey, remember cutting a hole in the fence at Father Mac's and going into the pool? Cops chase us out, we wait in the woods for an hour, go back in. Played street hockey for hours up there. And I remember Ray D'Arcy and Jimmy Doyle back in those days were very good friends of mine and I often thought of this, if they ever went to Norwood High, *Jesus,* I might not have made the team, because those two guys were freakin' unbelievable! They were just two hell of a hockey players that came out of Norwood that went to Catholic Memorial. They were just two *great* hockey players.

"Oh my God, if they were there, oh my God, if they had gone to Norwood, we would have been there again! I swear to God, they were that good! Mikey Martin was just a sophomore, and he was gonna be good, you just knew he was gonna be good, you just knew it. D'Arcy and Doyle could have stepped in the league and taken us to a different level."

One of Norwood's greatest losses, not to a Catholic school and more than tempered by the great success of Billy Pieri—who lost one game in his career—was that of goalie Brian Petrovek to Connecticut's Hotchkiss School.

"Actually part of my decision," the future Harvard All-American explained, "the overriding one, had I gone to Norwood as a ninth grader, the goalie at the time who was gonna be a senior was not somebody I actually thought I could beat out.[45] That could have been an aspect of it, but really the opportunity was to go to a place which had very rigorous academics, a world-class school, kind of the Mike Lyons story, but also a rink on campus, practice every day, they were building a new rink, and wealthy donors who already had made the commitment.

"The arena was basically under construction, so I knew I'd have a place to go and play every day, two rinks on campus, and the coach there was a former goaltender at Princeton. I said to myself I have a laboratory to go to, I can play every single day. I had a coach that also played my position, and a schedule that schools like Hotchkiss played at the time included some college freshman teams. Even though Norwood in the Bay State League was competitive, I really felt, you know, from whatever it was I could determine, that if I went to Hotchkiss and played four years, I'd be playing against the most competitive brand, and I'd have a chance to up my game better than in a public-school program. Even though Norwood had high expectations about state championships, it gave me a choice between getting fifteen shots a game and maybe practicing a couple times a week or go to a place that I could really focus my energies on, and that was the choice I made. I can remember being somewhat criticized for making that move, and not staying in the program that everyone was kinda growing up and aspiring to be part of, but it was the best decision I ever made."

If disasters were avoided when both Jack Cronin and Dickie Donovan remained in Norwood, catastrophe was averted when Peter Brown reached the same decision.

---

45 Brian Petrovek's freshman year would have been '69-'70. Norwood's starting goalie was Frank Eppich.

"Brian Petrovek's father Gus worked with my Uncle Al for years," Peter explained. "Mary Petrovek, absolute charming, classy, wonderful, beautiful people. Brian and I were on bantams together and Paul Kelley, (BU coach) Jack Kelley's son, was on the team. And between you and I, Jack Kelley started recruiting Brian and I on that bantam team. I mean, basically Brian went to Hotchkiss and I did my freshman year at Norwood High, and then I went with Gus one weekend down to Hotchkiss with the goal of possibly transferring and playing down to Hotchkiss. I went down there. And between you and I, I think that was my sophomore year, I'd gone down there. Mrs. Horgan—remember Mrs. Horgan, the cheerleader coach? — her husband would go into the office where my mother worked, and my mother was like, *oh yeah Peter has an opportunity to go to Hotchkiss school*, and so Don got wind of it. And I go down there to meet the coach, Blades Braden or something, Blades, you know, and the baseball coach is called Bats or something, you know, prep school back in the day, the fur coats and shit, I'm like this isn't me, I wanna go up the Elks and fucking drink with Wheatie! Fuck *me!* So I wound up not going down, and my mother didn't talk to me for six months!"[46]

When asked if he had any regrets about not attending Norwood High School, Zeke Doyle paused a long, long moment. "Um...probably," he finally responded. "And I say that, maybe to a little degree, although reality, there was a lot of good people at CM, enjoyed it very much, not only hockey but the other things that you go through in high school. So I'm

---

[46] "We were both gonna go to BU, Jack Kelley had us wrapped up," Peter explained. "Jack Kelley went to coach the New England Whalers, and Brian and Gus went to Jack and said do you still want us to go to BU? If Jack Kelley had stayed at BU, Brian would have gone to BU, instead of Harvard. Mr. and Mrs. Petrovek—this is Norwood. I'm up at the Walpole Four Seasons, I don't know why, and Mr. and Mrs. Petrovek were there. They give me a card, and they give me a 1922 Silver Dollar. For good luck when I go to BU. And I swear except for the fact that I blew out my knee about five times, I swear it brought me good luck. Brian beat us in the Beanpot, but I swear it brought me good luck. And that is something that...and Brian and I didn't hang together in college, he was in Cambridge and we kind of went our separate ways, but it shows the incestuous-ness of hockey runs very deep, and not just about the hockey. If at all, yeah, if at all you can slide in that Peter Brown never forgets that the Petroveks gave him...I still have it. 1922, which is my mother's birth year. I went to BU, and Brian graduated from Harvard. We won't hold that against him."

sure I did to a degree, because again, most of the guys that were playing, like Tommy Taylor and Dickie Donovan and Mikey Martin after, Mark O'Connell and those guys, Peter Brown, well guess what, I grew up playing with them, so I knew them all. And they're all good kids too, good people too, so I think there's some of that there, but not to a large degree. But personally, I had a great experience at CM.

"Well, you know what? I've heard it from many people, but the fact is you guys, Norwood had a great program anyway and they really did, they had a style, they were hard-charging and they played well. So yeah, in some ways you do wish it, in some ways...but I don't, I never lost much sleep over it. Like I said, I didn't have much control over the decision anyway. (laughs) It turned out well for me. I think it did, as I look back, I think it worked out wonderfully. And again, I've still got some very good friends from there and especially now in life, that's more important than anything else."

"No, not at all," Ray D'Arcy answered the same question. "You know, our experience, and I'm sure Zeke will say the same thing, is that the experience we had at CM, beyond just the hockey and all I said about Joe Quinn and into college and getting scholarships to college and playing in college, that was kind of what we had our eye on. And you can't believe how many times when I used to go down to Lewis' and if I was with Zeke and we'd be sitting at the bar, there would be more people who would bring up those years and say, *if you guys went to Norwood High we would have won more state championships*, and you know, a high school championship, that's all well and good and we certainly had our opportunities at CM—we were better than Norwood's team when we were at CM—but we got more experience getting out of the town and for the first time, being out of the suburban environment, and going to school at CM which was basically an urban culture, and meeting all these, and getting an experience with people who grew up in Mattapan and Dorchester and Roxbury, and the whole experience with the Irish Christian Brothers and the education we got at CM. I wouldn't change that for the world. And getting to know Joe Quinn, he had the biggest influence in my life. We used to get that a lot, when we were out of college, for the years after that, the discussions, particularly down at Lewis' after a few beers, but I've absolutely no regrets whatsoever. The life experience I had at CM; it couldn't be replicated at Norwood High.

"I think Dickie Donovan was at CM his freshman year. I think he left after the freshman year. I don't recall what happened there, but it could have been money. Small money now, but I think it was $350 a year back then to go to CM, or maybe he just wanted to stay in Norwood, that's what he decided to do and it worked out well for him, that's for sure. He got into the Norwood hockey Hall of Fame, and at Bowdoin, I don't know, but he might still hold all the scoring records up there. I know he loved Bowdoin. Dickie Donovan was an inspiration to me."

Dickie Donovan reacted differently to CM. "I don't know," he explained, "I have no regrets about it. Once I was there, I went to a varsity game and there were no people there. I'm used to going to Norwood games, I went to my first Norwood game in 1961 and Donnie Smith was in the net, Alby Crowell was playing, Charley Donahue was an all-star. It was fabulous, I got hooked on it. I was addicted to hockey in 1961. I was ten. And I never became unaddicted to it. (laughs)

"They had a pretty good program, Allen Doyle was playing over there, defenseman, he was pretty good, they had about three or four all-stars over there, Dick McGlynn was pretty good, Bobby Kelly, I got to know him a little bit, but I said, man, I had a chance to play for Norwood, I said, you know, the Arena used to hold about 9,000 and it was always full, and I said I wanna go back and play. So my old man said yeah, go ahead. It worked out.

"I was ineligible to play as a sophomore, but I wasn't any good, I was too small," Dickie Donovan continued. "I was about five-foot-three, 110 pounds. I grew a ton after my sophomore year, to my junior year I grew five inches. Then I would look Jackie Cronin in the eye and he looked about the same size as me. He was a monster of a guy, not that tall but his legs were like Richie Hebner's, they looked like a pro football player. He was a fabulous player. I played with so many good guys!"

So...what if? What if Freddie Kinsman and Allen Doyle were with Richie Hebner and Tommy Smelstor in '65, would that have helped Norwood score one goal against Walpole in the state final? What if Allen Doyle was with Richie in '66 when his skate broke in the quarterfinals, could he have picked up the slack, and over-come the loss?

What if Dickie Donovan, on the short-list of everyone's all-time greatest Norwood skaters, had had Doyle and D'Arcy, whose futures included years of minor league hockey as well as a captaincy at Boston College, skating beside him in '69? Would that team have survived Herbie Pearl? Those Winter Street kids led Catholic Memorial to an undefeated season in '70 and were considered the only team capable of competing with Ftorek's mighty, mighty Needham, could they have improved Norwood's 9-5-4 record that season?

And what if All-American Brian Petrovek had played—ah, but no, he simply wasn't needed. But it is easy to imagine—that's what we do—the effect of adding these exceptional players to already star-studded Norwood rosters. Five times Norwood went to the state finals in eight seasons, could it have been seven times? Eight times? The two seasons following '72 saw Norwood win fifteen games in each; if they had Petrovek and Mikey Lyons, could they have won more? Easily we could add a trip to the finals in '66 and '69, could it have been possible for Norwood to have gone to the finals in *five consecutive years? Could Norwood have been in the state finals ten consecutive years?*

Well, maybe. Then again, how good would Catholic Memorial have been had Dickie Donovan stayed with Doyle and D'Arcy there?

It's Norwood hockey's great *what if...*

"Hockey meant the world to me," Ray D'Arcy said. "Not only, again, I get back to Joe Quinn, as my high school coach. First of all, my dad died when I was like fifteen years old. Joe Quinn kind of took me under his wing and not only taught me about hockey, but Joe had a birth defect where one of his arms didn't grow to the full length. And so he had kind of a short arm with a small hand, but he played and got a scholarship to BU, and played hockey at BU with his arm like that. And so whenever you said to him you couldn't accomplish something—you just wouldn't say it to him. He'd say, you can accomplish anything you put your mind to and if you're tough enough and put in the hard work. And so that has stayed with me. I'm turning sixty-nine pretty soon, but that influence on me to take that advice about how to set goals, how to accomplish things, I mean, being told you'll never play at BC, Ray, *Oh really? Okay, well I'll show you!* Because I had such confidence instilled in me that if I really wanted to accomplish something, I'd do it. I ran the Boston Marathon under three hours. I qualified for the Boston Marathon, I wanted to achieve that. In business I ultimately became the CEO of a multi-billion-dollar company. And I since retired about ten years ago.

"So those lessons I learned in hockey about challenges and setting goals and doing whatever you have to do to reach those goals, becoming captain of Boston College, and playing at Boston College on a regular basis, was something like being told you'll never do that, well, *yes I will!* (laughs) It was that influence that hockey, particularly in those years when I was a teenager with no father, with no money in the house, I needed to get a full scholarship to college. It just made me work hard, knowing I wasn't the Robbie Ftoreks or Zeke Doyles of the world. But I had enough inspiration and enough motivation to make the best of the talents that I had, and it served me well right up until, you know, now I'm a father and a grandfather. So it, it was certainly a sport that made me as successful as I think I've been for my life. That's the way I feel about the luck that I had. If I didn't go to CM, I don't think all this other stuff that was instilled in me would have happened."

"You know," Zeke Doyle said, "I mean, certainly I guess my years up to twenty-five, twenty-six, hockey meant everything to me. In some ways, it was the only thing I really cared about. And that's both good and bad. There's plusses and minuses to everything. But, you know, like I say, when I was in high school it was all about how good could you be in college. I got a full scholarship, well that's great, and so I didn't pay attention to other things I should have, but that's okay. I mean, because it just, maybe that's just more my personality. I just go at everything one hundred miles an hour and maybe forget about other things I should be concerned about, too.

"But I still love to watch the Bruins play, love to watch the Stanley Cup, stuff like that. Hockey meant quite a bit to me in my years growing up. So it did, it meant quite a bit to me and you know, I think hockey makes you, I think hockey people are generally pretty good people, too. You know, even if you look at sports today you look at hockey people versus others and while there's idiots in every sport, most hockey people are pretty good people. And so I think it shapes you in a way, I think it makes you a decent person.

"That's my cut, anyway."

SPORT SLANTS

NORWOOD AT THE MOVIES

What, one may well inquire, does *"Love means never having to say you're sorry"* have to do with, *"Puttin' on the foil, coach!"*? How, one may also ask, does, *"There's no crying in baseball!"* relate to a Rotten Tomatoes-caliber hockey movie with no memorable line? Is it possible that Ryan O'Neil, Ali MacGraw, Burt Reynolds, Russell Crowe, Tom Hanks, Geena Davis, Paul Newman, Madonna, and Michele Pfeiffer's husband have a connection to Norwood athletics?

Well, yeah...but like the start of a good workout, it requires some stretching...

I love the smell of napalm in the morning!

The first is indeed a stretch, as it has nothing to do with athletics. Charles B. Rheault, Jr. grew up on Nahatan Street just over the Westwood line. His father had purchased a large portion of the former Forbes estate in 1928, subsequently selling acreage to Matthew Naughton in 1947, who in turn sold the lot to Vito Guisti upon which was developed Crestwood Circle. An adjacent lot Rheault sold directly to Anne and Dr. Roy Lydon in 1949, upon which they constructed their mini compound. Remaining land constituted the Rheault estate, whose grand house stands today, second in toward Norwood center, from Clapboardtree Street.

A West Point graduate and Korean War Silver Star-winner considered fast-tracked to become an Army general, Colonel Charles Rheault, Jr. garnered national attention in 1969 when he, at the height of the war and as head of 5th Special Forces Group, was accused of executing suspected Vietnamese double agent Thai Khac Chuyen in Nha Trang, Vietnam. The resulting "Green Beret Affair" culminated in Rheault's and several subordinates' court-marshals.

The trial is said to have made popular the CIA expression, "terminate with extreme prejudice," a now-familiar euphemism for the word,

"Kill." His gracing, if that is the appropriate word, the November 1969 cover of *Life Magazine* prompted the Colonel's eleven-year-old son Charles Rheault, III to notably comment, "What is all the fuss about? I thought that was what Dad was in Vietnam for, to kill Viet Cong."[47] When the CIA refused to allow its members to testify and with the U.S. Army chain of command deservedly nervous, the charges were dropped. Facing the impossibility of ever again being promoted, Rheault requested and was granted immediate retirement from the Army and returned to Westwood.

My brother Gordon, employed as a part-time groundskeeper on the Rheault estate, would sometimes see Rheault practicing pistol-shooting in the fields behind their house. Mike Lydon remembered his "next door" neighbor—their houses were several hundred yards apart—and the origin of his family's cabin, which for a generation of Norwood kids became almost a rite of passage to visit.

"Well, Charley Rheault, Sr. at the time was the oldest living Royal Canadian Mounted policeman, I mean, ex-policeman alive at the time," Mike Lydon recounted. "He married Ellie Rheault, she was the money, and he had a cabin out behind the house. A Swiss slate shingled, big stone hearth fireplace. When I was a kid we had a canvas pup tent, we were camping out in the field, it was his property, we wake up and there's cops pointing guns at me! He finds out it was Doc Lydon's kids, cuz he and Roy got along real well. He said you know Roy, we got a cabin out in the woods up there, comes apart, if you wanna take it apart and take it down to your property you're welcome to it, which he did. That's why there was a big hole we had to patch, because that's where the fireplace was. I'm gonna say that was early '60s, I'd say. I do remember when it wasn't there, but all through high school it was there, and I started high school in '66."

The movie connection? Director Frances Ford Coppola and screenwriter John Milius have both stated that the model for Colonel Walter Kurtz, the psychologically impaired, off-the-reservation rogue warrior played by Marlon Brando in their epic 1979 movie, *Apocalypse Now*, was none other than Colonel Charles B. Rheault, Jr. The Colonel can be seen interviewed in episode three of Ken Burns' and Lynn Novick's

---

47 Despite his Brahmin-esque appellation Charles Rheault, III, the son did not escape the neighborhood's blue collar influence, being nicknamed, "Skid."

quintessential PBS documentary series, *The Vietnam War*. Colonel Rheault retired to Owls Head, Maine where he died in 2013.

Love means never having to say you're sorry.

If the first was a stretch, this is within arms' reach. In 1969 Hollywood reached out to Harvard freshman hockey coach Bill Cleary for assistance in filming a movie based upon a Harvard hockey player and his ill-fated Radcliffe love interest. The screenplay was written by Erich Segal, whose 1958 Harvard graduating class included his friend Bob Cleary, Bill's brother. And what producers Howard Minsky and David Golden needed was a rink and players capable of bringing off a credible representation of college hockey, to which Bill Cleary happily reacted.

"They needed people that could skate," Bill Cleary said. "So I said, hey, we got the Harvard hockey team."

Among players chosen to participate was an eighteen-year-old freshman goaltender, who a year earlier had broken Norwood's collective heart with Arlington's overtime 1968 state final victory.

"People are fascinated by it because it's not that often you get to appear in a movie," Joe Bertagna said. "They were filming for a week or so in October of 1969 and they used, actually there were three heavy, full days of filming and they used the varsity all three days, and they allowed the freshmen to get involved the third day. Movie making is not really exciting because they come up with an idea and they film it six times one way and six times another way, and then there's an hour between activity and you're just sitting there the whole day.

"Watson Rink at the time was a cinder block and bleacher, spartan-type rink, and they had about a hundred and fifty extras and they would move those hundred and fifty people around depending on where the camera was pointing to create the illusion of a full rink. And they used, all of us could be either Harvard players, or Cornell players, or Dartmouth players, and then for one particular scene they got a guy from BU named Mike Hyndman who was a great defenseman. He was supposed to play this villain from Cornell who spoke French and they used Mike in that scene. I ended up having one scene, the puck comes to me, I stop it and I steer it to the left, and I give it to Billy Cleary, who's Ryan O'Neil's stuntman. Billy takes it behind the net and we filmed that a few times. And later they just took O'Neil and stood him behind the net and shot him from like the letters up, because he couldn't skate very well, so they didn't want to show his ankles.

"Bobby Havern was in it, don't recall Billy Corkery being in it. The opening hockey scene in the movie is a close-up from this camera of Bobby Havern stickhandling, but the point of view is from just behind the puck on the ice. So you're seeing the stick going back and forth, and you're hearing the sound it's making, that's how they introduced the first hockey scene in the movie. The other Harvard goalie, Bruce Durno, who was our starting goalie, he played the Cornell and Dartmouth goalies. Mike LoPresti was the backup on the varsity, he ended up being a state senator from East Boston. His family owned all the concessions at the airport at one time, he and I played the Harvard goalie. We were supposed to be the same goalie, so I wore his mask when I had my one day of scenes. I wore his jersey. The only thing is, he caught with his right hand and I caught with my left hand so in the movie, the same guy, same mask, same jersey but we were catching two different ways!

"So it was fun," Joe Bertagna continued. "We got invited to the world premiere at the Cleveland Circle Theater, we couldn't get any compensation cuz of eligibility. They gave the varsity red blazers, we just got invited to the movie and fifty years later they started doing all these reminising recollections of it. It was fifty years last year that they filmed it, fifty years this year that it actually debuted."

Love Story, starring Ali MacGraw and Ryan O'Neil, was released in December 1970. Enmeshed in the release were fascinating sidebars. Erich Segal based his protagonist Oliver Barrett IV on two very real Harvard students, Al Gore and his roommate Tommy Lee Jones. Jones, an All-Ivy League football star, had played in the famous 1968 Harvard-Yale football game, earned his first movie part in *Love Story*. Encouraged to take advantage of the coming film and quickly write and release a novelette based on his screenplay, Segal's literary reputation was destroyed when, after selling more copies than any other novel in 1970, the novel was nominated for a National Book Award only to have the nomination withdrawn when Award Judge William Styron declared it, "a banal book which simply doesn't qualify as literature."

Both film and novel, of course, were huge successes, despite savage reviews.

"I thought it was a little sappy," Joe Bertagna admitted. "I mean, it was kinda simply tugging at the heartstrings—and a story that wasn't completely believable. I tell people I didn't want to get typecast as a goaltender, so I've been rejecting scripts ever since..."

Another anecdote involved coach Cleary screaming at actor O'Neil for walking across concrete in skates borrowed from one of the team's stars, an incident sharp enough that Cleary was apprehensive meeting O'Neil years later. The Harvard star's name? None other than Dan DiMichele, Richie Hebner's dentist from Cranston East.

"O'Neil didn't have an appreciation for, I mean, a southern California guy he never really skated much or played hockey," Joe Bertagna related. "So he'd take phone calls and back then we didn't have cell phones so there were pay phones, whatever, and he'd step off of a mat and onto the concrete, and Billy the first time we saw it he said heyheyheyheyhey you'll ruin those blades, and kind of got in his face a little bit, and people said hey Billy you can't yell at the star, but Billy was actually the liaison between the Harvard community and the movie company. So he had a specific role, and when O'Neil did it again, I guess Billy *really* got in his face. So you jump ahead to five years ago, Ryan O'Neil and Ali MacGraw are in Boston performing a play called *Love Letters*. It's a play that shows the relationship between a man and a woman over many, many years through the letters they've written each other, and the staging of the play is the male actor is at one end of the podium and the female actress is at the other podium when they read these letters. So it happens that this version has the two people in it that were in *Love Story*.

"So Billy goes to the play and the fellow he was with was Eddie Gallagher, who was a coach at Belmont Hill for many years. Eddie says to Billy, you ought to go backstage and see Ryan O'Neil, talk to him. He probably won't remember me, Billy protests, and they talk him into it. Billy somehow talks his way into getting backstage and O'Neil comes out and gives him a huge hug, a very warm welcome, and immediately says boy do I remember the day you chewed me out for walking on the concrete! So he remembered! I've heard Billy say it was DeMichele's skates, so

I'm gonna take him at his word, that he remembers it correctly. I have no reason to question it."

My favorite response to the movie came from the Harvard hockey captain. Asked his opinion of a best-selling novel's film representation in the process of earning over $100 million dollars at the box office, a movie that had coined the famous line, "Love means never having to say you're sorry," the movie that made a star of actress Ali MacGraw and saw future star Tommy Lee Jones in his first acting role, asked his opinion, he replied from deep within the psyche of your typical hockey player:

"We never lost to Cornell."

There's no crying in baseball!

Continuing the Harvard thread, we bring it home. I recently attended Ed Hickey's Bowling for Buffalo fund raiser at the Norwood Elks. Sitting with Paul Hartnett (class of '71") and several '72 classmates, Mark Linehan, Bucky Sexton, and Barry Sullivan, we had mentioned fellow classmate Bob Bernstein's son Ed, who, pitching for Tufts, had set an unbreakable collegiate record when he had ended his senior season with an ERA of 0.00. *You can't beat a 0.00 ERA...*

"I have a record at Harvard that can't be beat, either," Mark Linehan, former Norwood High pitcher, offered. "I lost both ends of a double-header!" But it is not Mark's collegiate achievement that provides our next movie thread, but the career of Mark's mother Rhoda, who had played for the 1946 Ft. Wayne Daisies of the All-American Girls Baseball League.

The league, of course, was made famous with the 1992 release of director Penny Marshall's *A League of Their Own*, starring a host of celebrities including Tom Hanks, Geena Davis, Madonna, and Rosie O'Donnell. The film portrays the efforts of MLB executives to keep baseball in the hearts and minds of fans while droves of professionals, like Norwood's Ray Martin, went to war. Interestingly, lead actress Geena Davis was born and raised in Wareham, Massachusetts, barely fifteen miles from Somerset, from which an eighteen-year-old, left-handed batting/right-handed-throwing softball star named Rhoda "Nicky" Leonard had emerged.

"It's pretty cool, when my kids went to school and had show-and-tell, they'd bring a baseball card of their grandmother!" Mark Linehan related. "That's pretty awesome."

"She grew up in Somerset near Fall River and she played softball and baseball in church leagues. I'm gonna say at least four or five women from that team played in that league. Before she went out there, she played on the church team, and they played in their town league, and they were an advanced group from that league they played in, there were five of them.

"She loved the movie! She thought it was very true to the way it really was, with the etiquette classes, the uniforms were spot on, she was actually younger than most of the others, she couldn't go to the bars like the older girls. They came from all over to play, people couldn't read, some stuff like that, she felt it was accurate. A lot they talked about, they had to go to classes to learn lady skills, it captured a lot of the stuff they were trying to do. They showed them as athletes, but also showed them as women.

"She played in nine games and went 2-for-21. We busted her chops! *.091?! You could have done better with your eyes closed!* But the others were so good. In a way, many of them were out of her league. She talked about not playing that much, she only got up twenty-one times or something, and because she was younger, she didn't really fit in, because she was eighteen and she couldn't go to bars.

"She went straight from graduating high school and went to Indiana for only like three months, then came back and went to Bridgewater. I mean, I grew up playing catch with my mother! We'd have neighborhood games and my mother would be the first one picked! She played in a local women's league in Norwood until she was in her late thirties. You know, it's one thing to play well locally, and then playing against the best. My mother and Jean Brown, Larry Brown's mother, started the girls Little League in Norwood. She was elected to her high school Hall of Fame in its first class along with Jerry Remy, they were both second basemen.

"I think it was when the baseball cards and the movie came out it really started. Then all of a sudden, she'd get requests from little girls sending their cards to autograph, and she'd always do it, she'd bought extra cards to give out. They sent each player an allotment of cards, and my mother bought extra. She got requests not just from little girls, but from collectors, but that part was a huge deal. And then when that thing opened at the Baseball Hall of Fame, she realized this is a really big deal. They traveled by train and bus, she never traveled by plane, and it's why she didn't attend the reunion. She was invited, but she opted not to go.

"It *was* a big deal. I think it was the New England Sports Hall of Fame who came and asked her for her glove. She always got a kick out of the fact she was in Cooperstown, and then they came to get her glove. But I think the baseball card is what triggered that it was a really big deal. The cards came out around the time of the movie, because obviously there was a lot more interest. I think it was when my kids and my sisters' kids made a big deal about the cards, you know, it was something that gave her a little more energy. Once it went off on the interest, it just...she'd have letters from people asking for a card, some would send a baseball, and she'd sign it and send it back. It was mostly later-on that she got a sense of it...

"I just think it was such a great thing. So few people were part of it, I'm just shocked that my mother, that was brought up in Somerset—her parents were pretty strict—I'm shocked they let her go, and also that she could play at that level! I mean, not me, not my kids, none of us came close to playing in any professional league. It just distinguished her and she never made a big deal about it, and it was only when she became a grandmother that she enjoyed talking about it.

"I look at the movie and you see people...the best for me is at the very end when they have the extended time at the reunion, because they were my mother's generation. It was a time when people excelled without any help. Now things are so structured, they learned this stuff on their own. Her father had polio and her mother didn't have a clue about sports, so it was kind of an odd thing to happen. That's the part that amazes me, that she could get to that level without any structure, or any real parental encouragement. My mother would be thrilled to know she was part of a project like this."

Puttin' on the foil, coach!

In 1967 when Norwood's Dennis Hebner, Tommy Taylor, and Ken Reddick faced off against Framingham South's Scott Kimball, Kevin Anderson, and

Ned Dowd, I was not the only sibling harboring literary aspirations in the stands. Across the Loring Arena stands sat Nancy Dowd, who a handful of years after would write the screenplay, *Slap Shot*.

After graduating from Framingham South, Ned Dowd, who played the deranged goon Ogie Oglethorpe in the movie, was a teammate of Crestwood Circle's Dickie Donovan at Bowdoin. Vancouver native Michael Ontkean, who played college graduate Ned Braden in the movie, was a University of New Hampshire Hall of Fame hockey star, and played against Ken Reddick at the University of Massachusetts.

Dowd played two seasons of professional hockey for the Johnstown Jets of the North American Hockey League, a league notorious for the era's rough house play and exemplified by a certain Syracuse Blazer by name of Bill "Goldie" Goldthorpe. A left winger who attained a second moniker "Harpo" for his shroud of frizzled, blonde hair, Goldthorpe was the consummate "goon" who well understood his best chance at making an NHL or WHA roster was as an enforcer. When Nancy Dowd visited her brother during the 1974-75 season, her sights fell on Harpo Goldthorpe, and thus began the formulation of one of hockey's most notorious screen legends.

Goldthorpe was the un-real deal. Jailed at least eighteen times, he was once allowed out only for practices and games. Producers of *Slap Shot* considered offering him the role to play himself but demurred after the player broke a bottle in a dressing room while being visited by Paul Newman's brother. This resulted in the Ogie Oglethorpe role falling to Ned Dowd. Goldthorpe's enthusiasm for never backing down either on or off-ice came to an end when in 1980 he brought his fists to a gunfight. Defending an ex-girlfriend from a drug dealer, he was shot in the stomach, the ensuing two-year recovery effectively ending his playing career. Before this end, however, he literally ran into a couple of Norwood's finest.

"In 1977, my first year playing in the minors," Peter Brown recalled, "I was playing for the Dayton Gems. Zeke Doyle was playing for the Columbus Owls. His teammate for the first month of that year was Billy Goldthorpe trying out for the Columbus team. My first game, I got the puck behind the net, I move it, guy comes in lifts me right off my feet with an elbow. Now he's yapping at me, big blonde afro, I'm like, who the fuck *is* this guy? It wasn't college hockey anymore! He's yapping at me, he pulls the telephone that they use to call up to the press box, and fucking *throws* it at me. I'm like, what the fuck is going on, I've got to play ninety more games of this shit?

"So two weeks later we're playing them again. I think it was the end of pre-season games. Zeke comes to me, Mikey Powers who played at BC was on that team, they come up to me—they were late getting to the rink—you wouldn't believe what happened! Goldthorpe was such an asshole on the bus to the bus driver, the bus driver on the way from Columbus to Dayton pulled over and said I'm not driving another foot until you come out here and I'm gonna beat the shit out of you! And the bus driver and Goldthorpe were gonna have a fucking fight on the side of the fucking highway on the way to the hockey game! He tried out for the Sudbury Wolves in junior hockey, got cut, opened up the arena, back door, opened up the boards, drove his car onto the ice, fucking left it there, said I ain't moving! That's Billy Goldthorpe.

"There's more," Peter Brown continued. "So my first year in Atlanta's camp, I hear about this guy who played in the North American Hockey League, Dave Hanson was his name. They called him, 'Killer'. We had a rookie game against St. Louis, one minute into the game he's pounding the shit out of somebody. I'm like, oh, he can really fight, someone says oh yeah, that's Dave Hanson! He was in *Slap Shot*. I'm like, what? I'd never heard of it. This is the fall of '76, the movie hadn't come out yet. So Dave Hanson, before the movie, I knew him from Atlanta's camp.

"Then, the last year I played, I was in the Whalers' camp with Jack Carlson, one of the Carlson brothers. And he was another one who would splatter your nose from six feet back, he had real long arms. He wasn't a great hockey player, but he was a really good fighter."

Nancy Dowd's creative vision coalesced around her brother's colorful teammates as she traveled with the team during the 1974-75 season. Three Carlson brothers from Minnesota and a tough from Wisconsin named Dave Hanson combined for over 800 penalty minutes—and 82 goals—for the Johnstown team. When filming began, all four were scheduled to play roles, but when Jack Carlson was called up to the Edmonton Oilers of the WHA, Dave Hanson took his place alongside brothers Jeff and Steve Carlson to form hockey's most infamous line.

Despite lukewarm reviews and a disappointing box office, *Slap Shot* emerged as a cult classic, beloved by hockey fans. Dickie Donovan shrugged when his Bowdoin teammate and friend came up in our conversation. "One of the best players I played with in college was this kid out of Framingham South, his name is Ned Dowd," Dickie said. "His sister wrote the screenplay for *Slap Shot*. And he got to hang around with Paul Newman, they'd fool around together all the time. I know those long-haired—that's how I looked in college, Ned played with them. The Hanson brothers. I was in Montreal that year and I was trying to find him, I was like you gotta get me out there! Didn't work." And as in many hockey conversations, threads were followed.

"Those are the guys from the mill towns, the mining towns up there, you don't want to fight them," Dickie continued. "Ned Dowd could fly. He was as fast as me, he had NHL speed. He was a big kid, but he didn't like to rough it up. (laughs) He went to play in the minor leagues and played for the Johnstown Jets, and, you know, back in those days they wanted you to fight. Peter Brown didn't want to fight, and that's why he wasn't drafted that high. Mike Milbury would fight, so he played for a lot of years. But he was half the player Peter Brown was. *Maybe*. Oh, it's fact. We played Walpole that year, Milbury was a junior, we beat 'em 3-1 and 5-1. We had no problem beating him."

"You learn, right?" Peter Brown continued. "In the minors, there weren't many Americans kicking around. There's this guy, he's from Red Deer, I'd say to my roommate from Saskatchewan, is he a righty? Not, how many goals does he have, how many assists, no. Hey Al, is he a righty, or a lefty? Because if you're reaching for one and you grab the wrong one, you're gonna throw what I used to call a no-hitter. You know what a no-hitter is? A no-hitter is when a guy's got you like this and he's pulling you and punching you, and you're kinda going like this trying to grab hold, so when you skate by your own bench bloodied, they go, *nice no-hitter, Pete!* (interviewer laughs) Not that funny, Don!"

Paul Newman maintained his own memories. In 1984 he told *Time Magazine*, "There's a hangover from characters sometimes. There are things that stick. Since *Slap Shot*, my language is right out of the locker room!" The screen legend went on to say that making *Slap Shot* was the most fun he'd had making a movie, and that Reggie Dunlop was one of his favorite rolls.

The young woman on the other side of the Loring Arena stands did all right. After penning one of the most beloved sports screenplays of all, Nancy Dowd collaborated on the screenplay for *Coming Home*, for which she received the 1979 Academy Award for Best Screenplay Written Directly for the Screen. Perhaps there is no better tribute to her work and the characters she created, than to have Jon Voight win an Academy Award for Best Actor, and Jane Fonda win an Academy Award for Best Actress, for their roles in the film.

No memorable line

Our next movie connection is to the much-maligned 1999 Walt Disney production, *Mystery, Alaska*.

This story actually begins in 1905, when adventurers from the gold-mining town of Dawson City, Yukon challenged the reigning champion Ottawa Silver Seven for the Stanley Cup. The Klondikers' four-thousand-mile odyssey by dog sled, narrow gauge train, steamship, and cross-country train to Ottawa, only to lose by the greatest margin in Stanley Cup history, is hockey legend. After stumbling into Dawson City while on an Alaska/Yukon trip with Mike Lydon in 1987, I also stumbled upon this story. My novel documenting the legend, *Dawson City Seven*, was published in 1993.

Vancouver literary agent Donna Wong Juliani represented the novel in Hollywood where, she reported, Walt Disney had a meeting in which their "hockey movie" decision came down to either *Dawson City Seven*, or *Mighty Ducks III*. They went with "the franchise," releasing the movie in 1996, which also released, not to this writer's chagrin, invective from Roger Ebert and Gene Siskel. "*D3: The Mighty Ducks*," Ebert wrote in the *Chicago Sun Times*, "is a truly dreadful film, a lifeless, massive, childish exercise in failed comedy." Siskel piled on in his *Chicago Tribune* column, calling it "dull, stupid, brainless, and dim-witted."

Meanwhile, the good citizens of Dawson City, using *Dawson City Seven* as a blueprint, re-enacted the 1905 story. In 1997, accompanied by the invited author, a group of senior hockey players traveled four thousand miles by dog sled, bus, ferry, and cross-country train to play the Ottawa Senators alumni in Ottawa's Corel Center. Dawson, of course, lost badly once again, the likes of Laurie Boschman, Brad Marsh, Rick Smith and future Boston Bruins' coach Claude Julien too much for their middle-aged, beer league opponents.

As their 1905 predecessors had, the '97 odyssey resonated with Canada's hockey community, which was not missed by Walt Disney's ubiquitous eyes and ears. In the spring of 1998 three "suits" arrived in Dawson City to meet with the leaders of the Dawson re-enactment.

"They were three hours late," for their meeting in the Downtown Hotel, Kevin Anderson of the Dawson team related. "We were excited. We thought they wanted to make a movie about *us*, about what we'd done, but pretty quickly we realized they didn't want to make a movie about us, but something else. I walked out!"

In 1999 "something else" turned out to be Walt Disney's Americanized conversion of what we had done, entitled *Mystery, Alaska*. And once again, neither Bert Reynolds, Russell Crowe, nor a cameo by Mike Myers was enough to elevate the film, described by Roger Ebert as, "sweet, pleasant, low-key, inoffensive and unnecessary." It was a disappointing attempt by Michele Pfeiffer's writer-director husband to extend his brilliant TV success into movies.

David E. Kelley is among the most successful personalities in TV history, writing, directing, or creating a seemingly endless string of popular shows including *L. A. Law, Pickett Fences, Chicago Hope, The Practice*, and *Ally McBeal*. He married Michele Pfeiffer.

Born in Waterville, Maine, where family still maintains a ski lodge, he is the son of the late Jack Kelley, former coach of Boston University and the New England Whalers. During the 1960s and while coaching BU, the Kelley family lived in Walpole, which had no youth hockey program. And before his high school career at Belmont Hill—where he skated with Norwood's Mike Lyons—before his collegiate hockey career culminated in the captaincy of Princeton's 1978-79 hockey team, before attaining TV fame and fortune, before he married a movie star, before his remarkable life, David E. Kelley was a member of Tom Brown's Norwood Nuggets. Did I mention he married Michele Pfeiffer?

"Rosebud"

Our last movie connection is not even a stretch, but more homage to memory, and imagination.

Citizen Kane is a movie produced, co-written, directed, and starring Orson Welles. It has been lionized by learned experts as the greatest movie of all time. Released in 1941, it tells the tale of a famous newspaperman who, on his deathbed, holds a snow globe, utters the word, "Rosebud", and dies. The film follows the man's life through the eyes of an investigative reporter tasked with determining the significance of the deathbed remark. Covering the rise and extent of the legend's fame and fortune—allegedly based on William Randolph Hearst—the reporter is never able to discern the import of the remark. The last scene shows the late magnate's people clearing his mansion of a lifetime's detritus, the discarded items into a roaring furnace, including a boy's sled with the word "Rosebud" stenciled upon it.

The irony is obvious, that the man's last thought in the world, a man who'd achieved widespread wealth and influence, fell upon a childhood memory. It is a brilliant stroke of cinematic prose, so to speak, every writer's dream of revealing a universal, but normally unstated truth, which resonates with all.

"More than thirty years have passed since I last saw Ftorek skate for Needham," Brian MacQuarrie had written, "but his image still floods me with thoughts of a simpler time, and a smaller universe, and a reminder that when teenagers grow to adults, they need not leave their dreams behind."

"When I was working on the Richie Hebner documentary," Jack Tolman recalled, "I had been in touch with Richie back and forth setting up the interviews, and I wanted to get some footage. I didn't know what he had for memorabilia, so I asked him if I could come by the house. So I brought my equipment to the house and in a room off to the side he had his World Series ring in just a regular old drawer. To me, I would have had it on a big display, but it was just nothing special at the time for him, it was just something he had since 1971.

"So anyway, I said do you have anything else, and he said well I've got a room here with some pictures. So I go into the room and I look up on the wall and displayed prominently on the wall on a hanger was one of those old, grey, wool baseball shirts, and it was small and it said 'Tigers' and I think it had a Little League patch on it. I said what's that? He said that's my Little League team when we won the town championship with the Tigers! So I shot some video of that and then I look in the corner, and I see this white, kind of like a dish towel. It was just in the corner on the floor, and I said what's that over there? He said oh that musta fell down. It looks like a dish towel, he picks it up, and it's an old Pirates jersey with no sleeves, early '70s, and he says that's one of my Pirates shirts, yeah, they were kinda cheap, they were just recycling them. And you could see it was sewn up, and he said once they got so beat-up, they sent them down to the minor leagues but this one I got. And I just thought to myself, his Norwood Little League shirt is hanging on the wall and his Pirates shirt is on the ground, and to me, I just thought it was ironic what was hanging, and what was on the ground."

Little did a nine-year-old Nahatan Street kid in 1956, doing his best to win the Norwood Little League batting title, imagine that one day, far in his future, he would make the prose.

1972

A long, long time ago
I can still remember how that music
Used to make me smile
And I knew if I had my chance
That I could make those people dance...
— Don McLean, *American Pie*,
#1 song in America, March 1972

Mark Twain is credited with, "It's not the size of the dog in the fight, it's the size of the fight in the dog." It's a rare classic because it rings especially true. But I would ask, what if the dog with all the fight is also the biggest? And what if the biggest dog with all the fight also *wanted it?*

During the course of Leo McInerney's interview, he said, "Somebody sent me, this is interesting, oh I know who it was, you know Paul McAvoy? Mac sent me a thing about Neil, about his record of thirty shutouts. So I forwarded it to Jack, and I said yup, Neil holds the record with thirty shutouts and you were on the ice for every single one of 'em. How much credit did you get? And he just wrote back ha-ha. We were saying that to Billy Pieri, and Billy said—I thought this was very telling of Billy—he said, you know, that's really not an individual record, that's a team record. Billy only lost one game in his career, right? The personalities are terrific!"

> Pete Brown, 17, 190, 6-1 Sr, Has to be one of the top defensemen in the state this year. Last year he was a Bay State League all-star and is rated by Coach Wheeler as one of the most talented hockey players he has ever coached. Brown is a hard hitter and has one of the top shots in the state from his defense post. He has already been contacted by ten colleges for hockey.

"My family moved to Norwood from Dorchester when I was like four, we moved over to Ridgewood Drive," Peter Brown related. "My father was then transferred out to Chicago. That was only six or eight months, came back '61-ish to this house, Marlboro Street. At the time, it was the end of Norwood. It was the sandpits, they had just tarred this, they used to still shoot down the sand pits into the abandoned cars. But the first time I skated was out in Chicago. We lived across from a school and they flooded it, and I remember the first time skating. And then coming back here my father flooded right out there a couple times, I was probably eight. But what I'm babbling about, I was in the backyard here, there was no fence, no porch, no anything. The Bergerons lived right up there, and my brother came down that little hill there from delivering newspapers and said, you wanna sign up for hockey? That was like '63 or whatever, it was when Ernie Higgins had just started, they weren't even the Norwood Nuggets yet.

"Making the team as a freshman, obviously it was huge. The year before I broke my ankle and I played very little hockey. It was huge. I wanted to be like Richie Hebner. Richie Hebner made it as a freshman, so that was like the goal. The goal was to be Richie Hebner. He was the pinnacle. My freshman year, of course, looking back, that first practice was as big as any game at the Garden, any Beanpot, any national championship. I remember being unbelievably fired up. And I remember it being really fucking hard, really fucking hard. The memory I have were the competition drills, the forechecking drills, one on one, and there was no escape, right? I remember going with Teddy Curtis, he was a pretty good player, and Don flipping out, *a freshman just ate you up!* I remember we had holes in our gloves, I hit my hand and my hand was bleeding, at the time it was the most fired up I've ever been. But it taught me not to get beat in a drill, or you'd hear from Don.

"Another memory was like a week later; I was still with the team. I think it was the second Monday, a scrimmage at Brown University. I had Mrs. Shaw for English, detention. I was like ummm, what the fuck do I do? So, I was like, I'll like go and the bus really won't leave until three o'clock and I'll go, and she'll let me out early. Sitting there, remember the old clocks? Click, click, click...I'm like, CLICK, CLICK, CLICK God help me! *Peter Brown, please report to the office...*

"So Mrs. Shaw goes, Peter you can go. I go down, Wheeler's at the office, go get your stuff and get on the bus. I'm basically running down, by this time Wheeler's on the bus. I'm a freshman, Taylor, Arthur Harris, I come on the bus—what it was, I was too young and too inexperienced to know what I had just done. Halfway down somebody said something and I smirked, maybe a nervous thing, and these guys were like, who the *fuck* is this guy? I remember that, and later on at the game, Eddie Letts— so I'm a freshman, I'm trying, I don't know what the fuck is going on, but my brother Jeff was the manager in '66 and '67 and he was like a coach keeping an eye, so he'd tell me Wheeler's like this, you gotta work, work is the number one thing. So, anyway, I'm on the bench, we're playing Brown, here I am trying to figure things out...Eddie Letts, remember Eddie? Eddie took a shot from the point, the softest shot I had ever seen, barely made, the softest shot I've ever seen, everyone was swinging at it, it barely made it to the goalie. I was like hahaha, and Taylor turned and said *you're laughing? You laughing on the fucking bench? Don't laugh on the bench! No smiling!* I'm like, okaaay... See, I was still normal, I wasn't indoctrinated into it yet, right? (laughs)

"And then Don telling me you're gonna be on the team. We opened up against Framingham North, worst team in the state. But he goes, it's gonna be *baptism under fire*, it was like, you know, aw shit, I have to play against the Montreal Canadians today in my first high school game. I'm fourteen years old, we're playing Detroit, Canadians and the Bruins all at the same time. I taped a thing on my helmet because the year before I'd seen Tommy Shea, 'Beat Arlington,' so that was the thing to do for me. That was it. That was the thing. For the next four years I taped things to my helmet, I even did it at BU, from seeing Tommy Shea's picture in the *Patriot Ledger*.

"So my freshman year we're playing Framingham North. The day before in practice, Eat Up North. The day before, I was so fired up! Tommy goes, *What the fuck is that on your helmet?* I love Tommy! *What the fuck is that on your helmet? Fucken Eat up North...* I'm like, but I was ah ah, but I was fired up! We beat them 13-0 the next day. It was big, that's what I remember.

"I remember starting my first game against Walpole in a packed... fourteen years old, what I remember that time? It was the first time I ever stood for the National Anthem at a hockey game like I had watched the Bruins do, standing at the blueline looking at the flag. And I'm like, I gotta concentrate, I gotta concentrate... For the rest of my career part of my thing was using the National Anthem to focus, focus... In retrospect, I think I did it because I was nervous and that was Walpole, and it seemed like there were 85,000 people there. Maybe 90,000. I couldn't believe they could fit 90,000 people in Four Seasons Arena!"

> Ed King, 17, 180, 5-11 Sr, one of the players expected to make the Norwood team a Bay State League champion again. He had 11 goals as a junior last year and has the best shot on the team. King is a solid checker and one of the toughest players on the Norwood team. He will be the top goal scorer.

"I would have been introduced to hockey on the ponds behind Hawes Pool," Ed King recalled. "Just playing pond hockey, it was just fabulous going down after school, and back then the ice froze, so you'd be there all the time. I remember the guys from Alandale, the Taylor brothers—and sister—Bobby and Tommy, Paula Taylor, she played, ah, the Nolfis, the Saads, I can remember Dave Burke who lived above Wiseman's. It was Mr. Burke who drove me to Zwickers in Arlington to buy my first pair of Tacks. Don't know how that transpired, but I remember it was a 1967 Buick Grand Sport 400 yellow with a black top with the factory mag wheels. It was an automatic, the only downside. (laughs)

"We used to play there all the time. The beauty of growing up in South Norwood was we had Endean Farm up on Morse Hill, we had the Balch School, so you had two playgrounds. You'd have two playground leaders, shoot pucks down at Balch, having those two fields was fabulous. Yup. So, Endean Farm, so you could walk from the back of Alandale along Hawes Brook all the way up into Endean fields, it was woods, and a farm, and just a great place to hang out. And behind Banana Shanahan's house there was a field, he was a great pitcher. On Alandale Parkway it went Monkey Rosetski, Kevin McDonough, Banana Shanahan, Lucky... Lane? All good athletes. And of course we had the Saads, which were constant. I confirmed with Richie Saad it wasn't that he couldn't skate, cuz I always maintained if the Saads could skate we would have won more state championships. He said no, I could skate, it's just I went to freshman tryouts with Steve Fitzgerald and from skating on the ponds the skates were dull, and there was nowhere to get them sharpened. Blake Fitzgerald was Steve's younger brother, and they lived in the Saad house along with the Nolfis. In the back was an add-on apartment the Nolfis lived in, and the house itself was broken into I don't know how many various apartments that the Fitzgeralds lived in.

"Heroes growing up? I don't think I really looked at, well I wouldn't really call it a hero, Carl Yastrzemski, Ted Williams—before us, really—Bob Cousy. I remember watching his retirement where he got a Cadillac, his last day, they wheeled the Cadillac out on the floor for him, um, incredibly, the guy across the street from my father's store Lou Lamont had a Gulf station. As a little kid he let me hang out there. So as a little kid I'd say what's that? What's that Mr. Lamont? He was a Ford engineer. He let this little kid hang out and just talk about cars, and engines, and body work, and everything. Lou Lamont, he lived on Winter Street, the last house in Norwood, I think, or the first house in Westwood on the left as you go into Westwood. He and my father were good friends, so I wouldn't say I looked up to him, I just appreciated him. That's where I met Shotgun Seastrand. I met him at Lou Lamont's gas station. I think he lived in South Norwood or up on Morse Hill, and Lou Lamont introduced us. That's why they called him Shotgun, because he had such a hard shot. But growing up, I don't know if I admired him then, but just looking back, Leadfoot Clifford, Tom Clifford, what a wonderful person. Unbelievable, really. I didn't actually skate with him, very rarely, but later on I'd go up to Pettee's with him. Joe Wall used to have a program on Sunday nights, and Joe would come by and pick me up. That was Peter and Sails' brother who was a selectman, I forget where we used to go, but it was a rink and it was every Sunday night. It lasted a year or two, I think. So I wouldn't really say I had any real, I didn't really look up to many people as a role model.

"My driveway, we have the garage down the end, and we'd shoot pucks on each other. Shoot pucks. Mike Martin, we'd put end pillows on our legs, and he had a, remember wooden boxes that soda bottles came in? He'd stand there and I'm shooting, not that far away from him, and he's knocking down the pucks with the box and kicking them out with his legs, it was crazy! We'd shoot incessantly in the driveway and Mike was often times, and Phil Nolfi was often times there. Cuz at the store, the push carts at the store the wheels would wear out and get a flat and we'd switch them out and put new ones on, but we ended up with these, the front were probably four inches in diameter, the back ones were probably six to eight inches in diameter and I'd use those to shoot. Before a game I'd go out there and shoot there for fifteen minutes, these big, weighted pucks basically, and then you take a regular puck and it's like, completely light weight.

"Mike, I remember it was third grade and Mr. Martin came by on a Friday night and said we're gonna go to hockey. So it was Norwood youth hockey up at Four Seasons. And the season was halfway through the year, and somehow my father and Mr. Martin concocted to get us involved, so he drove us up. And I remember all I had was gloves, I don't know if I even had gloves, I had skates, and they gave us a white Nugget shirt, or a yellow Nugget shirt. And that's how we started."

The 1972 Norwood High School hockey team, whatever its destiny, was never considered a Cinderella team. It was an acknowledged powerhouse, rated first in the state from day one. It included not just core players Brown, Martin, King, Clifford, and Pieri from the previous season's undefeated-in-league-play squad, but the bounty of 1970's sophomore seeding, other three-year seniors described by Sails Wall as, Lou Parker, "perhaps the best back-up goalie in the state, and will be a fine college netminder," Bill Denehy, "hustler on the second line, a real good player who can dig in the corners," Al Skene, "expected to team with Brown as one of the biggest duo of defensemen in the state, a hardnosed player who loves to hit," and Don Reddick, "captain of the football team, a real tough customer, a hard hitter and has an excellent shot." Complementing was a duo of strong sophomores. "Greg Walker and Danny Bayer, they weren't playing to develop," Peter Brown recalled, "they were playing because they were good players." Juniors Kevin Hurley and Mark Balerna played significant roles, the team rounded out with underclassmen Frankie Baglione, Bobby Lawrie, Freddie Carbone, Mike Costello, Mike Smith, Ed McQuade, Roger Battles, Paul O'Day, and Greg Talbot.

Bob Thornton's assessment of Billy Pieri: "This guy here, for my money, and I said I played with Neil too, and Frankie Eppich and Artie

Harris, I played with four unbelievable goalies, this guy right here? Mr. Unassuming? Fucking *money*, baby!"

"Louis Parker would have been the best goalie in the Bay State League if Pierski didn't play," Peter Brown opined. "Except maybe Cap Raeder, and the kid from Wellesley was good, the lefty, went out to play at Notre Dame, Art Moehler." Louis Parker was matter of fact about his situation on the team.

"I respected Don because I thought he was a great coach and I thought he knew what he was talking about," the goaltender said. "I didn't like him personally, but that doesn't matter to me. It was almost like Bill Belichick; he has no personality; you're just doing your job and that's about all that goes with it. Nothing after, wasn't friendly and talkative, didn't explain much. He told me he thought Billy was better, and I'll get my chance if I keep playing hard. Okay, the coach wants to win and if I'm better then he's gonna play me. If I'm not better, he's not gonna play me. If Billy gets hurt, he's gonna play me. Until that time I gotta keep my head down and play. He explained that and I was happy with it. Okay, Billy beat me out. I'll play when I get a chance.

"There was one paper report there, you know how they do the preseason thing? They wrote me down at the best backup goaltender in the state. I would start for all but three teams in the state. It just happened that the second-best goaltender in the state was on the same team as me. The other one was Cap Raeder, then Billy, and I don't remember who they figured third, and I was figured fourth. I mean, what the hell. That's not bad, you know?"

"I'll tell ya," Ed King recalled, "Billy Clifford was the fastest skater, it was amazing how fast he was. Even at St. A's, he could just, he had jets, he could fly!"

"Billy Clifford was the greatest skater," Frank Baglione concurred. "I remember races, and I'd always get a good jump, but Billy always caught me with those strides. Byers was fast, the fastest guys on the team were Billy Clifford, Danny Byers, and Paul O'Day. They were pretty quick."

"I had strong legs, I could always run fast," Billy Clifford said. "I mean, sometimes I'd skate so fucking fast it scared me, out of control going that fast. Bayer says he could catch me, I said you're full of shit! I'd be going so fucking fast it was almost to the point of out of control!"

"Tommy Shea was the epitome of Don's forechecking system," Bobby Thornton said. "Donny Reddick reminded me of him. Swear to god, I played with both of them, just his physicality and everything."

"Donny Reddick was the only one I was scared of going into the corners with, because of his strength," Frank Baglione continued. "There was the drills where one guy goes in and one tries to score and the other tried to take the puck out, and I'd be up against him and I'd say, *fuuuck*..."

"Billy Denehy was the quintessential throwback in that he didn't play youth hockey," Peter Brown assessed. "Billy was a baseball player, and Don liked athletes more than, you know, dancers. But Billy was kind of that bridge between the old school of having very little hockey background and Don literally molding him into a player, and Billy responding, because he gave Don what he was looking for. Worked his balls off, good athlete, great attitude, he would work hard, and then just work harder, and Don ate that up. As a freshman, if you had told anybody Billy Denehy was gonna be part of a state championship team, you would have said, what are you smoking? But in the final game, our state final game, he gets two points. For someone to get two points in a state final game who, as a freshman, people wouldn't even give a chance to play varsity hockey, to me that's a real testament not only to Billy, but to Don's ethic, that work ethic that rubbed off on everybody else.

"Donny Reddick was a football player that played hockey. Growing up, he played youth hockey, played peewee, bantam hockey with us, so he had a hockey background, but when it came to high school, he was the go-to guy on the football team. Donny didn't play much hockey, he played during the season. Back then, in high school, we started specializing more. We played other sports, but we were hockey players. He had more of a hockey background than Billy Denehy, but his focus—he was putting his skates on for the first time the Monday after Thanksgiving. And the skills everybody else was working on in the summer and the spring and the fall, he didn't have a chance to. Donny Reddick was there as our enforcer, and I don't mean that in a derogatory way, I mean as a physical presence, that his physical presence was as outstanding as Mike Martin's talent. Mike had talent, but he didn't have what Donny brought in that size category, aggressive forechecking, as an athlete who would work his balls off. Another example of why Don would turn to a guy like that rather than maybe a more finesse player. Don liked athletes, he liked the hard work, and to him that was more important than anything else that you could bring to the table. Donny took the shot that Eddie McQuade tipped in against St. John's in the East-West state final game. Our third line doesn't score that goal, we don't win that game. Period. Full stop. So of six goals against Arlington and St. John's, the two state final games, these guys were in on half of them. Those are two examples that really exemplified, with our group, kind of a bridge between the old school with the new school."

"Well, I learned an awful lot from Peter," Alex Skene remembered. "We were never close, in fact at times we hated each other growing up, getting in battles playing street hockey down there and stuff, but we were never close. But that senior year we just got completely in sync. And the best, probably the best thing that Don did for me was, he'd always, you know the drill everyone loves to talk about, when he'd pair you off and throw the puck in the corner and just have you fight until it was just about time to drop your gloves and start swinging, he'd always pair me off with Peter. And Peter was so tough, he was a little more stable on his feet than I was, and he was a little stronger, so for me to go into the corner, I would say, going into the corner with *anybody, anywhere*, after that, looked easy, you know? I never felt overmatched after that, going into the corner with anybody after that, even if they had twenty pounds on me."

"Peter had such a hard shot," Billy Clifford said. "He'd get the puck and he'd wind up, I'd be in front of the net, I'd be shitting my pants, tip-ins, in front of the net looking for a tip-in, he could let it go. It was a hard, heavy shot, I'd shit my pants in front of the net! And one time, he took a shot, we were up at Four Seasons, it got deflected, you know how you have the goal light up on top with the metal casing around it? He took the shot; it deflected and shattered the casing!"

"So Eddie King was really like, he wasn't all that rah-rah verbally," Peter Brown said, "he wasn't. Like all of us would get into it, but on the ice, he was the quintessential, he was playing out what Wheeler was espousing. Eddie started as a defenseman. Solid as a rock, like a fucken brick shit house, strong skater, powerful skater. Started out at D, didn't really fit there his freshman, I think he played all his freshman year at D, and made the switch in the junior year. I would say Eddie probably personifies Don's ethic more than anybody else in that, well I'm talking about specifically his senior year, but over the course of the four years, he got switched from defense to forward, and it took him a little while to get used to that, but as a junior he was as good as anybody, as important a cog as anybody we had, because you need a deep team. We played soccer together, Billy, Mike, me, I went out for the soccer team the day before our first game and started the next day. I had never kicked a soccer ball in my life. Eddie played, so we were in pretty good shape and haircuts, you know the hair at the time, so haircuts came. Don, of course, *everybody gotta get your hair cut*...most people did as little as possible, or none, which went right up Don's ass. I remember I got my hair cut, it was long, I got it cut about an inch. I think that's what started our issue my senior year, I think my hair was too long. It was like the biggest thing, how long is your hair? I think my hair was too long, or some fucken thing, right? Right? It was like the biggest thing, how long is your hair? So Eddie comes high and tight, looked like a fucken Marine. Right then and there, he set the tone, unknowingly, for the whole year."

"Well Eddie, Eddie's just so much fun!" Alex Skene said. "He's such a fun human being. Such a buoyant spirit. I always loved hanging out with him. I mean he's wild, he used to scare me at times, (laughs) back when we were young and wild, and he played like an animal, strong, really strong. And he loved it, he loved it."

All of which cursorily covers kids who had survived the great Norwood hockey war of attrition, earning their right to don blue and gold, the exception being the preternatural athlete and remarkable character in our midst.

> Mike Martin, 17, 170, 5-11 Sr. First line center for this year's Norwood High sextet and is rated as one of the best in the state. Last year he was a Bay State League all-star and made the tourney all-stars. He led the league in scoring with 52 points and set a Norwood record with 29 assists.

"First time I ever met Mike Martin was down Pleasant Field," Peter Brown recalled. "We were watching a baseball game, he's got his bike and there's this mound of dirt and who's this kid riding his bike and getting air off the edge, doing this bike shit? Who is this fucking nut? Next thing I know, *wha, wha, what's your name?* I'm Pete. *I'm Mike Martin! M-M!*

Swear to God, this is the first time this kid goes, *M-M!* Next thing, *what are you?* What do you mean what am I, who's this fucking kid, *what are you, you Irish?* Here's Mike Martin!

"The next time I run into him I hear, this kid that just started playing on Friday nights, he's stickhandling by everybody, yeah, who's that, Mikey *Mah*tin! And yeah, from day one, nine, ten years old. So anyway, Mike was always a character. He's like, I don't know a character in literature you can compare him to, but he's unabashed, he would give you confidence playing with him, because he was very confident in his abilities and to take on the challenge of other teams, but in a way that was very different from the disciplined, hard-nosed compassionate hard-ass that Bobby Thornton was. Mike's, I'm trying hard to describe, he was like devil may care, don't give a shit, didn't seem overwhelmed by the big situations. Big games, the undisciplined wild guy who when push comes to shove was very much focused.

"His talent, great hands, his hands, he didn't have an overpowering shot at all, but his hands stickhandling, he was shifty, you could drive a truck through his legs, so straight ahead he didn't beat anybody, he wouldn't beat the people on speed, but he would beat people by moving laterally really quick. I played with Vic Stanfield at BU, going up and back was probably the slowest on the team. I used to call it the the no move move. It would seem guys would skate right by him, this way or that way, I used to see Mike go down, that lateral move, the quickness, great hands, great vision, and he was a great passer. Was very competitive, liked to score, right? Some guys don't have that real hunger to score, where Nolf had the hunger to score, but it was different. He was just a natural sniper. Where Nolf was a quintessential wing, back in the day wingers were supposed to get goals, centers were supposed to get assists. And that's what Mike did. Mike got a lot of goals, but his thing was moving the puck when he had to. Hands, the lateral quickness, and the vision and just being a good athlete, being smart, really smart. Mike, maybe one of the craziest fucks I know, goes back to the neuro psyche. We're all a compilation of strengths and weaknesses. I worked with a lot of kids who could not read, but they could take a car apart and put it back together. You don't want *me* taking your car apart and putting it back together! Mike Martin is one of the smartest guys I know, in certain ways. He's got a really innate sense of personal relationships, you know, and yeah, so, he was a character, really talented, will to win, and just a funny bastard!"

"I'll tell you a story about Mike Martin," Frank Baglione offered. "One time at practice he was skating with the JVs and he hung out, and he turned his stick upside down and stick-handled around us all and scored! With the knub end of his stick!"

"I'll tell ya, the kid could play hockey," Billy Clifford said. "Boy, I played with him all the way up. My sophomore year we didn't play much, because Mike was second line, I was third line. But even bantams and peewees we played together, and boy, he was just amazing what he could do. I mean, the talent he had, he was one of the best players to come out of Norwood, I think. You can talk about Hebner and Donovan, Mike was right up there, he was just phenomenal. Very unselfish, too. He never, with all the talent he had, he never hogged the puck, he'd pass it, he'd dish it off. He was a great baseball player, unbelievable golfer, he could go out not play for three years and shoot a 75. He was one of those type of persons, he just *had* it. He was just amazing, I enjoyed playing with him, we got along good."

"I had played golf down the cape," Ed King related. "This was a few years ago and my clubs are on the back porch and he takes the chipping wedge and three balls, puts them down, and he hits the balls one, two, three all to the base of a tree, like twenty-five yards away. Gets the balls, brings them back, goes *lefty*, turns the club head upside down, and does the exact same thing, three balls to the base of the tree, twenty-five yards away. I go, you're an asshole! But that's just Mike Martin. He's…" (shakes head and laughs)

"I, unlike Mike Martin, don't have the locked down memory. If you asked him these questions, he'd start rattling off facts. The story about Mike Martin, this is true, when you play golf, you have four shots, or eight shots, and you have to count 'em up so someone can write it down at the end of every hole. So I'm doing all I can to remember what I had for my shots on that hole. If you play with Mike Martin, on every hole, he knows everyone else all their shots, where they were from, and what everyone's score was. And more likely, for many holes in the past. If you look at the intellect that is required to see those three steps ahead of everyone else in hockey, that Wayne Gretzky-type thing, that's intelligence. At some level, that's intelligence. Everyone doesn't have that. Mikey had that. He was moving the puck with the idea that some other people he suspects would react and open up the play, and the next one was the one he was gunning for. I think he had that. And very few people have that."

"Mikey's just an amazing human being," Alex Skene assessed. "I don't think I ever played with or against a better player, anywhere, all the places I've played, before, after, and at times I wound up skating with or against guys who played in the pros, various places. Yeah, I think he was the absolute best. The way he could control the pace of the game and hold the puck, set people up. I remember our senior year that often times if Pete went in the corner to get the puck, I'd drop behind the net, if it was clear he was gonna take possession, and as soon as I'd drop behind the net I'd be looking for Mikey in the middle, and if I could see a clear path I'd fire it at him, just rip it, and make sure nobody could touch it, and no matter where I put it, in his skates, if I lofted it at one arm he'd catch it and drop it, he'd always collect the puck. That's one of my best memories of him. One of my best memories. And then, next couple of steps, those two steps, and he already knows where he was going with the puck, you know? We loved that center breakout, we used that a lot with him, because you just fire it at him, and he collected it."

"To encapsulate Mike," Peter Brown concluded, "the bottom line is, besides being crazy, besides being a funny bastard, besides having an unusual talent to know people and all that stuff, as far as the hockey goes, he could just flat out play against anybody, at any level. The other thing, he was never intimidated. The bigger the situation, the more he was into it. He was never intimidated, he was always *fuck them*, know what I'm saying? Ah, the elevator doesn't go to the top floor! (laughs) I say Mike wasn't intimidated, because Mike was a cocky little prick. As far as sports go, it *helps* you, it doesn't *hurt* you, you know what I'm saying? There's so much to Mike; as far as the hockey, he could just flat out play."

Our fathers shared the same experiences, and we looked to the same places for heroes as our predecessors had. Bobby Thornton's father had been a POW during WWII; Peter Brown's a Navy pilot. Louis Parker's father served in the Navy, on a minesweeper. My father graduated from Sharon High School in the spring of '45 and rushed to join the Navy before the war ended.

"In '43 when he finished BC," Alex Skene said of his father, "I guess he'd been training as an officer's reserve or something, so he went in the Air Force and trained as a B-25 pilot. Yeah, it was interesting, cuz he was in Nebraska, there was a big base out there, and they trained them very quickly and he was at a point where it wasn't long before he was gonna be sent to England and you know, be flying B-25s into Germany. And the commander of the base called him in, the commander of the base was the father of someone he had skated with at BC, either BC or in high school, and unfortunately his son, my father's friend, had been killed in the war. And the commander of the base said, you know what? I'm not sending you over there. I'm gonna keep you here. Cuz, he didn't want to see him get killed. Yeah, yeah. Said I got plenty for you to do here, gonna train pilots and ferry things around, keep you here. The war was won, by that time it was '44. So hockey kept him from getting sent to, not quite a certain death, but a high probability. A hockey connection."

"Well, he left high school at seventeen years old, and was on the aircraft carrier *Ticonderoga*," Billy Clifford recalled of his father. "He grew up on Mission Hill. Roxbury. He had a hard life, his mother died, his mother passed away when he was thirteen, so he was the oldest. His father was an alcoholic, drank all the time, right off the boat from Ireland, so my father basically raised the kids until he went off to the war. He has five battle stars, they were in Leyte Gulf, I forget the other battles, South China Sea, five big battles, with the kamikazes and everything. He helped the chaplain; he'd go down with the chaplain and help take the bodies up. My father was very religious, went to Mission High with the Brothers, and he always stayed in touch with at least two of the Brothers, long after. So he saw a lot, he saw a lot...my mother used to say he'd wake up in the middle of the night just screaming..."

"Who were my heroes?" Peter Brown replied. "There's a picture that George Usevitch has next door, he wants to show it to Richie Hebner. I said show it to Richie—cuz they work together sometimes down the funeral home—and when he's done, I wanna show it to Donny Reddick. It's a picture of the '65 team that your brother was on, you were like, *fucking Donny's brother that fucken lucky prick*, same thing I used to say about Jackie Clifford, *Jackie has two brothers that played that lucky prick*, right? So that picture of everyone in their suit and tie getting ready to go to Washington... I believe, at the time, if the Boston Bruins, if Eddie Shore,

Gordie Howe, maybe Bobby Hull—no, Bobby Hull I knew about, he was a star at the time—but if Gordie Howe was there, if Jacque Plante were there, I would not give a fuck about those guys. It would be the Norwood High guys, *Richie Hebner! Are you kidding me?*

"Dana Maus was one of my heroes. Timmy Twomey was an early one, because I remember my brother talking about him. In the Arena, he was number 7, Tobin was number 7, Thornton, T-T-T number 7, so to answer your question, the local kids growing up? Bigger than life. Bigger. Then. *Life.* Going into the Arena. I'm not sure I wanted to get my teeth knocked out, but I certainly wanted to be one of the guys in the huddle at the goal, saying our Father, you know what I'm talking about? That was like the biggest thing ever. Things you think about, coming onto the ice, things you think about, yeah but that whole Boston Arena thing, that made it bigger than life. Going into Boston, *oh jeezus!*"

"Ah, God, that's a tough one," Alex Skene replied. "I would say some of the, ah, the previous players in the area. Like Richie Hebner, of course, I always looked up to Tommy Taylor. My father coached bantams for a while and I used to go to the games with him, Tommy Taylor, and Johnnie Ranalli, and Arthur Harris, I remember they all loved my father. So yeah, I looked up to those guys. I remember that clearly. Real heroes? I'm trying to think, who else was around, I don't know, I don't know. Richie, he was a freak, yeah. I remember watching him in Four Seasons, how much older is he than us? I never had the opportunity to get to know him, I wish I had."

"Growing up?" Billy Clifford responded. "Well, of course Bobby Orr, that had to be one. Derek Sanderson. I think there were more hockey players, Yastrzemski too, I liked too, baseball. Actually, Dickie Donovan, I was a big fan of him. I just thought he was a great hockey player. And even before that, I saw Richie play. I thought Dickie was very clever with the puck, he handled it well, he could put points on the board, I thought he was very crafty, smart, smart on the ice, saw the ice. Who else, Jackie Cronin, I liked Jackie. Cuz he was going out with my girlfriend's sister. Anne Liddy was Jackie's girlfriend, and I was going out with Karen at the time. There were a few, that's probably it."

There was no question who my heroes were. I used to sit with my brother on his bed as he mentally prepared for his '67 games; afterward, I would rush from my father's car into the house to be first to tell my mother how he'd done. In 1969 I'd throw my stick and bag into my mother's trunk along with Dickie Donovan and Gary Sortevik's gear, as we were driven to school each morning. I had watched, with growing awe and excitement, kids I'd known since awareness, the Hebner brothers, Neil Higgins, and Dickie, become stars.

Eddie King—*such a buoyant spirit*—who had struggled to identify his heroes, got back to me. "Johnny McKenzie," he said. "Remember he was always pushing up his shoulder pads? I tried to emulate him. And Leah Riley as a cook. I used to call her every Wednesday with the *Boston Globe* weekend cooking section and discuss the articles!"

And then there was Don Wheeler. Perhaps because two players were in their fourth season with him and a host of others their third, trying relationships common between mentor and *mentees* had time to metastasize. A half century later, his players still try to reconcile the team's success with its pain and suffering. Not all opinions align.

"You know," Ed King said, "I think, you have to look at it he was a great coach, you just have to look at his record. I think he had an unusual motivation scheme, apparently worked enough to do the go-go forechecking. It was an effective scheme for many years. He got the Tommy Taylors, Tommy Shea, the epitome of forechecking, as Don used to call it the BU school of go-go forechecking. He said he used to go in and watch BU practice, that would have been with Jack Kelley, that was what he was trying to emulate, dump it in and forecheck the hell out of it. For me, looking back on it personally, I think I would have got a lot more out of it had we discussed more the flow of the game, instead of just go out, skate as hard as you can for one minute, get off the ice. There wasn't much puck control, unless the guys who did it naturally like Mike, Dickie Donovan, they'd just hold onto the puck anyway.

"Tell you a funny story, I didn't know Don that well. And when we were sophomores, if you remember, the seniors didn't like Don for whatever reason, so they were always bitching and moaning, bitching and moaning. So I'm with Billy Sullivan at the Needham game where Ftorek scored like 11 goals, or 9 goals, it was the game where from behind the net he just flipped it up off the goalie's back and in. It was the state championship game. So I'm sitting next to this guy with Billy Sullivan, you know, wise ass, right? And oh, you're from Norwood, what do you think of the coach? Ah, ah, he's, we don't like him, he's blah blah blah this and blah blah blah that. I didn't really have an opinion of him, I didn't play, I didn't really know him. He goes, well, Don's a good friend of mine. Uh-oh! It was Mike Adessa, Randolph, he had been at Holy Cross, he was a good friend of Don's, they used to have hockey camps together. So the first practice the next year, we're getting off the bus up at Walpole arena, Four Seasons, and Don says Ed King can I see you for a minute? Yes, coach. So I understand you have a poor opinion of me. I went blah blah blah blah blah, well, I don't' really have an opinion of you, but I was just mouthing off. And he said okay, work hard. That's all he said. He wanted me to know he knew. He left me off the hook completely. Just said okay, go out there and work as hard as you can."

"Don?" Peter Brown said. "As far as Don, the pattern I saw with Don, a lot of times guys got to be seniors and leaders and he used them to show the rest of the kids, I'm gonna kick his ass and have him respond appropriately to teach you how to do that. Yeah, I saw a lot of that. I'm gonna shit on this guy, and he's gonna stand up to it, and say fuck you and work his balls off, and that's gonna teach. Don didn't *say* that, but that's a pattern of behavior that I saw with Don.

"There's a thousand things in retrospect you can look at, but you can't blame kids...Don used to pull that card from time to time. If you talk to Billy, Billy feels as though Don blames him for '71. Why was it a tough year between he and I? I don't know. My hair was too long? I don't know. I rushed the puck one time? I don't know. He was all about stripping guys down, stripping you down. Don's intention was not to have a pleasant experience. Because he often, he taught, he verbalized it, I don't care if you hate me, he wanted the team to be in unison against him.

"Did he ever bend? We don't know, we don't know, and you know why? If he bent, he did it in a way that wouldn't show it. And I gotta believe, to be that subtle takes a fine instrument. Don was a blunt instrument. Now, is a blunt instrument gonna do the job? Yeeeeah. Is it going to beat the fuck out of a lot of things around it? Yeeeeah. But is a blunt instrument gonna get the nail driven? Yup."

"I got thrown off every year," Billy Clifford recalled. "My sophomore year he threw me off. My junior year he threw me off. My senior year he threw me off. So every year, *Clifford, get off the bus.* I'd walk home from the high school with my bag over my shoulder. I used to have to—my free period he made me come up to his room, sit in front of him. He'd sit at his desk and I was in the front row and right in front of him, and I'd just sit there and stare at him, the whole period, and not say a word. I'd just sit there like this and stare at him. That was my punishment. I had to do that every fucking free period during the hockey season. I think it all started my freshman year, going down the hallway and Mary McTernan was coming the other way, and during the summer we had gotten together, nothing serious, and the joke became we were going to get married and this and that. First day of school I run into Mary McTernan *oh when are we getting married*—Don was right there! So that kinda put the fucking, and then going out with Karen, oh *Jesus*, he'd always catch me walking in the halls with Karen, you know?

"Kevin Hurley's junior year, he had a good junior year, he did. I don't know, but he did something. I don't know if Wheeler saw him drinking on the bus going home, but he was in the doghouse his whole senior year. He was on the shit list with Wheeler. I don't think he even played much. He did a good job. I can remember me and Mike, going down to Burrillville to play Burrillville, me and Mike are on the JVs, (laughs) we beat 'em 19-2, Mike got like 8 goals! The next day we go into the Arena, you know the pullovers, red was first line, he'd always give them out. We're in the locker room, he gives Nolfi one, he gives Martin one, then he turns to me, he looks at me and *fires* it right in my face! I'll tell ya, I'll tell ya. I don't know if I've told you this, he got inducted into the Hall of Fame in Norwood? So afterwards we went down to talk to him, shooting the shit, Mary Jane was there, I loved her, I always loved her. So he goes to me, geeze he goes, how's your father doing? Well, he passed away, he passed away about three or four years ago. I'm sorry to hear that. I liked your father. I didn't like you, but I liked your father. I should have said you know what, Don? I didn't like you at all, either."

"Like most of us, I would say I had what amounted to a love-hate relationship," Alex Skene said. "I always remember my sophomore year, like mid-season, I was playing quite a lot but I was struggling at times. I remember I was paired with Tommy Lyons, and we were playing a lot.

And I got sick. I used to get sick sometimes in the winter with tonsillitis, probably from eating the fucking snow off the ice, because there were no water bottles. I was sick as a dog for like a week, high fever and everything, and I come back Monday and I was really weak, and the team had lost, and I was dreading it because I knew he was gonna put a beating on us, and sure enough he calls the practice off about, last fifteen minutes is nothing but wind sprints. And I hit a point where I can barely pick my feet up off the ice, and I'll never forget, as I turned to drag my ass up the ice, he whaled me in the ass with his stick. And I'll never forget that. I came really close to spinning around and killing him, you know? Of course I didn't, but every chance I got after that scrimmaging with him, I'd go right after him in the corners. Bang him against the boards, yeah, yup, yup.

"Like I said, my feelings are sorta love-hate. I mean, I respected him, and any bitterness you might have had are wiped away by winning the state tournament. I mean, it's hard to have any bad feelings after, for anyone who was involved with him after that, but when he hit me that time, boy, that hurt me."

"I would say," Peter Brown continued, "if you look at the big picture, what impacted us the most by his coaching was that Marine thing, unite the group against me or whatever, doesn't matter. You're pissed off at me? It's good you're pissed off about something. If you're pissed off at me, now you're gonna be pissed off at your opponent. Right? He used to say, an athlete will take any excuse to lose. If you give an athlete an excuse to lose, he will. I heard that a trillion times. If you give yourself an excuse, you have an out. No excuses. That was early on in Don's thing. You don't feel well? That's too fucking bad. You have the flu? Too fucking bad. Throw up? Okay, is it all out? Now skate your balls off. Oh, but I don't feel—too fucking bad. You don't feel good, don't play. See ya, next! Like the barber, who's up next? Back then it was who was gonna work the hardest. And even with us, who's gonna work the fucking hardest? Yeah, you're good, but you gotta outwork them on top of it. We were all equal opportunity assholes.

"I think that was a gigantic piece that gave us, we went into every game, we're gonna out-work them, we're gonna be stronger than them in the third period. We're gonna out-shoot them, and the total expectation was to win the fucking game. Did you pay a price? Yeah, we paid a price. Was our emotional experience of the hockey rewarding? No, no! The payoff was the hard work and the sacrifice was its own reward. By far. Even if we hadn't won the state championship our senior year, I hope that we would all be talking in a similar fashion now. We're way better off, there were ups and downs, like everything, literally everything, but were we better off? Oh, yeah."

"My senior year," Billy Clifford continued, "we're going into the tournament. You know how we'd walk down the stairs and he'd sit up top of the stairs when you walked in, when you're going down to the locker room? He always sat at the top there, so he calls me over and he says to me, he goes, Clifford, are you fucking around with your broad again? So I looked at him and said no I'm not fucking around with my broad again! Of course, I was. He said *if you fuck up this year I'll come and get you personally*. Quote, unquote. Seventeen-year-old kid, you know? So...oh, yeah. *You refuse to backcheck*. I think he said that after the game, after the '71 game."

"I think it was that senior year he quit scrimmaging with us at the end of practice," Alex Skene said. "I like to feel I should get some credit for that. (laughs) That was back in the day when all the coaches would scrimmage with us at the end of practice. You probably remember the freshman team we had, Chris Lee, I always remember him, he was an animal out there. Luckily, he couldn't skate all that well, but I remember getting pissed off because he was banging Pat Riley around and I remember lining him up in the corner and fucking hammering him, because he couldn't skate. I remember saying I'll get that motherfucker cuz he can't skate, and I did! Because I was pissed off the way he treated Bumper, my pal, I mean that was just wrong. That was just wrong. Speaking of characters, he was quite the character. He and Don were really close friends, which seemed like an odd pairing."

"Don back in the day, thought we were spoiled," Peter Brown said. "Cuz we were good hockey players; we had come up playing on actual rinks. These fucking kids can play. He wanted us to aspire to be where he wanted us to be, not by putting the puck through somebody's leg and dancing around, but fucking going head-first into the post and having the puck go in off your shoulder. He would rather that than, I think, honest to goodness, I think '71, that era was a big adjustment for him. Right? And '67 and '68 was the turning point. A bunch of those players didn't start skating until they started high school. Yeah, Wheeler basically molded them, created them. And people used to knock him for dumping the puck in, but what are you gonna do, fucken turn it over at the blueline every time? Right?"

"I really think if we didn't win in '72, he would have committed suicide!" Billy Clifford laughed. "I swear to God, he would have jumped off the fucken Bourne Bridge! I put up with a lot of his shit in three years. More so than probably anyone in the *history* of Norwood hockey, and I mean that. Every year I was thrown off, I'd have to go up and sit in front of him in my free period. I mean I went through hell with him, but I never quit. And I always made sure I was the first one to finish the sprints. Always. No one ever fucking beat me in sprints, I didn't care how dead I was, I made sure no one fucking beat me."

"I was just listening to this thing on the radio," Peter Brown said. "Student walks into this math class like five minutes late, there are two problems on the board. He assumes they're fucking homework. Takes 'em home, does 'em, but they're more harder than he's used to. Brings them in the next day, says here. Professor goes, what's this? He goes, the homework. Professor says that wasn't homework, those were two examples of problems that can't be solved. And he solved them. Because the expectation was not laid that this is undoable. I'm listening to this, and it creates a good environment for yourself in sports. Don's expectations was absolutely we win every, single, game. Oh, they're Needham, they're twenty years in a row state champs? Doesn't matter, we expect to beat them, and that expectation goes a long fucking way."

Yes, Don Wheeler's expectation was that we win every, single, game. And we did.

"We were 16-0-2 our junior year, so we expected to go undefeated our senior year," Billy Clifford said. "That was the mentality. And we had a couple of tough ones, Braintree was good, Dedham was always decent, you'd have to go out and play Framingham, South was always pretty good, you never knew what could happen out there, but I think we knew we could go undefeated. I knew we had a good team. I knew we could get back there again, and I hoped it would be Arlington, you know? I knew they had a good team; they had a lot returning, they were kinda in the same boat we were."

"So Eddie blossomed," Peter Brown said, "he had the banner year. Raeder might have been the most talented player, but he wasn't more valuable than Eddie King.[48] Our senior year, he was the MVP of the team, and deservedly so. He had a spectacular senior year. The year before, Bobby had four great years, but he also had a crazy senior year. Eddie had a crazy senior year, without that crazy senior year, we don't go undefeated. We don't beat Braintree at Braintree on a Wednesday afternoon. Eddie scored—only slapshot he ever took, he took a slapshot from in between the red line—ask him! —between the red line and the blue line and blew it by the goalie, the goalie was Cusack, pretty good goalie. It was a 1-1 game, they had a good team that year, they had Woodsie, Cleary, Sunderland, and Eddie fucken *Bam!* From outside the blueline!"

"You mean the only slapshot in high school I took in a game?" Ed King laughed. "It's true! The reason I took a slap shot was I was tired and I was dumping it in, I was so tired I didn't want to take a wrist shot so I took a slap shot and fell down! That was against Braintree with Stevie Woods at center, Sunderland the defenseman, yup. I took the slapshot and never saw it go in because I fell, and Alex Skene's father said it had a tail on it, and it kind of curved into the net over the guy's glove, or under the glove..." (laughs)

"So Eddie, senior year, without that goal we don't go undefeated," Peter Brown continued. "We might have popped one, but my feeling in that game was, we're skating uphill here. It was a Wednesday afternoon and they were a good team. They finished second that year, the only losses they had were to us. It was down on a Wednesday afternoon at Braintree, it was 1-1 or 2-2, and Eddie got that, huge.

"So anyways, he was just, Eddie was that go-to guy that came up big time. But another thing, we don't do shit without one of the best seasons of any defenseman I saw, Alex Skene. I mean, Alex didn't score a hundred goals, didn't skate by many people, but every time he passed to me it was

---

48 In 1972, the Bay State League MVP Award was shared by Ed King and Needham goalie Cap Raeder.

on my stick, ready to move. Alex was a very good passer, very underrated, very cool in big games. Especially in the playoffs, I remember Alex playing fucking great hockey, great hockey. Kevin Hurley, too, especially in the Arlington game, Kevin and Alex, especially Alex, was as good as any player on the ice."

Goals, assists, points, wins; all team records fell. Five of six starters were named to the Bay State League all-star team. After our final game of the season, we held a record 37-game unbeaten streak in league play. "Many fond memories," Frank Baglione recalled. "A fact that not many people know, that in that glorious 1972 year, not only did the varsity team never lose a game, but the JV team, of which I was on the first line with Mike Costello and Ed McQuade, *also* never lost a game. That fact should also be told."

Nevertheless, one of Don Wheeler's maxims, "never rest on your laurels", needed reminding. The coach sought the best competition possible in preparation of the state tournament and, as usual, looked toward Rhode Island. The game played between Norwood and Mount St. Charles might have been the greatest high school hockey game of 1972.

"I remember going down to Cranston, Mount St. Charles, and then we played 'em up at Four Seasons later in the year, Billy Clifford recalled. "Mount St. Charles had a good team, they had Tommy Songin, Guisti, and Kilduff."

"It was high school hockey at its best at the Four seasons Arena in Walpole on Wednesday night," Frank Wall wrote. "Close to 2,000 fans were on hand to see the Norwood High School team of the Bay State League and the leading team in Rhode Island, Mount St. Charles battle to a 3-3 thrilling tie. It was a game of hard-hitting and tournament hockey."

"Mount St. Charles," Peter Brown nodded. "Remember Tommy Songin running Donny Reddick? We were on the side, as you come in, on the left side. In between the red line and the blue line, he was like on the boards, and Tommy Songin like fucking ran him, and the puck came up and I ran Tommy Songin. It was bang-bang, I got him like that. Puck comes to me at the point, I shoot, he runs at me and I go ass over tea kettle, puck goes into the corner going straight at him, running him from behind, and we both get penalties. We're yapping at each other, people are like, *you're like you're ol' man,* but it started because I think he took the run at Donny because Donny had scored earlier! He ran at Donny, I ran at him, he ran at me, I ran at him, yeah. And that was one of the best high school games we ever fucking played. That one with Mount St. Charles was at Walpole, because of the Walpole guys, Songin, Brooks, Kilduff, Guisti, it was fucking packed. We were the best team in Massachusetts, they were the Rhode Island state champs. And it was a great game, it was a tie. That Mount St. Charles game was a big, it was almost like a Norwood-Walpole state championship game, great players, they had all kinds of players."

Frank Wall wrote, "One of the finest games seen this year in high school hockey certainly took place at the Four Seasons and that Mount St. Charles team was sure something, but then again, so was Norwood." We had been tied, our first "blemish" of the season, and though it didn't count in any standings, the message, the wake-up call was clear: there would be no laurels rested upon.

"There were other good teams," Billy Clifford said. "Archie Bills were a good team, bunch of individuals but they were a good team. We beat Matignon in the semis, Braintree had a very good team at that time. Matignon beat Braintree in the quarterfinals I think, to go to the semis. Melrose had a good team, so there was some really good teams. So it wasn't going to be easy."

Seeded number one, we headed into the tournament. The *Boston Globe* covered our first game,

> Norwood's 4 in 4 Minutes Top MC. Top seeded Norwood, the team to beat in Division I of the annual Eastern Massachusetts Hockey Tournament, wasted little time showing its power last night before 5,000 at Boston Arena. The fans had hardly settled into their seats when high-powered offense of the Bay State League champions went bang-bang-bang-bang and in less than four minutes Norwood had four goals on the way to a 6-2 win.

It had been Clifford, Clifford, King, Reddick in the flurry, sending us once again into Boston Garden, where we defeated Revere to set up a memorable semifinal match against Matignon. The Cambridge team was led by future Notre Dame All-American defenseman Brian "Dukey" Walsh, but eyes were also on Arlington, who kept pace. Perhaps too many eyes were on Arlington, as on Saturday afternoon, Matignon put a beat-down 13 shots on goal in the first period, Billy Pieri spectacular in keeping it a 1-0 game.

Norwood came out swinging in the second period, matching their 13 shots of the first, but Matignon wing George Garaffo stunned Norwood's crowd silent when he scored his second goal of the game, and after two periods it was 2-0. This was an unfamiliar position for the team that had lost just one of its last 43 contests, and thousands that afternoon wondered how Norwood would react.

The personalities are terrific...

Three minutes into the third period, "Mike Martin grabbed a Pete Brown pass and blasted one into the twine from about 40 feet out," Frank Wall reported in his column. "It was now a 2-1 game and Norwood was a threat..." For almost seven minutes Norwood pressed Walsh and goalie Ray Rossi without success, an uneasy reminder of last season's first period against Arlington. Then we caught a break. With just over two minutes remaining, Greg Walker stickhandled past several defenders and threw a pass to fellow sophomore Danny Bayer, the puck glancing off Bayer's leg and into the net. After a frantic final two minutes, regulation time ended with the score tied, 2-2.

I don't remember the locker room; I don't remember anything—none of us seem to—before stepping back onto the ice for overtime. But we all remember what happened next.

"He started our line," Billy Clifford recalled, "Peter and Alex were on D, and we're halfway through the shift and I come down the wing and I took a slap shot, missed the net and it rimmed all the way around and back in our zone. I'm thinking *oh Don's gonna be all over me on this one*... In the meantime, Mike and Eddie had changed, they were on the bench, Peter got the puck and hit Billy Denehy on the wing, and I just took off up my wing, and Denehy put a pass right on my stick. I got over the blue line and took a slapshot, I saw it go into the goalie's pads and my momentum carried me into the zone, and I could see it break between the pads and it flops down, and its fucking just trickling like that, I can still see it in my mind, and I'm in the corner now of the rink, and I'm staring and the thing's just going...and it goes over the fucking line and I just went, *boom!*"

An overtime, oversold, overzealous Boston Garden crowd of 14,000 exploded with joyous triumph and groaning despair. Arlington won its game. Norwood would play Arlington in the state final game.

Again.

ARLINGTON, AND IMAGINATION

Most of our lives are spent getting ready for dramatic moments that don't take place. Or if they do, are less than we expected. About the time we say, "Well, nothing really big ever happens to me," you can get knocked down with something larger by far than you expected. All the frustrations of all the little narratives in your life that never had a real climax can be present in the rare denouement that life also offers once in a great while.

— Norman Mailer,
The Spooky Art, 2003

Who hasn't had a dream when all of a sudden you've got the puck and you're going in and do something crazy and score the goal, I mean, everybody does that...

— Bobby Dempsey

The burgeoning of organized sports toward the end of the 19th century engendered a corresponding literary expression. The first well-known fictional sports hero was Frank Merriwell, the creation of author Gilbert Patten writing under pseudonym Burt L. Standish. Appearing first as a magazine story in 1896, afterward morphing into over two hundred dime novels, radio shows, and comic books, the character reflected the age's consummate athletic hero whose (many!) attributes included "truth, faith, justice, the triumph of mother, home, friendship, loyalty, patriotism, the love of alma mater, duty, sacrifice, retribution and strength of soul as well as body."

The protagonist's name was created specifically to reflect them. "The name was symbolic of the chief characteristics I desired my hero to have," Patten once explained. "Frank for frankness, merry for a happy disposition, well for health and abounding vitality." So powerful was the effect and so embraced was this character by a rabid and expanding sports audience, that no less than Christy Mathewson was endowed with what was considered highest praise when routinely considered, "the true-life Frank Merriwell."

Born one month before Frank Merriwell first appeared in print was Clair Bee, who undoubtably became familiar with the literary star in early youth. In 1948 Bee's first of twenty-four Chip Hilton books, written for adolescent boys, was published by Grosset & Dunlap. This new fictional character combined Frank Merriwell's high character with an emerging prerequisite of the modern sports hero: he was a winner of championships.

My imagination had an element of actual experience. One of the first times I ever ran the football for Arthur Gulla was by mistake. Coach Gulla had grabbed my arm and given me the play—*131 dive*, the fullback right up the middle—and pushed me onto the field with instructions to replace halfback Cameron Kelly. When I ran toward the huddle, however, all-star fullback Chris Macauley saw me, his backup, running in, and immediately hustled past me toward the sidelines. I tried to stop him but there I stood, the huddle all looking to me for the play, and I stuttering 131 dive *but I'm not supposed to be running the ball, Chris is...* Quarterback Barry Sullivan, always in decisive control in the huddle, snapped the command: *"131 dive, on one BREAK!"* And so it went...*how many weeks had Mr. Higgins tied my skates for me? How many Saturday mornings had I risen at 5 a.m. to shiver stuffed in the backseat of Mr. Lynch's car on the way to Tabor ice? How many times had I prayed to be selected for Tom Brown's Norwood Nugget traveling team?*

I was hardly the only kid imagining athletic heroics.

"As a boy," Skip Lockwood wrote, "I fantasized batting against Warren Spahn and Sandy Koufax in the backyard of our little house in Norwood. I also pitched against Willie Mays and Hank Aaron, striking them out with men in scoring position...For as long as I can remember I pictured myself playing baseball. I dreamed in baseball terms. I slept with my uniform on. I envisioned myself batting, hitting home runs, or pitching, striking out batters in the late innings..."

I'm on the third line. The rotation through the season was usually one-two, one-two-three, so we didn't play as much as the first two lines.

In the '71 Arlington game we had barely played at all, and I knew if things were tight—and all suspected they were going to be—we might not see much ice this year, either. So...I remembered that long-past football gaff and saw myself, the game winding down, two minutes or so to play, the House that Orr Built a howling, pounding mass of sound and fury, and...I jump over the boards on my own when the first line comes off the ice *change up! change up!* forcing someone on the second line to hesitate, and Wheeler to react furiously.

"Reddick! REDDICK!"

I ignore slapping sticks on boards to garner attention, drive hard toward the action...*how many tennis balls had I shot into our two-by-four, chicken wire net? How many tennis balls slapped, chipped, and driven against the cinder blocks of my house's foundation? How many street hockey games at Lydon's, stickhandling and deking and firing, mimicking Juniors Perreault and Dionne? How many practices over four years, trying to score every day on Frankie Eppich and Billy Pieri and Louis Parker? How many one-on-ones against the likes of Bobby Thornton and Alex Skene and Peter Brown? How many freshmen and JV and varsity games and all those chances and just a few goals, and more than a few hit posts...*

"Most of our lives are spent getting ready for dramatic moments that don't take place," Mailer had written. *This was taking place! Again! And again! And again and AGAIN! And I'd witnessed '65 when Richie couldn't score—how do you settle for second best? And I'd witnessed '67 when Kenny couldn't score—I don't know if that's a compliment or not! And I'd witnessed '68 when Dennis scored twice and the inexplicable happened to Neil—where would the statue be? And I'd played in '71 when we outshot them badly in the first period yet lost by the biggest margin yet, and saw blue eyes crying in the rain...*

Anyone can score these goals. In 1957, Arlington captain Gerald Cronin scored *two* overtime goals in two tournament games and seven overtimes played over a five-day span. Billy Corkery, added to the varsity roster only late in his junior season, scored the winning goal in the '67 Arlington game. Sophomore Tom Deveaux scored twice in the first period of the '68 Arlington game, equaling his season's output. An unheralded Herbie Pearl scored Marblehead's overtime goal against Norwood in '69. Anyone can score these goals.

Thirty-odd skaters shifted nervously in two Boston Garden dressing rooms that evening, and I'm sure each and every one dreamed of scoring that winning goal—*everybody does that*—but I can only relate my own aspiration. *I wanted to score that goal!* But—alas! —continuing the literary metaphor, my aspiration more reflected another famous fictional character than Chip Hilton.

In 1901, a seven-year-old Columbus, Ohio boy lost an eye from an errant arrow while playing William Tell with his brother. The injury prevented the youngster's participation in sports and has been suggested as impetus for his developing creative imagination. And in 1939 near-blind James Thurber wrote a short story for *The New Yorker* magazine entitled, *The Secret Life of Walter Mitty*... The historic goal-scoring would fall to another.

"It changed my life," he would tell me late one night, forty-five years later.

GAME DAY

Where, may I ask, can be found a more enthusiastic audience than at a championship hockey match? The very roof-timbers seem to creak with excitement; yells and shrieks that would silence a band of Sioux warriors are heard from every nook and corner of the building. The clashing of sticks, the stamping of feet, the yah-yahs of the admirers when a long and well-aimed shot for goal is fired, or perhaps when one player more cunning for the time than the rest, by his superior judgment, and surprising ability, darts with the puck, gently coaxing it from one side to the other while travelling at lightning speed through an entire line of adversaries until finally, like a pistol shot, it cracks through the goals, when a thousand, yes five thousand throats shout and scream until the pandemonium reminds one of a dynamite factory cutting loose!

— GEORGE A. MEAGHER,
SKATING, 1900

...the Garden shook as if a thousand trains had collided full force down below in North Station...

— KEVIN PAUL DUPONT, *BOSTON GLOBE* WRITER,
ON BOBBY ORR'S 1970 STANLEY CUP WINNING GOAL

If after '68 it was personal, after '71 it was raw abuse. The very word "Arlington" became an epithet, a nemesis of Goliathan proportions. Bob Bartholomew's, "We considered Boston Garden home ice" morphed from humorous quip to exasperating taunt. It was Norwood's fifth appearance in a state final game in the last eight seasons. It was Norwood vs. Arlington playing for the championship of Massachusetts for the fourth time in six seasons. Two Corkery brothers had scored as many goals against Norwood as Norwood's entire team had scored against Arlington, and Maurie Corkery was captain of their '72 squad! *You know that name, Corkery?*

Other names had changed, from Havern and Byrnes to Shaughnessy and Carr to Noonan and Flannigan, but the uniforms remained the same, intimidating maroon jerseys, maroon striped helmets. And yet what a rival! Simply the greatest record in the history of Massachusetts schoolboy hockey, seven state championships, led by one already considered a legend, though he'd pace behind benches another twenty-five years. Norwood in 1972 was justifiably proud of its fifth appearance in a state final contest in the last eight years; Arlington had *won* it three times over the same timespan! And those damn cigars...and *another Marine!*

But if Arlington was King of schoolboy hockey, the Bay State League had certainly made its mark as the finest schoolboy league in Massachusetts. In the decade since '61, when Framingham beat Needham for the crown, there had been eleven appearances in the state final game by league members. Needham had won the championship three times, Walpole twice. The league had been represented in each of the last seven final contests. If last season's final was billed Ali-Frazier, the heavy-weight bout of all time, what was this?

"The pressure was so intense," Peter Brown remembered. "It was pretty intense all year long. Not to carry on, every game was like, after a while you had to turn it off. And the expectations of unless we won our senior year, unless we won it all, we'd be talking now a pretty big disappointment. Right? So throughout the year there was a lot of that pressure both self-imposed by each person, and by Don. There wasn't a person in Norwood who didn't say, *you gotta beat Arlington!*"

"I and everyone else were focused on winning the state championship that year," Ed King said. "As focused as high school kids could be. I think it was a common expectation. I remember Arlington was always the focus, it really was, even during the year, in the back of your mind. I remember Billy Clifford putting up, this was during the tournament, in the basketball court in the gym, he had cut out of the paper a picture of the Flanagan brothers and he had written at the bottom of it, *pussy freaks.* Cuz they almost had like Farah Fawcett hair!" (laughs)

Norwood players were aware of the history, as well as Eddie Burns' quote after the previous year's loss, about which Peter Brown observed, "Considering you have, except for '71, take '71 out, you got three state championship games determined by a total of three goals. To say that we'll take on anybody anytime is okay if it's 6-2, so there was a reason. Eddie Burns was a great coach, but like Jack Parker told me, you know what makes a good coach? Good players. Know what makes a great coach? *Great* players. Again, considering except for '71, take '71 out, you've got three state championship games decided by three goals."

"Do you remember what the weather was like?" Ed King asked. "It was March 13th, I think? My father had organized the buses to go in, I don't know how many busses, but a bunch of them left from the Balch School. So they had all left. Remember Susan Gately? So Allen Gately her father used to work in the store. I remember coming downstairs and it was only Allen, and I said Mr. Gately I hope you don't mind, but I'm gonna take a case of beer. And he said, do what you want! So I took my bag and put the beer in the bottom and my hockey equipment in it.

"I went and took a walk for half hour or forty-five minutes up Morse hill, and up and around, it was just like 60, whatever the temperature was. It was humid enough that fog was, this low hanging fog, so it may have been partial melted snow, just low-hanging fog. And it was warm out. I remember walking around just to get my thoughts straight.

"I remember walking into Sociology class earlier that day with Peter Hexter, and I walk in the class and he says *hey*, and he threw me his keys to his green Camaro, and he says, take a ride. That's all he said. I remember taking the walk, stashed the beer in the bottom of my green army bag."

"Believe it or not, I ate dinner the evening of the '72 game in the Corkery house, in Arlington," Ken Reddick recounted. "I played with Bobby Corkery at UMass, and we came home together to see the game. What amazed me is that they didn't take a bus to the game like we did but jumped in their cars and made their way over to the Garden!"

"The day of the Arlington game," Ernie Paciorkowski remembered, "Bucky Sexton and I were in George Usevitch's office and for whatever reason George had WMEX on the radio, and the DJ said that he was sick of Arlington always winning and wanted Norwood to win. Well, that's all

George needed to hear. He got Bucky and I out of school and piled into his Mach I—no Vet yet—and we drove into WMEX and George gave the DJ some tickets and they put him on the air! And as they say, the rest is history!"

We were driven to Boston Garden by one who had become part of the team. "They called Sansone's when they needed a bus, and a lotta the times I was available, my hours were flexible," Rusty Booth recalled. "Rusty, will you drive it? Yup, I'll take it. The more I think about it, I made myself available more for the hockey team. I couldn't play that sport, but I enjoyed taking that group. There was something about that group that I really enjoyed. I don't remember names, I'm no good with names. The only thing I still remember is picking the hockey team up and taking them to the different places to play. I think I decorated the bus once or twice, put stuff up. I just put paper things up, congratulations, and what do you call it, strings of tape, colored tape across when they entered the bus. I did that a couple of times when they won big games. They were a special group, oh, they were, they were."

"Oh my God, there were busloads and busloads," Cheryl Shaw, class of '72, recalled. "We didn't drive in; we went in on one of the busloads of the thousand busses that went from Norwood into the Garden. You walked in there and I think Norwood people were three quarters of that stadium. In all honesty, I've never seen, I've been to a lot of Norwood High School hockey games, from Walpole to Needham to Framingham to you name it, but when we walked into the Garden that night, I think the whole dang town was there. I don't think that there was a person that didn't go. And it was just like, you were lucky to have found a seat. It was such a hair-raising game. It was such a fast-paced, fast-moving game, but the only thing anyone cared about was whether we were gonna win or not!"

Fraught with emotion and nerves, the locker room saw events prescient, bizarre, and humorous.

"I do remember before the game some old street guy came in," Peter Brown recalled, "he was like, what's that movie with Robin Williams, *Fisher King*? Guy coming in, a divine premise, but he came in and said, *I know Norwood is gonna win!* Ask other guys, who knows, but I kinda remember that."

"I remember when someone came barging in shitfaced," Frank Baglione said. "He must have been a Norwood player, I remember that, it was the Arlington game." Arthur Harris had charged into the dressing room, rendering with twelve-pack eloquence his very own Knute Rockne impression. We sat on benches, our lines together, usual suspects jumping up and hollering, "firing" us up. Next to me was my center Mark Balerna, one of the quieter individuals on the club, who for the first time all year suddenly flung himself to his feet and ranted and raved, encouraging all on. Flopping back in his seat before a somewhat stunned room he leaned close and whispered, "Pretty good, eh?"

"The first time I went out onto the ice at the Garden," Billy Clifford remembered, "we came out of the side, and all I can remember is a wall of people, just a straight wall coming right down. I was like, wow. Just a wall! It was like a wall, freakin' *wow!* But it was quite a thrill, I'll tell you that. We were lucky, we were lucky."

Peter Brown looked back on the experience from his collegiate vantage point. "I had an advantage of other players, because I was used to playing in the Garden. The pressure of the Beanpot my freshman year was nothing compared to eight months earlier playing in the state tournament final for Norwood High, blew it away. We were young men in a really—Don created a very intense atmosphere, and we did it ourselves, we challenged ourselves, and challenged other people.

"There was a lot of pressure from a lot of people. Because it was like, you know, if we'd finished second in the league, or lost to Matignon, we would have been shit bums. The expectation-reality gap, very rarely does it line up. It lined up. Most of it's a blur, I remember their first goal, I don't even remember our first goal, it happened on the first shift, didn't it? Right? Early in the game we were up 1-0. He started the second line, because Arlington's second line was the Flanagans and right wing, Peter Noonan? Here's the other thing, Arlington had a lot of good college Division One players. The team we played against, Peter Noonan played four years at UNH, the Flanagans played at Brown, Maurie, Barts, Joey Keefe all over at BC, they played a little, Cremens the goalie played four years up at Williams. So, it wasn't like Eddie Burns was whipping up magic spells here, they had good players. Their top players always became really good college players. Havern over at Harvard, Corkery."

Jay Shaughnessy, Arlington's '71 captain, described our current opponents. "The crew we had; you didn't know if somebody was gonna be in jail for the next game. He had some fucking lunatics. These guys were just fucking—I think Burns was afraid of some of these guys. Kevin Bartholomew was a defenseman, Burns is talking about different guys, *Bartholomew, I wouldn't put murder past you*, we had some real ding-a-lings. Kevin Bartholomew, not Robert, his younger brother, the twins, the Flanagan twins, you had Cremens in the net. There were a few nuts on that one."

"Here's the story on the Flanagan twins," Maurie Corkery said. "They were my best friends growing up. We all grew up, went to the same grammar school, junior high, high school and prep school together. I had my best year playing with them, great, tough kids. They were 160-pound defensive linemen in Arlington High in football. Used to play Brockton, real tough, especially Michael, he was real tough. They were like closest friends growing up. Talent wise, they were great. Pat was a center, he was more dishing off, Michael was a wing, and he was big. Patrick was smaller."

Pre-game passion? In warmups, when both teams first gained the ice and skated in circles, passing each other at center ice, I was slashed by an Arlington player. Billy Clifford, harboring both ill-will toward our previous loss as well as his own coach's perceived grudge against him for his role in that game, was sky-high.

"Lining up for a faceoff," the winger recalled, "I think, I don't know if Don started the second line, because Arlington's second line was the top, the Flanagans, that was their top line. I think Don started our second line against their first line. But I can remember lining up against one of the Flanagans and giving him a ration of shit. *You pussy fucking freak, you pussy fucking freak, you and your brother are fucking*...and I remember him skating away and going over to his brother and saying something to his brother and coming back."

Sophomore Greg Walker stunned the crowd thirty-five seconds into the game, banging home a Danny Bayer-Billy Denehy rebound and erupting the Garden into a cascade of unraveling toilet paper. "Billy shot the puck at their goalie and then Danny took a whack at it," Greg Walker told Frank Wall. "I saw it loose in front of me and the goalie was down, so I just flipped it over him."

Arlington goalie Chuckie Cremens then began repeating his performance of the previous year, making save after save, "some lucky and some fantastic" Frank Wall later wrote. The first period ended 1-0, momentum Norwood's, but the beginning of the second period brought ominous tidings.

Maurice Corkery—*you know that name, Cork–YES WE KNOW THE NAME!* —set up Al Quinlan for Arlington's first goal just over a minute into the period. "Corkery intercepted a Norwood defenseman's pass and fired the puck across to Al Quinlan who was all alone in front of Pieri, and just flipped it over Pier's shoulder," Frank Wall wrote. A huge goal in the game, it was also notable for precipitating the most disgraceful incident in tournament history, when a human fetus was thrown onto the ice.

"I remember their first goal," Peter Brown said. "I don't remember the goal, but I remember afterward, thinking that there was like a dead baby pig on the ice. Did I see it? I swept it into the net. Their first goal, 1-1. Swept it into the net. All kinds of shit on the ice, they came out, rink attendants put it in a popcorn box, I remember. I remember sweeping it in, but I definitely remember them coming out and putting it in a popcorn box. How's that one?"

"Absolutely I remember," Billy Pieri recalled. "Goal was scored, and they threw all kinds of shit on the ice, tennis balls and things, and somebody threw a fetus on the ice, it was in my crease. I took it, I just kinda pushed it back into the net. It stayed there for the rest of the period. I wasn't exactly sure what it was, but it certainly was in a fetal position, and in between periods the guy cleaning the ice picked it up and put it in a popcorn box." The incident passed virtually unnoticed; most learned of it after the game.

Unlike '71, Norwood did not let up, outshooting their opponent 11-2 in the second period.

"I remember that we were all over them," Alex Skene recalled, "dominating them, but we couldn't get the puck in the net. We were all over them, and I remember giving up one bad goal, but all the time with the feeling we were gonna get 'em, the whole game I felt like we were gonna get 'em. The memory I have is having that bad game in the semifinals, but not really losing confidence. And the game went well except we weren't scoring. Just giving up one bad goal, trying, I remember somebody was coming down on me, as he started to lose the puck, as I forechecked him the puck got in between my skates and I fucking stepped on it and fell down, and they scored! And I was oh, God! Just a freak thing, you know. But other than that, it was a very good game. Pete and I were playing well, I remember that, and the puck was in their end all the time. I remember having that feeling, we were gonna win that game, even when we were down 2-1."

Peter Brown: "I remember stepping up to hit Pat Flanagan and him passing to Mike and it being offsides and thinking lucky thing they called that, because if not I would have really fucked up. Pat and Mike were coming down, and I made Pat swerve at the blue line. I played him, but it was really like an isolated two on one and I shouldn't have done it, but Don had it so reamed in our heads so much you had to play him, if you make a guy go laterally at the blueline, it throws the other guys off. For a defenseman to go at an oncoming forward, it was all or nothing. So I was able to get him, and I got him, but just before I got him, he slid the puck over and Mike Flanagan who to this day claims he was onsides, but he was offsides. He was offsides. Tell him he was offsides, even if he wasn't, tell him he was offsides!"

"To me," Billy Pieri said, "the biggest thing was after the second period we were tied, I believe, and Mikey Martin stood up and said, there's no fucking way we're gonna lose this game! He came up to me and said Pierski, there's *no fucking way* we're gonna lose this game, and he was just walking around the locker room, I can remember motivationally, yeah, we're *not* gonna lose this game! I thought that was the turning point. It was unbelievable. Mikey can be very good like that."

Two and one-half minutes into the third period, the Spy Ponders broke the tie. "Al Quinlan intercepted a clearing pass and hit Pete Noonan all alone in front and Noonan jammed it home and Arlington led 2-1, and it looked like the same old story would come true, but these Norwood kids just don't quit," Frank Wall wrote.

"We took the play to them right from the start," Don Wheeler told Marvin Pave of the *Boston Globe*. "We never let up. Even when we were down in the final minutes 2-1, I had this feeling inside that we'd still win."

With under five minutes remaining in the game, Norwood struck. "Kevin Hurley shot the puck from the points and Danny Bayer got it over to me, and I just flipped it in the open side," Billy Denehy told our *Messenger* scribe. All of which, after the tumultuous vibration lessened and again the ice was cleared of debris, turned a championship game into virtual sudden death.

With no apology for the triteness of the phrase, the stage was set.

"During the course of the game, you don't remember a lot of the stuff," Billy Clifford said, "but you remember the end of it. You know? It's funny because me and Eddie worked on that play a lot after practice. Couple minutes after practice, we'd go down, he'd go to the net and I'd feed it over to him, bang, paid off. Peter gets it to Mike in the slot, Mike fed me, I came down the wing, Eddie's flying down his side, and I fired it over to Eddie, almost on net. I mean, he was right on top of Bartholomew and Cremens when he scored it, and *bang*, in the net. And I jumped fucking so high out of my fucking skates! That guy got a good picture, that's for sure!"

"My recollection," Ed King said, "is Pete Brown passed to Mike Martin who carried it up through center, who passed it off to Billy on the right wing, I was able to skate in front of the defenseman and about the same time Billy fired it across, and I was lucky enough to have it hit my stick or skate. I just always remember seeing the puck go in, and the ref was right there and he went like this, *okay!* That's all I need to see!"

Ed King's goal with 2:41 remaining burst that now departed, legendary building into a hysterical, pounding, raging explosion of dancing delirium. *The Garden shook as if a thousand trains had collided full force down below in North Station...*

"And then," Ed King recalled, "do you remember Don, first time all year, then shifted up the forechecking assignments. Soon as that goal was scored, he said okay, center forecheck only, two wings stay back on their wings. So we weren't going after the puck, we were going to sit on it."

The last minutes were heart-in-your-throat desperation, each touch of the puck the most important moment of each player's career, every soul in that arena on their feet, their collective voice a chaotic cacophony of unrepressed anxiety...

...and...time...wound...down...

"I also remember the very last play of the game," Peter Brown said. "Maurie Corkery had the puck in center ice, he came down and took a shot just outside the blueline, I deflected it up and out of play. As I remember it, there were three or four seconds to go, Maurie takes a shot and I deflected it, and there was a faceoff, our end outside the blueline, that was the last faceoff, game over. That's all I remember, that's all I remember..."

"I was on the ice when the buzzer rang," Mike Martin told Jack Tolman, "and I no sooner threw my gloves in the air then Frank Wall was standing right next to me in the Garden, and I said what did you do, did you jump from the rafters? How did you get out here so quick? It was unbelievable! Incredible! I never seen a man so happy in my life. He was the happiest guy in the world, no doubt!"

"It was the strangest feeling," Billy Pieri remembered. "I just kind of felt numb, like surreal. Of course I was happy but I wasn't jumping up and screaming, like you would have scoring a winning goal or something, I just remember thinking, *we did it*. I remember thinking to myself, *I thought you'd be more excited*. It was just a surreal thing, all these years of hockey, all these years of practice and all these years of putting up with Don's shit, all these years of teams losing before us and we finally won. I don't know if it was so much my brain just shut down or what, but it was very surreal. I remember Mikey Martin coming up, *I'm fucking buying tonight!* A lot of people were jumping up and down, screaming, I remember hugging guys, but not going crazy. It just kinda felt surreal. Course, later on it kicked in, but not while on the ice. The locker room, that's where it really started. Everybody was just yelling and screaming and everything, I had my skates on and I walked on the ceramic tile to get some water and somebody said something and I said, I don't give a *fuck!*"

"Some may have been jealous of the '72 team, but not me," Bobby Thornton said. "I was *so* proud of them; I truly think that I was the first non-player who jumped onto the Garden ice when the clock ran out in March 1972 at the great Norwood 3-2 win over the hated Arlington group!"

"I was on the ice," Billy Clifford recalled, "remember Peter, everyone piling on everyone, I remember Pete and Mike and Eddie behind him, taking a stroll around the place, people going fucking crazy, and then, I had got cut over my eye, got stitched up in between periods, I think the quarterfinal game, I had five stitches put in. So afterwards they took me down to the locker room, and took the stitches out, and I can remember walking down the hallway to the locker room and people just patting me on the back *yah!* and Mike was coming the other way, he was going in to get stitches, and he's saying *Billy don't leave me! Don't leave me!* I said screw you, I'm going back to the locker room! So then when I get back to the locker room there's just bedlam in there, the beers are going, *Monbouquette's coming in, Monbouquette's coming in!*" (laughs)

"I remember coming off the ice and Bob Crocker was right there," Peter Brown recalled, "the recruiter for BU. I hugged him, and then it's like a blur. It's like, the locker room was mayhem, cigars, everything, it was pissa!"

"Remember Peter Thomas?" Billy Clifford asked. "He brought beer; he brought a six pack in the locker room. I had one, I forget who said to me, it might have been Eddie, put that down! Cuz Monbouquette was coming in the locker room, Piccirilli... We drank on the bus. We did get away with a lot, though, I'll tell you that!"

The dressing room was jubilant upheaval, the apex of hysterical shout. Dozens crowded; my father and brother Ken entered as well as Bobby Thornton, Dickie Donovan, Bobby Clifford, Tommy Shea, Jackie Cronin, Blaine Maus, Paul Angelo, Bobby Donahue, and Timmy Twomey. Norwood's hierarchy entered, Principal Jack Monbouquette, vice-principal John Piccirilli, selectmen Joe Curran and Joe Wall, Athletic Director Andy Scafati. Frank Wall was there, of course, cigar in the corner of his mouth, seeking comments.

Peter Brown: "Since this group was kids, we wanted to be champs. This year we had the team and the great coach and we went out and did it. This is unbelievable. To every kid on this team, it's been a dream since we were nine years old. No material thing could come close to this. It's unbelievable! Fantastic!"

Alex Skene: "We didn't do too much different from our past few games. The only difference was we were up. We've been waiting for this since last year. A lot of people have waited for this for a long time."

Even equipment manager John Kerr was quoted in the *Boston Globe*: "This is all so unbelievable... I can't believe it...it's unbelievable!"

Frank Wall noted, "Eddie King had four cigars neatly wrapped in a tube. They were Robert Burns cigars but Eddie crossed off the 'Robert' and replaced it with 'Eddie' and Wheeler smoked one and so did Jack O'Neil and some happy reporter by the name of Frank Wall whose birthday was Monday night."

Other teammates, in a remarkable demonstration of utter immunity in the presence of high school and town officials, pulled beer from their bags. I brought in a couple of Millers and recall sophomore Peter Thomas pulling out his six-pack. A few fathers made their thoughts known to reporters.

"After raising four daughters, this is what I've been waiting for!" Ed King, Sr. said. "I finally had two sons and what a thrill it is to see this game played. This I won't forget for a long, long time."

"I've been waiting for this since Billy was this high!" said Bill Clifford, Sr., the Clifford smile gleaming.

"After the game was over," Frank Wall wrote, "coach Wheeler and Eddie Burns exchanged handshakes and Wheeler didn't say anything and neither did Burns. Last year the Arlington coach did make some remarks about Norwood and the Bay State League, but on Monday the coach was mighty quiet…"

Boston Globe sportswriter Marvin Pave wrote, "Wheeler was almost speechless at times. He kept muttering words like "great…wonderful," but he was in another world. He had been Norwood's coach for ten seasons and has been to the Garden finals five times. This was the first celebration and he was enjoying it. "The kids were teed off tonight," Wheeler said, "and that's what did it. It's like an animal, when an animal is healthy, it's complacent; but when that animal is wounded… Last year left a bad taste in our mouths. There was no way we were blown off the ice last year, and the kids remembered this. Before the game, we knew we were going to win."

"That '72 game you guys totally beat us, from start to finish," Maurie Corkery recalled a half century later. "I don't know how many shots we had; we didn't have many. Yeah, you definitely outplayed us, I remember that."

Norwood had outshot Arlington, 44-10.

"We got behind, 2-1, in the third period," Billy Clifford told Dock Trust of the *Patriot Ledger*, "but we knew we'd come back. We just kept moving at them, putting pressure on them, and we capitalized on their mistakes. They're tough when they get ahead, but we got up mentally and physically for them. We just wanted it so much."

"This was a pride game for us," Peter Brown told a reporter, "and we had to prove we could win, and we did. You could see the pride, it just lifted us right off the ground. You could see the electricity in the air in this locker room when we came here tonight. We had a meeting with the coach yesterday, and we figured it would be a 50-50 game. Whoever wanted it the most would win. And we really wanted it."

"This is the greatest day of my life," Ed King told a reporter. "We knew we could do it and we did it. Even when we were behind, we knew that we would bounce back, for we wanted this win. I'm just so happy words can't describe my feelings... I knew we'd take them. We had come so far, and we weren't about to let them take this from us again. Every kid on this team wanted this championship and wanted it bad."

"For a while," Eddie Burns said in a quieter dressing room, "goalie Cremens looked like the spoiler. It was the greatest game Chuckie has ever played. Norwood was an inspired hockey team tonight. They outplayed us, but for a while in the third period, I thought we might steal the game. But they wanted it...wanted it too much."

Jimmy Gormley had said that Don Wheeler "could take any kid if they really wanted it, he could make him into a capable hockey player. But he said, *they've gotta want it!* That's the thing."

That's the thing.

Don Wheeler stood in the most euphoric, chaotic Norwood hockey dressing room of all, and exclaimed to a Boston sportswriter,

"I'll tell you, this has got to be the greatest team Norwood has ever had!"

Frank Wall described in the *Norwood Messenger* what followed,

> ...onto the bus and the yelling and shouting again. Coach Wheeler is smoking his Eddie Burns cigar, the kids are cheering and then the mob of cars and rooters waiting for the club in Norwood. The big parade, the reception—it had to be one of the greatest nights that the town of Norwood has ever had, and do you realize that this CHAMPIONSHIP CAME ON OUR 100TH ANNIVERSARY. OUR CENTENNIAL YEAR!

Billy Clifford: "So after the Arlington game, it was the biggest party this town has ever seen! The bus ride home, we were drinking beers on the bus ride home. Drinking on the bus, and on the back of the fire engine. People throwing beers up to us, and down to Angie's afterward. You couldn't move. You could feel the floor shaking, there were so many people, you couldn't move. Jammed packed. People giving us beers. I remember going down Shaw's house afterwards, drinking down there. We got away with murder, we really did! We were king of the fucking castle! Fucking unreal!"

Ed King: "Afterwards, well, we were drinking beer on 95 with the coaches, it was on the way home. I didn't open them up until the bus ride home, and I remember we were on 95 South and I brought beers up to Don and Jack O'Neil. They drank 'em! Everyone would be fired now!"

Peter Brown: "So it's like I came to at the beginning of the bus ride, I mean the fire engine ride going through downtown, people throwing beers at us, just amazing. It wasn't like I was feeling exuberance, I have no idea what I was feeling. It was so intense, it was like I was in a ball, a tsunami, but my recollection, like Norwood center was packed, we went to the old junior high and the rec center across the street, it was pretty big. And that's what I remember. I remember then going down to the Old Colonial, Timmy Twomey was there shitfaced, grabbed me like this, *tell Billy Pieri he grew up near me, tell him great job, okay Tim, just don't punch me!* I remember Frank Wall was happier than any one of the kids were. Right? Oh, man!

"My father drank at Angelo's so I never went down there, but we went in. I remember they picked me up and carried me across the Colonial, and they were doing it with every player that came in. That was what was going on, all night. At the Colonial, picked me up and carried me right across. But do I remember the feeling? No, I really don't. I know at some point it was like, ah, thank God that's fucking over!"

Billy Pieri: "That's what it meant, it meant I can do anything I want. It just meant that much. Did you make it down to Angelo's the night we won? I can remember walking in there, and he had pizzas and all kinds of stuff for the hockey players, and somebody would yell *another hockey player!* and they would just pick you up and pass you, like a mosh pit, and just passed you, like their hands above their heads, and passed me right through the restaurant! I remember thinking holy Christ these guys are fucking strong! Big fucking hands and passing you like a pillow right through the restaurant!"

Billy Clifford: "When we got back the fire engine waiting for us, Julie Turner, ah, who else, Karen, and Karen O'Neil, they were driving in the car before the fire engine. I remember people throwing beer up to us on the fire engine. (laughs) It will never happen again, how involved the town was, being there four previous times, and coming up short…"

Ed King: "I remember being at the Civic, and I remember they announced the high school was called off the next day. They were calling people up and congratulating them. Don said some words, Joe Curran spoke, Sails of course was narrating the whole thing. I don't know where we went after that."

Frank Baglione: "I remember when Walker scored, I jumped so high I fell over and hit my lip, people thought I'd played! I don't recall much of the game, what I remember is the fire engine ride, and getting kissed by girls before getting on there. I don't remember much in the locker room; I do recall Harris. I remember how bad the ice was, I remember the deafening cheers after we scored, but we heard that all year!"

Phil Nolfi: "I was first row in the Garden for the '72 game. I thought *we* won! I partied with them afterwards! I was going to Northeastern at the time and I missed a couple of practices!"

"I was at BC and it was during the season, and I dropped everything and went to that game, I could not miss that game," Jack Cronin remembered. "That was…obviously I was happy, I was proud, it was payback because it was Arlington. I was proud, happy to see not just the players, but I was happy to see Wheeler win it."

Billy Clifford: "Good memories out-weight the bad, you know, Dee? It was fun. Oh, God, we did like drinking, though. It was insane! That night, my mother wakes up my father at three in the morning, she goes hey Bill, he's not home yet! My father goes ahh, what can you do? and went back to sleep!"

Ed King: "I do remember driving around about two in the morning. Arthur Harris was driving, Tommy Taylor was in the front seat, and me and Mikey were in the back seat, and we got pulled over by the police on Nahatan Street, I'm sorry, Neponset Street. We got beers everywhere, you know, and all Arthur Harris said (Ed's jerking his thumb back over his shoulder) *State Champs! State Champs!* And the cop said, okay go ahead. That would never happen today! Arthur Harris and Tommy Taylor, how we ended up with them I don't know, just driving around drinking."

The next morning was amongst the bleariest-eyed in Norwood's history. But not all were wincing.

"I was in third grade at the Balch school and I got picked up at the bus stop," Jack Tolman remembered. "And every time the bus stopped and went to the next stop, you could hear these bottles rolling, and the bus driver—kids would get on and sit down—and he'd say each time, watch your feet, boys and girls, watch your feet, kids, the boys won last night! And when you came to the next stop they would roll, and I can remember looking down at my feet and lifting them up and seeing Schlitz, because I knew my father drank Schlitz, so I knew it was beer. But every time the bus stopped, they would roll up, and then roll down, depending on where he was. For some reason maybe they didn't clean the bus that night or maybe it was too late, but all I know is all the way to the Balch those bottles rolled back and forth every time he stopped, and we had to lift our feet. I don't think I realized till I got older that, oh my gosh! That was when they won the state championship!"

"I remember waking up probably the happiest I've ever been," Ed King remembered. "*Wait a minute*, I had to pinch myself, *holy shit, we just beat Arlington? Oh, wait a minute, did I get the goal? Oh my God! It was unbelievable!* But I can honestly say, and I believe this is true, hockey is such a team sport. Yeah, I ended up in front of the defenseman in front of the net, but you know, there were four other people on the ice that helped with that. So, I think if for nothing else, it has made me more humble with the realization that, you know, all these people want to say *oh, you scored the winning goal*, well I did but, to get there you need other people to help you. I remember what's his name, good guy from Dedham, defenseman, Hampe, Kevin Hampe, so I'm at the Colonial at the bar, and I recognized him and introduced myself and our wives are sitting there. And when I went to the men's room he said to Meg, what's he say about scoring the winning goal? And Meg said he always says it's a team sport and he was lucky to be where he was to score it. Thank you, Meg!"

Then again, not everyone woke up that morning. "Billy Denehy and I, we're out partying," Billy Pieri recalled. "Remember Paul Redihan had a barn or garage behind his house? Like a barn and stuff? Somehow a bunch of us ended up there, there were no cell phones, I never told my mother where I was, and we're walking back toward my house, and I feel bad about this, I pulled a newspaper out of a bundle of newspapers by Dacey's. I used to be a paperboy, you deliver papers and if you were one paper short it was a pain in the ass, but I pulled a paper out of this stack of papers. Sitting on the wall at the Shattuck School and we're reading about the game, which was pretty cool when you think about it. All of a sudden, my mother came by in the car and she was *bullshit!* She'd been calling around people's houses, is he there, is he there? It was the next morning, we stayed out all night!"

At about nine o'clock that morning I went down to McDonalds, where I saw Mikey Martin standing about eighth in line, his hockey helmet on his head. Mike had graced the dawn.

Framingham's Ted Casey, who had won a state championship a decade earlier, gave voice to the boys of '72. "Well, it's something, we're kind of special guys that did something that not many people could do. It's fun playing the game, but to win at it is even more fun. I mean everybody goes out with the idea they're gonna pick up a baseball bat and they're gonna be Mickey Mantle or Ted Williams, it never happens. It never happens. It's like you pick up a hockey stick and you want to be Rocket Richard or Jean Beliveau or Bobby Orr and that doesn't happen, either. But when you get into it and you can play, you have fun and you win, and it keeps you outta trouble because you're not hanging around the corner. We grew up at a time without computers and we didn't have phones, we played street hockey, it's what we did. It was a different time."

"In my opinion," Frank Baglione said, "that '72 team was the best not just in Massachusetts, or the U.S., but I don't think anyone in Canada could beat us. Mount St. Charles had a couple of pros and we even beat them! We beat the alumni team that had Hebner on it, these are stars coming back, my heroes! Richie Hebner, Ken Reddick—your brother was my hero! They used to fill that Four Seasons rink, remember the sound, people smoking, smoke over the ice, that was like watching the pros when

I was ten years old! I used to go to the games and watch the older guys, I became those guys when I played street hockey."

"It wouldn't be the same if we had won in the middle," Billy Clifford said. "It wouldn't have been the same if we hadn't beaten Arlington. Arch enemy. Unbelievable. I mean the fan base alone, we played in front of packed houses, even at Four Seasons, 4,000 people there for a high school game, and you get to the Arena's and it's full, I don't know how many, 9,000 at the Arena? And then you get to the Garden, 13,909, incredible. I tell people that, and they go you gotta be shitting me. I tell my players that, they think they have a big crowd when they had three or four hundred people there. I go this is nothing, we played in the Garden seven or eight times, quarterfinals, semifinals, finals, seven times. I tell them I used to play in front of 14,000 people."

"It's something that we're never gonna see again," Billy Pieri agreed. "Which I guess is okay. It will never be jammed packed crowds like Four Seasons, remember one game the bus had to stop at the top of the hill, we couldn't get down, we had to take out our bags and walk down? These are people coming to watch fifteen, sixteen, seventeen-year-old kids play hockey, you'll never see something like that again. It was just, my kids never saw anything like that, just their parents in the stands. So for me it was an era I think we were very fortunate to be part of. We experienced something I don't think high school players will ever experience again. That is one of the most amazing things. I think for one little town, it was a huge thing."

"You say hockey, I think of Richie Hebner," Bucky Sexton said. "He was a great baseball player, and that '72 hockey team—that will never happen again. The night you guys won it was probably the greatest night of my life. Without a doubt, I remember having a front seat in the balcony. Johnny Most couldn't have had a better seat, and when you won there was pandemonium! When King put the puck in the net and Billy was in the corner, that was a special moment, and a special moment for the whole town. The magic of Norwood hockey left that night, it was never the same. I think because that era—we were all eighteen, we were all athletes for the first years of our life. It was the perfect time for athletes, skating on the ponds, walking around town, we walked everywhere. Remember going downtown to McDonalds? It could've been below zero, and there we were all the time. Of all the things we lived through in the 1960s, Kennedy, Martin Luther King was killed, we went to the moon, it was a great era for sports, but our town had it all that night."

"I think the only thing that stands out in anybody's mind is that last goal," Cheryl Shaw recalled. "You've got Billy Clifford flying in the air and that shot that went through, and the pandemonium when you guys scored that goal, it was everybody down there that put their whole heart into scoring that goal. It wasn't just one of you, it was all of you. But when that puck went in, it was pandemonium in that stadium. My mother was beating, I don't know who it was sitting in front of my mother, but she had the program and she was beating him on the top of his head with her program. I mean literally beating him on the top of the head! I don't know who it was, but he turned around and asked her to stop. But it was sheer pandemonium in Boston Garden that night, it was like unbelievable. I think the whole night, the whole game was such a blur from the time you got there until the time you left, and on the way home the busses were never quiet. Everybody was yelling, everybody was screaming, it was like, it was just out of sheer thrill and happiness. You could really see at that point in time, not only what you guys meant as a team and what Don Wheeler and Jack O'Neil had done to bring you guys to the players that you were, but you could actually see the camaraderie within the town. There was no defenses from anyone, anywhere, you could totally dislike the person next to you, but nobody cared at that point in time. Nobody cared! You were hugging your worst enemy at that point in time! Nobody cared! That game was, I don't know, to the townspeople that night, that moment, that instant, was probably the highlight of Norwood High School history, not only because of the coaches, but because of you guys. The whole town was brought together that night. And *that* you guys can only thank yourselves for. You worked hard for that. That's all *you*. Every single one of you."

NORWOOD HOCKEY AND THE ARTS

Every artist dips his brush in his own soul, paints his own nature into his pictures.

— Henry Ward Beecher,
Proverbs from Plymouth Pulpit, 1887

The degree to which any history is appreciated can be discerned by its artistic realization. Grander scales of cities, regions, and countries, buffeted by incremental financial largess and the momentum of popularity, commonly express a consciousness. The statue of Bobby Orr in front of today's TD Garden, along with a plethora of books and documentaries about the '70-'72 Big, Bad, Bruins, an excellent Boston example. That a working-class town of 29,000, unremarkable in aspects historical or cultural, would produce its own varied artistic realization a half century later indicates nothing less than a thoroughly ingrained pride and appreciation of Norwood in the Time of Hockey.

JERRY KELLEHER
DOCUMENTARY FILMMAKER

"Probably the first memory I have of a live sporting event is of my father taking me to the Boston Garden in '72 when you guys were on a roll. I was nine years old and I remember it vividly, because when I was a kid, I used to check the coin return in the phone booths and I found seventy-five cents that night, three quarters! The mother lode! It was a miracle, it was huge to me, and as we were going in the old Garden, up the ramps to the balcony, I found another two dollars in cash on the sticky floor. It was the biggest game and jackpot in my life, and Norwood won! Of course, getting there was an adventure in itself. Like most, we were a one car family at the time, so me and Dad got dropped off at Hawes Pool and took the bus to Forest Hills.

"I don't watch a lot of movies really, except my own. (laughs) I'm not a film buff or anything. I was in print media all my life, then I became more of an ad agency, and clients wanted full service. About twelve years ago, I went to work for the state. The Department of Transportation was just starting up and I did the original logo and a lot of their public image stuff. After a while, they called on me to do more photos, videos and public service announcements. That was kind of a jumping off point for my hands-on film work. Eventually, I started to spend lots of time in my spare bedroom on nights and weekends writing and editing documentaries.

"I was selectman for nine years, three full terms. Norwood has nine voting districts, a couple of times I won all nine, thank you Norwood! Anyway, I didn't want to go out to bars too often, because my name was on the license, and people talk. So, myself and a few other guys would go to Brendan King's place. He had a nice big garage that he used to work on cars, him and his buddies, and we called it District 10. So that's what we called the company. One night after a few ginger ales, we decided to do a movie about the old Norwood Arena Speedway. Originally, the idea was to do a few short films for the town, a bygone era series, like 'The Norwood Experience,' and that's what I'm doing now. The first one was to be about Norwood Arena. But the thing was so huge, I didn't know what I was getting into, the track turned out to be prominent in NASCAR history. So, the film went national. We got photos, films and memorabilia from California, New York, Virginia, everywhere. And then the people start talking. As you know from researching and writing your books—somebody gives you a reference, call that guy, call that woman, her brother did this, he's got trophies, he's got this, she's got that, next thing you know, it became a real full-length movie.

"Neither of us had any movie experience. Brendan runs the business side. We travel the country together to interview people, and I go back to my room and make the movie. We chased down people. That's the way we work. It's part discovery, part treasure hunt. For *The Banner Years of Hockey*, we talked to Cap Raeder, who played for the old Hartford Whalers. He told us Robbie Ftorek of Needham was probably the greatest high school player ever, but he was kind of a recluse. So, we had to go to Lake Winnipesaukee to interview him. We went to Pittsburgh and filmed Eddie Johnston at his house, we went to Scranton to get Richie Hebner on video. We'll go anywhere! You just have to go where the story takes you!

"After we did *"Norwood Arena: The Movie"*, we just had to make another one! So here I am one day, thinking about doing another sports movie. And here's the thing. I was in the Rama Fitness Center, sitting in the sauna with a guy, Jimmy Piatelli, he used to own a little indoor rink down by the airport. And we were talking one day while we both were trying to lose a pound, and he asks me, when are you gonna do the Norwood hockey story? I said, I don't know Jim, is there an audience for it? It took a little convincing, you know. I would love to do that one, but I need footage! I need film, because it's a movie, you need visuals. Plus, what's the hook? Well, Norwood has had only had one state championship hockey team.

"Brendan and I decided to do it. I started to gather information and as I looked into the state records, and there were five teams that dominated the whole era, it was Norwood, Walpole, Needham, Melrose and Arlington, mostly Arlington. There turned out to be a lot of interest in it, plus my daughter was playing goalie for Norwood High at the time, so it was cool for her to learn some local sports history.

"It was a story that needed to be told. The premier at Norwood Theater was awesome! My concern was the film might stop in the middle! (laughs) So much pressure, you're putting yourself out there. With a book you're with one person at a time, with a film—there were seven hundred people there, and they'd paid money to see it, you're really hoping they enjoy it. I put two years into it, I didn't want it to bomb! And you're nervous, will they get the joke? Will they laugh at the right time?

"Afterwards people are coming up to me and hugging me and it's like it was *my* state championship. I can't skate, I can't drive a race car, and it showed how much it meant to guys. Robbie Ftorek was crying in my interview. Peter Brown told me the Ftorek interview was the best he'd ever seen of him. Raeder said the same thing, it showed his personal side, he told me, the side I know, not the image.

"Adding it up, it was a story that needed to be told. People told me they were crying on the way out, Bill Clifford, Mike Martin, coach Wheeler and all those guys from the other towns. I was representing them in a strange way. It's their story, I just tried to tell it in an entertaining way. I've done a lot of different things now, from artist to selectman to businessman, and now I make movies."

CHARLIE DONAHUE
COMMISSIONER OF ART

"About thirty years ago I had someone who worked for me in Boston, and he had these beautiful paintings on his wall, beautiful impressionist paintings." Charlie Donahue explained. "Said his friend was an artist and had a gallery over on Newbury Street. His name was Tom Dunlay. After I moved to Westwood, I read that Tom Dunlay was having a lecture at the library and I went and there were questions at the end, and he sounded like a regular guy. His kids were running around. I thought I'd like to get to know this guy, so I got to know this guy. He does these beautiful winter scenes and I said Tom, I'd like to commission you to do a painting of the town common, the iconic buildings, and I'd like to have my three sons in it."

Charley Donahue is a fixture in Norwood hockey. Idolized by many entering high school in the '60s, he is considered on the short list of his era's finest defensemen. Fifty-eight years after his graduation from Norwood High School, he easily recalled his team's fate.

"Our senior year, 1961 at Norwood High, Paul Johnson broke his ankle," the defenseman recalled. "Framingham came in third in the Bay State League in '61, after Norwood and Natick, and they won the state championship and the New England championship! If we hadn't lost our top center, we had a shot at it. Ted Casey was like a professional hockey player for Framingham, he'd go right through the whole team!

"I was paired on defense with Monk Jessick. Monk Jessick looked about 6' 5" tall and had no front teeth. He was a monster, and guys would come down on us and Monk would smile at them, they'd take one look at Monk and throw the puck in our zone and race to their bench!"

Charlie's commissioned painting came out a gem, depicting Norwood's town square with the United Church, St. Catherine's, and the town hall as background framing three boys, hockey bags slung over shoulder and sticks in hand, walking through the common. The quintessential winter scene quickly attained local iconic status. The painting now hangs in numerous Norwood homes, its Norman Rockwell-esque quality casting its spell, its nostalgic suggestion of a simpler youth, in a simpler time. Unsurprisingly, its appeal has not been restricted to Norwood.

"We gave Paul Angelo one for the OCC," the Brown University graduate said. "He told us, we had a guy in here and he's upstairs and this guy had been around, been around the world, and he says this is one of the most beautiful paintings he's ever seen. Today the technology exists to copy a painting and you can't tell it from the original. I have the original hanging in my living room. There are people from Canada asking for copies. It reminds everyone of some time in their lives. It means a lot to hockey people, it represents days in their past, in their youth."

Charlie Donahue and his wife Katherine have taken advantage of the painting's growing reputation to further worthy causes. "We have a scholarship fund we give each year to a kid who wants to be a teacher. We've been selling the painting for fifteen years; we give some to charities. The first one was probably about sixteen years ago."

The defenseman laughs in summation, revealing his desire to repay his universe in some way. "Well, I'm proud of that," he says, "and deep down there's a lot of us that believe the people that taught us hockey…it was transformative. I got into Brown because of hockey, not because I was a genius!"

DON REDDICK
NOVELIST

And in the beginning were the words. And phrases and sentences and thoughts and dreams, and they came when young, and I sensed I should scribble them. There was no inclination that they were exceptional or unique, momentous or memorable, but more the fashioning, the structuring of an order in my mind, my path, an unrefined but undeniable urge to write down words and phrases and sentences and thoughts and dreams. What they would become took years…and the profound imprint of experience.

I began writing a novel, completing *Faded and Changed* within a year. To my surprise and delight, it was deemed strong enough to retain an agent, who proceeded to present it to the finest publishers in the realm. I remember pacing back and forth, rubbing hands together and thinking, *this is easy, I can do this!* But alas, what my agent failed to tell me, what only harsh and direct responses would indicate, was that *Faded and*

Changed was, in fact, a poorly written book. The agent, himself chastened by prospective literary associates and weary of incessant phone queries from the rookie Boston writer, dumped me. The bruising effect of professional criticism, like tough love, forced a reassessment which chipped chunks of naivete and illusory expectations from any self-perceived literary ability.

"...he'd say you can do better. Yeah. Yeah. And here I'd get a little angry, and then I'd say, he's right. I CAN do better, I can do better. I need to work harder in practice. That's what he taught me..."

"I'm gonna tell it like it is. I'm not sugarcoating anything and if you come back here and think you're gonna get some sympathy from me, you're not gonna get it from me. The only way to get back to the big leagues is get better. Then you get back."

I was never taught to write. Never a Creative Writing class during my stint at the University of Massachusetts, never mind the Iowa's Writers' Workshop. Never a helping hand from family or friends, the son of a Bird & Son foreman lacking familial advantage in literary experience. Never, when adult, the class in novel writing at the local library or evening college. Never the companionship and encouragement of a writer's group. I had to teach myself how to write.

I purchased books on plotting, on characterization, I bought over forty books on every aspect of writing. I bought a Thesaurus and dictionary. I bought Strunk and White's tiny masterpiece on form; I bought the *Chicago Manual of Style*. I read Mentkin's incomparable, *The American Language*. I began watching movies with an eye toward character and story; began re-reading comedic novels, studying what made them funny. I listened carefully and watched closely those who attracted eyes in the crowd, sensing a correlation between characters who told stories around town and characters who held a reader's eye, buried within a book's binding.

"I was a good listener; I'd do everything I possibly could to get better at the game. I had the strongest desire to play...and I just kept working at it. Working, working..."

"And then I did everything I could to improve, skated every chance I got, spent hours in the garage shooting pucks..."

"He was the best in practice, he wanted to be, and it showed. He was first on the ice, last to leave..."

I made fundamental decisions. Though I had written poetry, short stories, and sent queries to magazines, I decided my focus would solely be writing novels. The difference in disciplines is substantial, like the difference between training for long-distance running versus sprinting. Writing a novel is long-distance, requiring much time—often years—of sustained, disciplined effort, and I needed to learn this. Writing a book requires the fundamental understanding of story structure, and I needed to learn it. Writing a novel requires discovering what voice works best for you. Writing a novel requires managing time, often at the expense of family and friends.

I set a goal to write five books in five years, with the last being publishable. Each would invoke a different discipline; I included *Faded and Changed* in this plan, which was a novel. The second would be its sequel. The third would be a non-fiction research book; the fourth a novel written in the third person, and the last, the fifth book, well, the last had to be whatever I could produce best.

"What Don taught us, or gave us an opportunity to get, was through just the repetition. It was about the repetition, of every day in practice. I remember, every day in practice, whaddaya mean? Every, fucking, day. Every, shift. And he taught us what it takes to prepare, not just to be a good athlete, but to win. The overall thing is that he really taught us what it takes to win. Without any of the nonsense. You gotta do this."

Queries continued, effort continued, learning continued, for years. It was discouraging to slowly sense that the forty books on writing I'd purchased told less truth about writing and publishing but played more to marketable hopes and dreams. You don't make a hockey team by *reading* about hockey! It would have been easy to become discouraged.

"If you give yourself an excuse to lose you have an out. No excuses. That was early on in Don's thing... You don't feel well? That's too fucking bad. You have the flu? Too fucking bad. Throw up? Okay, is it all out? Now skate your balls off. Oh, but I don't feel—too fucking bad. You don't feel good, don't play. See ya, next!"

From *A Literary Education, and Other Essays,* by Joseph Epstein,

As an occasional university teacher of would-be writers, I fairly regularly encounter young men and women who have what looks to me like that dazzling magical property, true talent. Many of them certainly have vastly more ability at deploying words than I had at their age. Yet, over two decades of observation, I have had to conclude that most among them, however much they think they want to be literary artists, apparently don't want it badly enough. They find themselves choosing other roads, devoting themselves to family, moneymaking, neurosis, and other of life's responsibilities, entanglements, entertainments, and sand traps. I think of them as possessing, to quote Carlyle again, "a high endowment with an insufficient will." Desire—hot breathed, unreasonable desire—is missing in them.

"...there'll be some talent, but what we're lacking in talent we'll make up with desire, dee-sire, that was his big word..."

"...this guy brought it to a new level, that's the truth. And you know what? I have friends who started way above me and a bunch of other people, and they went away because they didn't want to pay the price or didn't like it, or whatever."

I came to realize that I didn't need the Iowa Writer's Forum, nor a family history; I didn't need the assistance of clubs and associates. I realized I had already been taught to prepare, taught to practice, taught to persevere. Oh, and there was one more component. I had realized that anyone could succeed at writing if they really wanted it, anyone could turn into a capable writer. But *they've gotta want it!* That's the thing.

That's the thing.

> "For a while," Eddie Burns said in a quieter dressing room, "goalie Cremens looked like the spoiler. It was the greatest game Chuckie has ever played. Norwood was an inspired hockey team tonight. They outplayed us, but for a while in the third period, I thought we might steal the game. But they wanted it...wanted it too much."

In February of 1993, I received the phone call that all writers dream of. My novel—my fifth book—*Dawson City Seven* was to be published in Canada. *Killing Frank McGee* soon followed. Norwood not only provided a foundation of hockey knowledge, not only provided experiences from which I could then write what I know, but its personalities—*the personalities are terrific!* —inevitably found their way into my stories. In *Dawson City Seven* there is a locker room scene before the big game in which the quietest player on the team jumps up and renders a rousing call to triumphant action, plops down, leans close and whispers to a teammate, "Pretty good, eh?" In the 2001 *New Delta Review*, reviewer Andrew O'Malley wrote the following about Alf Smith, a true-life character in *Killing Frank McGee*,

> In Smith, Reddick creates a remarkable character; his insights into the brutal logic of the sport are coupled with a deep resentment of the wealthy promoters and administrators of his beloved game. The ice is, for Smith, a site on which an ugly class warfare is played out, where he seeks redress for the injustices (real and imagined) he has suffered at the hands of Ottawa's social elite.

Editor John Stevens made this observation of the same character during the working stages of *Killing Frank McGee*,

> In your presentation of Alf Smith, you certainly have the makings of a great portrait of a ferocious competitor, of a man who cannot comprehend anything but the fiercest will to win, who sees the world in raw, elemental terms...his rage and hate and contempt for the weak and effete are marvelously vivid and convincing.

Does this sound like anyone we know?

A few years later I received the review that all writers dream of. Andrew Rodger, in *The Voice of Sport,* wrote of my 2011 effort,

> I have been reading *The Trail Less Traveled* and I must say I am thoroughly enthralled—what a read—I can't put it down. The people described in the book are so interesting and full of life, the description of the northern landscapes is so vivid and wonderful, the way Reddick mixes and intertwines the historical account with the modern-day journey is masterful. It is a book I will be reading multiple times.
>
> I found myself filled with a sense of pride and gratitude. As a life-long hockey fan, I was proud of the game we all love and its rich history; a game that could inspire two Dawson City hockey teams to undertake such an epic journey. The gratitude is for Reddick himself, for sharing a journey with us, the readers, for following a dream and sharing it with the world. Upon completion of *The Trail Less Traveled*, I did something that I rarely do, something reserved for "the classics"...I turned to page one and began the book again. Much like the original Nuggets' challenge, *The Trail Less Traveled* has achieved the status of legend—a true classic.

Andrew Rodger ended his review with the standard, *Don Reddick lives in Vermont.* After posting the review online, the irony in a Bobby Dempsey reply comment was inescapable: "The heck with Vermont, *he's from Crestwood Circle!"*

REQUIEM FOR MEMORY, AND IMAGINATION

After two hours, he grew quiet, so I got off the bed and started to leave. "Wait," he said, as he waved to me to sit back down. It took a minute or two for him to regain enough energy to talk. "I had a lot of trepidation about this project," he finally said, referring to his decision to cooperate with this book. "I was really worried." "Why did you do it?" I asked. "I wanted my kids to know me."
— WALTER ISAACSON, *STEVE JOBS*, 2011

Talent observed within a small-town atmosphere can be imprecisely judged, perhaps exaggerated without contrast to larger exposure. Norwood's talent held up well under enlarged scrutiny.

"I played eighteen years in the big leagues, which I never would have thought, and I had some decent numbers," Richie Hebner said. Norwood's greatest athlete had made the ball *cry* on baseball's biggest stage, stroking 1,694 regular season hits, including 203 home runs. With Pittsburgh in 1971 he won a World Series, during which he hit a home run off Jim Palmer. But it was his blue-collar, grave-digging Norwood demeanor, as much as his athletic achievements, that endeared him to his hometown. "You talked to Richie?" Paul Angelo asked. "You know, I was with him the other day. He is no different than what he was like when he was fourteen years old, and I was twelve. He's the same guy. He's not a big shot, he's a real down to earth guy."

Dickie Donovan starred at Bowdoin College. "I was the first kid from Norwood to be named an All-American in hockey," he related. "I had a goal when I went to college. I wanted to be an All-American! I worked my ass off! My freshman year I watched the team play, and I saw two or three guys, they were in my fraternity, and they were All-Americans that year, and I said I'm gonna get those records. In 1973 I broke 'em all. They named me player of the year, ECAC player of the year. That's my favorite accomplishment in sports. They named me player of the year in the ECAC East, proud as hell." Dickie Donovan was inducted into Bowdoin's Hall of Fame in 2009.

Peter Brown played four years for Boston University, was elected captain, played in a national championship game and on the U.S. National Team. In 1976 he was a first team All-American and was named ECAC player of the year. The Marlboro Street kid was selected in the NHL draft by the Atlanta Flames and in the WHA draft by the New England Whalers. "Best player out of Norwood I ever saw was Peter Brown," Dickie Donovan insisted. "No doubt. No doubt. He was about as fast as I was. This is when he got to BU. I couldn't believe how quick he got. He ran the BU power play; Jack Parker has said he's one of the three best players he ever had at BU. I'm telling you, he could have played in the NHL. Easily. He was fabulous. We used to scrimmage BU my senior year, he was a freshman, and I'd say look at this kid play!" Pete Brown was inducted into the BU Hall of Fame in 1993.

Ed King attended St. Anselm College, played four years and was inducted into its Hall of Fame in 2003.

Louis Parker, backup goalie who never started a game for Norwood High School, starred for four years at the University of Connecticut. The apex of his collegiate career occurred in a 1975 game against Lowell Tech, when he set the UConn record for saves in a game with 63. "At UConn it's still the record for most saves in a game," Louis Parker said. "At the time, because I started as a freshman and we played every game, I played 89 games in a row, started in goal 89 games in a row. At the time it was the NCAA record, because I got to start as a freshman. Up until our freshman year, freshmen had to play freshman, so you could only play three years of varsity. I was in the first class that could play four years of varsity. So I could start for four years and set a record for games started by a goalie. I don't know if it's still a record, but it was at the time. I still like to brag about it!" (laughs)

The "what ifs" did Norwood proud. Allen Doyle, before starring in the Senior Golf Circuit, was selected to both the Catholic Memorial and Norwich Halls of Fame. Younger brother Zeke played at BC before a four-year stint in minor league hockey, and his life-long best friend Ray D'Arcy became captain at BC. Brian Petrovek, star goalie who chose Hotchkiss over Norwood High School and Harvard over BU, was selected All-American in 1975 and drafted by the LA Kings. Brian was inducted into Harvard's Hall of Fame in 1998.

"A few years ago," Frank Baglione said, "I asked Billy Clifford (head hockey coach for Norwood High School, 2002-2012) how many of his players were going to play college hockey, and he said maybe one! If you look at '72, almost every player played college hockey. Mike Smith was captain at AIC, I think Walker was captain at Merrimack, Peter Brown of course was captain at BU. I might have been captain at Norwich, but I blew out my knee my junior year, and missed the last ten games."

Injuries abrogated other dreams. Neil Higgins, the kid from Crestwood Circle whose high school records still stand a half century later, suffered a knee injury at BC, ending any hope of a professional career. Mike Martin, the kid from Spruce Road that Don Wheeler felt might be the best hockey player he had ever coached, was involved in a car accident, curtailing his BC career. Billy Clifford, the kid from Harrow Road who could skate as fast as doth a bird in the air or a bolt from a cross bow, and who was inducted into the Massachusetts State Hockey Coaches Association Hall of Fame, suffered torn knee ligaments at St. Anselm.

The real world beckoned. We were parochial pride ensconced in a hermetically sealed small town. The experience perhaps universal; that inevitable metamorphosis from childhood through adolescent years of great change and discovery, and ultimately adulthood. Change was often awareness; any strutting from Crestwood Circle as an eight-year-old onto Little League tryouts at Shattuck School abruptly tempered by the presence of Chris Dixon; any vaunted self-appraisals of toughness tempered when emerging from elementary school into junior high school and playing football with Joey Davis and Bobby Stivaletta.

Awareness was often sudden and drastic; eighteen-year-old Skip Lockwood physically assaulted in the Oakland Athletics' locker room his first day in the major leagues; nineteen-year-old Peter Oberlander in the Mekong Delta. For others it was the nervousness of college experience, and its subsequent awareness.

My own came at the University of Massachusetts. I had been toasted by towns, carried on the shoulders of friends and fans, placed atop fire engines, introduced, "he was on the state championship hockey team."

One morning in my first week at the University I found myself with another in the John Adams dormitory elevator. Awkwardly searching for something to say, I suddenly blurted, "I'm Don, 20th floor. I was on the state championship hockey team last year." The kid eyed me with tired, sophomore sophistication. "Listen pal," he said slowly, his entire facial expression devolving into a drip of condescension, *"nobody gives a fuck."*

"Opportunity came my way in the person of Neil Higgins, among the most influential and important mentors in my life. Without Neil Higgins believing in me and pulling greatness out of me, I don't know if I would have had the chance to realize my dream of playing major college hockey, which led to me playing in the World Championships, the Olympics, and the NHL."

Easton's Jim Craig had met Neil Higgins while being fitted for his goalie mask, and played for the former Norwood netminder at Massasoit Community College before attending BU. He wrote these words for his *Mentor Series*.

"It gives him tremendous satisfaction and fulfillment, and brings a smile to his face, Neil says, when he hears of what I'm doing, and successes I may achieve, for he knows that a considerable amount of this achievement is owed to what he impressed on and taught me as being vital and important: studying and learning, being open to being coached, and putting lessons to use. I am forever grateful to Neil Higgins and the opportunity he gave me, and the time he spent mentoring."

The qualities Neil Higgins carried from the town of Norwood that so influenced one of America's most storied hockey heroes, were fashioned not only from a great family and childhood neighborhood, but a developing Norwood hockey tradition.

"Don Wheeler," Neil Higgins said, "helped mold me into the man that I am and the man I became and the businessperson that I became, because he taught me that I can always do more. And not to settle for just one hundred percent or settle for *good*ness. He taught us that you can go for *great*ness, and you can keep going even further than that."

"It prepared you for real life, whether it's disappointments or success," Blaine Maus had said. "Enjoy your success while you can, because there's gonna be down moments, there's gonna be losing moments…"

"What did Norwood hockey mean to me?" Rusty Tobin repeated. "That's a tough one. You think about it too much, you come up with too much. It was the best time of my life. I got married, and that wasn't as good as playing for Norwood. It was the best time of my life, best I ever had. Best fun. I remember really missing it. I think one of the ways I thought I could stay on that level of being so good and happy was coaching. It was giving back because I love coaching, too. Playing for Norwood was the best time I ever had."

"I will always be thankful that Don Wheeler was part of my life," Jack Cronin declared. "I'm a fan! He taught me so much about myself and understanding that we each have so much more inside of us than we realize. Don helped me understand the importance of intestinal fortitude and mental toughness. These strengths have served me well over the years and I'm thankful to coach Wheeler. But if there is one person in the world that I owe a debt of gratitude to, it is Jim Gormley.

"His help with hockey and baseball in my life has been secondary to his encouragement and belief in me as a person. I attended Boston College on a hockey scholarship. Who would have thought I'd go from Father Mac's to McHugh Forum? No one, including the guidance counselors at Norwood High School, thought I had a chance of getting in. I remember Jim driving me to the Boston College library and tutoring me for the SATs. His mother helping me with Latin. He has always believed in me and has been a great role model."

"It changed my life," Bill Denehy said earnestly. "It was the greatest thing that ever happened to me. I learned I could do anything in life, anything. The entire Norwood hockey experience was the single most important lesson I ever learned in my life."

"What did it mean?" Alex Skene replied. "I mean, it was, it was the most powerful experience of my youth. That's what it means. A sense of how compelling it was to, to those who were involved in it in all the different ways, people played, the fans, everybody involved. A sense of how compelling and how powerful an experience it was, and maybe you could shed some light on it, cuz I don't know. I think a lot about it now. You know, I still play quite a lot of pond hockey up here, we still get a good amount of ice, and sometimes I'll come back from playing pond hockey and think about hockey in general, and invariably the thoughts wind back to the memories of, you know, sometimes all the way back to youth hockey, but more typically to playing in high school with various guys. So, you know, what does it mean? I don't know what it means. But it was very powerful. Remembering, still. Fifty years. It was such a big part of our lives."

"I would say it was an honor to play hockey at Norwood High School," Billy Clifford responded. "The tradition, the people, it was just an honor to play for Norwood High hockey. In our time. The history, the build-up of it, it was incredible. So I think that's what I have to say about it, it was an honor. Not too many could say they played for Norwood and were successful like we were. People would die to wear the fucking uniform. People were crushed to get cut, I mean *crushed*.

"I don't think you'll ever see the intensity, the fan base, just the whole atmosphere, I don't think you'll ever see it again. I don't think you'll see it in any sport. Really. It was a different time. Of course, the Bruins had something to do with it, I mean it was a hockey crazed city at the time, everybody wanted to play hockey. You know, the tradition, the fan base, the excitement about it, you'll never see it again, you really won't. In any sport. You're lucky to get five hundred people at a, that's a packed house now, you know? I can remember as a kid going up to see Hebner, for a Saturday game you had to buy a ticket Tuesday night to get in, or you didn't get in. You did, or you wouldn't get in. And the smoke, it was insane. It was crazy. You were a fucking hero in this town, you were! I mean, you couldn't do anything wrong. Well, do you think people would remember if it was just an average thing? I'm sure they'd have some memories, but not like we do."

"I loved playing," Dennis Hebner declared. "Those two years of hockey I played was the best time of my life, really. I loved going to every game and playing, big crowds and everything. It was great. It was just, I thought it was the best time of my young life, really. I even told you the practices, not the first week of practice because they were tough, you'd come home and you'd be so sore the next day, but once you got through the first week of practice, I looked forward to everything about hockey. I just loved it.

"Made a lot of friends too, all the kids I played hockey with. I don't see them that much, because everyone's moved around and everything, like I see Leo McInerney once in a while. When I saw Neil come up, I gave him a big hug, he lives down in Florida. He came up for his Hall of Fame thing, him and Jackie got into the Norwood High School Hall of Fame together, and he flew up from Florida, and I couldn't wait to see him and give him a big hug and talk to him for a while. We were best friends in high school, we used to double date all the time. He had that big 1950 Buick Special, I don't know if you remember that, you're probably too young. His father used to work part time for Buick and some old lady traded it in, and that car, I'd sit in the back seat and I'd put my legs out straight and I couldn't even touch the seats! It was great!"

"That is why we play the game, to learn about life," Bobby Thornton offered. "Because the sport, like life, is never all good, or all bad. But rather the sport—like life—is full of ups and downs and we must learn how to persevere through the ups and downs right through the finish line. One of the best quotes and life lessons I ever learned from coach Wheeler was that 'people always remember the last thing that we do in the game.' So, if you totally screw up in the first two periods by falling down and letting people blow by you to score a bunch of goals, do not dwell on it and hang your head. Why? Because if you wind up scoring the winning goal at the end of the game, what do you think people will remember? And conversely, if you score five goals in the first two periods and you start skating around smiling at the crowd and 'resting on your laurels,' but then you fall down and let their guy go right around you at the end of the game and he scores the winning goal, what do you suppose people will be buzzing about at the end of the game? Right. The way it ended! Great life lesson."

"Real important part of my life," Phil Nolfi said. "Real important part of it. I feel bad for the people that didn't get to do what we did. Cuz you'll never forget, ever. I mean, I had my own business, I played college hockey, part that you don't forget. And I think a part of it was there were a lot of good guys, a lot of good shits. Just a great bunch of people. And everybody was dedicated to the same thing. I don't think there was a selfish player in the group. I think just everybody wanted to win."

"Good question," Pete Tamulionis responded. He paused longer than a moment, then said, "It meant everything. Playing for Norwood High School and playing for the town, it was just, there was nothing to compare it to. Hockey players in Norwood High School back in those days, they were

Gods. I mean, all of us. People just, oh you're on the Norwood hockey team? It was unbelievable, it was just unbelievable. It was awesome, it was heaven. You were on the biggest stage, and you know what I always looked back to, Donny? When we were playing Needham, or Walpole, or Dedham, or anybody, and we're driving up Rt. 1 to go to Four Seasons Arena and the traffic would be like the Southeast Expressway coming home on a Friday afternoon. It was just *packed* with cars. And you'd go in there, get dressed and come out on the ice, and we're thinking there's 15,000 people there. It's jammed, people are shoulder to shoulder, and you know it might have been 4,500 or 5,000. It was a thrill; it was an absolute thrill! I can't even—I try to explain it to my sons, you guys, you just don't, this is unbelievable! Norwood High hockey was unbelievable! The Bay State League was *the* league.

"And socializing, meeting people, being together, just that whole team atmosphere, you know what I'm saying? It was great. Norwood High hockey was, it was like you felt like you were on the Boston Bruins. It was just amazing, it was amazing. You walked around and people knew you, and we're in that beautiful town we grew up in, and I'll never have a bad word about that town *evah*, because it was the greatest town in the world to grow up in. And I met so many great people, learned a lot. And I'll never forget it as long as I live."

"I asked Pete Brown, how do I make this team?" Frank Baglione recalled. "He said be first in line for all the drills, even if you're throwing up on your skates, be first in line, and I did. And that didn't apply to just hockey. When I was in the service, in boot camp they tried to wear you out. I was first in line. I did it in college, up front, make sure they see you, this is what Peter said, no matter how tired you are, even if you're throwing up on your skates. I was a sophomore, trying to make the team.

"Well, I think now hockey set me up for what I do today. Be first in line, don't be behind with the smokers and jokers, be first in line, have morals, have character, hustling in everything you try to do. That's what hockey's done for me. It got me a scholarship to Norwich. I became an officer in the Army. I'm running high-tech applications server-built project teams with a physical education degree. They took a chance on me, and why is that? Because I hustle, I get in line first, I don't care how tired I am, I'll be there. Even today if there's a conference call, I'm the first one on. And that was Peter Brown, saying you want to be on the team? Be first in line."

"I think it could be said about any team sports," Ed King reflected, "but I think it's more so in Norwood, at least at the time it was, that there was a real comradery of hockey players from years before and after, it was a real club almost. That, and I really remember thinking, you know, with all the history Norwood had gone through with Arlington, and the losses, it was really a win for, not generational, but for all the different years preceding us. And that's a nice thing to have. I think it really was, everybody shared the same pond hockey experiences, which is one of the best things in the world, as I look back on it. Al Skene still skates up in Maine, it's cold enough up there. His father used to drive around even when he was older with a pair of skates in his backseat in case he came across a cranberry bog, you know? But I think the whole Norwood experience was certainly a positive thing for us, and I think just team sports in general help with character, work ethic, social interactions. I did a lot of rink-ratting, so to speak, after in my older years. You can walk into any hockey rink and sit in a locker room with people you just met, and it's pretty much the same people! (laughs) Everyone sort of have the same values."

"To this day," Bobby Thornton continued, "so this is fifty years ago. I'll never forget driving up that hill on Rt. 1, and it was a steady incline, there were no jersey barriers back then, driving up the hill and my stomach is in my throat getting to the top of the hill where Grossman's was, and taking a left across Rt. 1 and seeing the sea of cars and getting off the bus and getting the equipment slung over my shoulder. They say they closed the doors an hour before the games against Walpole and Needham, whatever, the place you could not get another body in there and there was no smoking laws, so you walk in there, there was a smoky arena, French fries, ketchup, bubble gum and smoke. And you walk in there, and you'd have to squeeze your way through the crowd and when they saw your stick and everything you were like a rock star. To get to that little locker room downstairs. I was fourteen years old. And these kids today, they see their parents at a game and they say hey dad how you doin'? And we're in the fucking Garden, there are 14,000 people there…"

"Sparks memories good, bad, and ugly," Jack Cronin said. "I loved hearing the individual perspectives of what it meant to grow up in Norwood and aspire to be part of a successful hockey tradition. My experience playing hockey for Norwood High School was a privilege and honor. Every kid that stepped on the ice was entering a crash course in the realities of life. Good or bad, it was Don Wheeler's world. No one at that age wants to be told they're not working hard enough, over and over, again and again. Don was the judge and jury. In many ways it was a military boot camp both physically and mentally. He didn't care if everyone hated him. He wanted to be the focus of their anger and hate. I believe it was one of the major reasons for the success of his teams, and a reason he is disliked by many to this day. No in-fighting among teammates! No distractions! If you didn't play or didn't get enough ice time, it wasn't *your* fault, it was *Wheeler's!* Don never minced words. As far as I know he was always brutally honest about an individual's performance. Probably to a fault. I can tell you I was on the receiving end of some ass-kicking words from Don.

"People can say whatever they want about the coaching at Norwood but there was, it made me what I was as a hockey player. It made a lot of people better as hockey players, as far as understanding, maybe I was one of the fortunate ones, understanding what your ability, how far you can actually go. Just when you think you're at your limit, you can go further. And that's probably the Marine way, but I learned that from Don Wheeler. And I'll be the first to agree, he didn't have a charming personality. It's almost like he wasn't being paid to be a nice guy, and it was a lot more fun to win than it was to lose. And he raised the bar so damn high, and I'm sure it was the same for you guys. When we were on the ice, we never expected to lose. It was just not even part of our thought process, so that's because of Wheeler. His expectations.

"I guess I was just proud to be…you know there's a certain pride I have being part of the whole Norwood hockey tradition, and I'd be lying if I didn't like to be, like the players on the '72 team, or the '69 team, like I—I was respected, just like I respected the guys who were older than me, the Dana Mauses, the Blaine Mauses, and the Paul Angelos, there's a certain amount of respect knowing that we're part of the Norwood hockey program."

"It was a privilege to play for Norwood," Neil Higgins concluded. "Anybody who donned the blue, gold, and white, it was a privilege. You *earned* it. To be part of that, and to be part of that era when things were hockey, hockey, hockey, when Four Seasons was filled every single

Saturday night, or Loring Arena, or the rink in Braintree, which was surreal. You don't see people turning out for even football games anymore that have that kind of support and people. It was, it was hockey was almost a given thing, that you *had* to go to the games, to see and be seen, because that was the culture. And to me it was a privilege to be part of that culture. And I was blessed, that's all I can say. I was blessed that I was able to play in that era."

Don Wheeler, after beating Dedham to go undefeated in 1971, had words that perhaps encapsulate the entire hockey experience for a generation of Norwood boys. "These kids are branded now," the coach told a reporter. "This is something you can never take away from the kids. There are a lot of material things in a kid's life and in an adult's life, too, but those things come and go and you forget about them. But they'll always have this wherever they go."

We end with a tale of two poems, which ironically *do* represent the best of times, as well as the worst of times. The first was written by Sir Henry John Newbolt, born in Bilston of England's West Midlands, the second by Bruce Springsteen of Freehold, New Jersey.

The first was written in 1892 by a thirty-year-old poet and novelist, the son of the vicar of St. Mary's Church, the Reverend Henry Francis Newbolt. The second was written circa 1980 by a thirty-four-year-old American rock star, the son of a bus driver named Douglas "Dutch" Springsteen.

The first's author was educated at Clifton College and graduated from Corpus Christi College in Oxford, before being called to the bar at Lincoln's Inn, "recognized to be one of the world's most prestigious professional bodies of judges and lawyers." The second's author was a college drop-out and self-described draft evader.

The first was written in the worst of times, on a continent on the precipice of a half-century of conflict that would cost the lives of an estimated 40 million people. The second was written in the best of times, on a continent free from conflict on its soil for over a century.

Both works address athletic pursuits of youth and their life-long effect upon character. Springsteen's song evolved from a chance 1973 meeting with a former Little League teammate named Joe DePugh. It revels in disparagement of time-honored physical achievement. *Glory Days* appeared on the rock star's *Born in the U.S.A.* album, a commercial smash with over thirty million copies sold, and recognized as one of the greatest albums of all rock time. Copyright concerns prevent the inclusion of Springsteen's lyrics. My contemporaries will remember the words and, more importantly, their dismissive gist.

Where any working-class bar provides an appropriate setting for Springsteen's words, Sir Newbolt's poem *Vitae Lampada* requires a more formal pageantry. It emanates from cricket matches played in the Clifton College Close, a "close" in British parlance meaning an enclosed venue. The engagement referenced is the 1885 Battle of Abu Klea in Sudan, during an ill-fated attempt to rescue General Gordon. An infantry square was a British infantry combat formation in close order, normally resorted to in great peril. The title is a quotation from Lucretius, meaning "the torch of life."

Vitae Lampada

There's a breathless hush in the Close to-night—
Ten to make and the match to win—
A bumping pitch and a blinding light,
An hour to play and the last man in.
And it's not for the sake of a ribboned coat,
Or the selfish hope of a season's fame,
But his captain's hand on his shoulder smote
"Play up! play up! and play the game!"

The sand of the desert is sodden red,
Red with the wreck of a square that broke;
The Gatling's jammed and the Colonel dead,
And the regiment blind with dust and smoke.
The river of death has brimmed his banks,
And England's far, and Honour a name,
But the voice of a schoolboy rallies the ranks:
"Play up! play up! and play the game!"

> This is the word that year by year,
> While in her place the school is set,
> Every one of her sons must hear,
> And none that hears it dare forget.
> This they all with a joyful mind
> Bear through life like a torch in flame,
> And falling fling to the host behind—
> "Play up! play up! and play the game!"

One poem exemplifies a profound, historical appreciation of the role athletics play in developing the character of every society, the other a shallow misunderstanding of the context in which we now live. "It seems to me that any sport is a kind of practice, perhaps unconscious, for the life-and-death struggle for survival," John Steinbeck, whose lifetime spanned the brunt of the worst of times, wrote. "Our team sports simulate war, with its strategy, tactics, logistics, heroism and cowardice. Individual competition of all kinds has surely ingredients of single combat, which for millions of years was the means of going on living."

We were sons and daughters of World War II, brothers and sisters of Vietnam. We were the boys of winter conditioned not to revel in *Glory Days*, but to pass a torch of knowledge and experience. *We old men are old chronicles, and when our tongues go, they are not clocks to tell only the time present, but large books unclasped; and our speeches, like leaves turned over and over, discover wonders that are long since past.*

At a recent reunion of UMass dormmates, yesterday a coterie of nervous eighteen-year-olds and today in our late sixties, one of my friends raised a glass and acknowledged that we were now, "in the fourth quarter." When I contacted Joe Bertagna, he informed that he was writing a book on his own life-long hockey experiences entitled, *Late in the Third*. Paul Flaherty, who so ardently encouraged me to write of Norwood hockey, would never see this book, indeed, did not even see the beginning of it. Jeff Brown, Peter's older brother and manager of the '67 hockey team, is gone. Reverend Dan Young is gone. Frank Wall collapsed and died of a heart attack while managing a Little League game at Endean Field, within sight of the house he grew up in. Bobby Donahue, captain of the '66 team, passed away. It's a tough time of life; Tommy Shea is gone,

'71 teammates Jackie Clifford, Teddy Curtis and Johnnie Lawrie are gone, as well as Johnnie's younger brother and '72 teammate, Bobby Lawrie. Since beginning this chapter in February of '20, Bobby Clifford and Billy Hasenfus have passed away, and now word is received that Arthur Harris has died.

Tragedy, edging the bizarre, encroached upon both hockey towns. Bobby Havern, Billy Corkery, and Eddie Burns all passed away from brain tumors within a couple of years of one another, causing concern in Arlington of a potential rink-related environmental issue. In 2006, the Hebner family was shocked when three of the five brothers, Billy, Brian, and Dennis, lost their wives within days of one another.

Brian Moloney, of the goaltending Moloney brothers, passed away after a long battle with cancer. Part of his obituary read, "Brian was raised in Norwood's Crestwood Circle, attended Xaverian Brothers Class of '69, where he was the winning goalie for the Catholic Conference Championship team, and Providence College, where he played freshman hockey." It is the only obituary I have ever read that mentioned the street grown up on, indicating pride in the old neighborhood, until the end.

Thoreau had a great line, "Maturity is when all your mirrors turn into windows." There was a long time when I would not miss a moment of a Bruins game. Today, I try not to miss a moment with my grandchildren. Instead of telling them I skated in Boston Garden and that my entire generation tried our damnedest to win it all and finally did, I encourage their own efforts, their own aspirations, knowing full well the lessons are universal. And heck, someday they might walk the path to Father Mac's pond and notice the hole I dug and inquire cause and occasion of the same; maybe someday they might wonder, after their own mirrors have become windows, of the Old Man's dreams, and read this book. I hope they do; I want our kids to know us.

> *But the people are dispersing. The sun is just setting. Some linger, and seem reluctant to leave. If you too, reader, linger and feel reluctant to leave Norwood, I shall be rejoiced and repaid for the long way over which I have led you.*
>
> — HENRY WARD BEECHER, THE LAST LINES OF
> NORWOOD; OR, VILLAGE LIFE IN NEW ENGLAND